THE
ARMENIANS

John M. Douglas

THE
ARMENIANS

John M. Douglas

J. J. Winthrop Corp.
Publisher

Library of Congress Cataloging in Publication Data

Douglas, John M.
  The Armenians
  Includes Index
     I. Armenia—History
   1. Title
ISBN 0-9631381-0-3

DOUGLAS, JOHN. M.
The Armenians
J. J. Winthrop Corp..

© 1992 by J. J. Winthrop Corp.

Printed in the United States of America

10 9 8 7 6 5 4 3

J. J. Winthrop Corp.
244 W. 54th St., Suite 800
New York, NY 10019

CONTENTS

CHAPTER SEVENTEEN

THE KINGDOM OF CILICIA 216

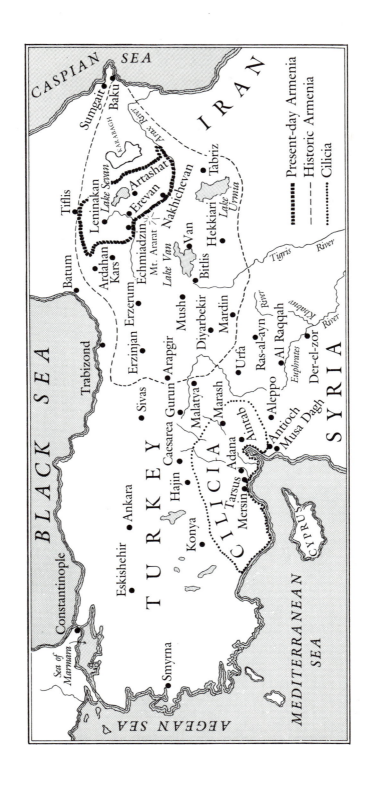

This is the story of the Armenian people, written in narrative form. Data, events, scenes, and characters can be verified. While most of the quotations and passages of dialogue in the book can be authenticated, there are some whose only source are the people I have come in contact with in the process of my research.

For the scenes described in Chapters Twenty-two and Twenty-seven I am indebted to the refugees living in the Armenian refugee camps in the Middle East whose eyewitness accounts I have tried to describe as accurately and coherently as possible. These refugees had an invaluable accumulation of vignettes regarding the Armenian Genocide of 1915. These vignettes are not unusual, however, in magnitude nor in character. Every Armenian family has a story similar to these. The accounts described in Chapters Twenty-two and Twenty-seven are in consonance with a great deal of documentation already in existence.

I would like to make a general statement of acknowledgment to the authors whose books I have read in the process of my research. Specific indebtedness goes to my wife for her discerning collaboration and invaluable comments and suggestions in connection with the interpretation and analysis of historical events. Without her this book would not have been published.

J. M. D.

CHAPTER ONE

THE PEOPLE

I began this project in December 1988. I was in a taxicab headed towards New York's LaGuardia Airport going home after five days of meetings. As the taxi was about to enter the Midtown Tunnel on the way to Long Island, the evening news program over the car's radio began to report about a major earthquake in the area between northern Iran and eastern Turkey. The early reports were sketchy. Four people were dead and many were left homeless. By the time we reached the airport the news became clearer - a major earthquake in the State of Armenia, a town had disappeared, two large cities devastated, tens of thousands were dead, children trapped in school buildings, voices from the ruins crying for help. The following morning the disaster was reported as headline news over the international wire services. Two days later the world learned of the magnitude of one of nature's worst calamities. Around 100,000 had died, 12,000 injured, and half a million were left homeless. Scientists called it one of the worst earthquakes in the history of man. Once again tragedy had hit the Armenian people.

The impact of this disaster propelled me to write this book. It was then that I embarked on a long journey through the pages of the history of these people, the Armenians. In years past I have traveled extensively and visited the Armenian communities around the world. I have lived in Armenian refugee camps and gathered innumerable eyewitness reports from the survivors of the Armenian Genocide. I began to assemble the papers that I had collected since my youth. I read books, stu-

1

died maps and examined manuscripts. I read the works of classical historians and recorded the results of their discoveries to develop a pattern of cause and effect. My father was a learned man. His scholarship and extensive knowledge of the history of the Ottoman Turks and his fluency in the old Turkish language had helped me in the past to study the Ottomans and read documents, mostly unpublished, which were then in the possession of my father that he himself had meticulously collected in his capacity as the editor of a newspaper during the first decade of this century. I studied the works of noteworthy historians, and the works of those who had chosen to make deliberate attempts to rewrite history and manipulate historic facts out of existence.

In spite of the voluminous works and unusual abundance of literature about the Armenians, the scope of my research was limited. Most of the wealth of these people's history remains buried today in the ruins of the ancient land. Literature about the Armenians is largely the result of archeological investigations conducted in the State of Armenia which comprises only about ten percent of the ancient Armenian territory. The Greater Armenian land is still occupied by the Turks who have stubbornly refused to allow archeological excavations in areas that were once inhabited by the Armenians. There were some historical discoveries made during the reign of the Ottoman Sultans in the early part of the Nineteenth century. These discoveries have enormously enriched our knowledge about the early Armenians. All studies about the Armenians were discontinued, however, when anti-Armenian sentiments became prevalent in Turkey in the early part of the Twentieth century. Since then the Turkish authorities have either deliberately destroyed Armenian antiquities in their control, or prevented historians and archeologists to dig the ancient Armenian sites. Spectacular discoveries made by Russian archeologists in the ancient Armenian city of Ani in the early part of this century were callously destroyed by the Turks when Ani came under the Turkish jurisdiction.

In recent years discoveries fundamental to Armenian history were deliberately mislabeled by Turkish historians and all efforts to identify monuments, ruins, or sculptures as Armenian were suppressed. In the mid-1970's the Turkish government began the construction of huge hydroelectric dams on the Euphrates and Tigris river system covering an area of nearly 30,000 square miles of the old Armenian provinces. The project known as the Southeastern Anatolian Project is destined to submerge important archeological sites. There is danger, therefore, that traces of the ancient Armenian civilization will be completely obliterated. While I have tried to record the results of modern historical findings, no ancient history of this magnitude can be set in concrete with uncontestable accuracy until Turkey, the occupier of large chunks of the Armenian territory, agrees to apply the rules of justice and equity and allow historians to make their investigations.

The historical experience of the Armenian people is quite unusual. On every page, in every book there is tragedy and disaster that have become their unfortunate lot since the beginning of time. They are raised in violence and nurtured in fear. Rarely have they seen periods of tranquility. They have been conquered, persecuted, oppressed, massacred, and exiled. They have seen their children slaughtered, their properties confiscated, and their churches burned. They have tried to worship their God but have been prevented to do so most of the time. They have tried to create a homeland but have been prevented to live there in peace. They have written books but the books were burned before they were read. They have composed music but rarely did they have the occasion to sing happily.

I confronted these people's past. Despite their sufferings, few in the world have demonstrated courage to acknowledge the grave injustices that have inflicted the Armenian people for so long. They lived by the grace of others and found themselves in the crossfire of military and political upheavals. But in spite of all their tribulations they were able to mold their people into a nation before others developed their own nationhood.

Who are these people? Most cultures are measured in centuries, but the Armenian culture is measured in millennia. The Armenians were there when the Greeks and Romans were writing the pages of their history. They were there with the Babylonians, the Assyrians, and the Egyptians at the dawn of civilization carving their own niche in the history of man in the cradle of civilization.

The Armenians are an ancient race about 3,000 years old. They are descended from the Proto-Indo-Europeans who originated in Anatolia, the home of the Proto-Armenians, and migrated east and west. The Armenian homeland is the plains of Mount Ararat stretching from the Caucasian mountain range in the east to the Euphrates River in the west. The nation itself is the result of a fusion of various tribes of Indo-Europeans who returned to Anatolia around 1200 B.C., merged with the remnants of other tribes who inhabited the plains of Mount Ararat, established organic communities, developed concepts for the rise and growth of man's civilization, and finally formed the Armenian nation around 600 B.C.

The Armenians reached the height of their power during the First century B.C. when an Armenian king, Tigran the Great, formed an empire that stretched from the Caspian Sea to the Mediterranean, from the Caucasus to Palestine. After the collapse of their empire the country became a vassal state of Rome, Persia, and the Byzantine Greeks successively. It was besieged by the Arabs, then the Mongol tribes came from the east and swept the country until the arrival of the predatory Turks. First came the Seljuk Turks followed by the Ottomans. Waves of Turkic tribes from the steppes of central Asia marched westward and conquered the Arab and Christian kingdoms in the east and west.

Armenia remained under the Turkish domination for over 500 years, forcing some Armenians to emigrate to other countries and establish communities in Europe and the Middle East. A group of Armenian noblemen migrated to Asia Minor and established the Kingdom of Cilicia that lasted until the end of the Fourteenth century. The majority of Armenians remained under the Turkish rule, kept their national institutions, preserved their culture and traditions, and became loyal subjects to the Ottoman Sultans. As merchants and bankers the Armenians made significant contributions to the growth and development of the Ottoman Empire. They lived in segregated communities and continued to maintain their Christian faith and national identity.

During the Sixteenth century while the Ottoman Empire was growing in size and prosperity, the Russians in the north began to form their own empire. They adopted an expansionist policy and with a powerful military organization made their way to the south of the Caucasus. They chased the Turks out of the region during the first quarter of the Nineteenth century, conquered Eastern Armenia and dissected the Armenian people into two groups. Western Armenia remained under the Turkish rule and Eastern Armenia became a province of the Russian Empire. The Eastern Armenians fared well under the Russian Czars who accepted the Armenians as industrious and faithful subjects. The Armenians, in turn, regarded the Russians as their liberators and the ultimate protectors against the Turkish oppression.

Tension began to develop both in the east and west towards the end of the Nineteenth century. In Eastern Armenia the Russians sought to Russify the territory under their control and replace the Armenian language with Russian and forced the Armenian Church to accept the authority of the Russian Orthodox Church. The situation was worse in Western Armenia. The rise of nationalism and the emergence of revolutionary parties placed the Turks against the Armenians. The Armenians demanded self-determination in Western Armenia and the Turks took measures to suppress the Armenian nationalist movement. When the Armenian revolt spread to other regions of the Ottoman Empire the Turks decided to put an end to the Armenian presence in Turkey. In the spring of 1915 the Turkish government organized a genocide and exterminated one and a half million Armenians and deported the survivors to the deserts of northern Syria.

The collapse of Czarist Russia and the rise of the Bolsheviks prompted the Armenian nationalists to seize the opportunity of political anarchy and establish an independent republic in Eastern Armenia with Erevan as its capital. By then Western Armenia had been emptied of Armenians. The Armenian Republic lasted two and a half years. In November 1920 the country was taken over by the Communists and eventually became one of the republics of the Soviet Union.

There is no reliable census as to the number of Armenians living in the world today. This is principally due to the fluid nature of the Armenian diaspora and the constant process of migration and change. Historians estimate that there were about 5 million at the beginning of the Christian era and the current figure is not too far from that. According to the Population Reference Bureau of Washington, D.C. there are about 5.4 million Armenians in the world with 4.7 million living in the Soviet Union. The rest are scattered around the world, largely in

Europe and North America. According to Armenian scholars of the State of Armenia, there are 6.9 million Armenians, with 3.3 million living in the State of Armenia, 1.5 million in 14 Soviet republics, 1 million in North America, 650,000 in the Middle East, and 500,000 in Europe.

The Armenians speak a language which is identified as Indo-European, one of the oldest in the human race. After migrating east and west from Anatolia the Proto-Indo-Europeans split into four groups and began to develop their languages. The modern philologists classify these four groups as Anatolian, representing the languages of the Hittites and the Luwians among others; Aryano-Greco-Armenic, representing the languages of Armenians, Greeks, Persians, Bengali, Urdu, and Hindi, among others; Celto-Italo, representing the languages of Latin, Italian, Romanian, French, Spanish, Portuguese, Scottish, Irish, and Welsh among others; and Balto-Slavo-Germanic, representing the languages of English, German, Latvian, Lithuanian, Slavic, Russian, Polish, Slovak, Bulgarian, Serbian, Ukrainian, Flemish, Dutch, Norwegian, and Swedish, among others.

It is no wonder today that the Armenians seem to take pride, at times, for having been the people whose homeland was once the cradle of civilization and the birthplace of the ancestors of modern nations. While they considered themselves a small nation among the great ones, they achieved more and endured longer while others disappeared. The contemporaries of the Armenians and the societies of antiquity had their religions, laws, powerful leaders, and great institutions but they were all discarded to the pages of antiquity.

What made the Armenians, who also had laws, religion, powerful leaders, and great institutions, succeed in their struggle for survival while others vanished? The answer may lie in the character of the people and the distinguishable individuality of their civilization. The Armenians are known as hardworking, robust, impetuous, with quickness of mind. But these are not supernatural qualities that helped them endure. It was perhaps their passion to be creative, their will to stay alive, and their profound respect for ancestral traditions that gave them the momentum to survive and guaranteed their existence through the vicissitudes of history. Their legacy was like a torch in flame that one generation kept passing to the next. At the end of each period of national disaster, whenever they found themselves at the edge of an abyss, they demonstrated some inner push for a new birth, starting from the beginning over and over, without losing the continuity of their national rhythm.

Not all facets of man's civilization can be measured in actual numbers. The Armenians have chosen to acquire some civilized convictions, and have developed ideas and institutions which made them aspire to far more than their physical existence. But they remained unheralded in the annals of history. The world knew them more for their sufferings than for their accomplishments and their story was put away from memory most of the time. But if their history was a history of endurance through the turbulent periods of human life, it is their ideas and institutions that helped shape the history of man and formed the basis of western thought.

From the cities of the Fertile Crescent to the Empire of Rome and the birth of Christ, the Armenians were there with their contributions for the development of the fundamentals of civilized life. They were there when mankind's earliest thinkers were formulating their thoughts. The value of their civilization lies in the continuity of the process of perpetuating their traditions from one generation to the next, while others lost their stamina to continue, became stagnant, and perished.

The Armenians were first to adopt Christianity as their national religion, placing them in the cockpit of Christianity as the pioneer believers of Christian virtue. This claim looms large in historical perspective. Through the centuries the Armenians have proudly and fiercely guarded the exclusivity of that claim with no timidity to remind anyone who cared to listen that they were in fact the first nation that was civilized enough to accept a civilized faith at a time when most of the world continued to worship its gods in the darkest days of paganism.

The Armenians lived in a country which was oriented by nature to be the crossroads between east and west. The Tigris and Euphrates valleys made the land of Armenia the center of gravity for world affairs. It was from here that the center eventually moved to Egypt, Athens, and Rome. Their history is interwoven with the history of great powers. The people lived in perpetual conflict between national survival and national subordination and suffered cruelly at the hands of their neighbors and mightier forces. They lived in the shadow of fear but in spite of their undignified treatment by others, they stood tall on the horizon of history as one of the most dignified men on earth. It may have been the land that made these people exceedingly individualistic, annoyingly stubborn, and unreasonably sensitive to criticism. They have a phenomenal persistence to endure and their recuperative and regenerative capacities have enabled them to transform tragedy into happiness, despair into hope, defeat into inspiration, ordeal into challenge. Their history has been a chronicle of incessant sufferings unparalleled both in degree and continuity in the history of any other race. But suffering seemed to have strengthened rather than weakened their will to survive. Perpetual sufferings have often shaken their faith in human decency and justice and they have grown to be intolerant about the unwillingness of others to help them.

They fiercely demand recognition today from the world at large and cling to any source which may offer them some degree of that recognition, particularly when one of their sons achieves international repute. They do not regard themselves easterners even though their origin was the east and their country is located in Western Asia. They have been unjustly identified with other races in the Middle East. They regard the Turks as their ancestral enemy and consider the Armenian Genocide of 1915 as one of history's greatest tragedies.

We live in a period of growing concern for the small nations and increasing responsibility of the great powers to understand the political aspirations of the people at large. History's rapid pace continues to show signs of trouble for the Armenian people. There is trouble in the homeland today and the hostility with its neighbors threatens to weaken the strength to build a new order. A new era is about to emerge. After 3,000 years of maturity, the Armenians yearn for the day when the world would make some conscious search for knowledge of their history and offer them a niche in the family of nations that they rightly deserve. If this book can stimulate such a search for that knowledge, its purpose will have been accomplished.

CHAPTER TWO

THE LAND

Armenia is a country with magnificent vistas. The spectacular beauty of this mountainous land offers a picturesque panorama of unusual dimension. The mountains are harsh and unforgiving. But their harshness is redeemed by a coastline of lakes and the beauty of the rivers.

The land covers approximately 100,000 square miles, extending from Asia Minor to Persia with two mountain ranges serving as protective shields. In the north there is the Pontic range and in the south the Taurus mountains. Between them lies a vast region of extinct volcanoes. Today only about ten percent of this ancient land is in Armenian hands, politically organized as the State of Armenia. The rest is occupied by the Turks and Azeri Moslems. The Turks have Western Armenia and the Azeris control the Armenian provinces of Nakhichevan and Karabagh.

In the middle of the Armenian tableland stand the two summits of Mount Ararat. Unlike any other mountain peak, Ararat emerges as a dominant centerpiece in a lowland surrounded with no other mountains. The distance between the two summits is seven miles and it takes two days to walk around the base. Ararat is an extinct volcano that rises to 17,000 feet and is one of the highest mountains in the world. This is the legendary mountain of Noah's Ark. According to the Bible, the Ark "rested upon the mountains of Ararat on the seventh month, on the seventeenth day of the month". After the floodwater receded Noah disembarked with his family and began to repopulate the world.

Ararat has a special meaning to the Armenians. They called it the "mother of the world". It symbolizes the Armenian soul and the national experience. Its primeval beauty has inspired poets and writers for centuries. With its majestic splendor it has guarded the sanctity of the Armenian history. It has witnessed the birth, the glory, and the misfortune of these people who lived at its foot for over 2,600 years. This grand old mountain stands all alone with no intrusion to block its view.

Armenia is gifted with hundreds of rivers flowing through plains, gorges, and canyons. Among them three have historical importance, the Euphrates, the Tigris, and the Arax, with hundreds of tributaries flowing into them. The Arax River takes its rise near the Armenian city of Erzerum at the foot of Mount Ararat, flows southeast, and empties its waters into the Caspian Sea. Most of the ancient capitals of Armenia were located along the banks of this river. The Euphrates and the Tigris born in the Armenian upland flow in a southerly direction toward the Persian Gulf.

Toward the west of Mount Ararat is the snow-capped peak of Mount Arakatz which rises to 13,410 feet. South of Erzerum there is the mountain of Bingol Dagh with 10,770 feet and further south Mount Souphan Dagh rises to 14,540 feet.

Armenia has two important lakes; Lake Van with 1,460 square miles is the largest. It is located on the eastern side of the country, and Lake Sevan, with 497 square miles, is located in the northeast. The country is gifted with rich pastures and fertile land. The soil is abundantly rich in mineral ore, among them the most important are gold, silver, copper, and iron.

The Armenian winters are very severe and the summers are almost torrid in their heat. The extensive snow in the winter makes most mountain roads impassable for at least seven months a year. It is this climate and the ruggedness of the land that have helped shape the character of the Armenian people. The snow-capped mountains provide water to the farm land below even during the driest season of the year. This has made the valleys extremely fertile, producing a prosperous agricultural life for the Armenian farmers.

THE NEIGHBORS

Many races and nationalities have lived in this region side by side as neighbors since the days of recorded history, but peaceful coexistence has not been their way of life. There has been a constant struggle for superiority precipitated by fanatic nationalism. Most of the neighbors who were the rulers of the ancient world have now disappeared. During the time of its birth Armenia had the Babylonians and the Assyrians in the south. They were later replaced by the Medes and Parthians. The Persians replaced the Parthians in the east. The Romans appeared in the western portion of Armenia until the emergence of the Byzantine Greeks who ruled the territory for 1,200 years. Byzantium fell in 1453 and the Turks occupied the Byzantine land which was identified as Anatolia, which in Greek means "the land in the east."

The Taurus mountains in the south separated Armenia from its southern neighbors, the Kurds, the descendants of the Medes. Throughout their history the Armenians rarely ventured to enter the Kurdish territory. The barbarism of the Kurds was well known. The Kurds lived in the impregnable region of the Taurus mountains as independent tribes with no cohesive unity. Their history is one of perpetual warfare, with a reputation of being one of the most unpredictable and savage peoples in Western Asia. In the north of Armenia is the narrow strip of land from Trabizond to the eastern bend of the Black Sea inhabited by the people of Lazistan who were equally ferocious in their savagery. The Armenians never dared to enter this territory either. Lazistan prevented the Armenians to have access to the Black Sea.

In the east of Armenia there are the Moslem Azeris who developed their nationhood during the Eleventh century when Turkish tribes followed their warriors into the territory on the west side of the Caspian Sea. They assimilated with the northern Persians and settled in an area which was referred to by the Persians as "the land of fire", Azerbeijan, because of the abundance of oil in the region (Azer means fire in Persian). They are Turkic in origin identified as Tatars or Caucasian Turks until the beginning of the Twentieth century.

The Georgians in the north are the only Christian neighbors of Armenia. Russia gradually began to extend its domination in the beginning of the Nineteenth century and annexed Georgia, Azerbeijan and Eastern Armenia to the Russian Empire and called the region Transcaucasia. The Russian occupation of the region fused the Georgians into one ethnic group but divided the Azeris and the Armenians into two parts. One group of Azeris remained in Azerbeijan under Russian rule and the other in Persia under Persian rule. Today the Azeris in Iran constitute the largest ethnic minority in northern Iran south of the Caspian Sea. The Armenians on the east side remained under Russian rule and constitute what is now the State of Armenia and the Armenians in the west were under Turkish rule until their forced deportation from the area in 1915. While there is a strong bond between the Armenians and Georgians, there is none between the Armenians and the Azeris. Both have distrusted each other for many centuries.

The boundaries of Armenia were never well defined. The borders changed as the fortune of the people changed. But this was the place which the Armenians called home. Most of the Armenian land is now part of the Turkish territory. Hordes of foreign invaders, from Alexander the Great, to the Persians, the Romans, the Arabs, the Tatars, the Memluks, and the Mongols came and occupied a portion of this land from time to time, but none of them had any aspiration to consider the land as their final resting place until the Turks came and called it their own.

There was a time when the land of Armenia was the center of gravity for world affairs. It witnessed the dawn of civilization and became the crucible for the culture of civilized man. There was also a time when this region witnessed history's greatest convulsions. Men fought their wars here for greed and religious superiority, each group pursuing its own political interest.

There was a time when this was a land of milk and honey, beauty and culture with laughter, songs, the smell of wheat and sun filled harvest. There was also a time when this land was a land of oppression, bloodshed and terror.

There was a time when courageous men of the past built a nation with an unbridled devotion to human liberty. Inch by inch they carved a niche in the history of the human race and in the process became one of the most dignified people of this planet. There was a time when industrious men of the past sewed the fabric of a society with the highest standards of human values and for 2,600 years valiantly fought to uphold those values.

There was a time when this was the home of the Armenian people. Western Armenia is now paradise lost. A God-forsaken place where no man dares to live and no flower dares to bloom. The sun does not shine here anymore. Other men came and destroyed the country, ransacked the homes, slaughtered the people and threw the survivors to the inhospitable deserts to perish. But the history of this people remains imperishable.

The Babylonian Empire was founded by Hammurabi around 2100 B.C. and the Assyrians became a powerful military force around 1400 B.C. Both were Semitic people with their origins going back to the dawn of the pre-historic civilization of Sumer. The Assyrians had developed a powerful military machine which they used to subjugate people from the Upper Euphrates Valley down to the River Nile. Their military conquests brought cultural achievements. The Assyrian kings made the capital city of Nineveh a civilized center for science and culture with a library containing thousands of tablets. It is mostly through these tablets that the world learned about the events that shaped the history of man in the early days of his civilization.

THE HITTITES

In the melange of the tribes and races in central Asia Minor the Hittites represented one of the most organized and powerful groups. They rose to power around 1700 B.C. and ruled this world of ancient man for 500 years. The Hittites were a mixed people of Asian origin. They entered Asia Minor from the Caucasus around 2000 B.C. and gradually moved westward and finally settled around the Halys River in central Anatolia. The previous inhabitants of the region were the Khattians, with Hurrians on their eastern border. As newcomers to the area the Hittites adopted the vocabulary of the Khattians and the gods of the Hurrians. They first appeared on the horizon of history during the formation of city-states which marked the beginning of man's early civilization.

The formation of a city-state under a governmental system was made possible after the fundamentals of civilized life were discovered. These fundamentals were agriculture and urbanization. Agriculture was the first most important science for the development of a civilized community. It produced food which is the basic ingredient for human existence. Civilization in its rudimentary form began not only when the supply of food became abundant but also when man learned how to cultivate the land to make food continuously available. The development of agriculture stimulated prosperity which led to the conversion of village life into urban communities.

Before the development of urbanization man kept moving in search of food. His sole concern was his daily struggle for existence. He hunted animals but kept wandering around in search of new hunting grounds. Man made his first experiment in farming and agriculture in the river valleys of the Tigris and Euphrates and in the plain of Mount Ararat as early as 4000 B.C. The successful experiments in agriculture initiated the process of producing food and making it available to the community. This evolution from food storage into food production, coupled with the domestication of animals, marked the beginning of a civilized life. Food production created social stability. Man did not have to wander around anymore in search of food. He settled down and raised his pigs, sheep, and goats and produced food for his daily sustenance.

By 2000 B.C. there were thousands of farming communities and villages around the Euphrates Valley and central Anatolia. The people lived in huts with clay walls and stone foundations. They domesticated the horse which provided them with an important means of transportation. They cleared forests and used the logs as beams for their buildings. They developed the technique of converting the mountainous terrains into pastures for agriculture and farming. These communities eventually grew into city-states with a class society and a centralized form of government.

With the advancement of agriculture and cattle breeding the science of mining and metallurgy was developed. Around 2000 B.C. man discovered silver and coined it for money and mixed copper with tin and created a stronger metal, bronze, which he used to manufacture weapons and tools. The discovery of bronze was a dramatic event in the history of early man. This metal changed the course of human history by replacing the crude implements of copper, bone, stone, and wood. Farmers used tools made of bronze to cultivate their lands. Ships were built with bronze devices and equipment, allowing man to sail to distant lands.

This gradual advancement in agriculture, mining, and metallurgy created the need to conduct commerce with the neighboring tribes. As wealth increased, urban communities were organized into larger communities. This led to the creation of small kingdoms. A procedure of paying taxes and duties was developed. People were required to pay tax to the local king who had the sole authority to govern the city-state.

By 1700 B.C. Caparnas, a powerful prince of a large city-state, founded the ruling house of the Hittites and declared himself as the King of the Hittites. He took other city-states in his fold and gradually expanded his territory in central Anatolia. This coalescence in a strong city-state required new methods of governing the territorial unity. Soon the institution of government was formed and subsequent kings were elected by an assembly of elders.

The Hittites were not alone.

There were other city-states in their immediate neighborhood, the Hurrians, the Mittanis, and the Hayasa-Azzis. The society of these divergent groups, however, was basically the same. They all had the same agrarian life style. The Hurrians were farmers and artisans. They lived in patriarchal families headed by a chief or a *euri*. When a *euri* of a family died it was the practice of the neighboring families to adopt the family of the deceased *euri*. This patriarchal system unified the families which eventually led to the development of a village, a town, and a city-state with a government of its own.

The Hayasa-Azzi located in the upper Euphrates Valley was a tribal confederation consisting of two separate groups, the Hayasas, and the Azzis with one common ruler. There was considerable hostility and warfare between the Hittites and the Hayasa-Azzis but the confederation was not strong enough to withstand the onslaught of the Hittites. It disintegrated in 1300 B.C. The country lost its political organization and the people scattered around central Anatolia to be assimilated eventually by the Thraco-Phrygians.

The Hittites were the first organized state in Asia Minor. They occupied the central plateau of Anatolia and were protected by the ruggedness of the mountainous region. Although the climate was severe, very cold in the winter and very hot in the summer, the land had abundant resources for agriculture. The Hittites did farming and cattle breeding in the river valleys and used the copper, silver, and iron deposits in the mountains for metal working. The Hittite kings ruled the vast regions of their empire through a feudal system in which local kings pledged their allegiance to the great king of the Hittites. Their king was the ruler of the land as well as the high priest and the supreme judge. He was given superhuman attributes and was referred to as the Sun-God.

The kingdom of the Hittites lasted until 1200 B.C. when the Thraco-Phrygians crushed the empire, captured the capital city of Hattusas and established their own kingdom. They built their capital on the Sangarius River and gradually expanded into the neighboring countries. The Thraco-Phrygians were noted as skilled craftsmen and referred to as horse-breeders and valiant warriors in the epic poems of Homer. Legend told of the Phrygian king, Midas, whose touch converted objects into gold.

After the destruction of the capital the Hittite Kingdom disintegrated but the civilization of the Hittites did not disappear. Elements of their culture and tradition were carried on by the Luwians and the Melids. The Melid Kingdom was the southern neighbor of the Thraco-Phrygians. With the adoption of the language and traditions of the Hittites the Melids became the legitimate heirs of the Hittites. They ran an independent democracy and were powerful enough to maintain their autonomy from the Assyrians who by then had become the most militant force in the Near East. In the Old Testament the Hebrew prophet Yezekiel mentions the house of Togarmah as the Kingdom of Melid. The recorded history of the ancient world uses the words Togarmah and Melid interchangeably. Historian Movses Khorenatsi refers to the people of Torgom or Togarmah as the ancestors of Armenians.

Around 900 B.C. the melting pot that eventually gave birth to the Armenian people consisted of the Thraco-Phrygians, the Melids, the Luwians, the Hurrians, the Hayasas, and the Azzis. But the process of assimilation was not yet complete. Another group will come and be an important component of the melting pot.

THE SCYTHIANS AND CIMMERIANS

Tribes called Scythian and Cimmerian emerged from the Chinese frontiers in the interior of Asia and around 900 B.C. began their journey westward. They settled around the northern shores of the Black Sea and a hundred years later began to spread towards Asia Minor. They crossed the Bosporus in the west and the Caucasus in the east and proceeded towards central Anatolia, where the pre-Armenians lived.

They were barbaric warriors bent on plunder and destruction. The hordes ravaged the Thraco-Phrygian towns and terrorized the people. Unable to protect themselves against the ferocity of the Scythian-Cimmerian attacks the pre-Armenians receded eastward, crossed the Euphrates, and proceeded towards the Lake Van region and around 700 B.C. settled in what came to be known as their national homeland. This unified group formed a kingdom and became the new occupants of the plain of Mount Ararat. The country around Lake Van where they finally rested was called Arme and this new group came to be known as the Armenians. They became a vigorous and industrious people, attached to their new homeland and were prepared to sacrifice everything for the cause of human liberty and freedom. A new nation was born from the fragments of the Thraco-Phrygians, the Melids, the Luwians, the Hurrians, the Hayasas, and Azzis. All of them provided the vital nucleus that formed the lifeblood of this new people.

But the formation of the Armenian people was not yet complete. Another group will eventually be welded into their backbone creating a stronger nation, more vigorous and powerful, destined to exercise its influence as a forerunner of man's civilization in the ancient world.

CHAPTER FOUR

THE URARTIANS

One of the great mysteries of modern history was the emergence of the Kingdom of Urartu. It appeared into the light of history only in the Nineteenth century A.D. when archeological investigations in the region around Lake Van revealed the existence of a highly civilized society with a prosperous economy and a political life. The people were called Urartians and lived in this part of the world some 2,400 years earlier. There is little known as to the origin of the Urartians as a people. Urartu means Ararat in Hebrew and Urartians mean the people of Ararat. The terms Urartu and Urartians are mentioned several times in the Old Testament.

According to some scholars there is a resemblance, both in language and in culture, between the Urartians of Lake Van and the Etruscans of northern Italy. There is some speculation that the Etruscans may have originated from the same geographic area where the Urartians lived. This Etruscan migratory movement may have taken place around 900 B.C. when Urartu was emerging as a nation. It is possible that the Urartians, like the Armenians, came to the plain of Mount Ararat from somewhere else. But the exact direction of their migration is unknown. Culturally they were close to the Hittites but spoke a language which was neither Hittitic, Semitic, nor Indo-European. They first appeared as a group of nomadic tribes around 1350 B.C. possibly out of the remnants of the Hurrians, wandered around in Anatolia awhile and finally settled around Lake Van and called their country Nairi after the name of one of their tribes.

Urartu's history as a nation begins around 860 B.C. with its first king, Aramu, and ends in 585 B.C. when Urartu was conquered by the Medes. The nation disappeared into oblivion around 550 B.C. when the Urartians were finally assimilated by the neighboring Armenians. For almost 300 years Urartu was a theater of an advanced civilization and the Urartian kings ruled their country through one of the most organically centralized governmental systems known to man.

Urartu acquired political and military significance during the reign of Sarduri I who rose to power in 834 B.C. Sarduri developed a powerful military organization and allied himself with neighboring countries to protect the region from Assyrian encroachment. Assyria, then a great power in Western Asia, was Urartu's principal rival. Both of them were in the process of consolidating their hold on their respective territories, extending the frontiers of their countries generally at the expense of the other. The Assyrians lived in the Upper Tigris River on the southeast corner of Urartu, controlling the strategic heartland of Mesopotamia. Before the emergence of the Urartians they had invaded Babylonia and established important trading colonies all around southern Anatolia. With no rival to check their advance the Assyrians were successful in extending their territory to the west around 1300 B.C., establishing the first Assyrian Empire across the arch of the Fertile Crescent, making themselves the legitimate heirs of the Babylonian civilization which had vanished by then. The Assyrian power began to decline gradually, however, when the Urartians came to power around the Ninth century B.C. In establishing their empires the two rivals had adopted different strategies. While the Assyrians colonized territories by killing or deporting the inhabitants of the conquered land, the Urartians were more political. They preferred to form federations with the conquered states, allowing each to govern itself within the administrative framework of the Urartian Empire.

Sarduri I was succeeded by his son Ishpuini in 824 B.C. But before he died Sarduri made Tushpa on the east coast of Lake Van the capital of Urartu. Tushpa was strategically located in the center of the country protected by mountains and Lake Van which never froze in the winter, allowing the Urartians to sail their ships in all seasons to transport supplies, arms, and troops to other regions of the kingdom. The new king erected fortresses and temples around the country and built defense barriers to protect the country from Assyrian incursions. But it was Ishpuini's son, Menua, who organized a formidable force and elevated the country's military might to a level comparable to that of the Assyrians.

Like his father, Menua also built temples and citadels in Tushpa, extended the boundaries of his kingdom, and strengthened the central authority of his government. He is credited with the concept of a new irrigation system, an elaborate network of aqueducts and water channels which helped the development of agricultural communities and consolidated villages into larger urban centers. Menua built gardens, public parks, and vineyards, and reclaimed new land watered by controlled irrigation for farming. He discarded the old fashioned hieroglyphic script and replaced it with the more modern cuneiform style. This change prompted the development of record keeping and encouraged cultural activity.

RELIGION

Menua's reign initiated a period of growth and economic prosperity in the Urartian history. It also marked the beginning of religious consciousness and a reawakening. New gods were adopted and conceived to ensure the nation's economic growth and to preside over the activities of community life. Their chief god, Chaldis, was not enough to protect them against the elemental forces of nature and control its adverse effect on human life. Along with Chaldis they adopted Teishuba, the god of storms, which was related to the Hurrian god, Teshub, and the sun god, Shirini. They adopted gods of the sea, water, mountains, and caves. They had a huge gathering of gods for every function. In addition to the gods worshipped on a national level, each village or town venerated its own local god.

The number of gods was inexhaustible. This polytheistic society had gods for every occasion. The more gods they had the more secure they felt against the uncertainties and vagaries of nature, and the more protected they felt against the forces of heaven, earth, and sea. For them each human activity required some divine protection. The gods had immortal power to control the universe and direct the destiny of man. They were the omnipotent figures of the community and the Urartians sought their intermediation to guide and bless all human activities, in times of planting, in times of harvest, or in times of war. In this assembly of gods, Chaldis, the warrior god, was the most important. He was concerned with the important issues facing the nation. His task was to strenghten the nation's military might and provide internal security and tranquility. The worship of gods was conducted in distinctive temples and Urartu was studded with them. During the rituals the priests offered prayers and sacrifices and officiated the religious feasts and festivals.

THE ECONOMY

Menua brought economic prosperity to Urartu. He extended communication with the neighboring states and made Urartu an important center for commercial activity. He extended Urartu's frontier as far down as northern Syria, thus controlling the caravan route between east and west. Urartu became prosperous as tributes were collected from merchants passing through the Urartian territory. During Menua's reign the Urartians began to exploit the abundant resources of copper. They mixed copper with tin and produced bronze and made extensive use of this metal for farm implements, tools, and armaments.

The Urartians had an extensive economic organization. They were skilled traders and their commercial contacts with their neighbors stimulated the development of foreign markets for their goods. The country had an extensive system of merchant housing establishments helping local businesses to find markets for their products and facilitating the collection of tolls and custom dues for goods in transit by foreign merchants.

Urartu was the crossroad between east and west, north and south. Caravans of camels, oxen, and donkeys used the Urartian trade routes to transport textiles, perfumes, spices, and dyes from the Far East to the eastern Mediterranean and ports on the Black Sea. When northern Syria came under the Urartian domination the Orontes River ports were used to carry goods to and from Egypt, Greece, and the islands of the Aegean Sea. Urartu's principal products for export were furniture, accessories in bronze, gold, silver, iron, and the Urartian timber which was used extensively to build chariots in Egypt.

Urartu had a prosperous middle class, particularly during the height of its power, and a cadre of professional people such as doctors, teachers, scribes, clerks, and craftsmen. Slaves were used extensively for the construction of government projects. The country had large metallurgical installations as Urartu was well known for its deposits of gold, silver, copper, tin, and iron. The metallurgical techniques were so advanced that the Urartians knew how to produce steel and smelt bronze. Since zinc and manganese were plentiful, they also knew how to produce glass, a technique which will be developed by other countries much later.

THE EMPIRE

Menua died in 785 B.C. and his son Arghisti succeeded him to the throne. Arghisti's principal objective was to annex the territories in the east and extend the Urartian borders to the coast of the Mediterranean.

To strenghten his hold on the eastern borders Arghisti built the city of Erebuni in 782 B.C. at the site where Erevan, the present capital of the State of Armenia is now located. Erebuni became an important base for the Urartian expansion in the east with an administration to supervise the necessary link with the central government in the nation's capital. With the expansion of his empire Arghisti successfully pushed Assyria into a secondary position, militarily, economically, and politically. Countries that were previously occupied by Assyria now gave allegiance to Urartu. He shifted the center of gravity through the use of his formidable army which now represented the most powerful force of Western Asia. He led expeditions into Assyria and maintained the security of Urartian borders. His military might protected the country from foreign invasions and created internal tranquility which in turn promoted unbridled economic growth and prosperity.

After building the city of Erebuni Arghisti built Argishtihinili. This city represented the center of Urartian economic activity. While Arghisti ruled the districts through local governors he maintained a system of centralization with unusual statecraft and administrative skill. At the time of his death Urartu had reached the zenith of its military and economic power. Arghisti's son Sarduri II succeeded him to the Urartian throne in 750 B.C. He continued his father's expansionist policies and established numerous economic centers in the kingdom.

THE ASSYRIAN THREAT

Sarduri's objective was to subjugate and later assimilate the tribes living around Lake Sevan and incorporate a large geographic area in the northeastern corridor with the Urartian Kingdom. But trouble was brewing in the southern border. Assyrians, annoyed by the increasing military and economic power of the Urartians, decided to attack the Urartian force in northern Syria. A military expedition was organized by one of the most ruthless kings in Assyrian history, Tiglath-Pileser II. He launched a successful attack and chased the Urartians back to their original frontiers. Sarduri II fled and took refuge in his impregnable fortress in Tushpa. The king was saved but the country around the fortress was destroyed.

This was a dramatic blow to the prestige and power of the Urartians. No organized power had ever threatened Urartu before. The Assyrian military attacks were frequent around the outlying areas of Urartu but never in the nation's heartland. The assault, however, was not perilous to the unity of the Urartian administration. After Assyrian forces withdrew from Urartu, Sarduri resumed control of his government and maintained the integrity of his kingdom. He consolidated his power, reorganized the army, and set about to reconquer the territories lost to the Assyrians.

Upon Sarduri's death his son, Rusa I ascended the Urartian throne. Rusa's problems were more formidable than his father's. Not only did he have an external problem with the Assyrians but also an internal strife. The central authority of the king was being challenged by the administrative governors of the various regions who were demanding autonomy to run their individual tributary districts. The disloyalty of the governors and consolidation of local power were a major concern for the new king. With swift and remarkable administrative skill Rusa removed the rebellious governors and replaced them with viceroys who had previously taken an oath of allegiance to the king. He introduced a major reform of governing the regions, centralized his power, and launched a massive program of reconstruction. Rusa tried to avoid military confrontation with the Assyrians. He was concerned more with restoring the security of his frontiers and took necessary steps to turn the country to economic recovery and growth. Trade was revived and Urartian influence extended once more throughout Western Asia.

The peaceful coexistence between Urartu and Assyria did not last long. When Assyrian King, Sargon rose to power, he turned his attention to the perennial enemy in the north. In 714 B.C. Sargon organized a massive military campaign against Urartu. With a large caravan of camels, donkeys, and troops Sargon crossed the Urartian frontier through mountainous passes and forests and reached the Urartian province of Zikirtu, whose governor, afraid of an Assyrian onslaught, had abandoned the city earlier and fled to the mountains. From Zikirtu Sargon proceeded towards the eastern shore of Lake Urmiah, conquered the region and directed his attention towards the Lake Van region which represented the nerve center of the Urartian power. The Assyrian troops entered the land of Nairi and staged a successful attack on the country of Musasir, which was an ally to Urartu. They destroyed Musasir and Sargon ordained himself as the king of Musasir. When Rusa heard that Musasir had been destroyed and the Assyrians were at his doorstep, he took an iron dagger and committed suicide.

This was again a temporary setback for Urartu. After Rusa's death, his son, Arghisti II succeeded him to the throne. The task for the new king was to consolidate his power and reorganize the army to protect the country from further Assyrian encroachments. This was a turning point for Urartu. They no longer wanted territorial acquisitions. They only wanted to secure their existing borders and maintain internal peace, tranquility and political stability.

The Assyrian King Sargon died in 705 B.C. and the Urartians were granted breathing space and an opportunity to rebuild the country. The new king of Assyria became preoccupied with military expeditions against Babylon, Syria, Palestine and Egypt and left the Urartians alone. The Assyrians' preoccupation with the countries in the south provided the stimulus for the Urartians to reconstruct their country. Arghisti built a city, called Titumnia, on the shore of Lake Van with beautiful gardens, an artificial lake and a canal. On the banks of the Upper Euphrates he built a fortress with massive walls and made it the administrative center for the northern region.

Arghisti's son Rusa II ascended the throne after his father's death. It was during Rusa's reign that Urartu enjoyed internal stability and found itself on the road to recovery. Assyria was threatened by new alliances in the north. The Scythian and the

Cimmerian tribes, after chasing the Armenians and pushing them to the country of Arme, proceeded towards the Assyrian frontiers. The new Urartian king began to establish a friendly relationship with these new tribes to protect Urartu from Assyria. This alliance with the Scythians and the Cimmerians made Urartu one of the most powerful and militant states in Western Asia.

Near the capital city of Tushpa, Rusa built a new city, Rusahinili and a new palace for himself on the peak of the mountain overlooking Lake Van. He built gardens, canals, lakes, and vineyards surrounding the palace, and erected new houses of worship for the Urartian gods. But his most important accomplishment was the construction of an enormous fortress in the city of Teishabaini. The fortress, a veritable hallmark of the Urartian civilization, came to symbolize Urartu's Golden Age and the period of prosperity. The remains of this fortress were excavated in Karmir-Blur, near Erevan. This was a huge citadel built on a ten-acre land containing 150 apartments and a large courtyard protected by massive walls of up to 12 feet in thickness and 24 feet in height. It had sanctuaries and rooms for worship containing the statues of gods. The fortress was named after Teishaba, the god of war, storm, and thunder. The temple inside was surrounded by wine cellars and storage rooms for grain.

This particular center of political activity not only revealed the existence of a highly centralized political administration but also an advanced state of economic activity with stock-rearing, cattle breeding, dairy farming, and cheese making operations. Work was processed in Teishabaini and distributed to other parts of the kingdom. Commercial products included not only agricultural commodities but also woolen yarn, woolen cloth, and fabrics. Excavations in Teishabaini disclosed a highly developed Urartian economy and an elaborate system of account-keeping to record income and expenditures and to prepare summary balance statements. Urartians had scrupulous concern for proper record keeping for the manufacturing of goods and their transportation to the various market centers of the kingdom.

Rusa II died in 654 B.C. and his son Sarduri III succeeded him to the throne. If Rusa's reign marked the beginning of the Golden Age in Urartian history, Sarduri's reign marked the beginning of an era in which this great civilization was drawing to an end. A series of powerless kings impaired the authority of the central government and the integrity of the empire. The non-Urartian districts of the empire gradually broke away from Urartu to form independent states and local governors and viceroys caused the breakdown of the king's central authority with their constant bickering.

THE FALL OF URARTU

The internal struggle was not enough to precipitate the decline of this highly civilized kingdom. A new power was emerging in Western Asia with more ferocity and barbarism than the Assyrians. The Medes, the ancestors of the present day Kurds, appeared on the horizon, and with the help of the Scythians, began to conquer lands and destroy everything in sight. While the Medes as a people were in existence since 856 B.C., their kingdom was not organized until 650 B.C. The Median Kingdom came into prominence when it extended its rule over the Persians in the south. By 620 B.C. the Medes were unquestionably the most powerful force in Western Asia. They destroyed Assyria in 614 B.C. and after the fall of Carchemish in 605 B.C., the Assyrian Kingdom ceased to exist, and Assyria vanished from the pages of history.

With the central authority of the government perilously weakened, Urartu was now thrown open to the Median raids and the local regions were left to their own resources. The Medes invaded Urartu in 585 B.C. with merciless barbarism. They massacred people, looted temples, plundered palaces and devastated the country, all in a matter of a few days. The Urartian kingdom crumbled away after the Medes destroyed Teishabaini in the north and Tushpa in the south. Disintegration brought anarchy and Urartu fell into political oblivion.

FUSION WITH THE ARMENIANS

The twilight of Urartu brought the ascendancy of the Armenians. The Armenians from the country of Arme located in the southwest corner of Lake Van began to spread into the land of Urartu and occupied most of the Urartian territory. The fall of Urartu gave the Armenians the opportunity to expand their homeland. The name Urartu gradually disappeared from historical records and was replaced by Armenia.

The population of Urartu around 585 B.C. was approximately three million and that of Arme was two million. The Armenian expansion into the Urartian territory initiated a long period of assimilation of these two races. Gradually the two peoples were welded together with Urartians forming the bulk of the new society. This period of assimilation lasted several generations. The ruggedness of geography and differences in language made the fusion between the two peoples painfully slow. During this period of great fusion the people spoke a mixed language. Some spoke Luwian, others spoke Hurrian and the Urartians spoke Urartian.

This society of many races and languages created a demand for a common language to evolve as a medium for communication. The unavoidable chemistry between the two races was very complex with no form of government powerful enough to preserve the continuity of its existence. While pages of Urartian history had been adorned with kings and heroes who had added luster to the civilization of the ancient world, the Armenians had no history of any particular accomplishments. They had a nomadic existence until 585 B.C. with an unusual docility of letting others merge with them during their long pursuit of a national homeland. But never had they had a better qualified partner than the Urartians. This mixture was not unusual for the Urartians. When the Urartian King Arghisti I founded Erebuni in 782 B.C. he brought Luwians and Hurrians to populate the new city. In the history of Urartu ethnic mixing had occurred many times and on a large scale. Their fusion with the Armenians, therefore, was not an extraordinary event.

The fusion gave a new name and identity to the Armenian people. The non-Armenians called these people Armenian after the name of their country, Arme, but the Armenians called themselves *Hay*. The origin of this word goes back to the Hittites. While the Hittites had disappeared from the scene a long while ago, the Urartians continued to call the people living on the west side of their kingdom as Hittites and the people living on the west side of the Euphrates as *Hate*. Before the demise of the Urartian Kingdom, the Armenians lived on both sides of the Euphrates River. After the fall of Urartu and during the period of assimilation the Armenians called their language Hittitic. When the Urartians merged with the Armenians and changed their language to Armenian, the language continued to be identified as Hittitic. In the old Armenian the word Hittite may have sounded like *Hatiyos*, according to the phonetics of the old language. *Hatiyos* eventually evolved into *Hayo*, therefore, the Armenians called themselves *Hay* and their country *Hayastan*.

The Urartians constituted the principal portion of the Armenian nation. The final phase for the formation of the people was completed around 550 B.C. It was during this time that the Persian and Greek sources began to refer to the country as Armenia and the people as Armenian. Herodotus was the first to identify them as Armenic.

The history of the Armenian people is the continuation of the history of the Thraco-Phrygians, the Hurrians, the Luwians, the Hayasa-Azzis, the Melids, and the Urartians. Out of the embroidery of this racial amalgam rose a new nation whose origin goes back to the time around 1200 B.C. when the Thraco-Phrygians crossed the Bosporus and entered Asia Minor. While it is accurate to say that the history of the Armenian people began in 585 B.C. when the Armenians and Urartians were fused to design a new united political destiny, it is equally accurate to say that the organization of the multiracial society of the Armenian people began around 1200 B.C. when the Thraco-Phrygians initiated the period of assimilation which eventually led to the formation of the Armenian people.

The successive processes by which Armenia achieved the unity of culture and language are obscure. Cohesion of the two peoples was achieved first at the lower stratum of the society when intermarriages united the two cultures and later at a higher level when the elite united to strengthen its protective shield against the Medes and the Persians. The result was a territorial unity of the land of Armenia with that of Urartu. Eventually the territorial units consolidated into some sort of kingdom under a central authority. But history does not record the establishment of an Armenian kingdom until 220 years later. Presumably the central government was in the hands of nobility. A prominent member of a noble family may have been selected as royal and a kingship may have been established through the same hereditary descent of the old Urartians. This is only speculation. There is only fragmentary evidence of dubious authenticity that records the activities of this people during this period. A tremendous sense of community spirit may have guided them for 220 years and kept them together as Armenians.

The amalgamation of the Armenians with the Urartians was an accidental refinement of the foundation of the Armenian people. The union produced a more rigorous race with a firmer momentum for survival. It was a manifestation of a new cohesive order in the uncertain and fragile world of Western Asia. Living in the ominous shadow of the belligerent Medes the racial unity provided the people with the strength to insulate the freshly minted group against foreign adversity.

The restless spirit of the Luwians, the passion of the Hayasa-Azzis, the intellect of the Melids, the tenacity of the Urartians, and the stubborn perseverance of the Thraco-Phrygians gave birth to a new and dynamic nation. Armed with the highest qualities of each racial component the nation was now on its way to design its own destiny. After wandering for nearly 600 years from the Bosporus to central Anatolia, they had finally found their resting place in the plains of Mount Ararat and called it their national homeland.

CHAPTER FIVE

ON THE ROAD TO KINGDOM

After the fall of Urartu the Median Kingdom became the principal power in Western Asia. The Medes under King Cyaxares expanded their empire into Anatolia, reached Lydia and made the Halys River their western frontier. While they had the most organized army equipped with the latest weaponry and ferocious barbarism they will eventually be overwhelmed by Cyrus the Great who will establish the Persian Empire and maintain tight political control. During the interlude between the fall of the Assyrian Empire in 612 B.C. and the establishment of the Persian Empire in 550 B.C., the center of gravity in Western Asia shifted north to Media.

This interlude was relatively peaceful. Armenia after the great merger with Urartu became incorporated into Media and as a vassal state contributed greatly to the administration of the Median Empire. Armenians enjoyed political autonomy. For Armenia this was the period of a new start. After the turbulent process of amalgamation with the Urartians, the Median occupation gave the Armenians the vigor to transform their seminomadic way of life into a new system of national unity. The Median Empire did not last long. Cyrus the Great defeated the Medes in 550 B.C. and made Media a vassal state of the Persian Empire. With the fall of Media, Armenia became an integral part of the Persian Kingdom.

THE PERSIAN RULE

Persia will exert a tremendous influence on Armenia for the next one thousand years. As rulers and neighbors of Armenia their influence on the Armenian language, culture, tradition, religion, and political life will be overwhelming. The history of Armenia from this point on will be interwoven with that of Persia. Kingdoms will be established and wars will be fought for the preservation of the Armenian political identity at the discretion of the Persian king who will, at times, design the destiny of Armenia in the most cruel and capricious manner. For one thousand years Armenians will be involved one way or another with the turbulent periods of Persian history. But despite the political subjugation and distinguishable trace of the Persian influence, Armenians, through the stubborn tenacity of their character, were able to retain their identity as a people.

The empire that Cyrus built stretched from the Mediterranean to the steppes of central Asia, encompassing or bordering five large bodies of water, the Mediterranean, the Black Sea, the Caspian Sea, the Persian Gulf, and the Indian Ocean.

The origin of the Persians goes back to 1000 B.C. when the Aryan Persians entered Western Asia from the interior of Asia. They were warrior horsemen, who traveled in groups in search of favorable pasture for food and settlement. Their migratory movements took them to the lower part of the Caspian Sea and settled in the region which consisted of a great central plateau of desert surrounded by a series of mountains. Concomitantly, two other Aryan groups, the Medes, and the Parthians, entered the region. The Medes occupied the northern region and the Parthians took the eastern portion. This land called Persia in the southern part of the Caspian Sea became a corridor between central and Western Asia.

The southern region of the Caspian Sea was the natural route of these Aryans who came in successive waves of migration but were blocked to proceed westward by the established kingdoms of Urartu and Assyria. They were forced to settle down in the desert and the mountainous regions and gradually organized city-states with nomadic chieftains as their rulers. The Persian city-states were always a target for the Urartians and the Assyrians whose kings raided, plundered, and exacted taxes every time they had the opportunity to do so.

Urbanization brought civilization to the land of Persia whose rulers began to exploit the resources of the land and initiated a program of populating Persia with artisans and craftsmen from Urartu and Assyria. The Persians were thus influenced by

Urartian and Assyrian culture and traditions. With the technique of craftsmanship came the introduction of weapons which the Persians used to defend their land.

PERSIA UNDER THE ACHAEMENIDS

The Persian element of this Aryan group gradually became the dominant factor in the political life of Persia. Around the time when the Medes were on the ascendancy, a Persian ruler founded the state of Parsumash in the Elamite territory of Persia. His name was Achaemenes from whom the successive Persian kings were called Achaemenids. The successors of Achaemenes accepted the suzerainty of the Medes until Cyrus the Achaemenid rose to the throne in 559 B.C. and changed the political direction.

After defeating the Medes, Cyrus extended his kingdom over the neighboring city-states and gradually unified the various regions and consolidated his power. With administrative skill and military genius he accepted many elements of the subject peoples of his Empire into the army, and organized one of the mightiest military forces of Western Asia; and within a single generation extended his Empire from the Indian Ocean to the Mediterranean Sea.

Armenia became one of the components of his Empire. With no distinguishable ruler of its own, Armenia governed itself as a vassal state to Cyrus. But Cyrus was a benevolent ruler. He maintained the integrity of his Empire with tolerance and respect for the native traditions and customs of the various ethnic groups. He spared the lives of the defeated kings who accepted him as a liberator and were eager to pledge their allegiance. He organized a royal council of advisors and called himself the "first among equals".

Cyrus was succeeded by his son, Cambyses who became the victim of internal revolt and was succeeded by Darius, the son of a Parthian king. It was Darius who initiated the systematic restructuring of the Persian Empire that Cyrus founded but was unable to hold. During his long reign of 36 years he managed to give the empire sanctions of authority and political administration and through them a hereditary descent. Although not a member of the Achaemenid dynasty he wanted to be recognized as one to maintain the hereditary continuity. He structured his Kingdom on the sanctions of religion and considered himself as the protege of Ahura Mazda, the chief god of the Persians.

Darius' religious inclination was primarily due to his close contact with Zoroaster, the religious reformer and prophet, who appeared in eastern Persia around the time when Darius was growing up in his father's court. Hounded by the established priesthood, Zoroaster found refuge with the father of Darius, then the king of Parthia.

The Aryan nomads brought with them a composite of religious practices from Asia during their migratory movements. The basic tenets of their religious beliefs were based on Indo-European doctrines which recognized two deities - the Deva meaning the celestials and the Ahura, meaning the masters.

When the settlements of the Aryans in Persia were completed and the Persians began to structure their communities into city-states, they refined the theological system by separating the two gods. They took the Deva as the demon and accepted Ahura as the true gods. Among the Ahura gods they selected one, the Ahura Mazda, to be the greatest of them all. They worshipped him as the supreme god of the universe.

It was Zoroaster, however, that made the Ahura-Mazda the only god of the universe, thus establishing the concept of monotheism in Persia. For him Ahura-Mazda was the omnipotent god, endowed with supernatural qualities, the creator of the world, and the embodiment of the highest ethical qualities governing the activities of man by universal principles of justice and truth.

Zoroastrianism believed that man is responsible for his acts and at the end of time a Messiah will appear and will resurrect the dead. A molten lava will destroy the entire world bringing the last judgment, during which the bad people will be burned in hell and the good people will live forever in heaven. Some of these concepts of Zoroaster were incorporated into Christianity by the early preachers of Christ's religion.

Darius shared Zoroaster's monotheistic concepts which provoked a religious revolution in Persia. But for him the political unity of his empire was more important than the dissemination of religious doctrines. While his predecessors left Armenia alone to govern itself under Persian jurisdiction, Darius ruled the empire through a system of provincial governments, called satrapies. He segmented his Empire into large territorial units. Each unit was governed by a satrap, who was a governor officially appointed by the king. There were altogether 30 satrapies. Armenia was divided into two, one was the 13th satrapy which included the land north of the Euphrates, and the other was the 14th satrapy which was the land east of the Arax River including the plain of Mount Ararat. The satraps were members of the Persian nobility, usually close friends or relatives of the king. They had the authority to govern the province with direct responsibility to the king under a loose framework which allowed a considerable degree of freedom to the subject people. But to solidify the Persian element of his empire, Darius made the Persians a privileged group with no obligations to pay taxes.

The Armenians were treated well. They continued to progress economically under the administrative rule of the satrap who allowed them to have a free hand to continue to practice their native customs in return for their loyalty to Persia. The satraps imposed a tribute and required Armenians to serve in the military to fight Persia's wars. The Persian rule was not oppressive. The Armenians were allowed to maintain their national institutions and worship their gods in an atmosphere of religious tolerance and civil liberties. The Persians exercised a benevolent rule with scrupulous concern for the welfare of the Armenians. They accepted the cultural primacy of the Armenians and considered them the most civilized among the subject peoples of the Empire. The non-oppressive rule of the Persians was extremely important during this critical time of the formative years of the Armenian people. The Armenians had been moving towards a more cohesive form as a people after their great merger with the Urartians. A harsher control by the Persians would have placed their national identity in the most precarious and vulnerable position.

The Persian rule did not affect the economic and agricultural activities of the Armenians. The Armenian communities remained fundamentally stable and prosperous, a testimonial to the benevolent rule of the Persians. New irrigation projects were constructed to reclaim land for farming. As the privileged class of the empire the Persians took little part in the economic life of the provinces. Their principal concern was to collect taxes and tributes. The political tolerance and tranquility in the region gave the Armenians the opportunity to continue to play their traditional role as merchants and traders. The loss of political independence did not prevent them to conduct trade within the empire and with countries outside the periphery of the Persian rule. The benevolent rule of the Persians stimulated economic growth which brought prosperity to Armenia. With no identifiable political life of its own, Armenia continued to forge commercial ties with Phoenicia and Syria in search of new markets for its manufactured goods. The transportation of goods was made possible by a network of new roads that Darius constructed to link the various regions of the empire together to preserve the administrative unity and to maintain a centralized authority in the empire.

ADVERSITY WITH THE GREEKS

With all their formidable power of empire building Darius and his successor, Xerxes, were frustrated in their efforts to subdue the Greek colonies in the western side of the Persian world. Earlier Cyrus the Great had conquered the Greek outposts, Ionia and Lydia, in the southern section of Asia Minor. But his successors realized that in order to hold the Persian Empire together it was necessary for them to enter Europe. The independent Greeks in the Hellenic peninsula continued to maintain cultural and political ties with their cousins in Ionia and Lydia, disturbing the political unity of the Persian rule.

A new chapter was about to be written in both Greek and Persian histories. The Greeks considered themselves in danger of the Persian might which was always ready to cross the Aegean Sea and conquer the Greek Peninsula. The political and economic well-being of the Greeks, therefore, was seriously affected by their military activities to stand ready to defend themselves against a possible Persian onslaught. The Persians in turn were affected by the spread of Hellenic culture in their territory. It was the Greeks who coined the Persian capital Persopolis, which meant the city of the Persians. It was from Persopolis that Darius and his successors ruled their vast empire.

Darius died in 486 B.C. and his successor, Xerxes, immediately began to organize a large scale military campaign to subjugate the Greek Peninsula into the Persian rule. Despite tremendous war power and the military resources at his command, Xerxes was defeated by a heroic and unified force of the

Greek city-states. The Greek victory stopped the Persian encroachments and political intrusion into Greece. It also enabled Greece to continue to move towards a panhellenic political coalition under a democratic form of government. New alliances among the various city-states began to coalesce into a Hellenic league with Athens and Sparta having the pre-eminent position in the alliance.

The Persian Wars also produced a historian of international renown, Herodotus, who traveled widely through the Persian Empire and wrote about the history of the wars and the various cultures of the Persian world. Among the groups of different nationalities, he found the Armenians worthy of consideration. With an inquiring mind he depicted the community life in the towns and villages of Armenia. He found the Armenian dwellings elegant and equipped with many utensils. He reported that Armenians had plenty of provisions and kept their wine in cemented cisterns. Some of the people were living in underground dwellings he observed.

Herodotus was fascinated by the extraordinary qualities and the work ethic of the Armenians. His book provided the first authentic information on Armenia during the formative years of the people. His honesty of thought and sophisticated search for truth earned him the universal reputation as the "father of history".

ALEXANDER THE GREAT

The Greek victory over Persia also shifted the focus of history from Persia to strong new powers of the Hellenic world. New political organizations were being formed among the various city-states of the Greek Peninsula. The prestige of the Greek civilization was on the rise. And while the Persians continued to hold a strong foothold in Western Asia there were signs of political decay in their empire. The empire was plagued by intrigue and revolt. The successors of Darius gradually adopted oppressive policies to rule the subject peoples, which resulted in frequent revolts and loss of loyalty to the Persian government.

The consolidation of city-states in Greece coalesced into a strong monarchy when Philip II of Macedonia incorporated the various regions under one administrative union in 348 B.C. Earlier each unit wanted to enjoy an autonomous existence. But

no unit was powerful enough to stabilize the peninsula and assure a lasting peace. Philip II ended the period of political disunity by welding the Greek states together.   But it was his son,
Alexander, who opened one of the most illustrious pages in the
history of the ancient world and initiated a new era of Hellenic
civilization. He inherited his father's kingdom of Macedonia in
336 B.C. at the age of twenty and when he died 13 years later he
had stretched the Hellenic Empire from Greece to northwestern
India and Turkestan. His military conquests shaped the destiny
of man for generations to come. He was the first to bring the
west and the east together which both the Persians and the
Greeks before him failed to accomplish. He destroyed the old
political frontiers and established new ones, and during the process gave the Greeks the opportunity to disseminate the elements of their culture.   Inspired by his teacher, Aristotle,
Alexander initiated a new epoch of Hellenization.   People
learned about the thought provoking ideas of the Greek philosophers which helped change the future direction of civilized man.
Alexander also gave the Armenians the opportunity to transform their vassal state into an independent kingdom.

THE END OF ACHAEMENID RULE OF ARMENIA

With an organized and well trained army, cavalry, and naval
complement, Alexander began his campaign of military conquests. He acquired land after land, territory after territory without losing his political and administrative ties with the
Macedonian capital. He was the military hero as well as the
political genius able to maintain the acquired land under his
control. His principal target was the Persian Empire which was
then ruled by an inexperienced king, Darius III. At the time of
Alexander's rise to power the provincial satraps had shaken the
central authority of the Persian king. Unlike his great predecessors, Darius III had abandoned the traditional rule of political
and religious tolerance for the subject peoples who accepted
Alexander as their liberator from Persian oppression.

Alexander entered Asia Minor and liberated the Greek
colonies from the Persian rule. He proceeded east to the Euphrates and entered Armenia. He abolished the Persian satrapy
system and replaced the satraps with a pro-Armenian Persian by
the name of Mihran as the governor of one of the satrapies and

Yervand as the governor of the other. It was Yervand who founded the Yervandian Dynasty in 322 B.C. which will rule Armenia until the establishment of the Armenian kingdom in 190 B.C.

Fragmentary evidence reveals the names of some of Yervand's successors with no particular distinction or accomplishments. The list of successors has gaps with no continuity of rule, and includes names of dubious authenticity. We know little of the events that shaped the course of Armenian history until the formation of the Armenian kingdom. There are no records, Armenian or foreign, that would show the way the Armenians carried on their business and were able to perpetuate the traditions of their society. This period can best be characterized as merely the prelude to freedom and independence and the period during which Hellenic thought was crystallized into Armenian national life.

Within a few years Alexander conquered all the territories of the Persian Empire. And when he was ready to crush the nerve center of Persia in Persopolis he was already invested with the titles of Pharaoh of Egypt, Great King of Persia, King of Sumer, King of Akkad, Lord of the Universe, and most importantly the liberator of the oppressed peoples of the Persian world. He entered Persopolis with ease. The organized resistance of Persia was already broken. He demolished the palace of Xerxes, symbolizing the Greek revenge of Persia. Darius III was killed during his flight but was offered a royal burial by the man who was now recognized as the most powerful and the absolute ruler of all men on earth. Alexander died in 336 B.C. at the age of 33 in Babylon when he contracted fever. The death of Darius III symbolized the end of the Achaemenid Dynasty in Persia which had begun when Cyrus the Great came to power in 559 B.C. The Armenians were now liberated from the oppression of the Persian satraps but they were not quite ready to chart their own political destiny.

THE SELEUCID KINGDOM

Alexander ruled his empire by the force of his personality. He commanded respect and the people recognized him as the absolute ruler with universal power. For some he was even regarded as one with divine attributes. His administrative purpose was to bring about a union among his people without distinction of race, color, and creed. But his vision for the brotherhood of man remained unaccomplished by his premature death.

The result of his death was political chaos. There was no provision made for his succession. Alexander's generals were quick to divide the vast empire among themselves. With no concern to pursue Alexander's plans for unification and driven only by personal interest and the aggrandizement of their power, Alexander's successors divided the empire into three segments. One took Macedonia, the other Egypt, and the third was Seleucus Nicator who acquired the bulk of the old Persian Empire.

General Seleucus founded a kingdom and became King Seleucus I. He ruled the empire by a system of satrap government for which the Persian Empire had given the precedent. The two Armenian satraps became part of the Seleucid Empire. He ruled his empire from his capital in Antioch which became the most important political center of the Seleucids, housing the palace and the court of the king. The Seleucid rule over Armenia lasted 140 years from 330 B.C. until 190 B.C.

Around 200 B.C. Antiochus the Great, a successor to Seleucus appointed two Armenian governors over the two provinces of Armenia. One was Artashes who became the governor of the larger province of Armenia and the other was Zareh, the governor of the smaller province. Armenia under the governorship of Artashes and Zareh enjoyed an autonomous status. The Seleucids left them alone in exchange for some military assistance and a moderate payment of tribute. The Armenians were allowed to practice their own customs and maintain their national institutions. The Seleucids avoided interference in the internal affairs of Armenia. They only wanted to carry on Alexander's Hellenization program to provide a homogeneity of Greek culture among the various groups of people in the empire. To pursue their policy they populated Armenia and other parts of the empire with Greek and Macedonian immigrants.

HELLENIC CULTURE IN ARMENIA

Armenians welcomed the infusion of Greek culture into their national life. The Greek settlers in Armenia brought with them a considerable amount of knowledge and information about Greek thought and civilization. A wave of Greek influence began to penetrate Armenia's national life. The intellectual curiosity of the Armenians was stimulated by the works of Socrates, Aristotle, and Plato. After 360 years of Persian satrapial rule which produced no particular cultural heritage, the Armenians were now taught about the universality of man's intellectual pursuits.

The overwhelming interest of the Armenians in their own traditions and culture did not prevent them to extend their horizon beyond the confines of the Armenian scholarship. Devoid of any alphabet of their own, they adopted the Greek letters to express their ideas and used them as a means of communication. They minted their coins bearing Greek inscriptions and used them to facilitate trade. They began to read the Greek writings on science, philosophy, government, and welfare and compared the Greek philosophy with their own thought. The treasures of Hellenic literature were now open to the Armenians. The texts of Homer, the lyric poets, the Greek tragedies, the works of the famous orators, the writings of Greek historians became part of the intellectual repertoire that the Armenian mind sorely needed. Greek drama as a means of entertainment became popular.

This was the Golden Age of Greece. From the Greek peninsula the Hellenic revolution in thought and culture was widely diffused, east to Asia Minor and the lands beyond the Caucasus, and south to Egypt, Palestine, and Phoenicia. Alexander's conquest of the east opened the door for the elements of the Greek genius to flow into non-Greek areas of the empire. They were there for the taking but not everybody was receptive. With the exception of a small community of Jews in Alexandria, other peoples and races of the Seleucid Empire took little interest in Greek civilization. Perhaps the Thraco-Phrygian element of the Armenian people was responsible for the Hellenic cultural movement in the Armenian national life. The Greeks themselves were excited by the unbridled enthusiasm of the Armenians in Hellenic culture. The Armenian society became more cosmopolitan. They became aware of the world beyond Armenia. They learned the techniques of craftsmanship, architecture and the principle of writing without losing the identity of their own culture. They adapted the sophisticated culture of Greece to their own needs, but continued to preserve the integrity of their own civilization with the Greek influence acting as a catalyst.

After living in the dark ages for 360 years and after a period of oppressive political subjugation by the Persians, the Armenians around 200 B.C. felt like the displaced person of the philosopher Diogenes who advocated the value of the individual person. Diogenes lived as a wanderer, devoid of any material comforts of life but always in search of truth and the virtues of human life. He walked around Athens in bright daylight carrying a lighted candle. When asked why, he answered he was looking for an honest man. There was a difference, however, between Diogenes and the Armenian person of 200 B.C. Diogenes considered himself homeless and denied the ties of family and society. The Armenian person also carried a lighted candle in the bright daylight of Armenia in search of truth without, however, changing the fundamentals of his national heritage. He accepted his ties of family and society as the basic foundation for his existence, just like Plato who advocated man could not live without society.

The political ideas and philosophical teachings of Plato had a profound effect on Armenia's political structure during the governorship of Artashes and Zareh. Plato taught about the need to establish a just society in which man could achieve a good life. In his works he created an ideal political system of a city-state in which both the individual and the state play a vital role in the fulfillment of man's happiness. The individual would express his own abilities and the state, through its political organization, would provide the opportunity for such expression. But it was Aristotle who was mainly responsible for the large scale Hellenistic movement in Armenia. Aristotle gave Alexander the Great the idea to disseminate the elements of Greek culture in the conquered lands. This prompted the great general to take along a group of scientists and scholars on his military campaign into the Persian Empire.

With an autonomous status and ruled by Armenian governors, Armenia around 200 B.C. was on the road to establish its own kingdom which would be the first after years of travail, mergers, fusion, sufferings, and oppression. On the road to kingdom Aristotle's ideas offered the prototype from which Armenians will develop the foundation of their kingdom. The great philosopher believed that a country should be ruled only by those who are most qualified to rule. The government, he preached, should be in the hands of a great man chosen from among the intellectual elite of the community.

Armenia needed imaginative leadership to organize a durable political structure. Artashes, among the two governors of Armenia was the one most qualified to be the first king of Armenia. He appears in the history of Armenia as a pivotal figure whose dynasty would mark the beginning of a new epoch, the Artashesian Age, that will last for 190 years until the beginning of the new millennium. He broke the mold of the Dark Age which had obscured Armenia for 360 years, and through political and military accomplishments shaped the direction of subsequent history. With a remarkable combination of leadership and administrative ability he established the condition which inspired Armenians not to be satisfied with their lot, to seek freedom and national liberation and create an independent kingdom without the intrusion of foreign rulers.

By the eve of the creation of the Armenian kingdom, the Armenians had established the fundamental institutions of their political destiny. It is from this point on that one will begin to notice the distinguishable individuality of the Armenian culture. There will be another ten years, however, before Artashes establishes the Armenian throne. The changes of political tides to which Armenia was exposed were not yet favorable for the creation of an independent kingdom.

CHAPTER SIX

THE ARMENIAN KINGDOM

The Seleucid Empire lacked political unity. Dynastic quarrels and unwieldy administrative structure were responsible for the gradual decay of the Seleucid authority in Western Asia. Seleucus I had a number of prominent successors who fought valiantly to hold their empire together, but their power crumbled away as a result of a diversity of political, racial, and economic problems. New powers were emerging in the eastern horizon of the empire. Persia broke away from the Seleucid fold and the governor of Bactria (present Afghanistan) renounced the Seleucid authority and formed an independent kingdom. In central Anatolia the kingdoms of Cappadocia and Pontus, both lying on the western side of Armenia, were being organized. But the most important development for the future direction of the Armenian people was the emergence of Parthia in the southeastern corner of the Caspian Sea as an independent kingdom under Arsaces - Arshak I. The subsequent influence of Parthia on Armenia's political development will be considerable.

The Parthians were the ancient Persians who settled in the northeastern section of Persia around 1500 B.C. and spoke a language called Pahlevi. The decline of the Seleucid authority in the eastern provinces gave the Parthians the opportunity to consolidate all of Persia. The Achaemenid Persians were already gone and there was a political vacuum which needed to be filled. The Parthians extended their kingdom into Mesopotamia and successfully pushed the Seleucids to the west of the Euphrates River. Another power was also on the rise. The expansion of Roman influence around 200 B.C. played a decisive role in the political reorganization of Western Asia. The Seleucids were puzzled by the unexpected Roman interest in the Near East. The Seleucid King, Antiochus III, attempted to stop the Roman military campaigns in Asia Minor but was defeated in 190 B.C. The Parthians in the east and the Romans in the west will eventually supplant the Seleucids as the two great powers of the Near East. The Euphrates River will provide the natural dividing line between the two giants.

THE CREATION OF THE ARMENIAN KINGDOM

The decline of the Seleucid power and the rise of the Roman influence in the Near East gave the two governors of Armenia the opportunity to finally shake off the suzerainty of the Seleucids over Armenia. In 190 B.C. Artashes I declared himself as the king of Greater Armenia, thus becoming the first king of the Armenian people, and Zareh declared himself as the king of Lesser Armenia. It would be Artashes, however, who would become more prominent and provide the royal succession. Zareh's line of succession would be discontinued after his death.

With administrative and political skill Artashes I immediately began the difficult task of building and maintaining an independent state. To gain political clout and to protect the new state against the increasing power of the Parthians he adroitly allied himself to Rome. He expanded his kingdom to the north to include the land formerly occupied by the Urartians and to the east to include Lakes Sevan and Urmiah. Artashes's expansion into the lands beyond Armenia proper was met with hostility. Local governors and princes wanted to maintain their political autonomy and were unwilling to accept the king's authority over their affairs. There was resentment over the ascendancy of the Armenian power in Western Asia. The rapid disintegration of the Seleucid Empire had created a political vacuum and the agility of the native rulers to fill the void was important to succeed in their struggle for survival. Artashes was quick to bestow titles and offer special favors to local governors, but was equally quick to eliminate political rivals and force others to come to terms with the royal authority.

With the creation of the Armenian Kingdom an elite group of people also began to develop. The emergence of the Armenian nobility as a separate class of people played a criti-

cal, and at times, a perilous role for the maintenance and the
continuity of the Armenian Kingdom. The members of the nobility were aristocrats chosen by the king to help him run the
administration of the country. They were the king's compan-
ions, friends, or office-holders in the high stratum of society and
lived in fortified castles and maintained small army units for
their own protection. It was the king's prerogative to nationalize
these garrisons in time of national war. The nobles were members of the inner circle of great families. They managed their
estates in times of peace and led army units in times of war.
The Armenian nobility was structured on a hierarchical system.
The political strength of the noble was measured by the family's
proximity to the crown. The noble immediately below the king
obviously was the most influential. The king had the absolute
authority and the nobles served as members and advisors of the
royal council and magistrates. While there was intense rivalry
among members of the Armenian nobility, they kept the throne
secure in a hereditary descent. The Armenian nobles were
known as Nakharars. They played a dominant role in the history of Armenia but their relationship with the king was not always amicable. In the case of Artashes there was political unity
among the nobles that protected the Armenian throne against
foreign intrusion. This unity was solidified mainly by the king's
largesse of granting huge estates to the Armenian Nakharars.

THE NATION'S CAPITAL

With the creation of a new kingdom, Artashes needed a new
capital. The old capital, Armavir, built by the Yervandian Dynasty, was not adequate for the growing administrative requirements of the new kingdom. The location of Armavir on the
bank of the Arax River was not suitable to offer a protective
shield. Meanwhile in the west Rome was concluding its war
against the Carthaginians whose leader, Hannibal had valiantly
fought against the Roman forces but was finally defeated. Hannibal fled to Asia Minor and took political refuge in Armenia.
Legend has it that it was Hannibal who suggested the discon-
tinuance of Armavir and helped Artashes plan the construction
of a new capital. Artashes selected a site where the Medzamor
River empties into the Arax, and built the new capital strategically protected by the river's junction. He built a palace for

himself and a fortified wall around the city. He called the city Artashat, after his name. He created a defensible core to serve as a base for his new government, and built theaters, temples and, as he was an ardent patron of literature, established libraries, and entertained artists. He organized the city as a city-state to house the political institutions that were essential to run an effective system of government. The ruins of Artashat may be seen today near the village of Khorvirab, located within a short distance south of Erevan, the present capital of the State of Armenia.

With the help of the Armenian nobles Artashes expanded its borders and converted the peripheral areas into provinces and built fortifications at strategic locations of his kingdom. He improved the road system and assigned new land for settlement and cultivation. Artashes expanded the villages to service the caravans passing through Armenia and consolidated the Armenian hold on trade routes. Artashes expanded towards the west and through an expansionist program reminiscent of the Urartian era, colonized most of the communities west of the Euphrates and brought them under the Armenian fold. Within a period of thirty-one years he brilliantly succeeded to transform his little kingdom into a strong, independent, and prosperous state. This transformation would have been difficult, however, without Roman help. The creation of the Armenian Kingdom itself would have been difficult without Roman support. It was the Roman Senate that approved the installation of Artashes and Zareh on their respective thrones in 190 B.C. It is important, therefore, to turn back and trace the development of the Roman influence in the east.

THE RISE OF ROME

The history of the Roman interest in the east began around 215 B.C. when Philip V of Macedonia joined Hannibal of Carthage against the Roman Empire. Earlier, Rome had been influenced by the cultural diffusion of the Greek civilization and had established commercial ties with the various city-states of the Hellenic peninsula. There was a large colony of Greeks living in the southern tip of Italy and Rome's involvement with the Hellenic world was primarily to protect the trade and shipping routes between Italy and Greece. Rome used Philip's alliance with Hannibal as an imperialist pretext for intervention. After a triumphant victory in Carthage the Roman army landed in Greece to fight Philip V. Unable to defend the country against the superior strength of Rome, Philip agreed to a peace settlement which obliterated his prestige in the Hellenic world and confirmed the rise of Roman power. Philip was required to give up all his possessions outside of Macedonia and deliver heavy indemnity to Rome.

The victory over Macedonia opened the doors of Asia Minor. The triumphant Romans marched through Greece and crossed into Asia Minor, crushing the last remnants of the Seleucid power. By 150 B.C. the Roman troops had conquered most of Asia Minor and subjugated the kingdoms of the Greek peninsula. Within a period of 50 years the Romans had successfully extended their interest to the eastern shore of the Mediterranean and had begun to establish a new order in the world in which they will play a dominant role for centuries to come. They too adopted the elements of Greek culture into their own institutions and developed new thoughts on government, philosophy, literature, and art, making a significant contribution for the development and preservation of western civilization.

Rome's military supremacy and its ability to maintain the integrity of the empire will influence Armenia's political life for several centuries.

ARMENIA AFTER ARTASHES

Artashes died in 160 B.C. and was succeeded by his son Ardavazd who was afflicted by a mental disorder and committed suicide soon after becoming king. The new Armenian king, Tigran I, who rose to power in 149 B.C. was unable to protect Artashes' kingdom against the increasing encroachments of the Parthians in the east. By now the Parthians had consolidated all of Persia and had successfully conquered the lands east of Mesopotamia. Their kings had assumed the title of Arshak. It was Arshak Mithridates II who rose to power in 114 B.C. and turned his attention to the Armenian Kingdom. The increasing power of the Armenians had undermined Mithridates' efforts to proceed west and consolidate the newly created kingdoms of Cappadocia and Pontus into his domain. Even without Armenia in the middle this wouldn't have been an easy task. By 100 B.C.

the Kingdom of Pontus on the west side of Armenia had grown to be a serious adversary to the rising power of Rome in Asia Minor. While Rome was at war in the Italian peninsula, the King of Pontus decided to oust the Romans from the east and re-establish a Greek hegemony in Anatolia. This was an ambitious Greek response to the increasing dominance of Rome.

Rome's objective in the east was to expand its empire, establish a durable political entity, and control the more consequential parts of Western Asia. These objectives were accepted by the people of Western Asia with some degree of enthusiasm. But there were exceptions. The Parthians in the east and the rulers of Pontus in Anatolia wanted to chase the Romans out and create their own empires on the ruins of the Seleucid Kingdom. Armenia was precariously in the middle between these two belligerent antagonists. The concern for the Armenian king was two-fold: To preserve the independence of Armenia in the event of a military conflict and to continue to conduct trade with the provinces of the Roman Empire.

There was a renaissance of prosperity in Armenia around 100 B.C. Artashat had become not only the political capital of the Armenian kingdom but its center of commerce as well, controlling the route of transit trade between east and west. Armenian products were being sold in markets in Italy and Europe and Roman traders moved into Armenia to conduct business. This reciprocity was beneficial to the economic welfare of Armenia whose nobles and the governing class received political support from Rome. But the political stability of Armenia was in a fragile condition. The Armenian King Tigran I died in 123 B.C. There followed a period of political turmoil when increased pressure from Parthia almost put an end to the newly created kingdom of Armenia. The balance of power in Western Asia which had been meticulously established by King Artashes I was in the process of being disturbed.

Ardavazd II rose to the Armenian throne and immediately began to reorganize the army and implement his predecessor's expansionist policies. He moved towards Media and Georgia and incorporated large territorial units to the Armenian Kingdom. He enlarged the city of Artashat and initiated new programs of increased trading activity with the west. His alliance with Rome helped him improve the commercial ties that Armenia maintained with the subject peoples of the Roman Empire.

The Roman Senate continued to send political and economic support to the Armenian king whose alliance to Rome was extremely crucial to preserve political equilibrium. It was obvious that Armenia provided a buffer zone between the two arch enemies of Rome, Parthia and Pontus. It was equally obvious that the destruction of the Armenian Kingdom would have unified Parthia and Pontus to the detriment of the Roman Empire. The merger of these two formidable powers would have disturbed Rome's ultimate goal to expand its empire to central Asia and India. The Caesars of Rome and the leaders of the Senate were anxious to establish their military supremacy in Western Asia and their support to the Armenian Kingdom was extended for that express purpose.

The Armenian king's expansionist move into Media and Georgia and his continued alliance with Rome infuriated Parthia, whose King Mithridates II finally decided that the time was ripe to strike in full force. The Parthian king organized a well-trained army and cavalry of Parthians, and barbaric mercenaries from Scythia and proceeded towards Armenia. But within a few days, his troops, vastly outnumbered, were decimated by the Armenian units. This was a humiliating defeat for the great Parthian whose colossal army earlier had won him great conquests in Asia and helped him compile a remarkable record of victories in his push towards Mesopotamia. His army devastated, Mithridates was forced to abandon his military expedition into Armenia. Armenia was victorious, but victory had its price. During the hostilities the Parthian forces had taken young Tigran, the heir apparent to the Armenian throne, as hostage. It will be this young man who will one day open one of the most illustrious pages in the history of Armenia. He will be remembered as Tigran the Great whose spectacular military conquests will place him among the world's greatest generals. He will be the ruler of an empire that will stretch from the Caucasus to the Persian Gulf, Palestine, Phoenicia, and the Mediterranean.

CHAPTER SEVEN

THE ARMENIAN EMPIRE

Tigran was the younger son of Tigran I. He was held hostage by the Parthians in the royal palace of Ecbatana, the capital city of greater Media, for several years. When King Ardavazd died in 94 B.C. the Parthians wisely decided to make concessions to the Armenians. Afraid of a possible takeover of the Armenian territories by the Romans, the Parthians agreed to return Tigran in exchange of territorial units in Media and Georgia taken earlier by Ardavazd. Tigran rose to the Armenian throne in 94 B.C. during a period of political instability in the east and became King Tigran II. His reign marked the beginning of a new epoch, the Heroic Age, in which Armenia achieved military supremacy in Western Asia and assumed the role of a world power. A page of glory is about to be written in the history of Armenia.

As a young career officer Tigran had a distinguished record of bravery during the military campaigns of his uncle, King Ardavazd. Ardavazd's territorial aggrandizement provided the stimulus for prosperity and there was unprecedented economic growth everywhere. The Armenian merchants were conducting business with the neighboring countries and with countries as far away as Egypt and Italy. It was important for the newly established kingdom, however, to expand its frontiers further to protect the trade routes, establish order, and guarantee economic security in the east. The departure of the Seleucids and the eventual disintegration of their empire had created a political vacuum. As a result, the region lacked political security and stability. Groups of mountaineers along the commercial routes and pirates around the Mediterranean shores began to operate. They kidnapped merchants, stole goods, plundered caravans, and raided villages. The towns and villages around the periphery of the Armenian Kingdom were constantly pillaged causing a serious economic problem and disrupting commercial activities of the merchants. Armenia needed a strong ruler to control the trade routes.

Tigran inherited the kingdom and with a remarkable combination of military and administrative acumen, chased the plunderers out, and established the security of the commercial routes. But if his predecessor wanted to expand the frontiers of Armenia solely for economic reasons, Tigran's interest was to create an empire and consequently change the face of Western Asia. He began his expeditions for colonization immediately after taking over the throne. He reorganized the administration of the government and built one of the mightiest armies in the east. The Armenian nobles accepted him as their commander-in-chief with supreme authority to declare and conduct war. He directed his attention first towards the western side of Armenia and in a swift campaign captured Cappadocia and made it a vassal state.

His army stopped at the border of Pontus whose king, Mithridates VI (not to be confused with King Mithridates II of Parthia) was in the midst of his military struggle with Rome. Mithridates began his hostilities against Rome by instigating the people of his land to massacre the Roman residents living in the east. His objective was to establish a powerful Hellenic state and chase the Romans out of Asia Minor. His savage disposition was well known throughout the east and the Mediterranean world. He had risen to power in Pontus by murdering his mother and brother and within a short period of time had extended his kingdom through deplorable means along the shores of the Black Sea. Mithridates ruled his kingdom by merciless cruelty and oppressed the land by heavy tribute. Tigran's strategy was to stay clear of Pontus. He wanted to organize his conquests in the interest of his own people without the intrusion of foreign elements. His great military project was the conquest of Persia, Syria, and Palestine and to proceed south to Egypt. He had no interest to go west even though Pontus presented no obstacles to his grandiose campaigns. The two rulers recognized the military and political necessity of dividing the Near East among themselves and removing the Romans from the area. As a sign of mutual respect they concluded a treaty of alliance in which they each pledged not to invade the territory of the other and give military aid in the event of an attack by another party. To solidify the friendship Mithridates VI offered his daughter, Cleopatra, to Tigran for marriage.

The death of Mithridates II of Parthia in 86 B.C. gave Tigran the opportunity to move eastward and recapture the territories previously seized by Armenia. His mission was to enlarge his kingdom and secure the eastern approaches to Armenia. His army was exceptionally well coordinated having its primary strength in the units of foot soldiers and the cavalry. Tigran entered the land of Greater Media and destroyed the capital city of Ecbatana, where he was once kept hostage. He then proceeded east and south and conquered the land of Persia and all the territorial units of Mesopotamia. He established supply and communication bases for his army as he went along. The country of Persia had no effective leadership during the reign of Tigran the Great. The death of Mithridates of Parthia created a political void not only in Parthia but also in Persia and Mesopotamia. From Persia Tigran proceeded south and west. He conquered Syria, Phoenicia, and Palestine and in 83 B.C. conquered Antioch, the old stronghold and capital of the Seleucids. He was now the supreme ruler of an empire that stretched from the Caspian Sea to Palestine, from the Black Sea to the Mediterranean. His military conquests were spectacular enough for him to assume the title of the "King of Kings". He ordered the Armenian coins to be minted with that inscription on them.

The army with which Tigran the Great began his military campaigns was small but exceptionally well trained. As he conquered land after land and territory after territory he took men of the native lands in his command. He used mercenaries and paid them by the treasury of the occupied countries but the core of his army was the Armenian contingent. Despite his military strength and the ability to structure a unified army, Tigran lacked an overall strategy for empire building. He was an able administrator but failed to maintain a centralized structure of government. He designed his military plans as he moved from one country to another but failed to connect the various regions of his empire with a central nerve center for control. As a ruler he adopted a policy of political prudence and religious tolerance for the subject peoples, but failed to build the foundation for a durable empire. The empire lacked a unity of purpose. Each group continued to have its own separate traditions and culture. The Armenians continued to live in Armenia proper and took no roots in the provinces and vassal states. The provinces of the empire were ruled by governors who collected tributes and reported directly to the emperor. Tigran spared the lives of the defeated kings but removed them from their respective thrones and brought them to Armenia to be his court attendants. He was aloof and dignified and had the skill to hold the loyalty of his men. He achieved this by continued military success rather than by sanctions of central authority.

After the victory in Antioch Tigran marched down the coast of the eastern Mediterranean. He took the principal seaports of Phoenicia and Palestine to secure the shipping routes and establish a commercial link between the Armenian mainland and the Mediterranean world. It took Tigran ten years to build an empire. Through his military genius he was able to convert a rudimentary kingdom into a world power. He brought down the old barriers and redrew a new political map for the east, and in the process became one of the most powerful rulers of the ancient world. He transformed the small inland kingdom of Armenia into an imperial framework within which various peoples lived.

A NEW CAPITAL

With the expansion of the Armenian Empire the capital city of Artashat became geographically remote. To rule his vast empire Tigran needed a new capital more centrally located and large enough to house his administrative headquarters.

In the southern part of Armenia not far from the Tigris River Tigran built a new capital and called it Tigranakert after his name. Tigranakert's strategic location insured political and administrative control and offered protection for commercial traffic that passed to the south. To exploit Armenia's important geographic position for trade, Tigran signed advantageous alliances and cultivated close commercial relationships with countries on the extremities of the empire. Tigranakert became a center of commerce as well as the political capital of the empire. The construction of the new capital prompted economic growth which brought unprecedented prosperity to the Armenian merchants and the aristocratic elite. The merchants funneled eastern and western trade through Tigranakert. The exotic goods from India and the east were reexported to the seaports in Phoenicia and Palestine, and the goods of the west and south Arabia were rerouted to the eastern provinces of the empire. The copper and silver of Armenia were exchanged for the timber of Phoenicia and the craft products of Antioch. A caravan route ran through the outskirts of the capital city which offered protection and warehousing facilities to the merchants. Uniform business methods were adopted which, together with the replacement of barter by a monetary economy, contributed greatly to economic expansion and prosperity.

Tigran built ostentatious palaces, temples, and citadels in the capital and fostered a luxurious court life. The great palace he built for himself became the symbol of Armenian glory. The palace with sumptuous rooms, spectacular surroundings, manicured gardens with statues of gods and goddesses, became the envy of the potentates of the east and west. It was an architectural masterpiece that marked the beginning of a golden age for Armenian political and cultural life. The entire city was surrounded by a wall which was 300 feet high with fortification, offering protection from outside invasion. Along with Armenians, Tigran populated the city with Greeks, Syrians, and Cappadocians and brought 300,000 Jews from Palestine and used them as slaves. The city represented the symbol of Armenia's rise to world power. The Armenians had built an empire. Their army had defeated all its enemies and their leader had successfully knit together the various political centers of the east. The Armenians, at 75 B.C. stood on the threshold of an unprecedented economic expansion and a new peak of prosperity.

HELLENIC CULTURE IN TIGRANAKERT

Along with palaces and citadels Tigran built theaters and libraries to disseminate the Hellenic culture in the east. Tigranakert reassuringly had Hellenic character. The political institutions of Armenia were closely associated with Greek culture and Hellenism was a vital force in the social, political, and religious life of Armenia. The official language of the Armenian court was Greek. The administration of the government as well as business transactions were conducted in Greek. The coins of the Armenian Kingdom were minted with Greek inscription and the non-Armenian aliens, including the Jewish slaves, spoke in Greek. The Armenian language was spoken only by the Armenian inhabitants of the city and it was regarded as a language only for the people living in the lower strata of society.

The kingdom was *de facto* an Armenian kingdom but under a Hellenic veneer. Tigran was more instrumental in spreading the Greek culture in the interior of Western Asia than the Greek kings around the Aegean Sea. He had a profound affinity towards everything Hellenic. The royal princes were taught in Greek, and Tigran's son, Ardavasd, wrote plays and dramas in Greek. The aristocratic and ruling class of Armenia in other cities of the kingdom also preferred to speak in Greek. The diffusion of Hellenic culture throughout the empire was the principal objective of the emperor who wanted to create homogeneity to consolidate the various provinces and unify the people. He wanted to transform the Armenian rural community into an urban community and convert Armenia into a more cosmopolitan state. His wife, Queen Cleopatra, played a decisive role in this Hellenic movement. She was a highly educated person, who had studied in Greece and was an expert in Greek prose writing and in the new schools of rhetoric and philosophy. Hordes of philosophers, writers, and celebrity performers from Greece flocked to Tigranakert to perform in theaters or teach in the schools. Tigranakert became an intellectual center. The Greek philosophers recognized the new individualism of the Armenian society and its willingness to adopt the nutrients of the Hellenic culture to the Armenian traditions and institutions. The Queen by dint of her intelligence became the most important person in Armenia's cultural life. Artists and writers came to Armenia to pay court and enjoy her gracious hospitality. She contributed generously, both in time and money, to the propagation of the Greek culture throughout the empire and created endowments for art and literature. She was a woman with infectious enthusiasm and people in the palace were stimulated by her intellectual activities and elegant demeanor.

While Cleopatra was the Queen of Armenia, polygamy and concubinage were still acceptable oriental traditions. Tigran the Great and the royal princes had a great number of concubines and several wives. The Emperor's family life, however, was an unfortunate one. He had three sons from Cleopatra but all three revolted against their father. One organized an open rebellion against the empire, the second forcibly took his father's tiara and placed it on his head and declared himself king when Tigran one day fell from his horse on a hunting trip. The third son left the family and organized an unsuccessful revolution against the empire with the help of the Parthian king. Tigran killed the first two sons with his own hands. A fourth son, Ardavazd, not a child of Cleopatra, succeeded him to the throne.

As the "King of Kings" Tigran believed in pageantry and in the proper decorum of royalty. He wore his tiara studded with precious stones and a tunic of white and purple symbolizing his purity and equal status with gods. The courtiers were ordered to wear special costumes and perform elaborate rituals whenever the Emperor entered the royal palace. But if Tigran was able to build a political and military power base in Tigranakert and flatteringly referred to himself as the "King of Kings", he was unable to consolidate his territories and maintain a coherent and durable organization which was necessary to govern a vast empire. Unlike the Roman emperors whose tentacles reached every corner of their empire, Tigran was not astute enough to build an imperial bureaucratic structure to preserve the integrity of his empire the way the Romans did. While he broke the old political molds and built an empire beyond the highest ambitions of his people, his empire lasted only a few decades, and it was soon torn apart by forces beyond his control. Rome was already at his doorstep.

CONFLICT WITH ROME

Armenia was an ally to Rome and Tigran followed a cautious policy with the Romans. But trouble was brewing in the west where his father-in-law, Mithridates VI of Pontus, was continuing to fight against the Roman forces and was determined to eradicate the Roman influence in the east. By 88 B.C. Mithridates had already extended his kingdom into the Hellenic peninsula and brought most of the Greek communities in Asia Minor and around the Black Sea under his jurisdiction. The expansion of Mithridates' power into areas bordering the Roman sphere of influence irritated the Roman Senate and threatened Rome's policy of aggrandizement into the east. The Senate was aware of the social unrest in the east and Mithridates' imperial ambitions to be the sole ruler of Asia Minor. The Senate was equally aware of the ill-feeling that the people had toward Mithridates. He had been a despotic ruler, ruthless, and barbaric at times, with ferocious implementation of his policies of violence and brutal deeds. In Asia Minor the Greeks predominated in population. They lived in freedom and maintained a harmonious relationship with their cousins in Greece. For them the price of freedom was nonparticipation in the struggle between Rome and Pontus. They had become prosperous by selling eastern goods in Italian markets and preferred political tranquility more than anything else. They had accepted Mithridates as their leader, not as a matter of choice, but as an exponent of politics and convenience.

To put an end to this annoying problem in the east the Roman Senate assigned Sulla, the consul in Rome and a general with an impeccable record of accomplishments, to go east and fight Mithridates. Sulla arrived in Greece with an organized army, took Athens with no difficulty, marched to Macedonia, and invaded Asia Minor from the north. He conquered the Greek principalities around the Black Sea and was on his way to the heartland of Pontus. Alarmed by Sulla's conspicuous military strength, Mithridates quickly negotiated a peace settlement. The terms of the settlement called for Mithridates to abandon his conquests in western Asia Minor and deliver his warships to the Roman general as indemnity for the war. This was a sweeping accomplishment for Sulla. He returned to Rome victorious and assumed the dictatorship of the Roman Empire. The conflict with Mithridates was not over. He returned to his capital to plan for his next confrontation with Rome.

Sulla died in 78 B.C. and Pompey rose to prominence in Rome. Pompey's first task was to put down an open rebellion in Spain that groups of dissidents were conducting in the western tip of the Roman Empire. The confusion in Rome and Pompey's preoccupation in Spain gave Mithridates the opportunity to denounce the terms of the settlement and open hostilities against Rome this time with the help of pirates around the Mediterranean Sea. Irate with this new development in Asia Minor the Roman Senate assigned Lucullus, another general of national renown, to go east and finish off Mithridates once and for all. Lucullus went to Asia Minor with one of the most powerful armies under his command, crushed Mithridates' power base and decimated the cities in Pontus. He destroyed, ransacked, and plundered the towns and villages of the kingdom. He subjugated the people to heavy taxes and took enormous sums of money as indemnity. Mithridates fled to Armenia and took refuge in his son-in-law's palace. Lucullus advanced towards Armenia and demanded the surrender of Mithridates. Tigran refused by declaring "the whole world and my conscience would condemn me if I should surrender the father of my wife to his enemy". Incensed by Tigran's refusal to cooperate, Lucullus invaded Armenia with a force of 18,000 and proceeded directly to Tigranakert. He took the heavily fortified suburbs of the city and stationed his troops outside the gates of the capital. Tigran fled, leaving all his treasures and his family behind. His recovery was quick, however, despite the damage inflicted on his army. He reorganized his troops in the northern part of Armenia and with the help of his vassal kings proceeded towards Tigranakert to chase the Romans out. He met the Roman army in 69 B.C. in the outskirts of the capital but the Roman military power was too formidable for him. With new reinforcements and supply Lucullus crushed Tigran's army with ease and entered Tigranakert. Tigran gathered his family and fled with Mithridates to the eastern section of Armenia.

The Roman troops ransacked the capital of the Armenian Empire, massacred the Armenian residents, looted and burned the palaces, but left the non-Armenian aliens alone. The Syrian, Cappadocian, and Greek inhabitants of the city helped the Romans to plunder and pillage with the promise that they will be allowed to repatriate to their respective homelands. Tigran reorganized his army again in the eastern region of Armenia and with the help of Mithridates proceeded towards Artashat, the old capital of the Armenian kingdom, to defend the last bastion of his empire. Tigran's plan was to cut off the Roman supply line, isolate the Roman troops and prevent them to receive supplies and reinforcements. But he did not need to use this strategy. The inclement weather and snow storms in eastern Armenia had forced Lucullus to abandon his plan and leave Armenia alone. The Roman troops were worn out. The severe weather in Armenia had prevented them to get supplies. Humiliated, Lucullus was forced to retreat to Mesopotamia and halt all military operations. The withdrawal of Roman forces gave Tigran and Mithridates the opportunity to reorganize the government, assume control of the country, and recapture the territories lost to the Romans.

Meanwhile in Rome victorious Pompey had returned from his successful military expeditions in Spain. The Roman Senate, impatient with Lucullus and outraged by the embarrassing failures in the east, ordered Lucullus to turn over his command to Pompey. With a remarkable talent for administration of war, Pompey organized a formidable army of Roman soldiers and mercenaries and began to march toward Artashat to finish off Tigran. His first target was Pontus. He entered Pontus with ease. There was hardly any resistance against the Roman forces because a few days earlier Mithridates had been murdered by his own son and the country had become leaderless. Pompey then turned toward Artashat. The Armenian forces were overwhelmed by the Romans. Tigran the Great was already in the twilight of his life. The old soldier was weary of war. After years of fighting, planning, organizing wars, and conquering lands, he had come to the end of the line. He gathered together a small regiment and proceeded toward the Roman camp where Pompey and his men were stationed. He was willing to accept any compromise offered by Rome. He rode his horse slowly to Pompey's private quarters, approached his adversary, descended from his horse, removed his tiara, and placed it on the ground in front of the Roman general. He requested truce and a peace settlement at any cost. Moved by the dignified appearance of the Armenian emperor, Pompey took the tiara and placed it back on Tigran's head. The war was over. Under the terms of the settlement Tigran agreed to relinquish all his territories in Western Asia, Syria, and Palestine and pay a war indemnity to Rome. The Armenian Empire was over. Armenia once again was reduced to its original borders. The once powerful kingdom became a subject ally to Rome and served only as a buffer zone between the Roman Asia Minor and the Parthians, who were once again emerging as an organically unified force in the east. Syria, Pontus, Cilicia, Cappadocia, and Palestine became provinces of the Roman Empire. Rome's sphere of influence was now extended to the Euphrates and small principalities near the Caucasus were converted into nominal allies to Rome.

For the remainder of his life Tigran held his throne on the sufferance and with the support of Rome. At the end he was all alone. His family had left him and his treasures were seized. He was no longer the King of Kings. He was only the titular head of the Armenian kingdom. Gone were the days of glory, pageantry, and the luxuriant life of the court. His capital city of Tigranakert which once represented the center of power and civilization in Western Asia was destroyed. He died in 54 B.C. He wanted to create a lasting empire and unify the peoples of the east under his command the way Alexander had attempted, but Rome proved to be too powerful for him to achieve his goal. At the end he died a defeated man. His empire was torn apart, and his ancestral homeland was reduced to a mere buffer zone between east and west and it will remain as such for the next 2,000 years. His greatness was short-lived but he wrote one of the most magnificent pages in the history of his people.

CHAPTER EIGHT

THE SUCCESSORS OF TIGRAN

In the years following Tigran's death Rome had to deal with the rising power of Parthia and the social discontent among the various peoples of the east who found themselves, once again, under the domination of a non-Asiatic ruler. This was the first time since Alexander the Great that the face of the east was being reshaped by a European power. At the time of Tigran's death the Roman Empire was vastly extended from the Black Sea to Palestine and the shores of the Mediterranean. The powerful rulers of Armenia and Pontus were gone. Pompey had singlehandedly organized the states of the east and transformed them into provinces of Rome. But Rome was not the only superpower in the world. By 50 B.C., Parthia, which was once a superpower in Western Asia before the rise of Tigran the Great, was emerging as a great power, threatening to challenge Rome's long standing interest in the east.

With the conquest of Armenia and the removal of Tigran, Pompey was able to establish peace and order and restructure governmental systems for the effective administration of the provinces. But his rule extended only to the Euphrates River. Beyond that and up to the Indian subcontinent was the world of Parthia led by the successors to Mithridates II. For the next several centuries Armenia will be squeezed between these two powers. Its fate will be decided upon alternately by Rome and Parthia, and its political, social, and cultural life will be influenced considerably by the relationships, alliances, and wars of these great powers. It will continue to have its own kings and central administration of government and it will be allowed to chart its own destiny in a quasi-autonomous environment. Its policies, however, will be affected by the great pendular swings between Rome and Parthia. Its strategic location will be considered by both an ideal buffer zone to insulate one from the other. The kings of Armenia will change political directions and alliances and adopt policies sometimes favoring Parthia and other times placating Rome. In the vicissitude of subsequent history, the viability of Armenia as a nation and its political fortune will be based on the wisdom or the foolishness of its kings.

Ardavazd rose to the Armenian throne upon the death of his great father in 54 B.C. As King Ardavazd II, he led the people with diplomatic vacillation and clumsiness, attempting to balance his allegiance between Rome and Parthia and playing on both sides of the spectrum to win the goodwill of whichever seemed to prevail at the moment. But in the end he failed and failed miserably, causing his tragic death and the misfortune of his family in the hands of the Romans. A man of intellectual disposition, erudite enough to write poems and dramas while growing up as a prince in his father's court in Tigranakert, Ardavazd inherited the throne as a natural successor to Tigran the Great. He was Tigran's last living issue and Pompey's only choice to be Armenia's king. Pompey trusted Ardavazd to be the leader of the vassal state with the expectation to receive assistance in the form of military materiel and manpower for Rome's ultimate conflict against Parthia. Ardavazd's first task as a king was to re-establish Artashat as the nation's capital. Tigranakert had been destroyed beyond recognition.

The establishment of an overseas empire and the necessity to preserve the superpower status required Rome to conclude its wars of conquest in the east by crushing Parthia and extending the empire to the Indian Ocean and the steppes of central Asia. But trouble was brewing in the west and Pompey had to return home to solve an essentially meaningless political quarrel among the various leaders of the Roman Senate. Pompey had the absolute power to lead the empire with the support of the people and the army. His great command in the east had given him the reputation of a powerful military leader with the ability to win wars. But politically he was weak. His struggle for political leadership overshadowed his military accomplishments. He felt threatened by Crassus who saw his personal power endangered by Pompey's popularity. Crassus was a figure admired by many in the Senate. But the Senate was fearful to allow either one of them to assume the sole leadership of the country. The Senators did not want the concentration of power to be in the hands of one man.

THE FIRST TRIUMVIRATE

A collective leadership was formed with Pompey, Crassus, and Julius Cæsar who was just entering upon a career which would eventually initiate a new direction in the history of the Roman Empire. The members of the Triumvirate were called upon to rule different portions of the empire, but the division of the territories was not made equitably. Crassus, with his enormous wealth and close relationship with the members of the Senate, dominated the political agenda of the day and established his own power base within the Triumvirate. Cæsar had his own ambitions, longterm perhaps, that compelled him to stay aloof and leave Pompey and Crassus alone with their personal animosities. From the outside he supported Pompey because of a marriage tie; Pompey had married Cæsar's daughter Julia. The division of the empire among the Triumvirs gave each specific assignments and responsibilities. Cæsar had the land of the Gauls, Britain, and Germany, Pompey had Spain, and Crassus had the much coveted portion of the empire, the East. While Pompey was a man of resolution with the political skill to bring the peoples of the east under the Roman flag, Crassus proved himself more infatuous, emotional at times, and less talented in military organization. The Roman objective in the east was to maintain the territories gained earlier by Pompey, crush the Parthians, and create a Roman hegemony. This was too large an undertaking for a man whose interest was more in the accumulation of material wealth than in organizing and fighting wars.

In 54 B.C. Crassus led a large army of forty thousand to attack Parthian strongholds from the deserts of Mesopotamia. King Ardavazd of Armenia offered to provide help. He put 10,000 Armenian cavalry and 30,000 infantry at the Roman's disposal with provisions of food and armaments. He also advised Crassus to advance towards Parthia by way of Armenia which offered a more favorable corridor than the Mesopotamian deserts. Ardavazd was aware of the Parthian ability to fight a desert war, and Rome's ineffectiveness to lead a successful expedition under the command of Crassus. Crassus refused to take the Armenian route. He crossed the Euphrates River and headed south towards the deserts. But Crassus was not Pompey. His limited military ability combined with the pitfalls of desert combat proved to be fatal. The Roman army had no chance against the well organized and coordinated Parthian troops, who, under the command of King Orodes, encircled the Roman garrisons in Carrhae at 53 B.C. and decimated them in the most ferocious manner. Crassus himself was treacherously murdered while attempting to negotiate a cease-fire.

When the news of the Roman defeat arrived in Armenia, Ardavazd immediately abandoned the Roman cause and ordered his troops to bring the severed head of Crassus to Armenia. The head was brought to Artashat, where King Ardavazd, having sought an immediate alliance with the Parthian king, was celebrating the marriage of his sister with the son of the Parthian king. During the wedding ceremony Ardavazd formally presented Crassus' head to King Orodes as a symbol of his new alliance with Parthia.

The death of Crassus created an imbalance in the Triumvirate. The survivors, Pompey and Caesar, immediately began to form separate alliances to build a political base and take over the helm of the government as the sole ruler. They looked upon each other as antagonists. The marriage between the two had been broken already by the death of Pompey's wife in 54 B.C. They became involved in a cruel and bitter struggle for leadership. The capital of the Empire fell into political chaos with rival gangs fighting each other in the streets. A veritable civil war was under way in Rome. The country was in the grip of a debilitating contest that was consuming the political resources of the government. Pompey sailed to Greece to assume control of the colonies as the protector of the state and Caesar attacked the Pompeian armies in Spain. From Greece Pompey sailed to Egypt and Caesar followed him in pursuit. To gain Caesar's friendship the fourteen year old king of Egypt had Pompey put to death soon after his arrival in Egypt. But Caesar did not take this kindly. While his adversary was out of the way and he was now accepted as the sole ruler of the Empire, the murder of Pompey by a non-Roman king was taken as an affront and insult to Rome's prestige at home and abroad. Upon his arrival in Egypt Cæsar deposed the young king and placed the king's wife and sister, Cleopatra, as the queen and ruler of Egypt. Victorious, Cæsar then returned to Rome and assumed the dictatorship of the government. His task was to organize the Roman republic, which had decayed by political turmoil.

ARMENIA ALLIED WITH PARTHIA

Meanwhile in Western Asia the political problems and the civil war in Rome had given the Parthians and the Armenians the opportunity to proceed south and gain control of Syria. In 51 B.C. they besieged Antioch and chased the Romans out of the area. The combined alliance of Parthia and Armenia ruled Syria unopposed for fifteen years until 36 B.C. when the successors to Cæsar, after restoring the much needed political stability in Rome, directed their attention to the east once again. For fifteen years Armenia under King Ardavazd II enjoyed political independence.

The defeat of Crassus had disbanded Armenia's vassalage to Rome. The military alliance, together with the marriage ties with the king of Parthia, gave the Armenians breathing space to restore the economy of the country and re-establish the commercial traffic with the neighboring countries. Economic expansion brought prosperity and the acquisition of Syria opened new markets on the shores of the Mediterranean. Armenian merchants began to cultivate commercial ties with their counterparts in other countries. Trade became profitable as deposits of precious metals such as silver and gold were mined and exchanged for the craftworks of Phoenicia and the textiles of Syria.

For fifteen years Armenia enjoyed a renaissance of economic prosperity. Artashat, despite the apparent inaccessibility, served as the focal point of caravan trade and Armenia itself acted as a land bridge for commerce between east and west. The capital city was enlarged and fortified. New palaces were built and new temples were constructed. Religion emerged as a new force as the government began to finance the operation of the sanctuaries. Ardavazd as a devotee of Greek culture and an ardent promoter of Hellenism began to build libraries, schools, and theaters and imported Greek intellectuals and scholarship reminiscent of the days of his father's court in Tigranakert.

Rome had accepted, at least for the time being, the consequences of its defeat in the east. The need to restore political tranquility at home compelled Rome to postpone its war of conquest against Parthia and leave Armenia alone. The temporary postponement of the war, however, did not remove the threat that Rome one day may thrust its military machine into the heartland of Western Asia. Rome was still recognized as potentially more powerful than the combined forces of Parthia and Armenia. The alliance of Parthia and Armenia tried to avoid military confrontation with Rome. They fancied no expansionist ambitions to extend the borders of their respective kingdoms beyond Antioch and Syria. If for Rome this was a war of conquest, for Armenia and Parthia it was a war of defense. The political reality forced them to join forces against the common enemy. But the alliance was a loose one ready to be changed in a moment's notice. While they both wanted to defend their states against Rome, the aim of each was essentially different. Militarily the alliance was lopsided. Armenia by no means was as powerful as Parthia. The two kings, Orodes and Ardavazd regarded each other with suspicion and distrust. But for fifteen years they managed to live on equal terms with one another.

THE SECOND TRIUMVIRATE

Julius Caesar was assassinated in 44 B.C. and the Roman Senate formed the Second Triumvirate consisting of Octavius, Caesar's adopted son; Mark Antony, the shrewd politician who delivered the famous eulogy at Caesar's funeral; and Lepidus, the renowned general who commanded a powerful legion stationed near Rome. Unlike its predecessor, this coalition had a unique blend of power and military dictatorship. Its objective was to restore peace and order immediately and reorganize the empire. The conspirators who planned the assassination of Caesar soon discovered that their aim of restructuring the republic could not be achieved because the republic of Rome was as dead as Caesar. Caesar was the central force of the republic, and his removal had destroyed the republic. The members of the new Triumvirate needed to provide the country with a different direction. It was important for them to resurrect the republic. It is the workings of this Triumvirate that initiated a new era which gave firmer momentum to the empire to endure for another two hundred years.

Rome had made enormous investments both in manpower and capital resources in the eastern provinces. But these investments had produced nothing but humiliating debacles. Parthia remained unconquered and Armenia was cut loose from the Roman sphere of influence. The only gain was the small principalities in Asia Minor which continued to maintain their nominal contacts with Rome. But Rome's defeats in the east and the political disturbances at home had severely damaged the ties of loyalty that these provincials had with their Roman patrons. The first task of the Triumvirate, therefore, was to reorganize the war of conquest in the east and finish up the job that Crassus had started. The administration of the Empire was divided among the Triumvirs. Mark Antony, having emerged as the strongest figure in the coalition, received the eastern provinces. He immediately began to prepare the stage to organize the military expeditions. He sailed to the east for the projected invasion of Parthia. But his interest was quickly diverted by the stunning beauty of Cleopatra of Egypt who had come to Asia Minor to greet him. Antony became captivated by Cleopatra whose mesmerizing charm forced him to put the affairs of the war aside and follow her to Alexandria. He stayed with Cleopatra for a long time and had a son by her and named him Alexander. While in Egypt he showed no great haste in preparing the war against Parthia.

It was only four years later in 36 B.C. that Mark Antony decided to go back to the business of war and attack the Parthians. It was time for King Ardavazd of Armenia to change sides. To win Rome's good will he made the suggestion once again to attack Parthia by advancing through Armenia. Antony accepted the offer remembering the fatal mistake of Crassus in the deserts of Mesopotamia. He needed the cooperation of the Armenian king for his military incursions into the heartland of Parthia. It was planned, therefore, for his army to detour inland and avoid the deserts. But Ardavazd played him false. While passing through the Armenian terrain on the way to Parthia, Ardavazd treacherously cut Antony's supply line and after the Roman army had penetrated through the Armenian mountains, advised the Parthians to encircle the Roman garrison and attack them from the rear. Antony lost 80,000 men. The fear of total annihilation forced him to retreat to the Mediterranean. This was a humiliating defeat. It caused tremendous damage to Antony's prestige whose goal was not only to crush the Parthian military might but also to win some laurels for himself to preserve his pre-eminent status in the Roman hierarchy. He had already affronted the Roman Senate by marrying Cleopatra and living with her congenially in Egypt. His lack of interest in the affairs of the state had given Octavius the opportunity to create a stronger image for himself. Antony needed to return and fight the Parthians to repair his reputation. He could not rely on Octavius for fresh troops and reinforcements. The rift between the two was made wider by Antony's contemptible defeat in Armenia. Rome was not interested to commit more troops for the eastern front. Desperate, Antony turned to Egypt and used Cleopatra to organize an army. His first task was to punish Ardavazd for his treacherous deed.

TRAGIC END OF KING ARDAVAZD

The combined army of Romans and Egyptians under the leadership of Mark Antony began to march in 34 B.C. from Asia Minor towards Western Armenia. Mark Antony set up a military camp on the outskirts of the Armenian border near Nicopolis and sent envoys to King Ardavazd inviting him to his camp on the pretext of planning the future attack on Parthia. Ardavazd walked into the trap. He was immediately captured, bound with golden chains, and together with his wife and children, taken to Alexandria to be exhibited in a victory parade. Only one of Ardavazd's sons managed to escape to Parthia and take refuge at the court of the Parthian king. A great festival and a triumphal parade were organized in Alexandria to celebrate Mark Antony's capture of the Armenian king. Antony and Cleopatra both sitting on golden thrones presided the parade. When the celebrations were over Mark Antony appointed his son, Alexander, to be the future king of Armenia. This spectacle did not sit well with Octavius and the Roman Senate. Events were moving rapidly and Antony's standing in Rome was at an all time low. Octavius decided to take action and take over the administration of the government. After securing an oath of loyalty to himself from each member of the Senate he declared war on Antony and Cleopatra. The Roman troops of Octavius fought the combined forces of Antony and Cleopatra at Actium in western Greece in 32 B.C. Octavius won the decisive battle and chased the royal couple to Alexandria.

Meanwhile the dethroned Armenian monarch was put in jail in Alexandria with his family. After her escape from Actium Cleopatra began to fear that Ardavazd may somehow escape from prison and collaborate with Octavius to topple the Egyptian throne and organize a political plot. In order to dispose of the possible threat, Cleopatra in 31 B.C. ordered Ardavazd to be beheaded. Shortly thereafter, Antony and Cleopatra, enmeshed in court intrigue and unable to continue the fight against the Roman forces, committed suicide. Octavius became the sole ruler of the Roman Empire. He was named Augustus by a decree of the Senate for his meritorious work of saving the Empire and, as Augustus, ruled the Empire for forty-five years. His foresight and ingenuity opened the doors of a new era for the civilization of Rome and for the peoples of the Empire from the Caspian Sea to the Atlantic Ocean.

One of the problems facing Augustus upon his return from Egypt was the restructuring of the eastern provinces. Upon the death of Ardavazd II in Alexandria the Armenian nobles in 30 B.C. had placed Artashes II, the oldest son of King Ardavazd upon the Armenian throne. Artashes had found refuge in Parthia when his father and the rest of the family were seized and taken to Alexandria. The demise of the Roman Triumvirate and the political uncertainty that followed had given the Parthian king the opportunity to move in immediately and persuade the Armenian nobles to install Artashes II to the throne to keep Armenia out of the Roman grip. The Armenian state was by no means powerful. The country was left leaderless for a long time and its governmental structure was in shambles. The interim government which was formed hastily by the nobles after the capture of Ardavazd, was supported only by the Parthians, whose ulterior motive was to safeguard their own interests. While Parthians and Armenians were engaged in re-establishing their mutual defense against Rome, Augustus had different plans for the organization of the east.

ROME'S POLICY OF ACCOMMODATION

Upon his return to Rome in 29 B.C. Augustus began the enormous task of reconstructing the Empire. The political strife and the civil war had demoralized the people and damaged the prestige that the Empire once enjoyed throughout the world. The government needed a complete overhaul. Unsuitable Senators and political malcontents needed to be removed or replaced. Augustus wanted to restore the old republic in the footsteps of his famous father, and shift the power base from the military to the educated elite. The assassination of his father had demonstrated the strength of the political process and durability of the Senate. He knew very well that the way to power lay through dictatorship rather than the democratic processes of the Senate. While he kept the Senate as a political institution, he used it only as a tool for the implementation of his policies.

As for Egypt and the east, Augustus wanted to change Rome's policy of military conquest. Mark Antony had made Egypt economically and politically an intrinsic component of the Roman world and shifted the center of gravity of the Roman Empire towards Egypt. But Augustus wanted to keep the power base in Rome, the historical center of the Roman civilization and accept the provinces only as colonies to the Empire. In the east he wanted to discontinue the war of conquest against Parthia. If Pompey, Crassus, Caesar, and Antony wanted to extend the Empire to the Indian subcontinent and considered Parthia a threat to Roman aggrandizement, Augustus made it clear to the Parthian king that Rome had no quarrel with him, and he was keenly interested to end the historical conflict in the east. He was content to establish his frontiers along the lines of the Euphrates and initiate a policy of diplomatic accord with Parthia. For him the east was not as important as the Mediterranean. His principal objective was to make the Mediterranean Sea a Roman lake after peace and tranquility were restored in the provinces. For Augustus Parthia was no longer a threat to maintain the territorial integrity of the empire. The dynastic struggle for the throne had weakened Parthia's military strength and polarized the central authority of the government. He wanted to maintain diplomatic ties with the Parthian king and discontinue the military campaigns provided that the buffer zone that Armenia had offered earlier remained within Rome's sphere of influence.

Augustus began his career as a soldier but became one of the great statesmen of Roman history. His was the rule of reconciliation and appeasement to win the cooperation of the people. That policy became important for the Armenian people who saw a new direction for their political life. Augustus was not interested to make Armenia a mere province of the Empire. He wanted the Armenians to preserve their kingdom in a quasi-autonomous environment within the purview of the Roman interest. It is to this end that Augustus appointed his great general and the stepson, Tiberius as his personal envoy in the east, with the responsibility of restructuring the Armenian Kingdom within the parameters of his foreign policy. For Tiberius, King Artashes II was not acceptable to remain as Armenia's king. He had been installed upon the Armenian throne by the Parthians and in the course of his short reign had favored Parthia over Rome. Tiberius' choice was Tigran III, Artashes' brother who had been taken to Rome from Alexandria after his father was beheaded. As a young prince Tigran was educated in Rome and had demonstrated loyalty to Augustus and accepted the principle of Roman primacy.

King Tigran III ruled Armenia as a vassal king to Rome and Armenia provided the essential buffer between Parthia and Rome. While the country was stripped of its autonomous freedom Tigran continued his father's economic policies. Rome used Armenia not only as a military buffer zone but also as the center of the caravan trade. Goods came from the east to Artashat and were redistributed to other commercial centers such as Palmyra and Damascus, and goods from the Mediterranean markets passed through Artashat from eastern trading posts.

THE END OF THE DYNASTY

Tigran III died in 6 B.C. and his son, Tigran IV and his daughter Erato succeeded him as the king and queen of Armenia. In accordance with oriental custom, Tigran IV had married his half sister, Erato, to safeguard the hereditary descent and ruled Armenia as a pair. This was the first time in the history of the Armenian Kingdom that the king and the queen shared the throne with equal authority and power. But Erato represented the real power behind the throne. She was more concerned with the promotion of her own interests than the affairs of state. The royal couple sponsored a luxuriant court life. There was some speculation that their lifestyle was supported by conspiratorial activities which involved the diversion of funds and taxes which were earmarked for Rome. The pair was also identified with a policy of hostility towards Tiberius. While there was some dispute about the authenticity of these charges, Tiberius deposed them both in 5 B.C. and installed Ardavazd III a cousin of Tigran IV upon the Armenian throne. Ardavazd was genuinely reluctant to accept the throne and made a futile attempt to get out of the responsibility of running the government.

Tigran IV and Queen Erato fled to Parthia to raise a force and forge an open rebellion against the Roman forces. The removal of the royal couple from the Armenian throne did not sit well with the Armenian nobles who were resentful of Tiberius' dictatorial intrusion into the affairs of this kingship. While he was an able administrator and helped promote prosperity in Armenia, Tiberius' tactless and arrogant policies had created problems between Armenia and Rome. Augustus was aware of his stepson's notorious indiscretions and lack of diplomatic skill but could not afford political strife in the east. He sent his godson, Caius Caesar to Armenia with instructions to crush the rebellion, bring about a reconciliation with the Armenian nobles, and restore peace and order in the region. But events were moving fast and the country was left leaderless. The newly crowned King Ardavazd III had died and the Armenian nobility was in disarray. The aristocratic families could not agree among themselves to choose a successor to the Armenian throne. Tigran IV was killed during the riots, and his wife, Queen Erato had managed to escape to Parthia.

Tigran's death in 2 A.D. marks the end of the Artashesian Dynasty which had begun one hundred ninety two years earlier when King Artashes I founded the Armenian Kingdom amid the ruins of the Seleucid Empire. The Artashesian kings and the successors to Tigran the Great created and maintained a unique military and political structure to form an organic community and mold Armenia into a kingdom, but in the end they failed to preserve the hereditary descent of the Armenian throne. The Armenian nobles tenaciously supported the national institutions and the dignity of the throne. They were successful in maintaining the balance of power by war and diplomacy. They were able to transform their small kingdom into a powerful empire and reshape the face of Western Asia. They were able to break down the old political barriers and erect new ones to suit their national interest. They were able to establish centers of culture and civilization and extend the horizon of their intellectual frontiers. But in the end when the test of unity required them to make a decision on a choice of a king, they broke apart. Throughout the history of this people the members of the aristocratic families, known as the Nakharars, left a legacy of disunity. They were divided by dynastic rivalries and at times used the king as their pawn. They were mainly interested in preserving the independence of their anachronistic individual fiefdoms without realizing that only a united Armenia could have played a decisive role in the survival of the people as a whole. The chaotic disunity among the nobles compelled Rome to install a foreign king upon the Armenian throne.

ARMENIA UNDER FOREIGN KINGS

If the first two hundred years of the Armenian Kingdom was a period of construction and national unity, the next two hundred years represented a period of confusion and political disarray. Not only did the Armenians lose their national independence but they were also forced to accept non-Armenian kings to rule their country. For the next two centuries Armenia as a vassal state will be governed by a series of non-Armenian kings who at times manipulated the Armenian political life to suit their own national interest. They were conspicuously anti-Armenian in some cases and were not concerned about the welfare of the people. The group included Medians, a Jew, several Parthians, Romans, a Syrian, and a pair of Georgians. They were mostly random selections by the two great powers of the day, chosen specifically to satisfy the political machinations of the country in power. Very few succeeded to transfer the royal crown to a person from his own family circle. The continuity of hereditary descent was constantly broken. When a king died or was removed from office, another was installed by either Rome or Parthia.

The installation of non-Armenian kings over the Armenian throne was mainly due to the political malaise created by the Armenian nobility immediately after the death of the last Artashesian king, Tigran IV. While Emperor Augustus avoided overt control of Armenia and wished merely to keep the country within the Roman sphere of influence, he failed to have exclusive power to make decisions for Armenia. Parthia, in the east, was also manifestly interested to keep Armenia within its political orbit.

THE NON-ARMENIAN MONARCHS

The first non-Armenian king was Ariobarzan, a Mede by origin, who was installed upon the Armenian throne by Augustus upon the death of Tigran IV. He was a man of pre-eminent qualities with a thorough understanding of the politics of the day. Ariobarzan was able to unite, at least temporarily, the various factions of the Armenian nobility and govern the people with the full collaboration of the aristocratic families. The Armenian nobles accepted him mainly because of his distinguished qualities of leadership and diplomatic skill. The Romans had given him the freedom of action to run the country, but the freedom was illusory. Economic and political decisions were made by Rome. Ariobarzan ruled Armenia for only three years. He died in an accident in 4 A.D. and his son succeeded him to the Armenian throne. As King of Armenia Ariobarzan's son assumed an Armenian name and ruled Armenia as Ardavazd IV. But unlike his father, Ardavazd was unable to unite the Armenian nobles and found himself in the middle of dynastic rivalries. While Ardavazd could convoke the assembly of nobles and run the institutions of the government to the best of his abilities, his seizure of the Armenian throne was taken as an offensive continuation of this non-Armenian family's intrusion into Armenia's political life. His reign over Armenia was short-lived. He was assassinated two years later while planning a conference of reconciliation between the crown and a group of nobles.

The political problems and internal dissensions in Armenia impaired Rome's ability to run the eastern section of the Roman Empire. While the implementation of Rome's foreign policy was in the hands of Augustus, the Empire was mostly run by surrogates who had pledged their allegiance to the emperor and had accepted the primacy of Rome. The emperor's aim was to provide political stability in the east within the framework of Pax Romana. By 6 A.D. Augustus had achieved the territorial unity of the Empire and had already converted the Mediterranean into a Roman lake. The client kingdoms and vassal states were ruled by local kings of his choice. But Armenia continued to cause problems. The role that Augustus wanted Armenia to play was not only that of buffer state between Parthia and his Empire but also to act as intermediary to provide the vital link of commerce between east and west. He wanted the caravan trade to flourish and planned to establish centers of commerce to make the luxury goods from the east available in the west.

The drive for economic prosperity forced Augustus to appoint a Jewish king over Armenia, since he did not have confidence in the loyalty of an Armenian to carry on the administration of the state. The assassination of King Ardavazd, Rome's appointed king, had further alienated the Armenian leaders from Rome. By the turn of the millennium the Jews had gained an international reputation of being good merchants with administrative skill to run the caravan trade and establish commercial centers to store and distribute goods from the east. Augustus judged that a Jewish king over Armenia could restore peace and promote international trade in the interest of the Roman Empire.

A Jewish prince believed to be the grandson of King Herod of Israel was installed as the King of Armenia in 6 A.D. The new king immediately began a period of reconstruction and economic revival for Armenia. To please the nobles he assumed an Armenian name and ruled Armenia as Tigran V. While he constructed cities and villages and restored peace and stability in the region, his principal aim was to serve his masters in Rome, particularly Augustus, who by now had risen to the zenith of his power as the omnipotent ruler of Europe, the east and north Africa.

Amid peace and prosperity, however, there were signs of decay of Armenian values and traditions. The non-Armenian king was not interested in maintaining the social structure or the cultural standards for which Armenia had become famous. The upper class was in pursuit of material wealth and the lower class was exploited by priests whose enormous influence was principally used to perpetuate their own self interests at the peril of national unity. The Jewish king was able, however, to reunite the warring factions and worked hard to maintain a comprehensive economic program to gain control of the important trade route between east and west. The King kept his royal authority and control over Armenia for eight years but lost the support of the nobles and the people in general when Emperor Augustus died in 14 A.D. He was expelled from Armenia shortly afterwards, and the Armenian Nakharars recalled Queen Erato, Tigran IV's wife and half sister, to return and reoccupy the throne.

This was a direct challenge to Rome. For the first time in almost fifty years the Armenians were choosing their own monarch without Rome's consent and had made the determination to run their own affairs without foreign interference. But this will only be a short interlude. In spite of her exuberant demonstration of energy, Erato was overthrown a year later, this time by Parthia. It was time for Armenia to be oscillated to the other side of the political fulcrum. Rome was preoccupied with problems of succession and had left Armenia in the care of its antagonist. The Parthian king appointed his son, Vonon, to succeed Erato as the King of Armenia with the design of making Armenia an integral part of the Parthian hegemony. Vonon attempted to merge Armenia with Parthia but the stubborn resistance of the nobles prevented him to do so.

THE END OF AUGUSTAN RULE

It didn't take long for the Roman Senate to find a suitable successor to Augustus. In the course of his long and brilliant reign of forty-five years the problem of succession was a major concern for the great Emperor. While the countries around the Mediterranean were securely held, the eastern provinces were a different matter. He knew how to deal with Parthia, and used the niceties of diplomacy rather than war, but he wasn't sure about Parthia's ultimate objectives in Western Asia. He was afraid that Rome's influence in the east would vanish after his demise and the continuity of Rome's authority would suffer if Parthia attempted to restructure a new political order for the countries around the eastern periphery of the Roman Empire.

The desire to maintain the *status quo* forced Augustus to recommend rather reluctantly his stepson Tiberius to succeed him to the Roman throne. While Tiberius was a man of brusque and austere temperament and lacked the essential elements of diplomacy, his expertise in the eastern affairs proved to be valuable to Rome in view of the increasingly growing power of Parthia.

As the administrator of Armenia and eastern provinces, Tiberius had served Augustus well and had successfully maintained the political stability of the region in the interest of the Empire. After taking over the reign, Tiberius wanted to settle the affairs of Armenia to the satisfaction of Rome. He appointed Zeno, the son of the Queen of Pontus, a faithful servant to Rome, as the King of Armenia.

Unlike his immediate predecessors, Zeno was popular in Armenia and knew the language well. Having lived in Armenia for a long time he had established an excellent rapport with the aristocratic families. He too adopted an Armenian name and ruled Armenia for sixteen years as King Artashes IV. The Nakharars acclaimed him as their leader and allowed him to reorganize the government in the interest of Rome and remove Armenia from the Parthian yoke. The King acted decisively to secure the Armenian borders and protect the integrity of the caravan trade.

Economic growth brought prosperity and the people felt good in witnessing the revitalization of the Armenian community based on social and religious reforms. The people became genuinely responsive to Artashes' policies to breathe new life into Armenia's political organization. There was little sentiment for a return of Parthian authority. The King had promoted a vigorous policy of Romanization and had successfully converted his office into a monarchy of the Augustan type, autocratic and yet diplomatic enough to compromise his views for the adoption of a dependable policy to placate both Rome and Parthia. Artashes IV died in 34 A.D. and the period of Romanization in Armenia came to an end. It was now Parthia's turn to swing the Armenian pendulum to the other side.

THE RULE OF THE SCOUNDRELS

In Rome Tiberius had run into difficulties in governing the Empire. The Senate had gained ground in the general administration of the government. While he wanted to work closely with the Senators as his father had, his frustration to make himself the sole ruler of the Empire finally forced him to leave Rome and live in seclusion on the Island of Capri. The paralysis in Rome gave the opportunity to the Parthian king to appoint his son, Arshak, to the Armenian throne. But the choice was not acceptable to Rome. There followed a period of a bitter struggle between Rome and Parthia over the control of Armenia. For the next twenty-five years Armenia will become a field for diplomatic and military struggle. Its political fortune will swing from one side to the other and its general role as an intermediary of international commerce will become seriously jeopardized. The country in power always blamed the Armenians with conspiracy to assist the other side.

It was during this political anarchy that an opportunist by the name of Mithridate from neighboring Georgia, managed to occupy the Armenian throne and declared himself as the King of Armenia. He acted first as ally to Rome but switched sides constantly to accomplish his covetous activities. His principal aim was to plunder the Armenian towns and villages and gain access to the Armenian national treasures in Artashat. He killed thousands of Armenians and forced the nobles to vacate their properties. He devastated the country and terrorized Armenia for fifteen years. He was finally killed in 51 A.D. by his nephew Hradamizd, who promptly occupied the Armenian throne and continued the brutal acts of his uncle.

There was little Rome or Parthia could do to rescue the Armenians from the ravages of these Georgians. After Tiberius' death in 37 A.D. the Senate appointed Gaius as the leader of the Empire. But Gaius was inexperienced to run the affairs of the vast Empire and by a unanimous verdict he was taken as a lunatic who at the age of 25 had forced the people to worship him as a living god. Parthia, in turn, was in the midst of political struggle. Dynastic rivalries had paralyzed its political system and had left the country leaderless.

THE RETURN TO NORMALCY

When Vagharsh of the Pahlevid family rose to power in Parthia, the fortune of Armenia turned for the better. He chased the Georgian rascal from the Armenian throne and appointed his younger brother, Trdat I as the King of Armenia in 52 A.D. It was now time for Parthia to be the architect of Armenia's destiny, but the switching of masters was taken with a sign of relief. The country was devastated after sixteen years of avaricious activities and terror. The national treasures were gone and the country was weakened by the migration of prominent aristocratic families to foreign lands. Less apparent but more potent than the physical destruction were the changes in community life and society in general. Gone were the days of cultural activities and intellectual pursuit. Writers, artists, and poets had left the country for safer havens. Libraries that once served as centers of culture were ransacked and destroyed. Armenia was on the threshold of social and political breakdown. A re-establishment of the old order was badly needed to breathe life into Armenia's social, cultural, and political structure.

The desire for reform and restoration of the old values propelled the new King to chart a new direction for Armenia. He initiated a vigorous campaign to rebuild the country. He sent word to the Armenian nobles to return home and help him to reorganize the government. He populated the capital city of Artashat with artisans, builders, and craftsmen to rebuild the palaces, libraries, and theaters. He created new administrative offices to run the affairs of the community. He forced the priests to relinquish some of their properties and distribute them to the farmers. The amount of cultivable land was increased and new methods of agriculture were instituted. The economic activity of the country began to flourish and caravans began to use Armenia again for trade between east and west.

While Trdat never aspired to gain complete independence from his brother in Parthia, he wanted to run Armenia in the interest of the Armenian people and keep the country insulated from the political intrigues of foreign powers. To accomplish his objectives he needed to reorganize the army and end the futile and debilitating rivalry among the principal members of the nobility. The nobles themselves wished to stop their petty wars, at least temporarily, to allow Trdat to unify the country and create a new military order. The mood of the country was to strengthen the national posture and reject foreign interference in Armenian affairs.

After completing his domestic programs Trdat directed his attention to the former possessions of Armenia which were taken over by Rome. He planned to reoccupy the territories and extend his authority past the Euphrates into Asia Minor. The plan involved danger of confrontation with Rome which was already irritated by Trdat's increasingly arrogant demonstration of militancy.

He worked hard to execute his plans peacefully and by skillfully attempting to convince the heads of the surrounding states to annex their territories to Armenia voluntarily and accept the Armenian rule over their affairs. He demonstrated statesmanship and unusual qualities of leadership and was determined to make his adopted country free from foreign intrusion. The prospects for the establishment of an autonomous Armenia, however, were not promising.

THE IRE OF EMPEROR NERO

In Rome Nero had come to power at the age of 16 with the help of his unscrupulous mother who had arranged to have Emperor Claudius poisoned to hasten her son's succession to power. It did not take long for Nero, however, to assume full control of the government and declare himself the sole ruler of the Empire. Within a short period of time he had his mother murdered and plotted the callous removal of all possible rivals to the throne. He ran the government with the help of his generals and applied autocratic rule without consent from the Senate to preserve the integrity of the vast Empire. His authority was soon challenged, however, by two unrelated but important developments, the rise of Christianity as a new religious force threatening to change the fabric of the Roman society, and the increasing power of the Armenian king in the east.

He assigned Corbulo, one of Rome's best generals to go east and stop Trdat's advances towards the Roman territories in Asia Minor. Corbulo organized a formidable army, well trained and coordinated, with Roman cavalry, foot soldiers, and thousands of mercenaries from the various parts of the Empire. He reached Armenia and proceeded directly to the nation's capital but found himself face to face with an equally powerful adversary.

It didn't take long for the Armenian troops to encircle the Romans and cut their line of communication and supply. Trdat had evacuated Artashat and had managed to get his men across the Euphrates to attack the Romans from the rear. The Armenian threat had become real. The Roman forces were subdued by the demonstration of invincible military power.

In desperation Corbulo moved his troops east to avoid heavy casualties and to assure his hold on Artashat. The capital city was left defenseless. In anger he set fire to the city and reduced it to rubble. Trdat continued his assault, broke the Roman formations, and concentrated on shattering the Roman supply line to prevent Corbulo to have access to fresh reinforcements. The Roman army was trapped. The danger of complete annihilation forced the Roman general to negotiate a cease-fire. This was a smashing victory for the little King against the powerful forces of the Roman Empire.

ACCOMMODATION WITH ROME

Trdat's defiance of Rome and the news of the humiliating defeat reached Rome. Nero, to save face, allowed the Armenian King to keep the territories adjoining Armenia. He also required Trdat to come to Rome to receive the crown from Nero personally, and pledge his allegiance to the Roman Emperor. Trdat knew very well that while he won the battle against the Roman general, a continued confrontation against the world's most powerful state was unrealistic. He also knew well that it was equally unrealistic to expect total autonomy from the two great powers of the day. He was not concerned about his brother's Parthia. The two had an amicable relationship and Parthia had left Armenia alone during its conflict with Rome. He considered it in the interest of the people, therefore, to shift the country to the Roman orbit and realign Armenia with Rome while continuing to maintain the same relationship with Parthia.

With a retinue of 3,000 horsemen, his wife, and Armenian dignitaries, Trdat traveled to Rome to accept the crown. When the group arrived on the Italian soil Nero sent royal chariots to bring the visitor to his palace. Rome was decorated with flags and emblems to welcome the Armenian monarch. Special races and gladiatorial events were organized in the coliseum. Festivities and banquets were the highlights of the spectacular ceremonies of the coronation during which Trdat formally pledged his allegiance and accepted the primacy of Rome.

This marked the beginning of a new period of accommodation between Rome and Parthia. They both agreed to rule Armenia with a king from the royal house of Parthia on condition that the king would receive his crown from the Roman emperor. This arrangement of dual control will not last long. It will be broken from time to time by one side or the other. Upon his return to Armenia Trdat immediately began to reconstruct the country. He rebuilt the city of Artashat and renamed it Neronia in honor of Emperor Nero. He built palaces and religious sanctuaries in Garni, a town that will gain national prominence in the years to come.

ARMENIA AFTER TRDAT I

King Trdat died in 75 A.D. leaving no heir to succeed him. In Rome Nero had committed suicide after losing the support of the people and Vespasian had succeeded him as the sole ruler of the Empire. Trouble was brewing around the various parts of the Roman world. The Roman system of holding the Empire together was being challenged. The Jews were in revolt in Judaea, and the Roman troops on the Rhine were experiencing difficulties in suppressing the rebellion of certain provincial governors. Trdat's death in Armenia created yet another problem for Rome. The eastern provinces were in a precarious situation. Parthia was continuing to exert its influence in Western Asia and Rome's vassal kingdoms were on the verge of switching masters. The east was hard hit. Its resources were depleted by continuous wars and political rivalries caused largely by pendular swings between Rome and Parthia.

Vespasian had risen to power mainly because of his illustrious military career and having had the ability to suppress the Jewish revolt. It was important for him to appoint a successor to Trdat to preserve the Roman influence and maintain the integrity of the eastern frontiers. He chose a non-Armenian to be the king of Armenia but the choice soon proved to be a poor one. The new king became an ineffective puppet to the Roman cause and antagonized the wealthy families. He was unable to contain the social unrest and did nothing to provide for the welfare of the country. He was overthrown by the Parthian king who placed his own nephew upon the Armenian throne.

There followed a period of political instability in Armenia. A series of Parthian kings, mostly related to the royal dynasty, ruled Armenia for the next twenty-five years with no particular accomplishments and political or economic innovation. Their principal interest was to keep the country within the Parthian sphere of influence and protect Armenia from Roman interference. Rome was preoccupied with its rapid growth of prosperity. The economy was flourishing and there was an abundant supply of money in circulation. The Empire was at the zenith of its territorial extent and the citizens of Rome were enjoying the fruits of *Pax Romana*.

ROMANS INVADE ARMENIA

Political stability was interrupted for a short period of time when Trajan rose to power in Rome in 98 A.D. He adopted an ambitious policy of empire building and planned to annex Armenia to the Roman Empire. He organized an army and marched towards Asia Minor. His aggressive policy towards Armenia was partly motivated by the weakness of the Parthian king, Khosrov II, who was engaged in a bitter struggle with the great landholders in the eastern part of his Kingdom. Trajan overran Armenia with ease, killed the Armenian king and advanced into northern Mesopotamia towards the Parthian capital, Ctesiphon. He was about to destroy the center of the Parthian Empire when suddenly his conquests began to crumble. The Parthian King had ingeniously incited the Jews in the eastern cities of the Roman Empire to rebel against Roman authority. This made Trajan divert his attention from Armenia and Parthia and concentrate on suppressing the Jews.

A period of economic and political stability followed Trajan's death. Emperor Hadrian, upon rising to power in Rome in 117 A.D., allowed the Armenian nobles to choose their own king. The country was devastated by Roman invasions and the government was left leaderless. The Armenian Nakharars chose a Parthian, Vagharsh I, to ascend the throne and helped him to reconstruct the country and re-establish the political order. His reign coincided with that of Hadrian whose benevolent attitude towards Armenia helped the Armenian King to chart a new direction for the people.

Vagharsh died in 140 and Rome named a Syrian, Sohemus, to occupy the Armenian throne. His reign was interrupted several times by military incursions from Parthia but he managed to rule Armenia peacefully for the next 45 years. Sohemus died in 185 and Armenia found itself in the middle of a religious upheaval. A new movement was spreading rapidly throughout the Roman Empire, a faith that will change the destiny of man and provide new meaning for the concept of God and the brotherhood of man.

CHAPTER TEN

CHRISTIANITY ENTERS ARMENIA

The period that began with the successor of Sohemus in 185 will be one of the most remarkable periods in the history of the Armenian people. It is during this period that the nation acquired a reorientation of thought and adopted a new religion based on the doctrines of a movement that had swept the orient by the beginning of the Third century. After living in political anarchy during which they witnessed the breakdown of their social and political system, Armenians began to search for a new god to help them in their difficulties and guide the nation towards a happier future. As the foreign rule became unbearable they began to reject the ideals of paganism and accept the concept of Christian God who had preached love, goodness, and the fellowship of man. The conversion from paganism into Christianity, however, will not be easy. There will be a fierce struggle between the old and the new before Christians establish a permanent foothold on the Armenian soil.

THE EARLY CHRISTIANS

When King Sohemus died in 185 the Armenian throne was bestowed upon yet another non-Armenian King, Sanatrouk, who ruled the country through a period of peace and tranquility. In Rome Commodus had risen to power after an illustrious reign by Marcus Aurelius, but found himself incapable of functioning as the sole ruler of a vast Empire. Inexperienced and vain, he let the subordinates run the government and treated the Senate with contempt. His death at the hands of a mistress in 192 led the Empire to a civil war and marked the beginning of the decline of the Roman Empire.

The Senate was unable to choose a successor to Commodus. The vacillation led the troops to take the selection process into their own hands. Half of the army acclaimed Niger, the commander in the east, as their emperor, and the other half supported Severus who had stationed a powerful legion in the outskirts of Rome. To make a show of force Severus advanced towards Rome and coerced the Senate to accept him as the sole emperor of the Empire. After consolidating his power Severus then directed his attention to the east to crush the forces of Niger and remove him from gaining control of the Roman throne. After winning a decisive victory over Niger's forces in Asia Minor, Severus then proceeded towards Parthia to punish the Parthian king, Vagharsh IV, and prevent him to take over the vassal kingdom of Armenia. Vagharsh earlier had offered aid to Niger and was threatening to invade the Roman possessions in the east. While King Sanatrouk of Armenia wished to remain neutral he was caught in the middle between the two antagonists. The conflict between the two superpowers cost him his life and left Armenia leaderless once again.

It was during Sanatrouk's reign that Christianity became a perceptible religious force in Armenia and legend has it that the Armenian King was the first to embrace the new religion. The appeal of the Christian faith had attracted many Armenians, including some members of the royal family, but the pagan priests later persuaded the king to renounce the new faith and send thousands, including his own daughter, to their martyrdom. While Christianity will not be accepted as a state religion in Armenia for another one hundred and ten years, Christian elements had begun to penetrate into Armenia as early as a century before Sanatrouk came to power.

Christianity as a new religious concept was first introduced in Armenia by two apostles of Jesus Christ, Thaddeus and Bartholomew, who traveled north to preach the new gospel, while Paul of Tarsus traveled west to convert pagans to Christianity. Because of this apostolic mission the Armenian Church calls itself Apostolic and considers its supreme head as the direct successor to the Apostles. The supernatural force of Jesus Christ who had suffered and died for the brotherhood of man helped Christianity to establish its roots in Armenia. This new religious

movement began to spread gradually from the south going
north to Antioch and finding its way through Asia Minor and
Armenia. The early Christian preachers were mostly Greek
and Syrian who traveled from province to province and systematically disseminated the word of Jesus to convert pagans into
the Christian faith. They gained their strength through discipline and orthodoxy and at times used militant fanaticism to
force the people to accept the new revolution in thought and
theology.

PAGAN CULT

For Armenians this was a new experiment totally different from
the religious ideology of their forefathers. Armenians over the
centuries had adopted a type of religion which was an accumulation of beliefs and practices developed into a theological
system and dominated mostly by irrational superstitions and
mythology of ancient man. Living in a polytheistic world, Armenians had gods for every occasion. The more gods they had
the more secure they felt against the uncertainties of life and the
vagaries of nature. Their religious ideology stemmed largely
from the Urartians and the people of Arme but new gods and
doctrines were introduced as the people came in contact with
other cultures and civilizations. Persian and Greco-Roman religious disciplines were the major components of their brand of
pagan cult and through the centuries they made these disciplines the foundation of the nation's social and political structure.

The pagan temple was the place of worship as well as the
center of power for the priesthood. They venerated their gods
by erecting statues. While most of their gods were humanized,
they were made to possess immortality. They believed in the
triad of gods, Aramazd, Anahit, and Meher, to guide the destiny of the people and to help the hungry and the downtrodden,
the poor, and the sick. In the parthenon of gods Anahit stood
out as the most prominent. She represented chastity and the
glory of the human race and played a decisive part in the creation of the universe as the matriarch of the heavenly bodies.
There were statues of Anahit in every temple of the country
with the principal statue, made of gold, located in Erzinjan.
The people went to Erzinjan in pilgrimage asking for help and

guidance. Meher was the god of truth and represented the light in heaven. He was Persian in origin and his statue was located in the village of Bagaritch. The month of February, known in Armenian as Mehegan, was dedicated as the month to celebrate the god Meher. Aramazd was the divinity of inspiration with the power to foretell the names of the people destined to die.

Besides these three deities the religious hierarchy contained other gods, secondary in nature and importance. Among these was Astghik, the goddess of love whose festival, known as Vartavar was celebrated at the beginning of each summer. Armenians today still hold this pagan festival. On that day they play games, fly pigeons, and sprinkle water on each other. Astghik's principal residence was in Mush. The Armenians believed that the goddess had a habit of taking a bath in a stream. To protect her privacy she had caused the entire area of Mush to be covered by fog. Mush is a derivation of the Armenian word, *Mshoush*, meaning fog. Nane, the daughter of Aramazd was the goddess of war and conquest. Persian in origin, she was introduced into the Armenian religion by Tigran the Great as the symbol of his victory over Persia. Vahagn was the national god representing power, courage, and vitality. He replaced Meher, occasionally as an important member of the galaxy of gods. Greek in origin, Vahagn was the Armenian prototype of Heracles and was introduced in Armenia's religious culture during the period of Hellenization. There was also Sandaramet, adopted from the Mazdeian religion of Persia, who represented piety, modesty, and the virtuous woman.

The traditional worship and festivals of pagan gods were administered by the priests. But the worship had a public character. The individual was not allowed to satisfy his religious feelings as Christianity would allow him to in the future. The priests were the representatives of the gods, charged with the responsibility of organizing the ritual of worship and running the affairs of the sanctuaries. They were enormously wealthy and influential and had made the practice of religion an important part of community life. The cults were supported by state funds and from collection of tithes, in cash or in kind, that each member of the community was expected to pay. While Armenians cultivated a wide range of foreign gods, they adopted their own version of paganism and conceived hybrid deities to suit their own national interest. Foreign powers which dominated Armenia from time to time demonstrated an astonishing docility with which they permitted the Armenians to exercise their religious practices. They let the people worship their chosen gods as long as the practice did not cloak political conspiracy and the religious affiliations did not place the country in the orbit of an opposing power.

COMMUNITY LIFE

While the national government was centralized around the royal court, the community life in Armenia was governed mostly by the Nakharars, who as feudal lords, ran a formalized bureaucracy over their assigned territories. Their functions extended to include regional activities, such as administering the agricultural output or protecting the caravan route that passed through their territory, as well as national assignments. They were individualistic men, arrogantly tough, proud of their heritage, and always ready to demonstrate their valor in combat, their skill in hunting, and persuasive ability in leading the community. They exhibited a remarkable brand of administration in running the various activities of their region with military units to protect their property from foreign as well as domestic incursions. They lived in luxurious estates surrounded by gardens and lakes and believed in pomp and pageantry. They wore golden tiaras, pearl necklaces, and expensive vestments encrusted with precious stones during official ceremonies and state functions. As feudal lords they were entitled to sit on a silver throne while the king used a golden one.

The head of the feudal house was known as *Ter* or *Nahabet*, the second in line was *Sepouh*. They had acquired their titles generally by hereditary descent with the advice and consent of the crown. There was tremendous rivalry among the leading dynastic families which numbered around sixty. Their political importance was measured by the clan's proximity to the crown. The Nakharars within the king's entourage wielded enormous influence and power. They were divided into two separate tiers, regional and national. The regional Nakharars were mostly engrossed in the affairs of their own community and the ones on the national level had specific duties assigned by the king to run the various institutions of the central government. Some were charged with the administration of the royal palace and others were the custodians of the national treasury. The Nakharar serving as the chief of staff to the king was called *Marzbed* and was necessarily a eunuch. He sat next to the king during state functions. The Nakharar serving as the prime minister or the grand vizier was called *Hazarabet* and the Nakharar serving as the commander-in-chief of the armed forces was called *Sparabet*. Other Nakharars had civil, judicial, and administrative positions. The Nakharar was the lord master of his feudal estate and ruled the inhabitants as his subjects. He guarded the integrity of his borders with great zeal even to the point of waging war against a neighboring Nakharar. His army unit was nationalized by the king only during national emergencies, but he was generally not involved with the overall policy of the king's government.

The Armenian society was hierarchical in nature with several different layers. There were the upper class, the middle class, the lower class, the serfs, and the slaves. The physical appearance of the towns was generally Urartian with separate residential quarters for each class of society. A sharp line of economic and social distinction was drawn among the different classes and the move from one residential zone to another was allowed only by feudal decree.

The upper class had the aristocrats and the privileged people needed for the task of the regional government. Below this was the middle class of merchants, artists, goldsmiths, artisans, doctors, and tailors. They were usually migratory and earned their living by wages or by profit from trade. They were educated people with a display of cultural interest and paid particular attention to family and community life. The lower class was made up of ordinary soldiers, and petty landowners, followed by the serfs, who were the field laborers attached to the soil. Below the serfs were the slaves known as *Strouks*, representing the lowest element of Armenian society. The *Strouks* were mostly prisoners of war and people who had declared bankruptcy. Armenia always had an abundant supply of slaves. The incessant wars had provided a good number of prisoners of war who were used first for public projects and then sold as slaves through an auction market. The slaves were sold or transferred by gift and contribution, and occasionally freed by royal decree. They were used by members of the upper class for field labor or domestic service in times of peace and as combat soldiers in times of war. Frequently the well educated slaves were used as tutors for the children of their masters and others helped the owners to run their businesses as skilled hands, secretaries, or accountants. As in other societies, there was a degree of vanity for an Armenian to advertise the number of slaves in his possession. But unlike other societies the slaves in Armenia were treated well. Such were the practices of religion and life in the community when Christianity began to establish a foothold in Armenia.

THE ARSHAKUNIAN DYNASTY

Upon the death of King Sanatrouk of Armenia the Parthian king appointed Vagharsh to ascend the Armenian throne. Though Vagharsh claimed descent from the Parthian house of the Arsacids, he pursued a policy in favor of his adopted country, and tilted Armenia towards Rome. His first act was to forge a military alliance against his blood relatives in Parthia and help the Romans to crush Ctesiphon, the great power base of the Parthian Empire. Vargharsh's reign will mark the beginning of a new dynasty in the history of Armenia. His descendants will rule Armenia for 236 years and call themselves Arshaks, meaning king in Parthian, hence the dynasty will come to be known as Arshakuni. It is during this period that the religious and cultural elements of Armenia's civilization will be permanently established, and the nation will acquire a different character.

A man with rare qualities of leadership and diplomatic skill, Vagharsh ruled Armenia in the interest of the people and helped the country assume its commercial pre-eminence in Western Asia. His important political innovation was the restructuring of the army and the appointment of the Nakharar to take over the military command of the armed forces. He made the army formidable enough to withstand the military forays of the Parthians. He created the post of *Hazarabet* and appointed a Nakharar to act as the prime minister to run the government. His most striking achievement, however, was in the area of culture and literature. He established centers of culture and introduced an Armenian calendar based on the solar year of the Persians with necessary intercalations to bring the seasons into proper relationship. He introduced the Feast of Navasard, or the New Year, and made it a part of the pagan cult to be celebrated in pomp and gaiety in the city of Bagavan. Vagharsh demonstrated an amazing degree of versatility in statesmanship and played the role of a diplomatic opportunist in dealing with his cousins in Parthia and the mighty rulers of the Roman Empire. Vagharsh was able to unite the regional Nakharars with those on the national level and conferred new titles of nobility to the prominent members of the aristocratic families of the country. He built a new city and called it Vagharshabad after his name.

Though he was a true supporter of the Roman cause, Vagharsh suffered politically when Emperor Severus died and his son Caracalla succeeded him to the Roman throne.

Caracalla was a despotic, enigmatic and arrogant man with imperial designs to make Armenia an appendage to Rome. He summoned King Vagharsh to Rome on the pretense to hold a political conference. This was a trap. Upon his arrival at the Emperor's palace, Vagharsh was arrested and put in jail. He died in prison in 216 and Armenians, upon hearing of the death of their popular king, organized an open rebellion against the Roman forces in Asia Minor.

TRDAT II

The Armenian revolt came to an end when Marcinus rose to power in Rome after engineering the assassination of Caracalla in 217. To placate the Armenians Marcinus immediately recognized Trdat II, the son of Vagharsh, as the King of Armenia and allowed Armenia to reoccupy its former territories in Asia Minor. One of the important events that took place during Trdat's twenty three year rule was the arrival of a group of prominent families from central Asia. Some of these families will play a dominant role in Armenia's political arena during the next several hundred years. Armenia's social structure was broken by continuous turmoil and the institutions of the central government had been shattered by the death of King Vagharsh. The perennial military conflicts between Rome and Parthia, with Armenia always taking the brunt from both sides, had driven people from their lands and dangerously reduced the commercial traffic that passed through Armenia. A fresh start was needed to inject new blood into Armenia's political mainstream.

The migration of prominent families from central Asia was principally motivated by their need to find better economic and political opportunities. The isolation of the hinterlands in central Asia and the Persian militarism in the east had forced the people to migrate west and find a new home for themselves. Trdat needed to organize a durable government to maintain Armenia's political viability in the great power struggle between east and west. He persuaded a group of prominent families in central Asia to settle in Armenia and help him restore stability in the country. Among these families two rose to prominence, the Kamsarakans and the Mamigonians, the first noted for statesmanship, the second for their military skill and superior ability of warmaking. Both became members of the country's ruling aristocracy and gradually began to exert their influence on Armenia's social, political and military affairs.

THE RISE OF SASSANIAN RULE IN PERSIA

After the destruction of Ctesiphon the Parthian power in Persia began to decline. A new and more formidable power is about to emerge which will eventually replace the Parthian rule, control the whole of the Near East, and dominate the political events of the region until the rise of Islam in the Seventh century after Christ. In 208 King Artashir of the Sassanian dynasty rose to power in Persia and immediately began to seize Parthian provinces adjacent to Persia. Parthian rulers already tottering precariously, could not suppress the increasingly damaging power of Artashir. In a battle in 224 Artashir defeated the Parthians and declared himself the King of Kings with absolute power over Parthia, Media, Persia, and the adjoining territories in Mesopotamia. A new nationalism had risen in Persia, ferociously militant and fanatically inspired, to restore the glory of the old Persian Empire of Darius the Great and establish a permanent hegemony in the east.

For the little Armenian Kingdom the emergence of the Sassanian power will mark the beginning of a new era. The tolerant rule of the Parthians will be replaced by the brutality and unsuppressed ruthlessness of the Sassanids. These new masters of Armenia will attempt to restructure the political, social, and religious foundation of the people and in the process systematically change the direction of subsequent history. The nationalistic zeal of the Sassanids gave rise to a new ecclesiastical revival in Persia. Artashir made Mazdeism, the orthodox branch of Zoroastrianism, the official religion of the state and ordered the priests to propagate the Mazdeic doctrines throughout the Empire.

Mazdeism believed in the sanctity of fire and the purity of the environment. The followers of Mazdeism were history's first environmentalists. They believed that the forces of nature, earth, fire, and water were important to human beings and the people were responsible to keep them sacred and pure at all times. The religious faith prevented the people to defile the earth and pollute the water. They worshipped their gods by blood sacrifices and forced the people to pay tribute to finance the operation of the temples.

PERSIANS INVADE ARMENIA

Artashir, after consolidating his power, began his military incursions into Armenia in 232. Roman Emperor Alexander sent a huge army to the east to protect Armenia and other Roman provinces from Persian onslaught. With the help of the Armenian troops the Persian forces were driven across the frontier. But the struggle will not be over. After the death of King Trdat II in 238 the Armenian throne was kept vacant for 15 years because of the political turmoil in the east and the vacillation of the Nakharars to find a suitable successor to Trdat.

Shahpur I after succeeding his father, Artashir, in Persia, resumed his hostilities in 252, pushed his army all the way to the coast of the Mediterranean Sea and extended his hold on Armenia by capturing the capital city of Artashat. Shahpur installed Ardavazd V to the Armenian throne in 253 and ordered the people to accept Mazdeism as the formal religion of the state. The occupation of Armenia secured Persia's northern frontier allowing Shahpur to move south and invade Syria. The political situation deteriorated, however, when Roman Emperor Valerian was taken prisoner by Persian forces during a battle in Syria. The Roman Empire was on the verge of losing the eastern provinces and Rome found itself in the most precarious situation. To rescue the Emperor, Rome asked for help from its reliable ally in the east, the powerful ruler of Palmyra, who had grown enormously rich on the profits of the caravan trade. Palmyra began to attack the Persians from the rear and Shahpur's army was forced to retreat back into Persian territory.

The Persian retreat created a political malaise in Armenia. King Ardavazd V, the Persian protege, wanted to pursue a cautious policy of neutrality but the nobles wanted to exploit the situation and shake off the Persian ruler once and for all. Ardavazd, in order to placate the Armenian nobles, advised Shahpur to release the Roman Emperor. Shahpur refused and Ardavazd abdicated the Armenian throne in 261.

Khosrov succeeded Ardavazd in 261 and found the country in the midst of political anarchy and chaos. The entire east was in turmoil. The Roman Emperor was imprisoned in Persia, the Palmyran king had died and his widow, Queen Zenobia, had assumed control of the Roman east, and Shahpur was continuing his plundering forays in Western Asia. In an attempt to annex Armenia to the Persian Empire, Shahpur engineered a plan to remove the Armenian king. He instructed a Parthian emissary by the name of Anak to plot the murder of King Khosrov. Anak assassinated the king and all the members of the royal family with the exception of an infant son, Trdat.

It will be a quarter of a century when fate will bring together the assassin's son, Grigor, and the infant boy, Trdat, to inspire the Armenians to accept the universality of the Christian God and forge a new epoch in the history of Armenia.

THE DISINTEGRATION OF THE ROMAN EMPIRE

It is difficult to pinpoint the period in which the Roman Empire began to disintegrate and the influence of Rome over the provinces began to vanish. It may have started when the military began the perilous exercise of appointing emperors during the period of anarchy between 235 and 285. It was during the same period that the Senate's ability to find a leader became irreparably damaged and revolt and civil war began to dominate the political events of the day.

The government of the Empire lost control of most of the provinces in the east and Rome's power began to dissipate rapidly. The loss of central authority and the rise of the Persian power may have been the major causes for the final breakdown of the Roman Empire. But the Empire will not fall. It will be reorganized, change its character, and form the cornerstone of another empire which will rule the east and western Europe from Constantinople until the arrival of the Turks in 1453. For Armenia the decline of the Roman power will place the country in the most hazardous path with profound consequences to the nation's political, social, and religious organization.

THE RISE OF TRDAT III

Diocletian rose to power in Rome in 285 and immediately began to reorganize the central government in an attempt to preserve the Roman supremacy. Buffeted by setbacks abroad and rising unrest at home, he was forced to break up the Empire to control the fringes of the Roman world more effectively. He dissected the Empire into two portions, east and west. He gave the western portion to Maximianus, and took the eastern side and ruled it from Nicomedia, a city near Byzantium in Asia Minor. While he continued to act as the senior ruler of the imperial unity, Diocletian was faced with a rapidly changing world in the east. His most important preoccupation was the damaging onslaughts of the Persians who were threatening to move west and occupy the Roman possessions in Asia Minor.

To insulate the eastern provinces and hold the Persians in check the Romans once again turned to Armenia to restore Armenia's traditional role to act as a buffer zone and protect the Roman interests in Asia Minor. The Armenian throne was left vacant after the assassination of King Khosrov. Trdat, the only surviving son of the murdered king had been smuggled to a Roman province and had grown up to become a popular gladiator in Nicomedia. In 287 he was brought to the attention of Diocletian who was looking for a surrogate in Armenia to maintain a balance of power in the east. He gave Trdat the Armenian crown and sent him to Armenia under heavy escort. King Trdat III managed to preserve political stability and ruled the country as a vassal state to Nicomedia, but his rule will soon be interrupted by the threatening power of the Persians.

King Narseh, the successor of Shahpur in Persia, began to attack Armenia in 294 and forced Trdat to abandon the throne and seek refuge in a Roman territory. Diocletian immediately organized a powerful army and dispatched his able general, Galerius, to attack the Persians in Armenia with the help of an Armenian contingent led by King Trdat. The Persians were speedily suppressed in 297 and Trdat was reinstated on the Armenian throne.

The smashing victory over Persia will provide Armenia with the opportunity to be in control of its own destiny. There will be peace and political tranquility for the next thirty years which will enable Trdat to devote his energy to guide the country. But a problem of a different nature is about to emerge on the horizon of the Armenian people.

CHRISTIANS IN ARMENIA

Christians were allowed to practice their religion throughout the Roman Empire. Emperor Gallienus' edict of toleration in 260 had left the followers of Christianity alone as long as their religious zeal did not interfere with the social and political order of the day. But suddenly in 303 Diocletian removed this veneer of tolerance and issued edicts designed to destroy the Christian God and eradicate the new faith. He saw a threat to his own power which was considered to be derived from the gods of Rome. During the period of toleration the Christian Church had grown in strength and thousands of people, including some members of prominent families, had been converted into Christianity. While Christians continued to be responsible citizens of the Empire, their growth in numbers and the intense heat of their movement were taken as a threat to the social and political equilibrium of the Empire. The new edict of the Emperor initiated a period of wholesale persecution in which Christianity was outlawed, church properties were destroyed and thousands of followers were sent to their martyrdom.

A group of 38 Christian women destined to be sent to their death by the executioners' sword escaped from the Roman territory of Asia Minor and went to Armenia to continue to practice the new faith in peace. After settling down in a secluded place near the city of Vagharshabad the group began its missionary work to convert Armenians into Christianity. Armenians were aroused with an insatiable curiousity about the teachings of the new religion but seemed to be more captivated by the exquisite beauty of the two women preachers, Hripsimeh and Gayaneh, who had asssociated themselves with a Parthian evangelist called Grigor Partev and had gone to the countryside to spread the word of the new God.

Grigor was the only surviving son of Anak, the Parthian prince who had engineered the assassination of King Trdat's father. Trdat after rising to power in Armenia had ordered the extermination of all the members of Anak's family. The order was carried out with one exception. The infant boy Grigor was saved and smuggled out of Armenia. He was taken to his uncle in Cæsarea who raised the boy in the Christian faith and motivated him to become a preacher. After receiving his ordination in Cæsarea, Grigor went to Armenia to spread the word of Jesus Christ with the hope of atoning his father's crime.

With stubborn tenacity and a profound conviction in Christian doctrines, Grigor began to preach the new religion first to small groups in the villages, then to the educated elite of the cities. Armenians found in Christianity a message different from that of paganism. They were told that Jesus, as the supreme protector of humanity, would help them in their present life and assure them immortality in the hereafter. For them Christianity communicated a new sense of hope. They found the personal nature of Christian worship more appealing than the pagan services. This was the first time that a religious ideology allowed anyone, rich or poor, free or slave, to become a member of the church and worship God together in a spirit of brotherly love and fellowship of man. It was a veritable revolution of thought powerful enough to shake the foundation of the old order.

At first the Christians in Armenia met in small groups and conducted their worship in the privacy of their homes. As they grew in number they began to assert their convictions openly and threatened to disrupt the social and political organization of the country. A clash was imminent. It did not take long for Christianity to come into an open ideological conflict with paganism. The hostility between the old and the new developed into a wholesale persecution of the Christians in Armenia. King Trdat ordered the execution of the women preachers and had Grigor arrested and thrown into a dungeon in the citadel of Artashat.

TRDAT ACCEPTS CHRISTIANITY

After sending the Christian leaders to martyrdom, Trdat became stricken by an incurable and mysterious disease. The prominent physicians in Armenia and Asia Minor tried in vain to cure the monarch. The pagan priests offered prayers and sacrifices to the gods for relief. But nothing helped. A suggestion was made by the monarch's sister to seek the help of Grigor who had demonstrated a miraculous power of Christianity while preaching the new faith. In desperation Trdat summoned Grigor from his prison cell who promptly offered his prayers and healed the King. Awed by the supernatural power of Christian God Trdat accepted Christianity as the state religion of Armenia and ordered the people to worship the new faith.

The year was 303. Some modern scholars move the year to 314. The event marked the beginning of a new era in the history of Armenia and made Armenians the first among nations to adopt Christianity.

CONFLICT WITH PAGANISM

After receiving the royal support to Christianize Armenia, Grigor went to Caesarea to accept the episcopal investiture from the Greek Metropolitan of the day. He was named the supreme head of the Armenian Church, took the title Catholicos, and was rechristened as Grigor Loussavorich, Grigor the Illuminator. Upon his return to Armenia he began to convert Armenians into the Christian faith through a remarkable demonstration of energy and ability. He decided that the way to conversion lay through the destruction of the old religion. Grigor ordered the pagan temples destroyed and the properties of the pagan priests confiscated. He demanded an absolute surrender from the pagans. He declared war against the adherents of paganism and enlisted the King's support to organize an army to crush the strongholds of the pagan cult. Christian troops demolished the pagan idols and slayed thousands of priests who refused to accept the Christian faith. The Armenian Nakharars took advantage of the religious revolution. The spoils were too great for them to wait long. While helping Grigor to evangelize the country, they began to loot the treasures of the pagan sanctuaries.

The pagan spirit was finally crushed when the struggle reached its climax in the village of Kissaneh. The pagan priests fought and died a violent death. Hundreds of pagans were butchered and others were stoned to death. From the lips of the last priest who was doomed to die at the Christian's sword came a resonant and electrifying curse which will proclaim the prophetic destiny of the Armenian people. "If you drive paganism away from Armenia, there shall never be rest for those who wish to reside here."

HOLY ECHMIADZIN

The religious revolution was over in 305 and the nation was evangelized in the Christian faith. This new religion will have a profound effect on the social, cultural, and political fabric of the Armenian people. The faith will knit the people together into a more homogeneous society. Grigor Loussavorich as the vigorous leader and the moving force of the new Church, founded and organized episcopal sees with urban and rural dioceses to govern the various activities of the Armenian Church. After consolidating his power he began his missionary work by sending preachers to neighboring Georgia to convert people into the Christian faith.

To govern this Church as the supreme Catholicos of all Armenians, Grigor, with the help of King Trdat, built a cathedral in the city of Echmiadzin. Built in 305 in the shadow of Mount Ararat, this Church with its majestic simplicity, is still in existence. It is the patriarchal see of the Armenian Catholicos, a title comparable to the Pope of the Roman Catholic Church. For Armenians today Echmiadzin is the planet's most venerable and sacred spot. Throughout the history of this people this Church has come to represent the focal point of national unity and the indomitable source of much of the nation's blessings. An enormous power has come to reside in Echmiadzin and in the person of the Catholicos, particularly at times when the Armenian throne was kept vacant and the people were left leaderless. In the subsequent history of Armenia the Catholicos will act not only as the spiritual leader of the people, but also as a surrogate king and the supreme arbiter of national disputes.

The Armenian today feels a surge of national pride when he visits this shrine of his ancestors. His mind wanders back across the centuries of sufferings and ponders how this place continues to exist for 1,700 years as the unperishable reminder of the golden age when his ancestors became the first to accept

the religion of the civilized man while the rest of the world continued to worship the gods of paganism.

CHAPTER ELEVEN

THE GOLDEN AGE

Armenia's new religion had implications which were political as well as spiritual. By being the first to accept a religious ideology which was fundamentally different from that practiced by Rome and Persia, Trdat paved the way for an independent Armenia with the hope of freeing the country from foreign intrusion. He sought independence through Christianity and with his momentous decision attempted to restore the unity among the people and create harmony among the warring factions of the aristocratic families. While the new religion will be a principal exponent for the uniqueness of their national character, it will not be enough to provide the people with the momentum necessary to preserve the race. The values and traditions of the Armenian civilization accumulated over a period of centuries made the society complex and cosmopolitan. The period of Hellenization that followed the conquests of Alexander the Great had made the Armenian society significantly different from that of other peoples in Western Asia. They were successful in adopting the Greco-Roman culture by making it a part of their civilization, but they were equally successful in continuing to adhere to their own values and institutions to maintain the purity of their identity and the integrity of their discipline. While they regarded themselves culturally different, they had no alphabet to call their own. From time immemorial they were forced to use someone else's letters to communicate and transmit the ingredients of their culture from one generation to the next. The transformation from paganism to Christianity made it imperative for the Armenians to have their own alphabet to preserve their religious conceptions and maintain the individuality of their culture. By adopting Christianity as the new religion of the country Trdat sought a new direction for the Armenian people. His decision will mark the end of the Greco-Roman influence and the beginning of a cultural scholarship based on Armenian tradition and thought.

A new age was about to emerge on the horizon with the freshness of new concepts based on Armenia's interpretations of Christian values and morality. It is this age that will reveal the true greatness of these people and separate them from others. After living in the shadow of Mount Ararat for 1,500 years the Armenian race had come to the age of maturity. The elements of the old culture which were thought not worth keeping will be discarded and those deemed to be valuable will be preserved. The process will bring a fundamental change in the character of the Armenian people, repave the course of their history and lead the way to a period that will subsequently be called the Golden Age of Armenia. But first we need to pass through a period of anarchy, assassination, and intrigue before we reach the golden gate.

In 305 Diocletian, already in poor health, decided to retire from public office and leave the Roman throne to his successors, Constantius, and Galerius. Constantius was killed in action shortly thereafter and the army acclaimed an able general, Constantine, as the ruler of the empire. To gain complete control of the provinces Constantine organized a military campaign in 312. According to Christian tradition, the night before a major battle was planned to be waged Constantine saw a flaming cross in the sky, and below it were the Greek words, "By this sign you will conquer". Constantine went into battle and won the throne of the Roman Empire. Constantine regarded the victory as the vindication of the power of the Christian God, renounced paganism, and accepted Christianity as the official religion of the Roman Empire.

After consolidating his power and removing all his enemies, he began the construction of a new capital on the site of an old Greek colony of Byzantium on the Bosporus, and called it Constantinople. It is from this strategic location at the crossroads between Europe and Asia, that he will rule the empire, shift the center of gravity from Rome to Asia Minor, and lay the foundation of another empire, called Byzantine, that will rule this part of the world for over one thousand years.

CHRISTIANITY AS THE PRINCIPAL RELIGION

Constantine regarded his conversion to Christianity as a sign of divine inspiration and considered himself as the representative of the Christian God. He took the new religion as a means of achieving unity and political stability of the Empire, and expected his subjects to accept him as the principal vanguard of Christian orthodoxy. To promote unity among church leaders he invited bishops from all parts of the Empire to attend an ecumenical conference in 325 in Nicaea, and help formulate a creed that will be the principal dogma of the new religion.

THE IRE OF THE PERSIANS

The entire Roman east, including the vassal states and the client kingdoms near the Euphrates, had now become Christian. The Persians regarded this alliance of the Christ worshipping kings and emperors as a serious threat to their religious and political organization. They were particularly outraged when King Trdat of Armenia openly aligned himself with Constantine and sent the Armenian Catholicos to attend the Nicaean Council. To stop the spread of Christianity and further the cause of Zoroastrianism, the Persians began subversive activities in Armenia. They dispatched a group of secret agents to Artashat to plot the assassination of King Trdat and install a more suitable monarch on the Armenian throne, one who would shift the country towards Persia and eradicate Christianity from the Armenian soil. With the help of the king's chamberlain, the Persians murdered Trdat in 330 by poisoning him during a hunting expedition.

The murder of the popular King aroused the Armenian Nakharars to organize an open rebellion and chase the Persians out of the country. They installed Trdat's son, Khosrov on the Armenian throne. Khosrov II, better known as Kotak, meaning little or short, ruled Armenia until 339. A man with no qualities of leadership or political acumen, he retained his throne mostly through the support of the Armenian Catholicos and the Commander-in-Chief of the armed forces, Vatcheh Mamigonian. He was, however, able to promote the caravan trade between east and west and inaugurate a period of economic growth and prosperity. His attempts to impose strict discipline offended the Nakharars and caused a political upheaval which

eventually led the country to open warfare between the crown
and prominent families of the aristocracy. One of the remarkable achievements of King Khosrov, however, was the construction of the city of Devin, which will be the future capital of
Armenia and play an important role in the political and religious development of the Armenian people.

When Emperor Constantine died in 337, Shahpur II of
Persia reopened hostilities against Armenia in an attempt to
bring the country within the Persian sphere of influence. In the
military conflict which followed, King Khosrov, with the help of
a powerful army led by Vatcheh Mamigonian, attempted to re-
pulse the Persians but in the end he was overpowered. The Persians had received the tacit support and collaboration of certain
Nakharars, who in acts of treason turned the conflict into a
battle of terror with the hope of toppling Armenia's Christian
government and reinstating paganism in the country.   They
killed the King and the Commander-in-Chief, along with thousands of Armenian troops. While the situation descended into
chaos, it failed to swing the country towards the Persian orbit.
The Christian Party was swift to install Khosrov's son, Tiran on
the Armenian throne, chase the Persians out, and restore stability in the country.

THE BRUTALITY OF KING TIRAN

A man with little qualities of administrative leadership, Tiran,
upon ascending the Armenian throne, began to antagonize the
Catholicos and strip away much of the political power of the
great Mamigonian family. He intrigued to upset the Nakharars
and was suspected of plotting with the pagans to reinstate paganism in the country. The reaction from the church was swift.
The Catholicos forbade Tiran to attend church services and
criticized him for his conduct in public and private life. The
church's criticism offered sufficient justification for the king to
order his guards to beat the Catholicos to death.

King Tiran ran the country with ruthless brutality but managed to maintain a neutral position between Persia and Rome.
This neutrality did not last long. When King Shahpur launched
a campaign of wholesale persecution of Christians in Western
Asia he tried to create political division in Armenia with the
hope of reinstating paganism in the country. He sent envoys to

win over Tiran to move the country towards the Persian orbit. Tiran refused to accept the Persian emissaries. Shahpur then invited the Armenian King to come to the Persian capital for consultation. This was a trap. He was thrown in jail and blinded. Tiran's son, Arshak II succeeded his father and ruled Armenia for seventeen years. Armenia continued to be a theater of warfare between Persia and Rome with no peace or tranquility.

TURMOIL IN CONSTANTINOPLE

Meanwhile, in Constantinople Emperor Constantine's death in 337 caused a family feud among the members of Constantine's family over the issue of succession. After a period of political malaise the Roman army put all the members of Constantine's family to death, leaving only his three sons, Constantius, Constantine II, and Constans, to share the Empire. The army divided the Roman world into three sections, Constantius ruled the east, Constantine II ruled the west, while Constans took the Italian peninsula and northern Africa under the nominal authority of Constantine II. This division did not last long. In 353 Constantius managed to get rid of his brothers and appointed his cousin, Julian to be his *aide-de-camp* to rule the Empire.

Constantius was a man of mediocre qualities. He ran the Empire with the help of bureaucratic functionaries who continued to adhere to pagan cults and refused to stamp out paganism in the provinces of the Empire. There was even a rumor that Julian, the designated heir to the throne, was secretly nurturing pagan sentiments and plotting to renounce Christianity as the state's religion.

Constantius' difficulties were more military than religious. Shahpur of Persia was continuing to threaten Armenia and the provinces of the Roman east and Rome's inability to suppress the Persians had reduced the respect that the army once had towards Constantius. When King Shahpur planned to invade Armenia, Arshak II asked for help from Constantinople. In a meeting held in Caesarea between Constantius and the Armenian King a plan was devised to organize a combined force to defend Armenia from Persian onslaught. But the plan was never materialized because of the sudden death of Constantius in 361. Julian succeeded Constantius and immediately began to launch a military campaign to crush the Sassanid power in Persia. With the help of King Arshak of Armenia he invaded Persia and pushed the combined Roman and Armenian forces to the gates of the Persian capital. But the war cost Julian his life.

ROMAN TREATY WITH PERSIA

Upon Julian's death the Roman army proclaimed Jovian, the commander of Julian's bodyguards, to be the emperor. Jovian was a man with no military experience. To continue Julian's move towards Persia, he pushed his troops to the Tigris River but was unable to cross the river and attack Persia from Mesopotamia. Shahpur prevented the Romans from advancing eastward. To break the stalemate the two powers agreed to sign a treaty. The pact was an example of international diplomacy in which each side pledged not to invade the territory of the other and leave Armenia to the mercy of the Persians.

The bilateral agreement without Armenian participation was not acceptable to the Nakharars. They continued to fight the Persians and prevented them to take over Armenia by force. They were confronted by a coalition between Persia and Rome which had offered Shahpur the opportunity to consolidate his power and prepare for a large scale operation to finish up Armenia.

HUNS INVADE EUROPE

Emperor Jovian died in 364 and the Empire found itself in a critical situation in the provinces above the Danube River. There were great migratory movements set in motion by the Mongolian Huns who had come from the vast reaches of central Asia and were moving rapidly towards western Europe. They had already destroyed the kingdom of eastern Goths known as Ostrogoths in the Ukraine and were on their way to destroy the kingdom of western Goths, known as Visigoths. They moved from east to west by ravaging the land of the Goths and seizing plunder from their villages and towns. Emperor Valens, who ascended the Roman throne in 375, allowed the Goths to move south and occupy the territory around the Bosporus. His goal was to protect the northern frontier by creating a buffer zone between Constantinople and the barbaric

Huns. While the placement of the Goths around the Bosporus effectively removed the threat of the Mongolian Huns, the forced migration of the Gothic people became too harsh to insure internal peace.

In the east the Armenian Kingdom of Arshak II was in a desperate situation. The country was ruined economically and the Persians were threatening to occupy Armenia by force. The Armenian troops led by the Mamigonian family kept the Persians in check but the almost continuous warfare had destroyed the morale of the military. A delegation headed by Catholicos Nerses was sent to Constantinople to ask for military aid from Emperor Valens. But Valens had a more serious problem in his own backyard. A revolt had broken out in the newly established Goth territory. The Goth migrants had begun to press against the frontiers and attack the Roman troops with ruthless barbarism. The corridor to the west had already been blocked and the Goths were threatening to control the routes to Constantinople.

KING ARSHAK MURDERED

In Armenia the struggle against Persia continued. When the delegation from Constantinople returned home empty-handed, King Arshak in desperation went to the Persian capital to plead Shahpur to leave Armenia alone. At first Shahpur accorded a royal welcome to the Armenian monarch but later ordered to have him arrested and killed.

King Arshak's death left the Armenian throne vacant and the country leaderless. The nation's military commander, Vassak Mamigonian, with the help of the Nakharars continued to fight the Persians but was overpowered by the trained and ferocious troops of the Persians. Shahpur's forces invaded Armenia in 367, occupied the capital city, captured General Mamigonian , and flayed him alive. The Persian occupation of Armenia did not last long. They were forced to leave the country and direct their attention to other territories around Mesopotamia.

KING PAP RISES TO POWER

King Arshak was succeeded by Pap, the twenty-two year old son of Queen Parantsem, who had married Arshak after her husband was treacherously murdered by the king's agents. Pap was installed on the Armenian throne through the auspices of Emperor Valens who had promised to revoke Jovian's treaty with Shahpur and protect Armenia against Persian encroachments. Pap ruled Armenia during one of the most turbulent periods in which the Romans and Persians found themselves at each other's throat. Armenia continued to be a fertile ground for foreign intrigue. While Pap attempted to placate both superpowers on an equal basis he saw more hope for an Armenian survival with Persia than with Constantinople.

Emperor Valens was led to suspect Pap's loyalty towards Rome as Pap continued his pro-Persian activities in Armenia. There was some speculation that Pap was preparing to make an alliance with Persia to attack the Roman forces in Asia Minor. With the encroachments by the rebellious Goths in the northwest and the threat of a united Persian-Armenian provocation on the eastern flank, Valens needed to secure the approaches to the Roman borders from both sides. There were fortified towns constructed on the western fringes to guard against the Gothic flare-ups but there was no organization to protect the land in the east. To stop the potential threat to Asia Minor Valens conspired to have King Pap murdered in 374 during a feast prepared by Roman generals in honor of the Armenian King.

Assassination which occurred quite frequently was not always the best way to gain control of Armenia. The Armenian lords, while unsupportive of their kings most of the time, felt incensed every time a foreign power treacherously plotted the savage removal of their monarch. It was easy for them to criticize the king of their own country but felt contempt when a foreign ruler attempted, through extortion or intrigue, to intervene in the selection and elimination of their leader. Such was the case when Valens appointed Pap's nephew Varazdat to ascend the Armenian throne. The Armenian nobles were not in favor of this appointment. They organized an open rebellion to oust the Roman appointee. The conflict between the crown and the Nakharars inaugurated a period of political turmoil in which Mushegh Mamigonian, the popular Commander-in-Chief of the armed forces, was killed and the economic condition of the country disrupted the continuation of trade between east and west. Faced with enormous social, economic, and political difficulties, King Varazdat was forced to flee the country in 378 and leave the leadership of Armenia to young Manuel Mamigonian who succeeded his father Mushegh as the Commander of the armed forces.

Two important events a year later changed the course of history and brought new governments in Constantinople and Persia. The general peace which had prevailed during the reign of Roman emperors was disrupted by the deaths of Emperor Valens in Constantinople and King Shahpur II in Persia. The demise of the two rulers caused instant warfare along the frontiers and the vassal kings began to jockey for political position in favor of one power or the other. The Roman army appointed Theodosius to occupy the Roman throne and Shahpur III succeeded his father in Persia. The period of transition gave the Armenian lords the opportunity to appoint their own king and put an end to the internal turmoil which had devastated the country for many years. The country's economic structure was in shambles, and the educated elite was concerned mainly with the teaching of the Christian doctrines to the masses. There was no interest on the part of the clergy to help the Nakharars to restore a semblance of political order. They had their hands full.

The new religion was still having its difficulties. Many Armenians considered Christianity a poor substitute for paganism. Others failed to understand the monotheistic nature of the new faith and questioned the theological differences between paganism and Christianity. Paganism believed in many gods, but there was only one principal god, the others functioned as subordinates. The Armenian pagans felt that the Christians were also practicing a sort of polytheism. They had a galaxy of gods. There was God and his Son, Jesus, who as the Son of God was also God. The Christians believed in the Holy Ghost who had God-like attributes, and a series of saints including Jesus' Mother and his disciples, endowed with supernatural powers as were the pagan gods.

While Christianity was firmly established on the Armenian soil, there were still pockets of people who continued to worship the pagan gods and accepted Christianity as an irrelevant religion and a schismatic sect of the Hebrews. Ever since the adoption of the new religion the successors of Trdat made it a practice to enlist Christians to help to run their political organizations. This made the position of the church strong, particularly at times when foreign powers attempted to disrupt Armenia's social and political system.

While the clergy and the educated elite were busy educating the people, the Nakharars were busy selecting a king for the Armenian throne. Vacillation and lack of unity made the selection process an impossible task. King Pap had two sons, and while both were unqualified to succeed their father, the lords could not agree to choose one to their liking. They finally agreed to appoint both as co-monarchs and share the throne on an equal basis. This was a glaring example of the ineptitude of the Nakharars to assert themselves as a cohesive body in times of national urgency.

THE PARTITION OF ARMENIA

Meanwhile in the west Theodosius had firmly established himself as the sole ruler of the Empire perhaps without realizing that he will be the last emperor of a unified Roman Empire. After his departure the Roman world will be forever divided and a new empire will emerge from the ruins of the old one. With a rare quality of leadership and diplomatic skill Theodosius was able to put down the Gothic rebellion by promising the Goths an independent enclave above the Danube basin within the jurisdiction of the Roman authority. In the east he concluded a treaty with Shahpur III under which Armenia was partitioned between the two powers. Greater Armenia became a vassal state of Persia and Lesser Armenia became a Roman colony.

Shahpur III appointed Khosrov IV to the Armenian throne in 385 but the new king lasted not quite two years. His conduct in foreign affairs offended the Persians who promptly dethroned him and forced him to live in confinement in the Persian capital. Khosrov's brother, Vramshapuh, rose to power with Persia's approval and ruled the country for twenty-eight years. In Persia Yazdegert I succeeded Shahpur. One of his first tasks was to ratify the election of Sahag to be the Catholicos of the Armenian Church and Sahag's son-in-law, Hamazasp Mamigonian, to be the Commander-in-Chief of the armed forces. The stage was now set for Armenians to develop a new style of communication and inaugurate a period of grandeur in which they will forever shed the alphabet of foreign lands and invent their own.

THE ALPHABET

Perhaps the most important single factor that affected the course of subsequent history and offered perpetuity and a new character to the Armenian civilization was the invention of the alphabet. The Armenian civilization as it was known by the beginning of the Fifth century, was a complex and cumbersome urban society whose records were kept in Greek or in Persian with no linguistic homogeneity. For 1,700 years, from the time when the Thraco-Phrygians crossed the Bosporus on their way to form the Armenian nation, the people used the letters of another country to record their historical events, make laws and regulations, and develop the thought and tradition of the society. In contrast to other cultures in Western Asia, the Armenian civilization had become complex by the multilingual character of the society and the need of the people to use a phonetically alien alphabet to express themselves.

Against this broad perspective one man stands alone as a pivotal figure whose achievement marked the beginning of a new era and gave new meaning to the word Armenian. His name was Mesrop Mashdotz. An erudite and intellectual man from the Taron region of Armenia, he initiated a cultural revolution by inventing the Armenian alphabet and caused the emergence of a new civilization uniquely Armenian and characteristically different from the cultures of the neighboring countries. The invention of the alphabet was in response to the needs of the society in general but more specifically to the needs of the teachers to preach the Christian Gospel. By the beginning of the Fifth century the society in Armenia and the doctrines of Christianity had become too complex to be transmitted orally. The preachers needed a continuity of religious education which would have been possible only through the use of reading and writing.

Although the Armenian civilization was a heritage from the period of Urartu and Arme, its basic character was formed during the period immediately following the conquests of Alexander the Great, when Armenians adopted the Hellenistic culture and classical traditions. It was during this period that the elements of the Armenian civilization were developed and the unity of race and language was achieved. This period, 600 years before the arrival of Christianity in Armenia, was the prelude to the flowering of the Golden Age in the beginning of the Fifth century. The catalyst for this renaissance was Christianity. But Christianity was a foreign religion. It was introduced in Armenia by foreign preachers, but despite the derivative nature of the Christian tradition, Armenians developed their own interpretations of the religious borrowings. They created their own church to satisfy their spiritual needs with no imitative characteristic with other branches of Christianity. Throughout history they clung tenaciously to the uniqueness of their church. While the church was Armenian in character, the worship was conducted in Syriac or Greek, thus impeding the growth of religion and separating the church from the community. Prayers and readings were occasionally translated into Armenian but the congregation remained illiterate. The people were unable to memorize the teachings of Christ or recite the prayers in Armenian.

MESROP THE PREACHER

Mesrop Mashdotz began to teach the Christian faith in the mountain districts of Armenia where pockets of people continued to worship the pagan gods. He saw the need to conduct the liturgy and deliver the sermon in the Armenian language and emancipate the Armenians from the tutelage of foreign preachers. With the support of Catholicos Sahag and King Vramshapuh he embarked on a project to invent an alphabet for his people. Mesrop was a polyglot. As an expert in the Greek, Syrian, and Persian languages he served as a royal secretary to the king but later had entered into the service of the church to pursue an intellectual career and devote his life to the teachings of Christ.

IN SEARCH OF AN ALPHABET

There was some speculation, judging from preserved historical records, that there was a set of Armenian characters in existence in the library of Syrian Bishop Daniel in Edesa. Mesrop studied this alphabet but found it to be inadequate and flawed. He then conducted an intensive search around the cultural centers of Asia Minor and the Near East to develop a type of letters that would satisfy the phonetic complements and sound symbols of the Armenian language. At first he experimented with sets of different variations, a group of consonants in combination with vowel sounds. But in 404 he created a set of 36 characters (two more letters were added in the Twelfth century) that satisfied the requirements and the grammatical structure of the Armenian language.[1]

With the invention of the alphabet and a system of spelling in place, the Armenians began to translate the Old and the New Testament, the works and the homilies of early Christian fathers, and the ecclesiastical history of the Christian Church. While the principal motive for the alphabet was to disseminate the Christian faith to all levels of society, the importance to transmit thoughts and records of history to the succeeding generations was immeasurable. The alphabet enabled the Armenian society to perpetuate itself and pass to the future generations the nation's institutions and traditions through a process of continuous refinement which ultimately formed the intrinsic foundation of the Armenian civilization. The invention of the alphabet was fundamental to Armenia's life. Armenians began to record their history only after the discovery of the alphabet.

THE AGE OF ENLIGHTENMENT

The new alphabetic script opened the door for other intellectual and cultural pursuits. The development of the alphabet was accompanied by a surge of creativity in literature, art, and philosophy. After translating the Christian writings the Armenians began to write hymns, poetry and philosophical essays. Their society had a sufficient repertoire of traditions and customs to provide the necessary ingredients for literary creativity. This great burst of intellectual energy revealed a high degree of sophistication. With genuine enthusiasm to create a new society Mesrop and his associates went around the country, built schools, and began to teach the new letters to the people on all levels of society. He sent trained scribes to the remote corners of the country to spread the knowledge of the new alphabet.

---

[1] It is interesting to note that Chairman Mao-tse-Tung in 1949 in an effort to modernize the Chinese society chose to adopt Mesrop's Armenian alphabet to replace the complexity of the Chinese characters, but later rejected the idea on the advice of his wife who represented the traditional cultural movement in the People's Republic of China.

THE TRANSLATORS

This cultural movement was sponsored and promoted by a group of clergy known as the Translators (Tarkmanich) who extended themselves to other fields of cultural endeavor. While emphasizing the importance of religious education they taught ethics, philosophy, and the basic sciences, and in the process introduced a new understanding of humanism and a new rationale of life for the community. They established a system of public education and, with the help of the King and the wealthy Nakharars, made it compulsory for the people to participate in the process of education.

This was indeed an intellectual transformation of the Armenian society. The people were receptive to the barrage of educational material and regarded Mesrop as a brilliant architect for the revival of Armenia's cultural spirit. In the past Armenians had shown little flair for educational tasks. A formal educational system was a privilege only for the children of the aristocratic families. The middle class was primarily interested in trades and professions, and the serfs and the slaves were engaged in serving the members of the upper class. With all the turmoil and political instability the Armenians had neither the taste nor the time to educate themselves. But the alphabet created a galvanizing force to thrust the nation into the age of enlightenment. In the cultural movement nurtured by the invention of the alphabet a galaxy of able scholars, such as Goriun, Yeznig, Pausdos, Yeghisheh, Parbetsi and others came into prominence. Together with Mesrop they founded a new social order to direct the spirit of Armenia for the succeeding generations.

CHAPTER TWELVE

THE BATTLE FOR RELIGIOUS FREEDOM

The period that followed the invention of the alphabet marked the beginning of a sad epoch in the history of Armenia in which the Arshakunian Dynasty will topple and the country will be governed by the will and caprice of the rulers of Persia with no occupants on the Armenian throne. This will also be a period in which the Armenians will be tested for their firmness in the Christian faith and for their ability to defend their religious freedom. The implicit hostility between pagan Persia and Christian Armenia will develop into a wholesale persecution of the Christians, culminating in a military confrontation in which Armenians will rather die than abjure their Christian convictions.

THE RETURN OF KING KHOSROV

When King Vramshapuh died in 414, Catholicos Sahag went to Persia to obtain Yazdegert's consent to release King Khosrov IV from his imprisonment in Persia and reinstate him on the Armenian throne. Khosrov occupied the throne in 415 but his reign lasted only a year. Forces beyond his control were moving rapidly and it became impossible for him to reverse the tide. Religious fanaticism dominated the events of the day. The Persian king issued edicts to stamp out Christianity in the Persian Empire and in the client kingdoms bordering Persia. Christian leaders in the Persian territories were arrested and churches burned. Heavy penalties were set for the clergy with their properties seized and their treasures confiscated. Most of them suffered martyrdom and others served as forced labor.

The anti-Christian fervor was triggered principally by an ill-conceived plan of an Assyrian bishop to set a Mazdeian temple on fire. This was an important shrine dedicated to the god who had a special appeal for the miraculous. The fire infuriated the Persian king who promptly declared an all out war to eradicate Christianity. Yazdegert, who suffered from an obsessive anxiety to preserve the prestige of his religion, was outraged by the disloyalty of his Christian subjects and the boldness of the clergy. The conflict no longer had ideological coloration. Conventional theological or philosophical differences between the two religious sects were set aside and militarism was in vogue to force people to demonstrate their loyalty to pagan gods. Yazdegert chose Armenia to provide the stage for his anti-Christian activity because Armenians were believed to be the staunchest defenders of the new faith and their country was regarded as the bastion of Christianity in Western Asia. He deposed King Khosrov IV in 416 and appointed his son, Shahpur, to be the governor of Armenia with the express purpose of introducing the cult of Zoroastrianism and running the administrative machinery of the state according to Mazdeian practices and requirements. The period that followed brought large scale persecutions of the Armenian Christians with the organization of the Church seriously jeopardized and most of the clergy thrown in jail. At the height of the crisis Yazdegert I was assassinated in Persia and his son, Shahpur, hurried home to claim the Persian throne.

The conflict in Persia was two-fold. Guerrilla warfare was conducted by a group of Persian political activists who wanted to install their own man on the throne, and the persecution of the Christian elements who courageously continued to defy the king's orders to renounce their faith. Shahpur's reign began with fresh hostilities against both factions. He too fell victim to the plots of the terrorists and was assassinated a few months later. Anarchy followed this second assassination and the Persian court was on the verge of losing its grip. Internal and external conflicts had weakened the structure of the government and demoralized the troops. The Persian Empire was plunged into a potentially dangerous upheaval and the country was exposed to encroachments from outside.

The situation was remedied and stability was restored somehow in 420 when Bahram V rose to power and through

diplomatic skill concluded a Hundred Years' Peace Treaty with
the Romans. Under the Treaty the Persians agreed to accord
religious freedom to Christians and the Romans promised to
permit the Persians in Asia Minor to worship Zoroaster. The
Treaty, however, served only as a camouflage for the sharp
cleavage between Zoroastrianism and Christianity. The Persian
court was legitimized by Mazdeian concepts and the Christian
elements continued to reject the irrationality of Zoroastrianism.
But the camouflage was good enough for the Armenian people
who craved for a semblance of tranquility and the cessation of
religious oppression. Under Governor Shahpur the country had
lost its political organization and the patriarchal seat, on which
the nation's strength generally rested, tottered under Mazdeian
pressure. The idealism of intellectual pursuit, which was the
fruit of the Golden Age a few years back, had been converted
into political reality. While educational programs continued to
be offered, expediency dictated the reduction of cultural activities with emphasis placed on the techniques of survival, political
as well as spiritual.

The elevation of Bahram to the Persian throne brought
salutary results to Armenia. The Persian hold on Armenia was
relaxed. Bahram in the spirit of good will allowed the Armenian grandees to appoint Vramshapuh's son, Artashes, as the
King of Armenia in 423. Christianity was tolerated and the
country returned to normalcy. The churchmen were released
from prison and cultural life began to flourish.

THE END OF KINGDOM

Political and religious stability lasted only five years. King Artashes was only seventeen when he ascended the throne. While
energetic enough to run the national government, he was too
young to demand loyalty from the Nakharars whose avaricious
greed created a financial drain on the nation's treasury and
brought the country to the verge of bankruptcy. During the
governorship of Shahpur the Nakharars hauled large sums of
money in the pretense of reorganizing the caravan trade between east and west. The appointment of the youthful King
threatened to put an end to the independence of their fiefdoms.
They were prepared to share with no one, not even the king,
the financial resources that they selfishly accumulated for their

own purposes and personal aggrandizement. There was a serious food shortage at the time and the King wanted to provide grain for the less privileged people who were not allowed to share in the amenities provided by the Nakharars. The nation's treasury was empty and the wealthy grandees refused to offer financial aid. Turmoil and anarchy plagued Armenia once again. The King was too weak and inexperienced to cope with the situation and maintain the vigilance necessary to keep the nobles in check. His authority was undermined by the consolidation of local power in the hands of wealthy families who, as a group, made a travesty of government. While Armenia remained as an important marketplace for goods from the east, a decline in trade had already begun which neither Artashes nor the Nakharars were able to check.

The struggle produced no accommodation between the crown and the Nakharars. Unable to topple the King themselves they planned to go to Persia and ask for the dethronement of the young King. Sahag, the esteemed head of the Armenian Church supported King Artashes and pleaded with the lords to leave the kingship intact. He was acutely aware that the removal of the King through the schemes formulated by the Nakharars would bring serious consequences, political as well as religious, and will make Armenia forever subservient to the Persian rule. With a remarkable quality of statesmanship he tried to dissuade the assembly of lords by proclaiming that "a sick lamb was preferable to a healthy wolf". But his advice was ignored and King Bahram of Persia promptly complied with the request of the Nakharars and dethroned King Artashes in 428.

Perhaps the Armenian nobles did not realize that by their recalcitrance they brought the end to the continuity of orderly succession initiated by the Arshakunian Dynasty which had ruled Armenia for the last 376 years. It had begun in 52 A.D. when Trdat I ascended the Armenian throne. For over three centuries the descendants of Trdat ruled Armenia to the best of their ability. After ousting the foreign kings from the Armenian throne they established a new order for the people, one that eventually led the nation to accept the religion of the civilized man and inaugurate a period of grandeur through the invention of the alphabet. While they generally ruled the country under the auspices of a foreign power, they managed to maintain the durability of the political system and the continuity of hereditary descent. They ran their courts with pageantry and opulence. The brilliant court life will now come to an end. The regimen of existence which had characterized the Arshakunian Dynasty will now disappear, and the result will be more tragic and far reaching than expected. For the next 457 years the Armenian people will have no kings and the country will be reduced to the status of a province with governors designated by foreign potentates who will rule the land with merciless brutality. While Armenians will retain their national identity, they will have no opportunity to claim political recognition. A dark age will obscure the country until the rise of a new dynasty centuries later. Perhaps the Nakharars should have taken heed of the sage advice of Catholicos Sahag.

RELIGIOUS PERSECUTION

The immediate result of King Artashes' removal was political chaos. Greater Armenia became a province of Persia ruled by governors known as Marzbans and Lesser Armenia became a province of the Byzantine Empire ruled by governors known as Curopalatis

In Persia Yazdegert II rose to power in 438 and immediately initiated a program of religious oppression to stamp out Christianity from Western Asia. He will soon be identified with a more militaristic Mazdeian rule at home and aggressive imperialism abroad. After repudiating the Hundred Years' Treaty of 420 he invaded Byzantine territories, massacring Christians and burning churches. His intent was to revive the Empire of Cyrus the Great and establish a Persian hegemony that would stretch from the Indian subcontinent to the Mediterranean Sea. He considered himself the first servant of Ahura-Mazda, and he initiated a program to blend his peoples in common loyalty toward his God.

Byzantine Emperor Theodosius II was unable to stop Yazdegert's encroachments in his territories. He had risen to power in 408 and ruled the Empire from Constantinople as his immediate predecessors had. His reign would later be regarded as the beginning of the Byzantine Empire which seemed to evolve as a logical continuation of the Roman Empire out of the era of Constantine the Great with Roman law as the basis for their political organization.

At the time when Theodosius ascended the throne there was a serious question whether the government in Constantinople would be able to survive under the continued pressure of the Gothic generals. As the Empire became weaker and weaker, the Goths gained considerable strength in Asia Minor through their barbaric activities. Theodosius was able to reverse the tide by playing one Gothic general against another and using small bands of mountaineer warriors to crush the power base of the Goths. But in Persia the situation was quite different. With Persia, Theodosius had a perennial enemy of centuries old, with unlimited resources and a religious fanaticism ferocious enough to destroy not only the political organization of his Empire but also eradicate Christianity and replace it with Mazdeism.

When Yazdegert II began his anti-Christian activities, Theodosius was in the midst of compiling a code which was to be the summation of all the edicts of the Roman emperors who had ruled the Empire from Constantinople. The preparation of the code which was designed to illuminate the society and the administrative rule of the Byzantine emperors, prevented Theodosius to take the field against Yazdegert. He was forced to conclude a treaty of noninterference with a mutual recognition of both empire's territorial limits.

With the Byzantine threat out of the way, Yazdegert prepared a formal ultimatum and a declaration of war against the Christian elements in Armenia. He summoned the Armenian Nakharars to his palace and ordered them to accept Mazdeism and renounce Christianity. Den-Shapuh, the Persian High Commissioner, tried a more amicable method. If Yazdegert's orders were militaristic, Den-Shapuh's methods were more diplomatic. He entertained the members of the prominent Armenian families lavishly and offered them properties and estates in exchange for religious conversion. He moved people to areas predominantly inhabited by Persians and attempted to establish inter-racial communities with the hope of inducing Armenians to acquire Persian practices and provoke a religious revolution in favor of Mazdeism. But no diplomatic nicety or royal decree was powerful enough to change the iron will of the people. They clung to their faith and steadfastly rejected all attempts for conversion. Frustrated, Den-Shapuh imposed oppressive taxes on properties and persons and offered a tax-free status to those who were willing to convert. He replaced the nation's Hazara-pet, Vahan Amatuni, with a Persian and appointed a Mazdeian priest as the chief justice of Armenia.

When diplomatic and political maneuvers failed to produce results, Yazdegert, through his Grand Vizier, Mihr-Narseh, issued an edict to the Armenian people, warning them to give up the foolishness of the Christian God and accept Mazdeism. He exhorted the Armenians to study the benefits and advantages of Mazdeism and absolve themselves from the sins and darkness of Christianity. The edict was delivered in person to Vassak Sewny, who was then the Marzban of Armenia, appointed by the Persians as the most trustworthy among the Armenian Nakharars. Vassak was a powerful Nakharar from the Sewniq region of Armenia which bordered the Persian frontier. A brilliant and wealthy prince, he had inherited his father's vast estate at an early age and governed his district with diplomacy and political acumen.

THE COUNCIL OF ARTASHAT

When Yazdegert's edict arrived in Armenia in 449, Vassak called for a general assembly in Artashat to discuss the order and prepare an appropriate response. His policy was that of *rapprochement*. As the principal Nakharar responsible to run the country as a surrogate to Persia, Vassak aspired to a higher position. Since the fall of the Arshakunian Dynasty and the removal of the last King of Armenia, he aspired someday to rise to the throne and crown himself as the King of Armenia. To achieve this he needed to play a skillful double game contriving to hold the confidence of the Persians while at the same time establishing himself as the leader of Armenia. To please the Persians he adopted a policy of appeasement even at the risk of forcing his countrymen to renounce Christianity and return to paganism. There was also another reason for his policy of appeasement. His two sons were kept as hostage in Persia and the Persians intended to use them as pawns to assure Vassak's continued support of the Persian intransigence.

The assembly was chaired by Catholicos Hovsep and attended by Nakharars, noblemen, bishops, monks, and prominent clergy whose representative was a courageous priest by the name of Ghevond Yeretz. The Council categorically rejected Vassak's conciliatory policies towards Persia. There was no question in the mind of the participants that Armenia, after 150 years of Christian life, would ever renounce Christianity. The nation had already adopted the principal tenets of the new religion and in the course of time it had changed the pagan practices in accordance with Christian traditions and institutions. Christianity was still new, however, and there were pockets of people, especially in the countryside who sought condemnation of Christianity along traditional pagan lines. The chief preoccupation of the participants of the assembly was to search for ways to defend the Christian concepts against the pagan elements at home and abroad. As a result of the brutal rule by Persia, contempt for Persia's religion had grown rapidly and no matter how benevolent Persian rulers pretended to be at times, the Armenians regarded them with extreme distrust and suspicion.

Respectful but firm, the Council rejected Yazdegert's edict and presented the following manifesto to the Persian King:

"Neither angels, nor man, neither fire nor sword can make us renounce our Christian faith. All our earthly possessions are in your hands; our bodies are before you, dispose of them as you will. If you let us live in our faith, we will on earth choose no other lord in your place, but in heaven choose no other God in place of Jesus. Because for us there is no other God than Him. But should you require anything beyond this great sacrifice our bodies are in your hands, do with them as you please. Generations ago our forefathers surrendered their goods, their possessions, and their bodies for the sake of the Christian faith. We are no better than our fathers. We are prepared to die for the love of Christ. But if we die as mortals Jesus may accept us as immortals."

YAZDEGERT SUMMONS THE NAKHARARS

Outraged by the Armenian response Yazdegert ordered the Nakharars to appear before him. Headed by Marzban Vassak and Vartan Mamigonian, a delegation of Armenian Nakharars headed for the Persian capital. "If you do not kneel before the Great and Magnificent Sun," Yazdegert exhorted the Nakharars, "and acknowledge it as your god, you will be imprisoned and chained, your wives and children will be exiled in foreign lands, and the Persian troops and herds of elephants will be sent to Armenia to demolish your churches and shrines". The Nakharars were dismissed from the King's presence and sent to Armenia accompanied by 700 pagan priests with instructions to convert the Armenian people into Mazdeism within a period of twelve months.

When the group of pagan priests arrived at the Armenian border a crowd of peasants, men and women, armed with clubs and slings, shields and swords, led by priest Ghevond Yeretz, began to attack the Persians, killing the pagans and chasing the survivors across the border back to Persia. The Nakharars, after returning home, held a general assembly chaired by Vartan Mamigonian. Vartan, as the prominent member of the Mamigonian family, which had given Armenia a general in almost every generation since the settlement of the Mamigonian dynasty in Armenia, assumed the leadership and advised his colleagues to fight the Persians to defend the church and the homeland.

The general assembly sent envoys to the Governor General of Western Armenia and to the Emperor in Constantinople to observe the ties of Christian unity and send military aid. The delegation to Constantinople came home empty-handed. The Byzantine Emperor was in no position to extend help to the Armenian Christians. Attila, the King of the barbaric Huns, who had already stretched their territory from the Caspian Sea to the Rhine in central Europe, was threatening to enter Constantinople and crush the Byzantine power base. The Goths on one side and the Huns on the other, the Byzantine Greeks were in no position to provide help. They themselves were in a perilous situation.

THE TREASON OF VASSAK

Armenia was in a state of emergency. The country was girding itself for a confrontation against the Persian might. When the pagan priests fled home, Yazdegert, in rage, ordered the Persian high command to begin preparations for an all out war against Armenia. To help the Persians, Vassak, frustrated in his attempt

to convince the Nakharars to accept Mazdeism, organized an
army of his own and began to attack the Armenian churches.
He changed his policy of *rapprochement* into one of total submission to the Persians.

THE BATTLE OF AVARAIR

In the spring of 451 the Persian forces, under the command of
Grand Vizier Mihr-Narseh, crossed the Arax River and positioned themselves at the Armenian frontier. Vartan Mamigonian, as the Commander-in-Chief of the Armenian forces, began
preparations to confront the Persians. He set up his camp near
the village of Avarair. A tributary of Arax separated the two
antagonists. There were 66,000 cavalry and infantry in the Armenian army recruited from the forces of the Nakharars with
thousands of civilian volunteers and clergy joining the army. In
a short period of time Vartan was able to harness the resources
of the country and turn Armenia into an ordered state of military readiness. The army became a professional force brigaded
into squadrons and companies of archers and infantry. They
were all skilled troops with a single-minded dedication to
uphold the faith. There was much that Vartan could depend on,
the courage and the profound respect for ancestral customs and
the principles of liberty that have been established in the course
of Armenia's political experience.

Vartan divided the army into four legionary formations.
He positioned the first on the right side under the command of
Khoren, the Prince of the Khorkhoruni family. The center was
under the command of Nershapuh Ardzruni. He took the left
wing and designated the fourth as the division for the reserves
under the command of his brother, Hamazasp. The foot soldiers were armed with archers, spears, and swords, and the
heavy cavalry was armor clad. The civilian volunteers, people
from all levels of society, were armed with pitchforks, clubs, and
slings.

The Persian army, on the other side of the river had
300,000 men, including Vassak's regiment of 40,000 Armenians.
After destroying the Armenian churches in his district and putting the clergy in jail, Vassak had taken his garrison to the Persian camp ready to fight his brother Armenians. As the
Marzban of Armenia, he had the national treasury in his custo-

dy. He used the funds to recruit mercenaries from the tribes in the Caucasian districts bordering Armenia. The center of the Persian army was held by a division of 10,000 horsemen and a herd of trained elephants, each carrying an iron tower with a bowman guiding the elephant.

On May 26, 451, the two enemies faced each other in battle array. The Commander of the Persian forces promised his men medals of valor to be presented by the King himself, while Vartan read the Holy Scriptures about the deeds of the Macabees who successfully fought against Antiochus in defense of their faith. "Stand firm by our resolute Commander, who shall never forget your deeds and valor", Vartan spoke. "For us it is a great distinction that God is performing this work through us, revealing His real power....Our Commander is not a mortal man, but the Commander-in-Chief of all martyrs. Fear is a sign of doubt, but as we have repudiated doubt long since, let fear also disappear from our hearts and minds."

Ghevond Yeretz, the fiery priest, who had previously galvanized the clergy to join the army, offered prayers and made the invocations "May God have mercy upon us", he chanted, "and may He not deliver our Church into the hands of the heathen". With a loud cry from both sides, raging with fury to destroy each other, the enemies began to fight. The Armenian cavalry crossed the river and burst on the Persians unexpectedly. The left wing of the Armenian army, however, was soon ambushed and began to retreat. Vartan Mamigonian immediately attacked the right wing of the Persian army and pushed the enemy back towards the elephants in the rear. With the elephants as his shield he surrounded the Persians and continued to attack. The Persian commander, noticing the disarray of his troops, ordered his regiment to rush to the spot where Vartan was fighting. Surrounded by the elephants and isolated from his men, Vartan tried to shield himself against the heavy assault of the Persians but his strategy proved to be fatal. He was killed instantly and his body was thrown to the elephants.

The Armenian troops could do little but adjust their positions as the Persians doggedly kept up their action and continued their attack. They planned to combine their forces to permit a holding action while the troops fought and inflicted heavy damage on the Persians. Their operation was endangered, however, by the treachery of Vassak, who showed the

Persians a way around to attack the Armenians from the rear. The fighting ceased toward evening. The Armenians were defeated and the battlefield was full of slain bodies. The complexion of the battle changed immediately as the survivors began to scatter over the hilltops. The Armenian army had no leader. The Commander-in-Chief, together with a distinguished Nakharar, had fallen in battle. The Persians began to plunder and burn Armenian towns and churches. Catholicos Hovsep and priest Ghevond Yeretz were murdered in cold blood. But beneath the flash of joy for the Persians there were strong tensions in the Persian High Command to leave the Armenians alone and merely accept the victory as an opportunity to influence Armenia's political structure with no religious intonation. This was not a gesture of charity but rather the recognition that the Armenian Christian tradition could not be wiped out. The Persians won the battle but seemed to have lost the zeal to continue to press for a religious conversion.

The Commander of the Persian forces advised Yazdegert to cease all military operations and consider the advantages of a policy of *laissez fair*, allowing Armenians to continue to worship their Christian God. He also advised Yazdegert to hold Vassak accountable for the Persian debacle. To the Persians Vassak was largely responsible for the inconclusive war at Avarair. The Persian victory on the battlefield had so inflated him with vanity that he intrigued his Persian masters to allow him to claim the Armenian throne immediately. He was suspected of plotting against the Persian High Command and was brought to trial in Persia and subsequently thrown in jail. For his treacherous deed he will be forever cursed by the Armenian people.

Vartan Mamigonian became a hero of legend whose martyrdom is still remembered. He is accepted as the true representative of the heroic age which cast a glow of nobility and helped Christianity to shape the political and social structure of the Armenian people. Until today Armenians throughout the world commemorate a day in February as a holy day of remembrance of the indomitable will of their ancestors who defended their faith against all odds.

Attempts to stamp out Christianity in Armenia failed. With the Battle of Avarair the Armenians established their lasting identity as a Christian people and became a model of Christian durability and resolute foes of change. But the battle was a turning point in the history of this people. The struggle between Persia and Armenia encouraged revolution and guerrilla warfare in Armenia where revolutionaries fought to gain freedom and liberate the country from Persian superintendence. Armenia continued to be Christian but internal stability and the political organization were shattered beyond recognition. Revolutionaries attempted to form alliances and coalitions to claim political recognition but there was no individual with marked superiority to assume the leadership of the country. For the next four centuries the Armenians will grope for peace but will fail to establish a political structure powerful enough to shed the foreign rule.

CHAPTER THIRTEEN

THE STRUGGLE FOR SURVIVAL

The almost immediate result of the Battle of Avarair was a systematic devastation of Armenia's political organization. The country had come to the brink of social disintegration and political anarchy. While granting the Armenians the freedom to worship their God, Yazdegert lost no time to ruin the country's political machine and impose rigid discipline to prevent the resurgence of an effective leadership. Thirty-five Nakharars were arrested and carried away to Afganistan in chains in 452 and held in exile for thirteen years. Their wives were tortured by mutilation and their children were sold into slavery. Their palaces were burned and looted and their wealth in gold was carried away as plunder. Without a central administrative authority and provincial governments Armenia virtually lost all its political structure and became a province of Persia with Marzbans governing the country as surrogates to the Persian ruler. Political devastation brought economic chaos. No longer were the services of the Armenian merchants needed for the east-west trade. Lack of political tranquility had diverted the caravan trade to other commercial centers of Western Asia. The nation's treasury was empty and the members of the upper class were forced to leave Armenia and migrate to other countries in search of safer havens and better opportunities.

Firuz succeeded his father Yazdegert II on the Persian throne and immediately began his own notoriety to bring Armenia into the fold of the Mazdeian religion. Instead of adopting his father's oppressive measures, he chose peaceful means through gifts and promotions, to persuade Armenians to accept

Persia's religion and worship the sun and fire as gods. His chief lieutenant in Armenia was Adr-Vshnasp, the Persian diplomat who had succeeded Vassak as the Marzban of Armenia. Vshnasp made gifts of gold and properties to the clergy and the members of the upper class, opened educational facilities for the people in the villages and towns, and sent Mazdeian priests to the countryside to persuade people to accept Persia's religion. Despite a vigorous campaign of cajolery, the program for religious conversion produced no result. Embittered and hopeless, the Armenians accepted Catholicos Gute as their leader to form a pro-Roman party with the support of the Mamigonian family to protect the country's religious freedom. The country desperately needed a military force. Patriarchal leadership was not adequate to organize an uprising against the Persian might. The Catholicos sent a delegation to the Byzantine Emperor, Leo I, soliciting military aid in the name of Christian unity. He was spied upon, however, by pro-Persian Armenians, promptly summoned to the Persian capital, and was divested of his patriarchal duties on charges of treason.

GUERRILLA WAR

Unable to withstand Persia's tremendous pressure for religious conversion, the Armenian people once again turned to the Mamigonian family for leadership. Vahan Mamigonian, the nephew of the martyred hero, was chosen as the new leader of Armenia with full authority to organize a military force and seek a new direction for the people to gain religious and political independence. As a youngster, Vahan and his younger brother had been kidnapped by Vassak and taken as hostage to the Persian capital and later released when Yazdegert granted general amnesty to hostages and prisoners of war as a gesture of good will, immediately following the Battle of Avarair. Vahan was a logical successor to Vartan as the Commander of the Armenian armed forces. Vartan Mamigonian had left no son and Vahan, after his return to Armenia, had assumed the helm of the Mamigonian family.

Taking advantage of a Georgian revolt against Persia, the Armenians organized an insurrection to chase the Persians out of the country. The Persian Marzban, unable to protect himself and his family, fled the country and an Armenian government was installed in 481 in the capital city of Devin, under the vigorous leadership of Sahag Bagratuni. During the next four years Vahan and his army regulars conducted a guerrilla war against the Persian elements in Armenia. Vastly outnumbered by Persian forces they raided the towns, crushing their enemies in battle, and through deeds of heroism chased the Persians out of the country.

The organized forces of Persia were unable to contain both Georgian and the Armenian rebellions at the same time. The entire region was fraught with peril. The Persians were overwhelmed by the ferocity of the revolt and were unable to curb the indiscriminate violence and terrorism. It was difficult for them to locate the enemy because the unity of their provincial governments had been destroyed and they were caught between insurgent and counterinsurgent campaigns. The headquarters of the Armenian rebels were hidden in the impregnable and rugged mountain fastnesses of Armenia and the Georgians were conducting their operation in the forests of Apkhasia.

In 484 King Firuz of Persia was assassinated and his brother, Vagharsh, succeeded him to the throne. As the new head of the Persian government Vagharsh wanted to settle the annoying problem of the Armenian rebellion as expeditiously as possible. The unrelenting hostilities had caused political upheaval within his Empire and the national policy issues were for a long time sidetracked by religious preoccupations. The kingdom was embittered by a strain of hostilities from all fronts. He sent his high commissioner to Armenia to make overtures of peace to Vahan Mamigonian and stop the seemingly futile and endless turmoil and violence. Vahan was prepared to lay down the arms if the Persians were willing to accept his conditions for a cease-fire.

THE TREATY OF NUVARSAK

A treaty between Vahan Mamigonian and the Persian commissioner was signed in the village of Nuvarsak. Under the Treaty the Armenians were given the freedom to conduct religious services in accordance with Christian faith and the Persians agreed to the immediate and unconditional removal of all Mazdeian altars from Armenia and the restoration of the rights and privileges of the Nakharars and the members of the upper class.

The accord also called for the appointment of Vahan as the new Marzban of Armenia with freedom to conduct his own affairs and run an autonomous government. Through valor and perseverence the Armenians finally succeeded in gaining their religious freedom. While they were unable to completely extricate themselves from the Persian sphere of influence, they at least were able to restore a semblance of a political organization within the framework of the Persian Empire and begin the difficult task of rebuilding the country after years of political decay. The treaty weakened, if not declawed, the pro-Persian elements in Armenia who had been brutal in their attempt to fuse Armenia's political and social structure with that of Persia.

The Treaty of Nuvarsak opened the doors for revival of economic growth and commercial trade. The schools were reopened and cultural activities began to flourish. Religious and ideological differences ceased to play a dominant role in the relation between Persia and Armenia, and the threat of military force was no longer an instrument of national policy. The leaders of Armenia wanted to assure the new king of Persia that their characteristically defensive instincts will never again become offensive if they were left alone to worship their god.

As Governor-Marzban of Armenia, Vahan Mamigonian ruled the country for twenty-five years and brought Armenia to the peak of prosperity. He abolished the Persian style system of governance in which the country's legal apparatus waxed and waned with the fortunes of the Marzbans and Persian kings. He removed all previously restricted religious regulations issued by the Persian court and encouraged the clergy to reinstate the religious campaign to propagate the Christian faith. This was the first time since the removal of the last king that a stable governmental organization with centralized authority was being put in place in Armenia. What little political system survived after the departure of King Artashes was virtually swept away during the tumultuous period following the Battle of Avarair.

Vahan's principal legacy was the formalization of the legal code invested with Christian values in which the rule of man was replaced with the rule of law. He issued a plethora of statutes covering all activities of society. Peace had finally come to the Armenian soil and the Persians left Armenia alone. This was not exactly an act of charity on the part of the Persians. They left Armenia alone, principally because they themselves were kept busy defending their Empire from Byzantine encroachments.

WESTERN ARMENIA UNDER BYZANTINE RULE

If Greater Armenia in the east began to enjoy political tranquility and economic growth, the situation in Western Armenia was quite different. The conditions of life were never easy in the west. Armenia in general, but this region in particular, occupied an unenviable position of crossroads between Byzantium and Persia. The Persian-Byzantine conflicts created the necessity for the Byzantine Emperor, Justinian, to reorganize the political structure of Western Armenia by suppressing the feudal prerogatives of the Nakharars living in that region and consolidating all military operations into one unit. Lack of unity divided the feudal system and the fragmentation of military forces provided an ineffective and inadequate defense posture for the rulers of Byzantium to protect the eastern fringes of their Empire.

After signing a peace treaty with Persia, Justinian in 532 began to dismantle Western Armenia's political organization to make that region an integral part of the Byzantine Empire. The intent was to abolish Armenia's national identity and remove any possible claims that the people of Armenia may have in the future to restore their political autonomy. The removal of political freedom stirred popular discontent. Members of the Mamigonian and Bagratuni families living in Western Armenia organized forces and began to foment an insurrection in 537 against the Byzantine authorities. The movement was provoked by the assassination of an Armenian prince by a Byzantine Pro-Consul. Within a matter of days the Armenian rebels massacred Byzantine troops and chased the survivors out of the country. This was only a temporary setback for the Byzantine forces. They re-entered the country, murdered the principal Nakharars and sent their families into exile to distant parts of the Empire. The precision and the brutality of their operation left a paralyzing effect on Western Armenia's military organization to the point that the Armenian leaders will never again attempt to seek political independence and for all practical purposes Western Armenia will cease to exist as an autonomous region. It will henceforth be a mere appendage to the Byzantine

Empire. The Armenians in Western Armenia will lead a wandering experience and constantly change their habitat in search of food and safety with no political unity.

Turning their attention to Greater Armenia, the Byzantine government began secret negotiations with the Armenian leaders in 570 to forge a rebellion against the Persian authorities in exchange of an affirmation that Byzantium will help liberate the country from the Persian yoke and recognize the territorial rights of Eastern Armenia. This was an affirmation and not a commitment. The Armenian rebellion and guerrilla warfare against the Persians supported by Byzantine commando units lasted two years during which the capital city of Devin was captured, the Persian Marzban was murdered, and the Persian forces were chased out of the country. But the Armenian insurrection precipitated an all out war between Byzantium and Persia which lasted until 579. After a series of humiliating defeats the Byzantine Emperor was forced to sign an accord with the Persians, recognizing Persia's territorial rights and granting a general amnesty to prisoners of war.

MAURICE, THE ARMENIAN

Not all the emperors of Byzantium were of Greek or Roman origin. The court of Constantinople had many foreign elements, and among them there was a group of Armenians who rose to power. The first Armenian who wore the imperial mantle in Byzantium was Maurice. Born in Cilicia in 539 Maurice attained the rank of general and won a series of decisive victories against Persia. He became emperor upon the death of his father-in-law, Emperor Tiberius Constantine in 582. During his reign of twenty years he became, paradoxically, one of the most vicious enemies of Armenia.

Maurice supported the Persian ruler, Khosrov II, against other pretenders to the Persian throne and helped Khosrov occupy the throne in 591 in exchange for a large portion of Eastern Armenia from Lake Van in the south to Lake Sevan in the northeast. The alliance between Persia and Byzantium was forged to establish zones of influence based on necessity and political expediency motivated primarily to neutralize Armenia and minimize the danger purportedly posed by Armenians. Emperor Maurice sent a letter to the Persian King, shortly after

the accord was signed, complaining about the unruly Armenians in their territories. "As long as these troublesome people
remain in their country you and I will never have peace", he
declared. It was then that the two powers decided to disperse
the Armenians and transfer their leaders and troops to distant
lands and ordered them to fight the enemies of Persia and Byzantium. Thousands of Armenians were deported to Asia and
central Europe and others were forced to develop lands for the
welfare of the two powers. Armenia was virtually emptied of
any political and military leadership. This forced migration was
the most devastating political event in Eastern Armenia, followed by equally tragic events in Western Armenia in which
Armenian leaders were murdered and thousands were forced
to leave their homes.

These two events, which occurred during a span of fifty
years, threatened the very existence of the Armenian people.
For the first time in many centuries Armenia was left alone without a protector. Promises of help and the affirmations of previous emperors to guarantee Armenia's territorial rights were
repudiated by no other than another Armenian who had risen
to power in Constantinople. After vacillating from one side to
the other the pendular swing of Armenia seemed to have gotten
stuck in the middle. While they were constantly intimidated in
the past by demonstrations of brutality, they somehow managed
to place themselves in a protective corner oscillating between
the two great powers of the day. Their fortunes changed alter-
natively with the tides of political movements. But this was the
first time they were being considered the enemies of both powers and threatened to be oppressed by the rulers of both empires with equal brutality.

Throughout their political experience, and since the creation of the Byzantine Empire, the Armenians wanted to be
shielded by the Byzantine Greeks against the savagery of the
Persians, preferring the control of the former to the ruthless authority of the latter. But more often than not the Greeks proved
that their only redeeming grace was their Christianity. They
were no better than their Persian contemporaries in waging ex-
tortionist acts against this small nation. While generally supporting the principle of Christian unity, they too often failed to put it
in practice. They ran their empire and venerated the Christian
God but when the time came to help the Armenian Christians,

they were stripped of any veneer of Christian charity they might have had. The leaders in Constantinople failed to fulfill the purpose of the Byzantium Church as the protector of the Christian faith.

The Greeks made skillful use of political chaos and took advantage of Armenia's political weakness to suppress the country's natural idealism which had served as a catalyst to propagate the Christian faith in the pagan world of Western Asia. Perhaps the Greeks felt that the Armenians had monopolized the teachings of the new religion, leaving no room for others to proselytize their own brand of Christianity.

THE DIVISION OF THE CHURCH

A favorite pastime for the Byzantine Greeks was the assertion of their claim that the Armenian Church was under the jurisdiction of Byzantium because of the consecration of Grigor Loussavorich, the first head of the Armenian Church, at the hands of the Archbishop of Caesarea which was then located within the confines of the Byzantine Empire. The Armenians refused to accept such claims, as theirs was an Apostolic Church founded by the two apostles of Jesus Christ, Thaddeus and Bartholemew, who at the conclusion of their missionary work in Western Asia, had traveled to Armenia to preach the Gospel.

The dogmatic differences between the two churches, which were fundamentally political in nature, became crystallized by the attitude taken by the Armenian Church leaders towards the Fourth Ecumenical Council of the Christian Church held in 451 in Chalcedon, a suburb of Constantinople, under the sponsorship of Emperor Marcianus. The Council was summoned to clarify the ambiguities in regard to the two nature doctrine of Jesus Christ, promulgated in the previous convocation of the church leaders held during the embryonic stages of the development of the church. After fierce deliberations the delegates at Chalcedon made a compromise and accepted the doctrine of duality, proclaiming that Jesus had two natures (diphysite), each distinct from the other, but united in one person. He was, therefore, both God and man.

The Armenian Church leaders could not attend the Council at Chalcedon primarily because they were busy preparing the country for the Battle of Avarair. At a council of their own, held in 506 in the capital city of Devin, the Armenian bishops officially rejected the duality of Christ's nature and the decrees of Chalcedon, and steadfastly upheld the original contention of the Christian Church, as decreed in Nicaea in 325, that Christ had but one nature (monophysite). The Armenians refused to accept the humanity of Jesus and considered him divine because they believed that only God would have been endowed with the power of resurrecting himself from the dead. For the Armenians, Christ's baptism, which is the manifestation of divinity, and Christ's birth, which is the manifestation of the human flesh, were one event. They celebrated both on the same day while others celebrated them as two separate events on two separate days. This was the principal reason for the irreparable factionalism of the Church, and one that affected trenchant criticism from the Orthodox Church of Byzantium and forever separated the Church of Armenia from the mainstream of Christian thinking. The Armenians insisted to remain loyal to their established principles and stay aloof from the quarrels of the churchmen of the day, who, at times, seemed to be more interested in dogmatic dissertations and theological differences than the willingness to help an embittered people against the brutality of the Persians.

It was this attitude of the Armenian Church towards the Council of Chalcedon that infuriated the Byzantine Greeks. For the next one thousand years the Greeks will apply pressure with an arrogant zeal, political or otherwise, to the suffering of the Armenian people, in their attempt to bring the Armenian Church into the fold of Byzantium's orthodoxy. But they will never succeed.

HERACLIUS, ANOTHER ARMENIAN

The fragile alliance between Persia and Byzantium collapsed and the antagonists went back to their original position of destructive rivalry, when Emperor Maurice was assassinated in 602 and revolt broke out among the warring families in Constantinople. Maurice was succeeded, after a brief interregnum, by another emperor of Armenian descent, Heraclius.

As the Exarch of Carthage, Heraclius sent a fleet against Constantinople to avenge the murder of Emperor Maurice. His military campaign was successful and he was coronated as the

Emperor of the Byzantium Empire in 610. Heraclius' rise to power will mark the end of the Roman period and the beginning of the new era in which the rulers of Constantinople will discard the heritage of decadent political life and give the Empire a more vigorous character to meet the challenges facing the state. Born in 575 of Armenian parents, Heraclius, blond, bearded, studious and fanatically religious, became one of the most dynamic rulers of Byzantium. At the time of his rise to power the Empire was in a sad state of economic and financial bankruptcy and the machine of the political organization had come to a standstill. The military structure of the Empire was in a pathetic condition and Byzantium had no money in its treasury to hire alien mercenaries to forge war against its enemies. Constantinople, then the principal center of the Christian world, was surrounded by enemies who were powerful enough to destroy the Empire. In the west there were the Slavs and the Avars who had come from the north and settled in the Balkans, and in the east the Persian King, who taking the occasion of Maurice's death, had seized the Armenian territories from the Byzantine forces and made the country a launching pad for his wars against Byzantium.

The Empire that Heraclius inherited was so weakened by a decayed political bureaucracy that it had become powerless to put up an adequate defense line against its enemies. The Emperor's army was defeated miserably when in 611 Heraclius attempted to reoccupy Armenia and chase the Persians out of the country. The Persian victory in Armenia gave the Persians the opportunity to move on all fronts. They went south and took Damascus. They went further south and occupied the Holy City of Jerusalem, and with the help of the persecuted Jews, stormed the city and massacred most of its inhabitants. After destroying the Church of Holy Sepulchre, the Persians took Christianity's most treasured relic, the Holy Cross, and carried it off with them to the Persian capital. By 619 they were in control of most of the provinces of Byzantium and had come close to the gates of Constantinople.

It was during this critical period that Heraclius, after overhauling the political structure of the government, made a fundamental change in the military organization of the Empire. He established large military zones in areas not yet occupied by the enemy. Each zone, or theme as it came to be known, had its own division of troops headed by a military superintendent with the responsibility to defend the district against enemy encroachments. This system of military themes will be Heraclius' greatest legacy and future emperors will preserve the system to keep the borders of the Empire protected against foreign intrusions.

One of these themes, called the Armeniakon, was organized with Armenian troops serving the emperor under the Byzantine flag. The Armenian theme made a decisive contribution to the Byzantine military organization and helped Heraclius to chase the Persians out of Armenia and Asia Minor. The Byzantine forces reoccupied Armenia and Heraclius, at the head of the Armeniakon theme, moved towards the Persian capital. He took the city with ease and after chasing the Persian King Khosrov out of the city, destroyed the fire temple of Zoroaster in revenge for the Persian destruction of Jerusalem. Heraclius established a government in Armenia and ran the Empire awhile from the Armenian soil. Byzantium had won the war on all fronts and the Persian army was decimated. Heraclius recovered the Holy Cross and reverently reinstated it in the Church of Holy Sepulchre in Jerusalem. The Age of Heraclius marks the beginning of a new epoch in the history of the Byzantine Empire. It marks the end of the Roman period and the beginning of the Greek element in the administration and political life of the state. Latin, which was recognized as the official language of the Empire, will gradually disappear and Greek will become the predominant language.

For the Armenians, however, the Age of Heraclius meant more pressure and brought a different type of crusade from the Byzantine Church to bring the Church of Armenia within its fold. While in Armenia, Emperor Heraclius held conferences with the Armenian Church leaders to convince his countrymen to embrace the Byzantine orthodoxy. His concern, politically motivated, was to preserve the unity within his Empire with ties of a common faith and remove all ecclesiastical complications that had threatened to erode the strength of his military apparatus. But the Armenians rejected such moves and continued to adhere to their religious doctrines.

For the rest of his life Heraclius will devote his reign to exalting the orthodoxy but fail to succeed in his attempts to restructure the Church of Armenia on the pattern of Byzantine theology. His religious life will be interrupted temporarily a few years later when he will be called upon, once again, to stop the movement of another religious force, created by a prophet who had received a divine inspiration to lay the foundation of a religious unity in the deserts of Arabia.

THE FALL OF THE PERSIAN EMPIRE

After ruling the Persian Empire for over four hundred years the Sassanian Dynasty had begun to crumble away. The powers of the Persian monarchs began to disintegrate rapidly. Their ability to defend their Empire was weakened by continued hostilities at home and abroad. The King of Persia was no longer the source of all favors. His exalted authority was diminished by lack of loyalty of the local governors, and in the vassal states the Persians failed to maintain the vigilance necessary to keep the Marzbans in hand. Marzban's authority was gradually undermined by consolidation of provincial governments organized by powerful Mazdeian priests who had begun to lose faith in the king's ability to pursue a policy of religious conversion in the Empire. Another and a more powerful force was about to emerge from the south. A new religious movement, more powerful, more militaristic and fanatic than Christianity was gaining momentum in the deserts of Arabia. This movement has laid the foundation to become a dominant power to impose a different ideology about man's relationship to God, and attempt to chart a new destiny for the peoples from central Asia to the shores of the Atlantic.

After the removal of King Artashes in 428 the Sassanid Persians ruled Armenia through a Marzbanic rule. In all, thirty-five Marzbans, appointed by the Persian kings, ruled Armenia for over two hundred years until the fall of the Sassanian Empire in 652. Throughout this period Armenia was held together through a network of feudal estates, which during the course of two centuries had risen in number generally at the expense of the peasantry and the rural elements of the society. The peasants were heavily taxed by the Marzbans, mostly through arbitrary exactions. There were land taxes, personal taxes, property taxes, poll taxes, taxes on agricultural products, and for the merchants, custom-house duties on export-imports.

While this was one of the darkest periods in the history of Armenia, there were some bright spots, particularly in the area

of commerce and cultural activity. Commercial activity flour-
ished and Armenia continued to provide the corridor for caravan trade. Spices, drugs, raw silk, and precious stones found
their way through the Armenian commercial centers of Devin,
Artashat, and Erzerum. The country became a producer and
exporter of goods, such as wine, dyes, grain, oil, rugs, textiles,
and copper. The commercial activity, however, mainly served
the interests of the rulers who exploited Armenia's strategic position for trade and held a monopoly on the production of goods.
The Armenians were generally employed as laborers and the
revenues were channelled to the treasury of the masters.

What is destined to be remembered in this period of Marzbanic rule, was the collapse of Armenia's political system, meticulously constructed by the Arshakunian kings. It was a period
of continuous struggle for survival, reduced in intensity only
through the benevolence of certain Marzbans during short spells
of peace when the seemingly incessant military confrontations
between the two powers were temporarily interrupted or, when
one side felt secure due to the weakness of the other and left the
other side alone. Throughout their political experience the Armenians attempted to make the best bargains possible with the
power of the day in their quest for peace and security. They
wanted from their masters nothing more than the freedom of
conscience, ensuring the right of the individual based on their
Christian beliefs.

The brutality of the Persian and Greek masters will now be
replaced with another force, much more oppressive, threatening, and ruthless. This new force will repress Armenia for
another two hundred years, chart a new direction, and attempt
to place a series of tragic punctuation marks in the history of
these people.

CHAPTER FOURTEEN

WHEN ARABS RULED ARMENIA

The rise of Islam produced one of the most spectacular events in the history of man and for Armenia it marked the beginning of a new epoch of anarchic barbarism in which the Armenians will again be tested for the firmness of their religious beliefs and the nation's structure for government will fall apart beyond recognition. In a single generation, Mohammed and his followers became the masters of an empire greater than that of Rome, stretching from Bay of Biscay to the Indus, and the outer reaches of China, and from the Aral Sea to the central regions of the African continent. The effects of this unprecedented expansion will shape the subsequent history of man. The Moslem Arabs broke the imperial molds of Persia and Byzantium and brought millions of people into their fold, forcing them to accept the new creed and recognize Mohammed as the founder of a true religion epitomized by a single phrase "There is no God but Allah, and Mohammed is his Prophet". In less than one hundred years after the death of this new prophet, his name, joined by the almighty Allah, will be called five times a day from the minarets scattered over the Islamic world.

It was not only a religious ideology that began to be prose-lytized by the Arabs but also an ambitious movement of culture at a time when Christianity had already been established and the principal features of the Greco-Roman civilization had already been assimilated by most of the peoples of the known world. With their religion, Arabs brought a new understanding of man's relationship to God and imposed a pattern of social conduct, which rapidly changed the face of Asia, the Near East, southern Europe, and northern Africa, and blended people in common loyalty. If Christian ideas made their way west, the Islamic movement expanded in all directions, east, west, north, and south, transcending all borders and frontiers, attempting to crush the last remnants of old kingdoms and break the decayed and decadent political barriers through a systematic process of religious and military expansion which came to be known as the Holy War of Islam.

While it was an Arab revolt, nurtured in the deserts of Arabia, it soon created the conditions to inspire other men to give it a universality with laws governing all aspects of society based on a common brotherhood and the principles of universal law as prescribed by Mohammed, the Prophet. With great energy, opportunism, and religious zeal, the Arabs consolidated their new territories, and brought races and peoples together, binding them through the cultural unity of Islam. They organized stable forms of governments and forced people to accept their political system with ideas and institutions engrafted into the nomadic traditions of the Arabs.

The cultural and religious unity, however, while characteristically Arabic, adopted the classical traditions of the past as a catalyst for the new movement. It extended man's horizons beyond the confines of the universal standards established by Greek, Roman, and Christian thinkers. Unlike Christianity this unity recognized only one language, the Arabic, as the common tongue of Islam and allowed people to speak to God in no other language, thus making the new religion more coherent, organically unified, and more subtle than Christianity. If it took Christianity three hundred years to gain momentum and acceptability, the rise of Islam was almost instantaneous. The greatly diminished resources of manpower and wealth in the west, the seemingly incessant conflict between Persia and Byzantium coupled with the great migratory movements of barbaric peoples from central Asia to Europe, had created a restless world causing the breakdown of political institutions. The internal weakness, military exhaustion, the shrinkage of political power, and the general lack of vitality in the west, encouraged the Arabs to move rapidly and introduce their new creed into areas eager to accept the Islamic orientation of thought and reject the rationality of the Christian doctrines. Most of the ideas of Mohammed were easily accommodated into the political organization and the social fabric of the countries that the Arabs occupied, whereas Christianity developed its doctrines only when it came into open conflict with paganism and built its foundation as a fundamentally religious movement with no political intonation.

Islam's appeal lay in the universal nature of worship, reinforced by observances of a moral code promulgated in the Koran and the traditions of the Prophet, collectively known as the Hadith. Both gave the worshipper a sense of security on earth and the hope of a better life in the hereafter. The religious doctrine itself was an offshoot of Judaism and Christianity, recognizing most of the tenets of Christian beliefs. It accepted God as being one and all powerful, the creator of the universe, rewarding those who carry out His commands, and punishing those who disregard them.

THE CALIPHATES

Immediately after Mohammed's death in 632 the reign of the Moslem world fell upon the Caliphs, who as the vicars of the Prophet, became the religious as well as political leaders of the Islamic movement. They were the protectors of the new faith and as such structured the political organizations of their governments into a theocracy closely associated with the teachings of the Prophet. Their first task was to organize a powerful military force to preserve and propagate the faith, with Islam being the ultimate basis for their military supremacy.

The first Caliph was Abu-Bakr, who ruled the Arab Empire until 634 followed by Caliph Umar, who ruled for ten years. Umar's successor Uthman was killed by a group of Moslem fanatics during an uprising in 656. Ali, the son-in-law of the Prophet, soon followed Uthman but his election to the Caliphate failed to gain unanimous support. Civil war and political unrest followed Ali's election. The conflict was between Muawiyah, the commander of the Arab forces in Syria and Caliph Ali.

Upon the assassination of Uthman, Muawiyah had proclaimed himself as the new Caliph but the more Orthodox Moslems had selected Ali for the Caliphate. The civil war ended with the murder of Ali in 661, thereupon Muawiyah was declared the sole ruler of the Empire. The dynastic wars between the two factions and the manner in which Muawiyah was elevated to the Caliphate were sufficient reasons to create an irreparable cleavage in the Moslem world which still continues to this day. The schism separated the Moslem society into two principal sects, the Sunnis, who considered the Caliphate as an elective office representing the Meccan tribe of the Prophet, and the Shiites who considered Ali and his descendants as the rightful successors to the Prophet.

THE MARCH TOWARD ARMENIA

Shortly after Mohammed's death, the Arabs, under the command of an able general, Khalid ibn-el-Walid, began to advance towards Syria and Palestine, which were then part of the Byzantine Empire. With unusual mobility of cavalry and camelry they occupied the territory and called it their own. They made Damascus, the principal city of Syria, the capital of their Empire, and continued to march north. Emperor Heraclius sent an army of 50,000 headed by an Armenian general, Vahan, to meet the Moslems at the River Yarmuk in Palestine, but the Arabs, far superior in potential strength, slaughtered the Christian troops, broke the resistance of the mighty Byzantine army, and paved the way to proceed towards the Taurus mountains and the northern limits of Syria.

The acquisition of Syria and Palestine and the humiliating defeat of the Byzantine forces, gave the Arabs the impetus and confidence for an onward push towards northern Mesopotamia and the plains of Mount Ararat. Under the command of General Abd-er-Rahman, 18,000 Moslem troops occupied the region of Lake Van, raided the fields, harassed the cities, and began to burn churches and slaughtered thousands of Armenians.

Before the Arabs arrived on the scene there were some differences of opinion among the Armenian leaders and Catholicos Nerses III on the proper action to be taken with regard to the Arabs. Before the Arabs occupied the Armenian territory the people of Armenia were living in a period of economic prosperity and cultural development, particularly in the fields of science and architecture. Catholicos Nerses who was surnamed *Shinogh*, or the "Builder", had built two architecturally magnificent churches in Armenia, Hripsime, and Zvartnotz, with massive pillars and spectacular domes. Anania Shirakatsi, a scientist of international renown, had made important breakthroughs in the fields of mathematics, astronomy, and geography. His books on mathematical theorems were used as standard texts throughout Western Asia and the Mediterranean world.

The dynasts of Armenia were concerned with Byzantium's treacherous motives and were willing to allow a Moslem protectorate over their land, but Catholicos Nerses was in favor of a Byzantine rule. Sembat Bagratuni, the military commander of the armed forces, and Theodore Rashtuni, the prince of a prominent family, wanted an Arab protectorate. While they were percipient enough to recognize the Arab danger, they were not willing to accede to Greek demands. They preferred the military control of the Arabs to the religious harassment of the Byzantines. The issue proved to be academic, however. While the Armenians vainly tried to reach a settlement, the brutality of the Moslems did not give them the opportunity to choose their masters.

After conquering the Lake Van region of Armenia the Arabs advanced towards Devin, the capital of Armenia. They sacked the city in 642, murdered 12,000 Armenians and carried off 25,000 in captivity to Arabia. Sembat Bagratuni and his Armenian forces could not stop the bloodshed. After witnessing the annihilation of his troops Bagratuni surrendered to the Caliph and agreed to pay a heavy tribute. With the capital of Armenia taken, the Moslems then proceeded to conquer villages and towns, seizing captives and confiscating properties, and carrying women and children into slavery. While the Moslem troops fought with profound conviction for the Islamic cause, they were mostly motivated by the Caliph's promise of offering plunder and dark-eyed Armenian virgins to those who achieved military success through valor.

ARABS DESTROY PERSIA

In the east the Arabs completed the acquisition of the mighty Persian Empire and began to lead expeditions into the Caucasus. At the time of their arrival the Persians were living in a period of incubation for revolt. Palace intrigues had given the usurpers the opportunity to assure the leadership of the Empire. The central structure of the Sassanid government had been shattered and the land of Persia had fallen into anarchy. The Persian Emperor and his troops had deserted the Persian capital, Ctesiphon, without a fight and the Arabs had entered the city in triumph. Soon after Yazdegert II, the ruler of Sassanid Persia was assassinated by one of his aides, toppling the Persian Empire and bringing an end to the Sassanid dynasty. Persia will not rise again for another 800 years. The annihilation of the Persian forces made the Arabs the sole masters of Western Asia and opened the door to spread the Islamic creed into central Asia and India. The fanatic Mazdeian Persians who were once anxious to impose their religious doctrines to others now fell victim to the Islamic faith and gradually accepted Islam as their new religion.

The conversion from Mazdeian fanaticism into the Islamic faith was not difficult to achieve. As worshippers of the sun and fire, the Persians had difficulty to accept a human being as divinity. It was difficult for the Christian missionaries in Persia to preach a doctrine which considered Jesus, a human being, to be the son of God. The Islamic approach was fundamentally different. For Moslems there was only one God, Allah, who had no sons but only Prophets, and Mohammed was his prophet. Unlike Christianity, Moslems did not worship Mohammed as God. The Islamic interpretation of divinity presented a more palatable course for the Persians than the doctrines of Christianity which they felt came close to polytheism.

In the south the Moslems raided Egypt and took the capital city of Alexandria which was then the base for the Byzantine navy. Soon entire Egypt, which served as the granary for Byzantium, came under Moslem domination. In less than a decade this unforseen power from the deserts of Arabia conquered north Africa and reached the borders of Morocco and Barbary, and in 713 they crossed the Strait of Gibralter and entered Europe through southern Spain. By then the Arabs had reduced the Byzantine Empire to the Anatolian peninsula, the Balkan coast, and the southern tip of Italy.

ARABS IN ARMENIA

After occupying the capital city of Devin and the plains of Mount Ararat the Arabs established a governorship in Armenia to rule the country as a tributary state to the Islamic Empire. The governors were known as Osticans, and during the next 200 years there will be twenty-six of them who will rule Armenia in accordance with the wishes of the Caliphate. The Armenian

Nakharars were speedily suppressed and the Arabs controlled the political system of the country. While the Arabs were successful in converting the Persians into the Islamic faith, they had no success in Armenia. The people were staunchly opposed to any religious campaign. For the next thirteen centuries, however, the Armenians will remain in close contact with Islam with varied degrees of interference by their Islamic masters.

When attempts to convert the Armenians became unsuccessful the Moslems took the Armenians as *dhimnis*, or the protected people. As *dhimnis* they were required to pay heavy taxes and put down their arms. They were exempt from military service since only a Moslem was allowed to fight for the defense of Islam. The Armenians and Moslems lived in separate communities observing their respective traditions and laws, within the framework of the Arab rule. The Armenians were governed by their church laws and the Moslems by the tenets of the Koran. Neither side accepted the religious laws of the other. In the legal framework of the Moslem jurisprudence the testimony of an Armenian could not be accepted against a Moslem because according to the Koran the Armenians had corrupted the texts of the Scriptures and could not be trusted.

Emperor Constans II of Byzantium expressed willingness to help the Armenians but his offer for help had its price. The Byzantine Greeks were ready to send an army to Armenia and free the country from the Moslems if the Armenians accepted the Orthodox brand of Christianity and brought their Church into unity with the Church of Byzantium. The Greeks regarded the Christian states in Western Asia as a sort of protectorate. They claimed to have the sole power to formulate a Christian policy and expected subservient cooperation from the Christian minorities. But the Armenians were different.

The bitter theological strife that had racked the Christian world a century earlier was still very much alive. As Christianity strived to formulate its doctrines, some of these disputes came close to silliness. Ecumenical conferences that were held from time to time were principally designed to make ecclesiastical absurdities sound respectable. At the time when the Armenians were being terrorized by the Arabs, the Byzantine Greeks were inquiring, with benign indifference, as to "how many angels could balance on the head of a pin".

The issue of Christ's nature, whether he was divine or human, was perhaps the most fundamental. To preserve the unity in the Christian world, particularly at a time when the Arabs were threatening to smash the strongholds of Christianity, it was important for the religious and political zealots of Byzantium, to solve this most irritant issue and maintain a cohesive posture against the danger of the Moslem expansion. The obsessive anxiety for religious unity is perhaps explained in part by the Byzantine's attitude towards life on earth. The Greeks regarded themselves as the chosen people of Christian God and interpreted Christ's teachings faithfully. "He who loses his life for my sake will find it", Jesus had said. Living in a disillusioned world in which life on earth was only a temporary stop for the eternal life in heaven, the Greeks shared the ecclesiastical preoccupations of their leaders. To attain the right path to heaven, they believed that theological differences, no matter how miniscule they appeared to be, must be resolved with the help of secular policy and military intervention if necessary, to achieve a perfect unity in the orthodoxy of the Christian world. The Emperor, while the head of the state, was also recognized as the Guardian of the Keys, the Pastor of the Flock, and the Prince of the Apostles. He was Christ's representative on earth and the self-ordained defender and champion of the Christian faith. He ruled the Empire by divine right. He was regarded as the visible manifestation of God on earth, and as such, he assumed the divine responsibility in bringing the Christian people into an ordered harmony under his rule as God would have done to regulate the heavenly order. The capital city of Constantinople was dedicated to Virgin Mary who was regarded as the spiritual guardian against the enemies of Christ. In the Emperor's palace the four Gospels were placed on an empty throne next to the monarch's to symbolize Christ's presence on earth.

HARASSMENT FROM BYZANTIUM

Constans II sent emissaries to Armenia to discuss church unity with the Nakharars, but the Armenians were too busy to discuss such issues. They were in the midst of an insurrection against the Arabs. General Hamazasp a short while earlier had successfully organized commando units to chase the Arabs out of the country, but the Arabs had proved to be overwhelmingly pow-

erful. They killed most of the Armenian guerrilla fighters together with 1,775 Armenian hostages held in custody on
instructions from Caliph Uthman. The atrocities against the Armenians stopped shortly after Caliph Uthman's assassination in
656.

Muawiyah after succeeding Uthman began his own campaign against the Armenians. The Byzantine Emperor once
again sent emissaries to persuade the Armenians to take an oath
of loyalty and accept his brand of Christianity. For the Armenian leaders this ecclesiastical harassment and the paternalistic
policy of the Greeks had national concern. While desirous of
ecumenical harmony in the Christian world, they believed that
the Church of Armenia was essentially national in character.
They deliberately wanted to maintain the schism and internecine strife between the two churches for the sole purpose of preserving the uniqueness of their Christian identity. This
unwavering attitude, however, left the Armenians alone and unprotected during one of the tragic periods of their history.

Infuriated by Byzantium's attitude towards Armenia the
Armenian leaders sent the following letter to the Emperor - "We
have received nothing but a trifling aid from you, even during
the most tragic period in our history. You are now asking us to
take an oath of loyalty to you. We have submitted ourselves to
you before but Byzantium has rewarded our submission with
insults. If we take an oath of loyalty, it will lead us to our destruction and death. Therefore, leave us alone to deal with our
present masters no matter how ruthless they may be."

Enraged by the Armenian response Constans II sent an
army to ravage Armenia. His troops destroyed the towns and
villages which had not yet been destroyed by the Arabs and
took 8,000 Armenian families and sent them to slavery in central
Europe. To force church unity he ordered the Catholicos to
be arrested and brought to Constantinople for trial. The Emperor's treatment of the Armenian Church leaders was similar to
his treatment of the Roman Catholic Church leaders. Earlier
Pope Martin, who had been elected Pope in Rome in 649 without the consent of Constantinople, had condemned the Byzantine Church for its views on the nature of Christ and had
excommunicated the Patriarch of Constantinople. This
prompted Constans II to move swiftly. He sent his representative to Rome with orders to arrest the Pope and bring him to

Constantinople for trial. Pope Martin was arrested and tried by
the Byzantine Senate on charges of high treason. He was then
banished to far off Cherson in the Crimea, where he died after
enduring hunger and privation. The Emperor planned to give
the same treatment to the Armenian Catholicos. He sent an
army unit to Devin to arrest the Catholicos and bring him to
Constantinople for trial. The Greek army could not accomplish
its mission, however, because by then the Arabs had assumed
control of Armenia and had made the country a part of the Islamic Empire.

OPPRESSION BY THE ARABS

Suspecting that the Armenians were planning another rebellion
against them, the Arabs overran the Ararat province, destroyed
the towns, razed villages, invaded monasteries and sent monks
into slavery. Neither the military nor the financial means of the
Armenian revolutionaries were adequate for a defensive campaign to stop the Arabs. To make Byzantium help the Armenians a plan was hatched by a group of Armenian princes living
in Byzantium to overthrow the Emperor, and seize the throne
from the Byzantine Greeks. Constans II was murdered in 668
and an Armenian, Mjej Gnuni, was proclaimed Emperor of Byzantium. The Armenian conspirators were arrested soon after
and executed, and Constans' son, Constantine IV rose to the
throne.

The murder of Constans II gave Caliph Muawiyah the opportunity to resume his military campaign in Asia Minor and
conquer the remaining provinces of the Byzantine Empire. His
army advanced towards Constantinople and for the first time
the Arab troops appeared before the walls of the capital of Byzantium. The new Emperor reorganized the army and chased
the Arabs away. The Caliph was compelled to sign a thirty-year
pact with Byzantium in 678 and agreed to pay the emperor
3,000 gold pieces annually as a tribute.

Constantine's son, Justinian II rose to power in 685 and
immediately began his own campaign to exert pressure on Armenia. He sent church leaders to Armenia to bring the Church
of Armenia within the Byzantine fold. He had by this time
brought the Georgian Church into his jurisdiction and the Armenians were the only ones left in Western Asia continuing to

remain independent. Georgia, Armenia's neighbor to the north, had been converted into Christianity through the missionary work of the Armenian Catholicos, Grigor Loussavorich. The Georgian Church had been under the jurisdiction of the Church of Armenia with the Armenian Catholicos acting as the head of the Georgian Church as well. The Georgians, unable to withstand the Greek pressure, finally seceded from the Armenian Church and accepted the Chalcedonian decrees. They elected their own Catholicos and brought their Church within the purview of the Patriarchate of Constantinople.

NEW WAVE OF TERROR

The Arab governor over Armenia who proved to be most inhuman and morbidly perverse was Abd-Allah. He arrested the Armenian leaders, among them Catholicos Sahag and Sembat Bagratuni, and sent them to Damascus in chains. He sacked and pillaged Armenian monasteries and blinded monks by torture. His successor, Emir Mohammed bin Merwan, continued Abd-Allah's reign of terror. In Nakhichevan he placed members of prominent Armenian families in a church and set the church on fire, burning the occupants alive. He demolished churches and replaced them with mosques. He had the tongues of the priests cut and their eyes perforated with hot metal rods. Thousands of Armenian families were forcibly torn from their homeland and sent to Arab territories. The Nakharars sent an envoy to plead with the Emir to exercise tolerance. A month later they received a gift from the Emir: the head of the envoy preserved in salt, wrapped in a black cloth with the defaced portrait of Jesus. The Moslem atrocities and the unsettled political situation in Armenia forced many prominent Armenians to leave the country and seek safer havens in the Byzantine territory. These Armenians gradually accepted the Orthodox communion and many of them rose to prominence in the Byzantine Empire. Several of them became emperors of Byzantium. Emperors Theodor, Manuel, Bardanes, Photius, Leo V, and Basil I were of Armenian descent.

Armenians of the lower class left the country to seek employment as mercenary soldiers in the Byzantine army. They were used by the Emperor for the defense of the Empire. Most of them, however, refused to accept the orthodox faith. While they proved to be able fighters for Byzantium's cause, they were at times treated harshly by its rulers. During an uprising the faces of one thousand Armenian mercenaries were tattooed "Armenian conspirator" and paraded in chains in Constantinople.

MISSION TO DAMASCUS

A decision was made in Devin to send Catholicos Hovhannes Otznetsi, a skillful church leader and diplomat, on a mission to Damascus to see Caliph Hesham and plead the case of Armenia. The journey to Damascus took many months, passing through Aleppo after crossing the Syrian desert. As the Catholicos entered the covered narrow streets of Damascus on horseback, a herald marching ahead of him called "make way before our lord, the Holy Man". The Arabs were fascinated by the impressive appearance of the Catholicos. He was dressed in embroidered silk with rich colors glowing with gems and gold powder sprinkled on his beard. As he entered the Caliph's palace the Catholicos himself was awed by the splendor of the surroundings. He was immediately taken to the audience chamber to meet the Caliph. The chamber was adorned with rugs, expensive curtains, cushions, and artificial trees of gold and silver around the periphery of the chamber. He noticed birds made of precious metals on the branches of the trees. As he looked outside the window he saw artificially dwarfed trees specially cultivated to yield fruits of rare varieties.

When the Caliph entered the audience chamber he promptly proceeded towards a square seat covered with richly embroidered cushions. In flowing robes he sat cross-legged. On his right were his paternal relatives and on his left his maternal relatives, with courtiers standing behind them. Noticing the Armenian prelate, the Caliph was surprised at the ostentatious attire of the Catholicos. He asked the Catholicos that if he was the spiritual leader of an impoverished country, why was he wearing such richly embroidered robes with precious gems and gold powder on his beard. The Catholicos responded by revealing a primitive hair cloth that he was wearing underneath. "you see, Your Excellency, he said, it is proper for me to appear in your presence, in the luxuriant surroundings of your palace, in this attire as a sign of respect towards the leader of the Moslem world, but I want you to know that underneath I carry the sufferings of my people. In my country I travel clad in a shabby cloak, I carry a sack of wheat, and a goatskin of water".

The Caliph was touched, looked at the Catholicos and said, "I would like to help you, but why do your people continue to worship this man Jesus. How could Jesus, who was unable to save himself from the Jews, deliver you from my hands. You should go back and tell your people to abjure him. In our Koran it is written, "Then the word went forth; O Earth! swallow up thy water, and O sky withhold thy rain....away with those who do wrong". "Your Excellency", the Catholicos responded, "four centuries ago our fathers chose Jesus to be their God. As Armenians we cling tenaciously to the heritage of our fathers and want to keep their faith as you wish to keep the faith of your fathers. We cannot change our fathers' traditions because we are no better than our fathers. Your Excellency, Mohammed taught that Christians be regarded as brothers and Allah disapproved unjust bloodshed. In the spirit of the teachings of the Prophet I plead you to leave us alone to worship our God". Touched by the Catholicos' eloquence, Caliph Hesham granted religious tolerance to the Armenians. However, trouble was brewing in the Arab world and the Umayyad Dynasty, which had ruled the Moslem Empire for one hundred years, was about to topple.

THE DEMISE OF THE UMAYYADS

By the beginning of the Eighth century the Arabs had already conquered most of the Mediterranean world and the Iberian peninsula. They were ready to proceed north into Europe when in 732 they were checked by Charles Martel in one of the most decisive battles of history fought in Poitiers, France. To expand the Arab rule into Europe the Moslems had withdrawn most of their garrisons from Armenia and Western Asia. The Arab military adventure in Europe gave the Armenians the opportunity to attempt to gain political autonomy.

The Armenians organized an army and began insurrections against the Arabs. To stop the Armenian revolt Caliph Marwan II adopted a policy of moderation and continued the religious tolerance granted by Caliph Hesham. He appointed an Armenian prince, Ashot Bagratuni, as the Governor of Armenia, replacing the Arab Ostican. The moderate Arab rule, however, was followed by a period of unmitigated Moslem terror in which three oppressive Arab governors, Suleiman, Bakkir, and Hussan, took turns to cause havoc and terrorize the Armenians. They demolished churches and butchered thousands of Armenians and took four thousand Armenian women forcibly and sent them to Damascus to serve as concubines.

Around 740 the power of the Umayyads in Damascus began to crumble. The family that brought mighty Persia to its knees began to lose its grip in the Moslem world. Moral standards gradually began to change and indulgence in luxury brought decadence in the ruling circles of the Moslem Empire. Material wealth was used to cultivate a comfortable lifestyle and corruption and laxity in central authority left the reign of the government to petty officials.

In 747 an Arab family known as the Abbasids, organized an open rebellion against the Umayyads in Damascus. Damascus fell with ease and the Umayyad palaces were destroyed. To conclude the victory, the Abbasid general organized a feast and invited eighty prominent members of the Umayyad family to the banquet under the pretense of signing a peace accord. While the banquet was in progress, the general ordered his aides to murder the guests. After spreading leathern over their dead bodies he continued his dinner with benign indulgence. The head of the Abbasid family was Abul-Abbas Al-Saffiah, which meant Abul-Abbas the Bloodletter.

ABBASIDS RULE ARMENIA

The Abbasids took over the Caliphate from the Umayyads and became one of the most savage rulers of Armenia. They gained their reputation of executing their policies by ruthless force and the leathern over the dead bodies in the banquet was never forgotten. To symbolize their brutality the Abbasid Caliphs had a practice of spreading leathern beside their throne, which served as a carpet for the executioners. The Abbasid Caliphs ruled the eastern part of the Moslem world for over 500 years when they themselves were crushed by people even more ferocious and cruel, the Mongols of central Asia.

BAGHDAD THE NEW CAPITAL

When the Abbasids took over the Caliphate they moved the Caliph's seat from Damascus to Baghdad, a city on the bank of the Tigris River. The transfer of the Moslem power from Damascus to the more distant Baghdad reduced the Moslem pressure on Constantinople. The rulers of Byzantium were now able to pursue a policy to enable them to recapture some of the territories lost to the Arabs. It was during this period that one section of the Armenian territory came under the Byzantine rule, and the other section continued to be governed by the Arabs.

The decision to shift the center of gravity of the Moslem world to Baghdad was an important one. "It is an excellent military camp", the Abbasid Caliph who founded Baghdad declared. "The Tigris River will put us in touch with lands as far as China and bring all the food products of Mesopotamia and Armenia, and the Euphrates River nearby will carry for us the products of Syria and the surrounding lands". The rivers provided a system of communication, helping the Arabs to bind together, politically and commercially, the diverse regions of the Islamic Empire. Baghdad opened the door for a more despotic Arab rule. With its geographic proximity to Persia it gradually came under the influence of Persian culture and civilization and brought a revival of Persian despotism.

One of the prominent Caliphs of the Abbasid Dynasty was Harun-el-Rashid who rose to power in 786. With a keen sense of appreciation for statecraft, Harun-el-Rashid pursued a more tolerant policy towards the Armenians than his immediate predecessors, and established diplomatic relationships with major powers of the day. His contemporary in the west was Charlemagne who cultivated el-Rashid as a possible ally against the Byzantine Empire. Harun-el-Rashid, in turn, wanted to use Charlemagne against his deadly cousins, the Umayyads in Cordoba, who were still in power in southern Spain. Baghdad, the new capital of Islam, became a center of wealth, culture, and splendor. Armenian laborers and craftsmen were very much in demand for the building of the city and they were used as white slaves to maintain it. Most of the architects who were responsible to build the royal palaces were Armenian.

While Harun-el-Rashid was a benevolent ruler, his lieutenants in Armenia were not. Despite the order from Baghdad, the Arab governors of Armenia, continued to loot churches and oppress the land by cruelty and heavy taxation. They invaded the holy monastery of Echmiadzin, arrested 42 priests, and put

them to death. A new reign of terror came upon Armenia.
Nakharars were murdered, churches were burned, the population of entire villages was put to the sword, and the survivors
were sent into slavery. Bogha, an Arab governor of Turkish
origin, conducted the most heinous acts against the Armenians.
He dug tunnels and buried thousands of Armenians alive. He
arrested monks and roasted them on spits. He ordered his
horsemen to take Armenian women, tie their hair to the tail of
the horse and run the horse, dragging the women behind.

THE ECONOMY

While the Armenians were suffering under the savage rule of
the Arabs, commercial trade in the region had begun to flourish. Arabs exploited Armenia's strategic position for international commerce. New routes were opened to encourage
trading opportunities between east and west and Armenia once
again became the crossroads for commercial traffic. Trade was
varied and extensive. Products from Tibet, China, and India
began to flow through Armenia where new markets were designed to procure goods not available in the acquired territories
of the Arabs. Along with Moslem troops there was a considerable number of Arab merchants who had settled in Armenia
and had organized open bazaars in Devin and other commercial centers of the country. Into these bazaars came porcelain
and silk from China, spices and dyes from India, rubies and
slaves from the land of the Turks in central Asia, honey and furs
from Russia. From the south the caravan brought rice and
grain from Egypt, and pearls and weapons from Arabia. Devin
became one of the most important administrative and commercial centers of the Moslem world. The wealth of Asia and the
Near East seemed to pour through the city. The Arab Dinars
were used as the principal currency for international commerce,
replacing the currency of Byzantium. Armenian slaves were
used to build highways in Mesopotamia and Persia to allow the
Arabs to travel to India, Tibet, and China.

While the rulers of Islam wanted to consolidate the various
regions of the Empire through the process of economic integra-
tion and attempt to bring a homogeneity among the various
peoples and races of their conquered lands, in Armenia the situation was quite different. Moslems lived in separate quarters

away from the Christian elements and the gulf remained quite wide between the native Armenians and the Moslem inhabitants. The Moslems who were most intolerant to the non-Moslems were the Shiite fundamentalists who were generally the cause of continuous bloodshed. Most of the Shiites in Armenia were the former Christians and Jews who had converted into the Islamic faith. There was also a considerable number of slaves. While the Koran did not accept the practice of slavery, the Arab governors continued the practice since the Old Testament had admitted the legality of slavery.

In the area of culture and civilization the Arab conquerors had nothing to offer but much to gain. This was the first time that the tent dwellers of the Arabian desert were coming in contact with the more advanced civilization of the west. They quickly began to assimilate and adopt with surprising versatility the cultures and traditions of the peoples they conquered and began the long process of learning just as the Romans did when they conquered Greece. Gradually they were fused to the patterns of a higher civilization and began to write literature, poetry, philosophy, and books of medical science and mathematics. After conquering Persia the Arabs began a scientific study of the Arabic language and structured a grammar with a striking resemblance to the Hellenic language.

While the development of writing proved valuable for the growth of the Islamic civilization, the culture of the Arabs lacked sophistication. Coming from the desert of Arabia they had no culture of their own, but they brought with them a keen sense of intellectual curiosity. They began to translate Greek and Armenian writings into Arabic and made the thought provoking works of the philosophers available to other parts of the Islamic world. It is this Hellenic, Persian, and Armenian influence on their culture that enabled the followers of Mohammed to redivert the stream of their culture to Europe and make tremendous advances in the fields of geography, mathematics, astronomy, and medicine.

As the crossroads between east and west, Armenia played a significant role as the conveyer of this cultural stream opening the way for a surge of scientific and cultural activity. Indian scientists and mathematicians traveled through Armenia and provided the early source of inspiration for the Arabs to write literature and learn about mathematics. Around 773 an Indian traveler in Armenia on the way to Baghdad taught the Arabs the science of astronomy and brought a treatise of mathematics through which the Arabs developed the numerals which were later adopted by the western world. The numerals that the West currently uses is called Arabic by the West, but Indian by the Arabs. Since the Hellenic peninsula was not under the Moslem jurisdiction, Armenia was used as the center for the dissemination of the Hellenic culture. It was the philosophy of Aristotle and Plato that served as an important catalyst for the development of the Islamic civilization. At the height of this Hellenic influence Caliph al-Mamun in 830 established the famous House of Wisdom in Baghdad which was a combination library, academy, and translation bureau built by Armenian laborers and which later became the most important educational institution in the Arab world.

While this age produced many accomplishments for the Arabs, it produced comparatively little in the way of creative scholarship for the Armenians. The merciless oppression by the Arabs brought with it the dwindling of cultural activity in Armenia. The constant struggle for survival made the people culturally sterile. There were some literary works written by monks which depicted mainly the tribulations of the Armenians under the Arabs, but the doctrinal disputes with Byzantium had exhausted most of the resources of the Church and checked the development of cultural activity. Armenian churches were replaced by mosques which served as centers for intellectual activity for the Arab inhabitants of Armenia. Cultural life in Armenia came to a halt as Armenians prayed for political stability.

A NEW RELIGIOUS MOVEMENT

The theological strife and the intellectual sterility in the Christian world provoked the emergence of a new religious movement based on the accumulation of beliefs and practices of pagan life. A heretic sect founded in 657 by Paul Samosata in Western Armenia became popular in both Armenia and Byzantium. The followers of the movement were known as the Paulikians and Tondrakians. They were the followers of the early Christian non-conformists who had redefined certain Christian concepts and moved into a world dominated by a new orientation of Christian values. They rejected the Old Testament and accepted Christ only as an angel invested with certain qualities of truth and justice. They considered the world without divine supervision in which only man was responsible for his religious orientation with the interference of the prophets.

At the time when the fortunes of the Christian Church were at their lowest ebb, the teachings of these people became more appealing to the masses than the traditional doctrines of the established Church. They preached asceticism and the value of private life for man. They renounced wealth, material assets, and the institution of marriage. They rejected ornaments, smashed crosses and refused to participate in church rituals. Their way of life was viewed as shameless and aggressive and their secret meetings were regarded as orgies of vice. They were accused of favoring promiscuity, homosexuality, adultery, and incest. These religious fanatics expanded their power beyond the Armenian borders and became a perceptible social force. They gained considerable strength and brought thousands of people into their fold. As they expanded their power, they came into open political and theological conflict with the established Church. Their militancy came to be regarded as a threat to both Armenia and Byzantium. They were chastised by the Armenian Church leaders and hounded by widespread persecution by the Byzantine emperors.

THE END OF THE ARAB RULE

By the middle of the Ninth century the Arabs began to lose their grip and the dynastic struggle weakened the Moslem Empire. The Caliph in Baghdad gradually lost his control in the administration of his vast Empire. The Byzantine Greeks, recognizing the general weakness of the Arabs in Western Asia, began to advance towards Mesopotamia and Syria in an attempt to drive the Arabs away.

In 867 an Armenian by the name of Basil I rose to the imperial throne in Constantinople. The new Emperor destroyed the defensive forces of the Arabs in Western Asia and pushed the menacing forces of Islam to the central regions of Syria. As the Arab power continued to disintegrate, political thinking sought justification for the Armenians to organize a military insurrection and strike the Arabs. The Armenians under the military leadership of Ashot Bagratuni began a successful revolt against the Moslems in Armenia. This was a period in which heroic acts were crystallized into a legend which later formed the theme of popular literature. A group of highlanders from Sasun attacked Moslem strongholds around the periphery of Armenia proper. They destroyed entire regiments, killed the Arab general and pushed the Moslems south of the border. The triumphant fight of the peasants of Sasun and the exploits of their leader were glorified and later became the theme for an Armenian epic poem, *Sasuntsi David.*

Finding himself faced with two enemies at the same time Caliph al-Motawakkil decided to grant political autonomy to Armenia to free himself to fight the Byzantine Greeks alone. He appointed Ashot Bagratuni as the Governor of Armenia and conferred the title Prince of Princes, and made Armenia an autonomous region within the framework of the Moslem Empire. This was not a noble gesture of generosity. It was primarily a diplomatic maneuver to win the Armenian support in the border war with Byzantium. Peace did not come easily, however. 80,000 Arab rebels under the command of Jahab invaded Armenia. The Armenians, led by Bagratuni, gave a crushing defeat to the Arabs on the banks of the Arax River. With a force of only 40,000 the Armenians slaughtered most of the Arabs and chased the survivors across the border.

Ashot Bagratuni was a diplomat and skilled politician. He had no illusions about the rapidly changing world in which Byzantium and Baghdad controlled the destiny of his people. While he trusted the Byzantine Greeks less than the Arabs, he viewed the world of superpowers with political clarity and wanted to maintain an amicable relationship with both. He established the political organization of the country and organized a military force and within a short period of time succeeded in restoring the frontier defenses around the periphery of Armenia proper. After a period of two hundred years of Moslem domination, systematic devastation and neglect, Armenia needed an imaginative leadership to regain political stability. Bagratuni rebuilt the country with remarkable rapidity and brought Armenia to the dawn of a new age which later will be characterized as one of the most prosperous and happiest periods in the history of this people.

ANI, THE NEW CAPITAL

Bagratuni's first task was to transfer the Armenian capital from Devin to Ani, a city located on an impregnable mountain fastness. Devin gradually began to dwindle away into oblivion. An earthquake in 893 devastated the city, destroying buildings and killing thousands of Armenians. Ani became a self-contained fortress with massive walls and deep ravines surrounding the city. The great gate of the city stood at a high point where a citadel protected the entrance. Soon Ani became the home of a large population. With little flair for political animosity, Bagratuni invited members of the Armenian upper class to move to Ani and establish residential headquarters. The Catholicos built a cathedral and churches in every district of the city and coined the city as the "city of one thousand and one churches". The Cathedral of Ani became one of the most beautiful churches in the Christian world. It represented the artistic expression of the Armenian architecture with its splendid edifice and majestic simplicity. There were monuments and memorials brought from all parts of Armenia and palatial residences that rivaled those of the princes of Constantinople. The residences of the rich were elaborately landscaped with interiors richly decorated, boasting gilded ceilings and gold plated furniture and luxuriant ornaments.

Ani became a prosperous center for international trade controlling the commercial traffic between east and west and drawing a host of merchants from Asia Minor and the Mediterranean world. Carved out of the mountain and birthed in freedom, Ani will endure as the capital of Armenia for the next two hundred years. It will be the center of Armenia's political life and will preserve the institutions of the Armenian civilization. It will inspire the leaders of the people to find new frontiers of culture. Ani will be the shining city on the mountain and the impregnable fortress of the nation's freedom and independence.

The Arab rule of Armenia was drawing to an end. After 427 years of Persian and Arab domination, with violence and bloodshed that failed to leave a scar on the nation's character, Armenia once again emerged as an independent nation and shed the rule of foreign oppressors. It was a miracle that a nation so frightfully fragile, that had been through so much, was now ready to establish a kingdom in one of the most inhospita-

ble places on earth. Its indomitable will to survive would have
permitted no lesser outcome.

CHAPTER FIFTEEN

THE DAWN OF A NEW AGE

The Mamigonian dynasty which had given Armenia a general in almost every generation since the migration of the Mamigonians from central Asia, gradually lost its prestige and the family went into oblivion. A new age of political stability and economic prosperity was about to emerge in Armenia initiated by another dynasty, the Bagratunis who will dominate the political scene for the next 800 years. The rise of the Bagratunis was a turning point in the rapidly changing world of Western Asia. Armenia will continue to be in the center of the struggle between east and west.

The conflict between the Moslems and the Byzantine Greeks encouraged the Arabs to undertake the most fundamental re-evaluation of their territorial policy since the death of the Prophet. This political reappraisal laid the groundwork for a new *rapprochement* towards Armenia which led to the establishment of an Armenian independence under the sponsorship of the Caliphate. The desire for political stability on the part of the Armenians was conducive to a cultural renaissance in which a galaxy of literary figures will come into prominence. The growth of philosophical speculation and scholarship made possible the flowering of a new golden age. New interests in art, architecture, liturgy, and literature will bring a new definition to the classical tradition making this golden age more practical than the grandeur and the dignity of the golden age five hundred years earlier.

The period will also mark the beginning of migratory invasions of nomadic tribes from central Asia that will introduce new elements into the population of Western Asia. These half savage nomads, the forefathers of the present day Turks, will emerge from the steppes of Asia and through the land corridors of the Caspian Sea will work their way into the cultivated region of the plains of Mount Ararat. With little skill in agriculture and farming, these migrants will gradually move into the political life of the peoples in Western Asia, adopt the religion of Islam, and eventually take over the reign of the Islamic Empire.

THE RISE OF THE BAGRATUNIS

The ancestral home of the Bagratunis was the district of Sber on the upper Jorokh River, a land of hills and upland farms protected by the impregnable ranges of the Armenian mountains. After dominating the political spectrum of Armenia for several hundred years under the superintendence of foreign potentates, the Bagratunis rose to prominence and eventually took over the reign of the government. Despite a series of successful insurrections organized by Bagratuni princes against the Arab Caliphate, the family did not gain political recognition until the emergence of Ashot Bagratuni as the Prince of Princes and the leader of a new coalition of the Armenian nobility. Ashot set the foundation of a national policy to secure the loyalty of the Nakharars and maintain a unity of purpose which was so badly needed after years of tribulations under foreign rule. With considerable skill and courage he restored the independence of Armenia by replacing pro-Moslem provincial governors with Armenian princes and within a short period of time shed the Arab control over the Armenian affairs.

The country's political structure had been damaged beyond recognition and years of political turmoil had encouraged the members of the upper class to migrate to the Byzantine territory. Thousands of Armenian families were forced to migrate to the Balkans and central Europe to help the Byzantine Greeks fight the enemies of Christianity. New groups of people had penetrated the Byzantine Empire and a tribe called Rus had come to challenge the Byzantine authority in the Danube basin. The Armenians were pushed to the west to fight these new groups of people and help the Byzantines to preserve the integrity of their Empire.

While the Armenian merchants continued their trade between east and west, there was a severe economic deprivation and the country had become a hopeless financial basket case. Ashot Bagratuni needed to work out concepts of political and economic unity and devise methods to bring a semblance of a political system to regain the country and run the administration of the government.

It was this unity that brought the Church and the nobility together to appeal to the superpowers to bestow a kingly title to Ashot. The Caliph in Baghdad, to further strengthen Armenia's political affiliations with the Islamic Empire, granted the royal regalia to Ashot and the Prince of Princes became the King of Armenia in 885. Two years later the Byzantine Emperor followed suit by recognizing Ashot as the King of Armenia. After a vacancy of 457 years the kingship was finally restored on Armenia's throne and for the next two hundred years the descendants of Bagratuni will rule Armenia as kings thrusting the country to the threshold of a new era.

King Ashot began to reconcile the institutions of the government with the need for strong leadership and international cooperation with the superpowers of the day. His purpose was to create a new society in Armenia with a profound respect for the classical past but paving the way for a new order. After establishing his throne in the new capital of Ani and restoring peace and tranquility, he cultivated a wide range of foreign affiliations. His first mission was to pay a visit to Byzantium to sign a treaty of alliance with Emperor Leo VI, an Armenian by descent, and reduce the pressure of theological strife between the two nations.

Ashot was welcomed in Constantinople in great triumph and the celebrations for this freshly minted king lasted for several days. The royal celebrations in the heart of Byzantium carried a political recognition that Armenia had, once again, become an independent state and for the first time in four centuries was attempting to seek a presence in the community of nations. The triumphant entry of the Armenian king in the Byzantine capital was publicized as the restoration of political unity between the two nations and the end of ecclesiastical strain between the two churches. Political and commercial treaties were signed by the two monarchs under which the Emperor promised to protect Armenia's political integrity and Ashot promised to help the Greeks fight the Bulgars in the north.

THE THREAT OF THE BULGARS

As Arab power continued to pound in the east Byzantium found itself confronted with yet another difficulty in the north. The Bulgars, in alliance with Slavic tribes, had penetrated the Byzantine territory and made continual inroads on the Balkan lands. The wars of conquest with the Arabs had drained the Byzantine Empire of its military resources and the Emperor needed help to strengthen his defense posture around the European periphery of Constantinople.

The Bulgars were a people of Turkic origin. In the days of Emperor Heraclius they had maintained friendly relations with Byzantium but later their kingdom had disintegrated under pressure from the Khazars, forcing them to leave their homeland in the east and seek safer territories elsewhere. The migration that followed brought the Bulgars to the land around the Danube River immediately adjacent to the Byzantine frontiers. Gradually the Bulgars moved west and penetrated into the Byzantine territory and after merging with the Slavs formed a unified kingdom of Slav-Bulgars in the northwestern part of the Black Sea between the Danube and the range of the Balkan mountains.

The ferocious militancy of these people forced the Byzantine Greeks to recognize the Bulgarian Kingdom as a *de facto* political entity on the Byzantine soil. As they gained military superiority and continued to expand their hegemony in the north the Bulgars began to attract other minorities in Western Asia, among them Armenians, who began to migrate to Bulgaria in search of safer havens. Thousands of Armenian families settled in the land of the Bulgars to escape the Islamic oppression. Most of these Armenians rose to prominence and some even succeeded to ascend the throne and became kings of Bulgaria.

At the time when Ashot Bagratuni became the King of Armenia, the Bulgars, led by a king of Armenian origin had posed a serious threat to Byzantium. The treaty that was signed by the two monarchs in Constantinople called for Armenian military assistance to help crush the Bulgarian power base. It was an unusual twist of fate that an Armenian on the imperial throne in Constantinople was seeking help from another Armenian, the King of Armenia, to make war against yet another Armenian, the King of Bulgaria. This was a welcome sign, however, for the newly formed Armenian Kingdom. The Byzantine appeal allowed Armenians to participate in the formulation of the Byzantine military policies.

THE RISE OF THE AZERIS

Ashot's son Sembat I succeeded his father in 890 and was given the mandate to assume full control of the country's leadership. After reorganizing the political administration of the governmental units and strengthening Armenia's military machine, King Sembat extended the country's frontiers to Colchids in the north and Karin in the southwest. He had the support of the powerful Nakharars who were prepared to hold the state together and push Armenia towards a territorial expansion and economic recovery after years of political decay and foreign domination. King Sembat I continued the amicable relations with the foreign powers which were meticulously established by his father. He extended Armenian influence in areas adjoining Armenia proper without provoking Moslem or Byzantine intervention. While he demonstrated a remarkable quality of statesmanship, his plans for expansion were viewed as menacing by the neighboring Azeri-Shiites.

The country of the Azeris located between Armenia and the Caspian Sea had historically provided a base for intrigue against Armenia and the Christian minorities in Western Asia. After the rise of Islam and during hectic activity of the Arab military expansion, Azerbeijan had become a pantheon of evil for Shiite fundamentalists who wished to maintain a quasi-autonomous entity within the framework of the Moslem Empire. The country was called Arran by the Arabs and Albania by others before it assumed the name Azerbeijan. The decline of the Arab power and the diminishing presence of the Byzantine Greeks in the east, had resulted in a new order in Western Asia in which uncultured and barbaric Azeris became a dominant power and established the territorial basis of their Shiite fundamentalist movement.

Administratively the newly organized Kingdom of Armenia was unprepared to preserve its political autonomy. The Moslem fanaticism in the east appeared to upset the *status quo* which was carefully designed by the superpowers in Baghdad and Byzantium. The Shiite dynasty of Sajids was rapidly building a military organization while maintaining a political link with the Caliphate in Baghdad. It was hardly possible for the Caliph to treat the Azeris in the same way as the other subjects of the Islamic Empire. The half savage Azeris with ferocious disposition had forced the Moslem ruler to stay away from their country. They were the inhabitants of an unruly state, governed by their own emirs and paid taxes to Baghdad whenever they pleased.

At the time when Sembat I rose to power in Armenia, the ruler of Azerbeijan was Emir Afshin who organized an army and advanced towards Armenia to check Sembat's territorial expansion in the east. Afshin's troups were crushed, however, at the foot of Mount Aragatz by the potentially more powerful and vastly outnumbered Armenian forces. The defeated Azeris then diverted their forces, entered Armenia through another corridor, and occupied the city of Kars.

The military confrontation with the Azeris interrupted Sembat's plans to organize a politically non-aligned government in Armenia and undermined his ability to make plans for national recovery. To put an end to the conflict Sembat offered to yield the territory east of Armenia and give his niece in marriage to Afshin in exchange for peace and alliance. He wanted to establish a suitable line of defense between the two territories and bring a fruitful political understanding between the Armenians and the Shiite Azeris. The alliance was short-lived, however. Afshin died and his brother Youssouph immediately resumed the hostilities against Armenia. He invaded the plains of Mount Ararat and after seizing a major portion of the Armenian territory, slaughtered thousands of Armenians and captured Sembat's son and nephew and put them to death.

Youssouph made military reinforcements before advancing towards Ani in pursuit of King Sembat. Control of the Armenian territory allowed Youssouph to replace some of the Azeri troops with more ferocious Turkomen who had begun to penetrate the Azeri territory. In the ensuing route the Armenians lost many men and Sembat's organized resistance became irreparably damaged by the combined forces of Azeris and Turkomens. King Sembat attempted to escape but Youssouph struck the great gates of Ani, captured the King, and threw him in a dungeon in Devin. The Azeris then proceeded to secure other cities in the Armenian Kingdom. Most of the towns surrendered to Azeri hordes voluntarily, but the city of Evanchak proved a formidable obstacle. The gates of Evanchak had been converted into an impregnable fortress. The walls were too massive and it was impossible for Youssouph's forces to batter them down. To prove to the inhabitants of this city that their King was in his custody, Youssouph ordered Sembat to be dragged in chains before the principal gates of Evanchak. Hopeless and separated from the rest of Armenia, the Governor of Evanchak ordered the gates to be lifted. The Azeris poured in and massacred the inhabitants. To round off his conquest of Armenia in 914 Emir Youssouph ordered King Sembat to be beheaded, his body taken to Devin and exhibited in the public square.

The Byzantine Greeks were not in a position to help the embittered Armenians. The imperial family in Constantinople was in the midst of a crisis of its own. The Bulgars had continued to exert immense political and military pressure on Byzantium. The local governor around the northern flank of the Empire had shaken the central authority and in the course of successive insurrections, decided to join the Bulgar forces against the Byzantine Emperor.

Leo VI died in 912 and his six year old son succeeded him to the throne with Leo's brother acting as regent. The Bulgarian Czar, Symeon, who was to become one of the greatest rulers of medieval Europe, attacked the Byzantine territory in 913, pushed his men across the frontier, and camped beneath the walls of the Byzantine capital.

KING ASHOT II

Sembat's son Ashot II succeeded his father in 914 and became a constructive statesman and one of the pivotal figures in the history of the Bagratuni dynasty. He inherited the kingdom from his father at a time when the country's political system had been damaged beyond repair and the governmental order which had been so carefully designed by his grandfather was in shambles. The Azeri terrorism had gripped Armenia's political scene, disrupting the growth of economic and cultural activity. Through a remarkable series of military accomplishments Ashot drove the enemy troops out of the country. His victories in battle won him the surname *Yergat*, or the iron.

Emir Youssouph, infuriated by Ashot's successes, reinforced his troops and attacked Armenia again, ravaged the cities, and took thousands of Armenian women and offered them to his Moslem troops. This latest Azeri terrorism disrupted all commercial activity and the traditional economic organization which had been designed to make Armenia productive and agriculturally self-sufficient. While the country was not gifted with an abundance of cultivable land, historically Armenians had planned the exploitation of their land in such a way that the greater part of their production was saved for future purposes. Agricultural products were accumulated in warehouses of the Nakharars through a system of planned production and economic planning, and the processing and distribution of food were regulated through governmental agencies under the direct supervision of the Nakharars.

The situation was different in neighboring Azerbeijan. The primitive Azeris had not gone through the transition from food gathering to food producing. Yet they knew how to reap harvest, but no sowing was done which was needed to establish a cycle for production. They were envious about Armenia's agricultural prowess and the abundance of food in Armenian warehouses. No political turmoil in the past, however, had disrupted this economic cycle until during the second phase of the Azeri terror. To punish Ashot, Youssouph ordered his troops to attack Armenia's agricultural heartland to destroy the warehouses, obliterate properties, slaughter the peasants, farmers, and their livestock. The result was a widespread famine with thousands of Armenians dead of starvation within a short period of time.

King Ashot appealed to Byzantium for help. He went to Constantinople and met with a fellow Armenian, Romanus Lecopenus, the son of an Armenian peasant who had risen to power through palace intrigue and had captured the imperial throne as co-emperor with his son-in-law, Constantine VII. Help was granted and King Ashot returned home with a contingent of Byzantine forces and chased the Azeris out of the country once and for all. After restoring relative peace in Armenia, Ashot abdicated the throne in 929, retired into private life, and spent the rest of his life as a recluse on an island in Lake Sevan. With no sons to succeed him, Ashot's brother, Abas, occupied the throne in 929 and ruled the country for twenty-four years.

The most significant event in Abas' reign was the complete elimination of the Azeri threat which allowed the new King to restore political order and initiate a vigorous campaign to construct the badly damaged cities and towns. His first task was to repair the fortifications at the city of Kars. He became the architect of a revitalized kingdom with expanded territories and firm assurances from both superpowers that Armenia's territorial integrity will always be protected against foreign intrusion. After expelling the Azeri terrorists, the capital city of Ani grew from a city of local importance to become the principal administrative and commercial center in Western Asia. During this period of reconstruction Armenians developed their kingdom into a unified state with a strong military presence to withstand foreign intervention.

The country was not completely immunized, however, from foreign mishaps. With the Abbasid Caliphate in Baghdad on the decline, minor Arab emirates had gained significant military and political importance in areas surrounding Armenia and Byzantium. One of these emirates was the Hamdanids of Aleppo who had established a political sovereignty of their own and had grown in prestige and authority outside the jurisdiction of the Islamic Empire. In 940 the Emir of the Hamdanids organized a military campaign to attack Christian strongholds in Asia Minor. Armenia once again became a theater for military conflict. The efforts of the Byzantine Greeks to form a joint defense line with the Armenians against this latest Moslem onslaught were ineffectual. Their war efforts on the eastern fringes of the Byzantine Empire had been crippled by dissension among the mercenary troops who were the half loyal hired hands of the Byzantine army. The damage of the Hamdanids was extensive, however. After a brief siege of Armenian cities, the Moslems withdrew their forces and returned to northern Syria.

THE FLOWERING OF A GOLDEN AGE

King Abas died in 953 and his son, Ashot III succeeded him to the throne. The country had been reconstructed from the ravages of the Moslem invaders and a new phase of economic recovery was about to begin. Foreign trade had made Armenia enormously wealthy and the political union among the principal families of nobility had brought the Armenians together again. For the first time in many centuries Armenians had become conscious of their political and military superiority in Western Asia.

The rapid growth of prosperity in the kingdom was facilitated by basic economic reforms. Ashot welded Armenia's economy into a single unit by formulating a new monetary policy and making the circulation of money plentiful for the enhancement of foreign and domestic trade. Coins replaced barter in the principal trading centers of Armenia. For the first time in many decades Armenia's mints were reopened and gold and silver coins began to be issued and circulated widely under the direct supervision of the king's treasurer.

Ashot III inaugurated his reign by the installation of a system of taxation earmarked for military build up and reconstruction of the country. Revenue from taxation was used to rebuild the abandoned cities and promote industry. People began to manufacture goods again and export them to Moslem and Byzantine territories. Woolen and cotton fabrics and carpets made in Armenia became important commodities for the Arabs. Objects of art, gold, jewelry, belts, bracelets, rings, earrings, began to be manufactured in Ani. There were factories to produce porcelain and copper vessels all around Armenia.

International commerce between east and west was revitalized and Ani, Bitlis, Kars, Van, Karin became important centers for commerce and industry. Armenia became a distribution agent for exotic and luxury products from India and Arabia. Farmers began to cultivate their lands and re-establish large scale production of grain, rice, cotton, and fruits. The country once again became covered by orchards and vineyards. Granaries were full and there was an abundance of food supply. The king ordered the digging of irrigation canals to help farmers cultivate thousands of acres of desolate lands. Livestock began to be exported to other parts of the known world in large quantities.

The general atmosphere in Armenia was one of hope and happiness. After years of terror and foreign oppression, Armenians yearned for nothing more than the restoration of peace and the opportunity to control their own destiny. It was the King, Ashot III, who laid the groundwork and provided the proper environment for a new revolution in thought and culture. New churches were erected and state funds were used to

build centers of learning. A new movement of cultural development was accompanied by a surge of creativity in art, literature,
and sciences. Ani, the shining city on the mountain, the jewel
of Western Asia, became the center of a new revival of intellectual pursuit. It had always been Armenia's political experience that whenever the country was allowed to have a breathing
spell, no matter how brief that period may have been, Armenians undertook cultural activity and began to write literature
and poetry, composed music, and built churches. In this particular period of the Armenian renaissance a renewed interest in
literature, science, and architecture revealed a new attitude of
mind, searching for new plateaus of cultural endeavor. Creative
works of literature, poetry, philosophical essays, and scholarly
activity under the patronage of the King began to flourish. The
burgeoning of this scholarship inaugurated a new period which
will rightfully be called the Golden Age of Armenia, the second
time around.

One of the most important literary events of this age was
created by Grigor Naregatsi, a recluse in the monastery of Nareg, who wrote elegies, odes, and homilies. His Book of Prayer,
called *Nareg*, contains the penitent's lamentations in profound
theological prose with meditations for longing for eternal holi-
ness in the form of conversations with God. For the next 900
years this book will exact a potent influence in the development
of religious thought and Armenians will consider it as their most
sacred book, second only to the Bible, with the power to offer a
source of inspiration and solace for the needy, the sick, the destitute, the widow, and the individual in search of comfort and
truth. The book contains a humanistic view of Armenian history with a reflection of the intellectual attitude of man's relationship with God. It was a custom for every Armenian household
to have a copy of Nareg.

Naregatsi was passionately concerned to make man's life
meaningful. A good and happy life could only be achieved, he
wrote, through association with God. The nourishment of the
soul, spirit, and wisdom, could be cultivated in large measure
by man himself but only if it is regulated by the power of divinity. He was against the comforts of luxury and the pursuit of a
materialistic life. He believed that the desire for food, shelter,
and the material things in life was not as important as the desire

to elevate one's soul to a high plateau. Only then will man be able to attain the state of perpetual happiness.

Monasteries, of which there were many, provided the source for creative energy. Ever since the adoption of Christianity, monastic life was sought by clergymen who wished to pursue a life of humility and penitence. While the monks never attained high ecclesiastical ranking in the hierarchy of the Church, they exercised enormous power over the affairs of the Church. Armenian monks were regarded in high esteem as the providers of heavenly guidance with healing grace to perform miracles. The monasteries were the place where new literary movements emerged, and new books were published. While monks devoted themselves to Christian life, they were conscious of their role as the providers of knowledge and found a receptive audience among the upper classes of Armenian society.

Members of nobility zealously guarded the tradition of their culture and the heritage of the classical past. They sought superiority through education and considered it their duty to educate their children. Ignorance was regarded as a social disgrace. An Armenian proverb declared "only he who can read is a man."

THE ARMENIAN LANGUAGE

Besides monasteries there were also educational facilities sponsored by the Church and liberally funded by the state. Foremost among the disciplines in these institutions was the grammar and the use of classical Armenian, called Grapar. By the end of the Eleventh century a new form of Armenian language, called Ashkharapar, was developed out of the vernacular spoken by the people, making Grapar solely used by the church, and Ashkharapar by the people. Although the Armenian language was partly the heritage from the period in which Indo-Europeans dominated Western Asia, its character was largely formed in the centuries which elapsed from the fall of Urartu to the invention of the Alphabet.

Around 4000 B.C. there existed in Western Asia a family of languages known as Indo-European with three branches spoken by various peoples, Anatolian, Indo-Iranian, and Thraco-Phrygian. The Anotolian branch dominated the western part of Asia Minor where Hittites used to live.   This language was forced out by the Thraco-Phrygians when the Hittite Kingdom fell and the Thraco-Phrygians occupied the country. The other group of Armenian ancestors, the Hurrians, and later the Urartians, spoke a Caucasian language called Nash-Daghestan. The successive steps by which the Armenian language achieved its final form are obscure and difficult to trace. It was probably developed during the period of the great fusion of the Hurrians, the Hayasas, the Azzis, the Luwians, and the Melids initiated by the Thraco-Phrygians between 1000 B. C. and 585 B.C.

When the Urartians lost their identity as a people during the influx of Armenians into the land of Urartu, elements of their language were gradually adopted by Armenians. Rapid growth of Persian, Greek, and Arabic influenced the language. French and other Romance languages later came to bring their influence on the Armenian language. Turkish elements entered the language when Turks began to rule the country. In addition to the principal language of the people there were several dozen different dialects with each region of Armenia speaking a dialect of its own. In spite of all these foreign elements, however, the people clung tenaciously to the heritage of the classical period and preserved the grammar of their language which until today remains independently unique.

THE LITERARY FIGURES

It was during this period that some of the most imaginative works of poetry and literature were written. Earlier a compendium of church hymns and chants, known as the Sharagans, was developed by Catholicos Gomidas in the Seventh century. A lady of aristocracy, by the name of Sahagdukht, in the Eighth century wrote and composed church hymns with somber profundity and offered singing lessons concealed behind a curtain to disguise her identity. There were musicians, poets, and philosophers. Bishop Khatchadour of Taron invented the musical notes, known as the *khaz*, or the neume, to enable people to read music.

Great works of secular literature were produced particularly in the area of history. Grigor Magistros, a linguist and a scholar, assiduously collected Armenian manuscripts and translated the works of Plato, and the Eulogy of Socrates. He was fascinated by Plato's concept of the ideal state in which man's social function was an expression of his own personality, with the state providing the proper environment to make such an expression possible. He believed that man's desire for social justice was associated with the organization of the state and the power of the government. Magistros wrote essays and poetry depicting the religious and political problems of the day. He was the first poet in Armenian literature who wrote poetry with rhyme, a literary technique that was introduced in Armenia by the Arabs. Stepanos Assoghig recognized the need to write about the world beyond Armenia and introduced new interests in historiography. Aristakes Lastivertatsi, one of the most prominent historians of the period, wrote the eye-witness account of the suffering of the Armenian people under the Arabs. Madteos Ourhayetsi, a historian of international repute wrote the history of the last two centuries in chronological order.

THE ARMENIAN CALENDAR

Hovhannes Sargavak stimulated interest in mathematical studies and explained the order of the universe. His books on mathematical theorems were used as standard texts throughout Western Asia. He measured the length of the solar year and lunar month and revised the Armenian calendar after discovering the flaws of the old system.

The ancient Armenians had their own method of reckoning time which was generally based on pagan practices and legendary events. The calendar was based on their observations of celestial phenomena, the movement of the sun, the moon, and the stars. Their practice was to refer events to the years which had elapsed from the legendary birthdate of the Armenian people, which according to tradition was August 11, 2492 B.C., the day when the nation's legendary forefather, Haig, defeated his enemy, Bel. To determine the Armenian year one needs to add the current year to 2492. The year 1993, for instance, will be 4485 (1993 plus 2492) for the Armenians.

The pagan Armenians had divided the year into twelve months of 30 days each and an additional month, called Haveliatz, with only five days, to make up the discrepancy with the solar year of 365 days. The names of the months were: Navasart, Horee, Sahmee, Dareh, Kaghotz, Aratz, Mehegan, Arek, Ahegan, Marery, Markatz, Heroditz, and Haveliatz. Each day of the month had a special name after some notable region or a legendary figure such as Arek, Hrant, Aram, Mihr, Vahakn. The day was divided into twenty four equal segments with a separate identification for each. There were the day hours, referred to as Ayk, Dzayk, Arpogh, and the night hours, Khavaroug, Gamavod, and Pavagan. This Armenian calendar was kept in use until the adoption of the Julian Calendar on July ll, 552. For Armenians the year 552 marks the beginning of the Christian era.

ART AND ARCHITECTURE

The Golden Age opened a new world of opportunity for Armenian artists and architects. Art and architecture found their fullest expression in this age of cultural accomplishments. Churches and palaces built in this period were examples of engineering skill and ingenious designs. The Cathedral of Ani, the ruins of which are still in existence, was one of the most remarkable buildings of antiquity. Its architectural design with triangular niches was far advanced of anything that was built in Europe during the same period.

Armenian church architecture acquired a distinctive style of its own with multiple vaulting. The dome and the centralized plan represented the principal architectural elements. It is a tribute to the genius of this people to have constructed churches with curved ceilings and crowning domes, making their architectural style uniquely distinguishable from the mainstream of Christian architecture. Though the churches were small in size with simple proportions, they had spaciousness and clarity, built generally in the form of a cross. The interior of the church was separated into two parts, one for the congregation, the other, the altar, for the clergy.

Armenians are known as church builders. It has been said that wherever they go they build their churches first before their homes. This is true even at times of tribulation and national suffering. Historically the size of the churches indicates political tranquility or the lack of it. The churches erected during the Golden Age of the Bagratunis appear to be larger than the ones built during the earlier periods, indicating political stability.

POLITICAL FRAGMENTATION

While this period witnessed a transformation of thought culturally, politically the society underwent a far reaching change.

The abundance of wealth and the economic recovery stimulated the development of small principalities outside the jurisdiction of the Armenian king. After gaining political recognition the rulers of these districts declared themselves kings, independent from the Kingdom of Ani, thus creating a political cleavage at a time when unity would have been a more effective tool to protect the country from foreign intrusion.

Small kingdoms were formed in Vaspouragan, Kars, and five other regions under the sponsorship of the Caliph in Baghdad who viewed Ani's unprecedented growth a threat to the Moslem presence in Western Asia. The Caliph had granted political autonomy to Armenia principally to gain Armenia's loyalty for the Arab cause against the Byzantine encroachments. The rapidity in which Armenia put its political house in order and became enormously prosperous was not in the interest of the Arabs. Such revivals in the heart of the Islamic Empire were contrary to the political schemes of the Moslems and were regarded unfavorably by the rulers of Baghdad. The policy of divide and conquer may have been the principal stimulant for the Arabs to create seven smaller Armenian kingdoms to prevent the establishment of an organically unified Armenian state which would have been to the detriment of Moslem hegemony. The fragmentation will eventually be mended, however, and a fruitful unity of culture among the Armenian kings will bring new vigor to the plains of Mount Ararat.

ANOTHER ARMENIAN EMPEROR

Meanwhile in Constantinople another Armenian had risen to power. Hovhannes Tchimishkik, a member of a prominent Armenian family in Byzantium and a general of great talent, had become Emperor of Byzantium through the treachery of his mistress, the wife of Emperor Nicephorus II Phocas, who had arranged the murder of her husband to pave the way for Tchimishkik to assume the throne. Tchimishkik became one of the greatest and most powerful emperors of Byzantine history. Through heroic deeds he recaptured most of the territories in Cilicia, Syria, and the coastal cities of Beirut and Sidon from the Arabs and invaded the land of the Bulgars to chase the Russians and the Patzinaks out of the area. King Ashot III of Armenia contributed to the military build up of the Byzantine army.

There was a contingent of 30,000 Armenian troops in Tchimish-kik's army at a time when the Arabs were concerned about Armenia's growing affiliation with Byzantium.

With the help of the Armenian troops the Byzantine forces occupied most of the principal cities of Palestine and came short of capturing the Holy City of Jerusalem. After his triumphant success Tchimishkik sent a letter to his friend and ally, King Ashot III of Armenia - "Hear and receive the wonderful tale, all Phoenicia, Palestine, and Syria are freed from the yoke of the Saracen". This was the first time since the rise of Islam that Byzantium had recaptured the territories lost to the Arabs.

A PERIOD OF EXUBERANCE

King Ashot died in 977 and was succeeded by his son, Sembat II whose major contribution was the building of a double wall and fortifications around the capital. Gagik I succeeded his brother Sembat II in 989 and ruled the country until 1020. During his reign, Gagik encouraged international trade between east and west which made the country enormously prosperous. For the next thirty years Armenia will enjoy a rare and unprecedented period of exuberance, political stability, and religious freedom. State festivals, singing, dancing in the streets, became common occurrences. When the King was in town, the government organized triumphant parades. On such occasions, the King wore his pearl laden crown, rode his white horse followed by soldiers clothed in their brilliantly embroidered attire, armed with swords, spears, and banners with the royal emblem. For the first time in many centuries the people were happy and were given the promise of a new era which will later be identified as one of the happiest periods in the history of Armenia.

BULGARS DEFEATED

Meanwhile in the west a dynamic ruler had risen to power in 976 destined to crush the barbaric Bulgars in the north and help convert the unruly Russians into Christianity. The Emperor Basil II occupied the throne amid a vicious internal rebellion against his rule. To consolidate his power in Byzantium, Basil II sought the help of Prince Vladimir of Kiev who sent a formidable army to Constantinople to crush the rebellion. As a reward the Emperor gave the Russian prince his sister Anne as a bride. This was the first time that a Byzantine princess born in the purple was marrying a foreigner. Their marriage will have a vast historical significance. It became the galvanizing force that inaugurated a new epoch in the relationship between Russia and Byzantium and helped convert the State of Kiev to Christianity in 988. The conversion into Christianity brought the entire Slavic region in the north into the spiritual fold of Byzantium with the Church of Russia coming under the superintendence of the Patriarchate of Constantinople.

The amicable relationship with the Slavs, however, did not extend to the Bulgars, whose Czar Samuel, the son of an Armenian immigrant, had gained the possession of all the land north of Byzantium and was on his way down to the Bosporus to harass the Byzantine lines of communication. Basil II mobilized a powerful army to assure his continued hold on the strategic fortifications surrounding the capital. After crushing the Bulgar forces around the periphery of Constantinople, he pushed Samuel's army to a narrow pass in the north and captured 14,000 Bulgar soldiers. Czar Samuel had successfully extricated himself from the battlefield and taking a small regiment with him retreated into the interior of Bulgaria. To put an end to the irritating problem of the Bulgars Basil blinded the Bulgar soldiers in his custody, leaving one man for every one hundred with one eye as a guide to lead the rest of the troops back to the Bulgars. When Samuel saw his gruesome army he was devastated and died two days later. Basil II entered the Bulgarian capital victoriously and received homage from the surviving members of the royal family. The problem of the Bulgars was finally solved and the land of the Bulgars became a mere appendage to Byzantium. For his deed Basil II was surnamed Bulgaroctonus, the killer of the Bulgars.

With the demise of the Bulgars, the entire Balkan peninsula came under the imperial rule of Byzantium, marking the beginning of one of the most prosperous periods in the history of the Byzantine Empire. Antioch and Aleppo came under the Byzantine rule and Russia, after legitimizing Christianity as a state religion, became a political ally to Byzantium. The subsequent era of comparative peace will represent the golden years of the revival of the Byzantine power in the Mediterranean world in which political equilibrium will be restored and the cultural unity of the Byzantine epoch will be established. The resurgence will accompany certain political events that will begin to foment problems for Byzantium and Armenia and shake the very structure of their govermnents. In the east the Seljuk Turks had begun to emerge as a ferocious power challenging to destabilize the political order, and in the west the Crusade fervor directed principally towards the infidels of Islam was gaining momentum among the kings and princes of the Holy Roman Empire.

THE ARRIVAL OF THE TURKS

King Gagik of Armenia died in 1020 and was succeeded by his inept son Hovhannes-Sembat III. Many feudal Nakharars refused to give their allegiance to the new king and encouraged the king's brother to claim the throne for himself. Sembat attempted to appease his brother by offering him territories along the Georgian and Persian frontiers.

The factional strife between the crown and the Armenian lords was overshadowed by the eruption of a horde of barbarians emerging from central Asia. A Turkomen tribe had developed into a powerful force at the foot of the Altaz mountains and after accepting the faith of Islam had begun to proceed west to ravage the fertile lands of the Caliph and the territories of the Greeks.

Around the Tenth century these Turkomens, under a leader by the name of Seljuk, settled in the vicinity of Bukhara and established a powerful empire. The impact of their wars in central Asia was not as damaging as the militarism of Seljuk's two grandsons, Chaghri Beg, and Toghril Beg, who wanted to establish their own country in Western Asia and dominate the political life of the west. They waged their wars with the heavy reliance on the loyalty of the nomadic Turks who wanted nothing but a good plunder as the group moved into the heartland of the Islamic Empire.

While the Arab Empire was still immensely wealthy, the power of the Caliphate in Baghdad had weakened considerably and the central authority of the Caliph was challenged by the formation of countless dynasties and quasi-dynasties. The powerful emirs who ruled their districts as private kingdoms had shaken the authority of the Caliph in Baghdad. The Fatamids had gained control in Egypt and the Ismailites were in Syria and Palestine. In the west the non-Moslems had assumed the administrative control of their territories, and the usual intrigue and series of murders had contributed to the rapid decay of the Arab power. Palace intrigues and fratricidal quarrels among the members of the Caliph's household offered the Seljuks the opportunity to assume the reign for Islamic supremacy. Toghril Beg became the *de facto* ruler of the Islamic Empire with the Caliph acting only as the religious leader. The Seljuks took over the administrative control of the Empire, and their leader came to be known as the Sultan.

The Seljuk Turks were warlike and predatory with no cultural heritage, no knowledge in farming and agriculture, and no appreciation of statecraft. They kept moving west in search of rich pastures and grazing land. They settled down in agriculturally rich communities awhile and became parasites on the community. When the food supply of the communities was exhausted they moved on to other communities to find new pastures. For them, war seemed to be the easiest solution to satisfy their basic needs. Their primary need of searching for food shaped their political and social behavior. At first their expeditions were raids for plunder, but eventually their occupation of the territories became firm conquests and gradually they began to coalesce into an Islamic society and acquired the patterns of the more civilized culture of the Arabs.

INVASION OF ARMENIA

The fields of Armenia became a magnet for the Seljuk nomads. Their first target was the province of Van. They began to raid the towns and villages, killing thousands of Armenians. Around 400,000 Armenians, unable to withstand the Seljuk onslaught, left Armenia and settled in the Byzantine territory which had always served as a sanctuary for Armenians fleeing from oppression.

After conquering Van, the Seljuks proceeded north and in 1021 invaded the capital city of Ani. The Kurdish governor, Khoudrig, allied himself with the Turks, and began to devastate the surrounding areas. He dug ditches and buried thousands of Armenians alive.

King Hovhannes-Sembat III asked for help from the Byzantine Emperor. He sent Catholicos Petros to Emperor Basil II with a letter promising to bequeath the entire Armenian territory to Byzantium after his death in exchange for military assistance. Basil II sent an army to Ani to stop the Seljuks. King Hovhannes-Sembat III died in 1041 and Emperor Michael IV, who had risen to power in 1034, invoked the rights to accept the bequest of the Armenian territory. The Armenian lords refused to honor the promise of their dead king. With the Turks at their doorstep, they organized a powerful resistance to stop the Byzantine encroachment and immediately installed sixteen year old Gagik II on the Armenian throne. Constantine IX Monamachus after succeeding Michael IV in 1041 sent an army to crush the Armenian resistance, but Gagik's forces stopped the Byzantines at the gate of Ani.

Unable to conquer Armenia by military force Constantine IX reverted to treachery. He bribed the Catholicos and a group of Armenian lords to persuade their king to accept an invitation to come to Constantinople on the pretense to sign a peace accord. After receiving the assurances from the Nakharars and the Catholicos that they will continue to remain faithful to his policies and loyal to the Armenian cause, Gagik made the journey to Constantinople. Upon arrival in the Byzantine capital he was immediately summoned to the imperial palace and was ordered to relinquish his throne and cede Armenia to Byzantium. The Emperor showed Gagik a letter signed by the Nakharars and the Catholicos promising to turn over the Armenian territory to Byzantium and hand over the keys of Ani to the Emperor. Betrayed by his own people, Gagik II abdicated in 1045.

The brilliant rule of the Bagratunis will now come to an end. For two hundred years they ruled Armenia and established a new political order which eventually led the nation to a period of grandeur and economic prosperity. Their cousins will continue to rule neighboring Georgia for another 700 years, but the Armenian throne will be kept vacant. For the next 150 years the people will wander around in search of a new homeland, attempting to grope for peace, tranquility, and religious freedom.

The demise of the Bagratunis brought the disintegration of the Armenian society. Some of the Armenian Nakharars and feudal lords settled in Byzantium and made significant contributions to the Byzantine Empire. Others simply vanished from the pages of Armenian history. Most of them migrated to the Kurdish territory with their families, servants, and armies and settled in the inaccessible mountain fastnesses. For a while they preserved their Armenian ethnic identity and maintained their Christian faith, but their succeeding generations lost their interest in Armenian affairs and were assimilated by the Kurds and Islamicized. During the period of Kurdish atrocities several centuries later when the Kurds were massacring Armenians in Western Armenia, some of the Kurdish chieftains were believed to be the descendants of these prominent Armenian dynasties. They carried Armenian names in Kurdish version, Mamikanli, Mendikanli, Rushkotanli, Bagranli.

GAGIK MURDERED

King Gagik was not allowed to return home. The Emperor gave him a palace in Constantinople and a small estate near Caesarea where he lived until his death in 1079. The Byzantine forces occupied Ani and inaugurated a period of religious oppression to force the people to accept the Orthodox faith. They imposed heavy taxes and instigated a struggle for power among the Armenian nobles convulsing the country and the Church with political strife. Some of the treacherous Nakharars were put to death when their usefulness as pawns disappeared. Catholicos Petros was summoned to Constantinople and was forced to live in exile for the rest of his life. In the history of the Armenian Church the treacherous act of this Catholicos will never be forgotten. Centuries later when his tomb was discovered during an archeological excavation, an Armenian priest, who later became Catholicos, took his bones and threw them to the wind exclaiming, "May the lord curse your bones for eternity".

While living in Byzantium, King Gagik did not find the Greeks particularly receptive to his presence. The Byzantine Greeks were contemptuous in their treatment of the deposed King. This was symptomatic of the considerable anti-Armenian sentiment in Caesarea prevailing at the time primarily because of the Armenians' stubborn refusal to unite their Church with the Greek Orthodox Church. In time, the dislike towards the Armenians was transformed into hostility. It soon became fashionable for the Greeks to insult the Armenian inhabitants of

Cæsarea by calling their dogs Armen. The Greeks criticized the Armenian King for his display of Armenian customs and traditions and for his desire to restore the Armenian Kingdom of Ani which was then securely held by the Byzantines. The anti-Armenian sentiment came to a climax when the Greeks hanged King Gagik on charges of organizing the murder of the Greek Archbishop of Cæsarea. The charge may have been true. The Archbishop had become an important protagonist of the anti-Armenian movement and his insolent behavior towards the Armenians by calling his dog Armen may have offended the sensibilities of the Armenian King. With Gagik's death, the Bagratuni Dynasty came to an end.

THE FALL OF ANI

The Greek hold on Armenia will not last long. Toghril Beg of the Seljuks, after instituting a system of salaried army of the Memluks from the highlands of the Caucasus, attacked Armenia in 1048 and ordered 140,000 Armenians to be butchered. His successor, Alp-Arslan, proved to be more cruel. With savage violence he pushed the Seljuk forces to the gates of Ani. The Byzantine forces began to flee. The Turks surrounded the city and after a short siege climbed over the mountains and entered Ani on June 6, 1064. They began a wholesale massacre of the people with blood flowing in torrents. Some people attempted to take refuge in churches. The Turks burned the churches, burning the people alive. Bellies of Armenian women were slashed open and the heads of infants were crushed against pavements. It was a veritable holocaust which lasted a week. Alp-Arslan plundered the wealth of Ani and replaced the churches with mosques. He took the great silver cross from the top of the Cathedral and placed it at the threshold of the Moslem mosque and ordered his troops to spit at it while walking over the cross to enter the mosque.

The fall of Ani shattered the perception of invincibility of the Byzantine soldiers and the infallibility of the Byzantine strategic planning. Their occupation of Armenia was regarded as the fulfillment of their Christian obligation to protect a Christian minority against the barbaric hordes. They entered Armenia to strengthen their defense posture in the east but became entangled in ecclesiastical issues by attempting to impose their religious doctrines on the Armenians. Their inept military strategy in the east, tainted with religious intonations, were ill-suited with regard to the war of savagery conducted by the Seljuks. The Greeks' clandestine activities and perverse myopia proved to be detrimental to the viability of their own Empire. As the Turks continued to expand, the Greeks continued to retreat. Ani was the gateway to the west. Its destruction allowed the Turks to enter the Byzantine territory in increasing numbers. Perhaps the Greeks should have protected this Christian outpost in the east. They may have prevented their own destruction by the cousins of the Seljuks some years later.

The beautiful city of Ani was now in ruins. It will never rise again. After the Seljuks, the Moslem Sheddadids ruled the city awhile. Then came the Shah-Armens and several Moslem emirates. A branch of the Bagratuni family, ruling neighboring Georgia, became increasingly powerful. In 1123 a Georgian Bagratuni, David II the Builder, invaded Armenia and took Ani and its fortifications. In 1126 the Sheddadids came back and reconquered the land and continued to exploit the suffering of the people. In 1236 the Mongols invaded Armenia and ravaged the towns and villages. The final blow to Ani came in 1300 when an earthquake destroyed whatever little remained of the city.

A tide of anarchy swept over Armenia. The wealth of the nation was plundered, churches were destroyed, and palaces were looted. The towns dwindled into isolation and the civilization came to an abrupt halt. Villages were abandoned and the people were enslaved or driven away to strange lands. Many in despair began to walk aimlessly with whatever belongings they could gather. It was during this period that approximately 600,000 Armenian men, women, and children left their homeland and proceeded north in search of safer havens. They began to walk towards the Caucasus with their horses and wagons. The journey was long and treacherous and the routes at times were impassable. They established trading posts along the way but their main line of migration was towards the hinterland of the Crimea and far away Moldavia and Poland. After leading a wandering existence for many years, they finally reached their destinations and settled down in stable communities. They failed, however, to perpetuate the tradition of the Armenian civilization. They lived in separate colonies awhile but eventually were fused with the local people and forever lost their ethnic identity.   There are many Poles today with Armenian last names. Their only link to their ancient heritage is their ability to recite the Lord's Prayer in Armenian.

A dark age will obscure Armenia. This was the first time since the formation of the Armenian people that Armenia's political structure will be completely demolished. While the people will continue to cling to their soil, Greater Armenia will cease to exist as a political entity. It will be 900 years before this part of Armenia will restructure itself into a new discipline, acquire a political regeneration, and gain independence from foreign rule.   For 1,500 years Armenia was conquered by the Achaemenid Persians, Alexander the Great, the Parthians, the Romans, the Sassanian Persians, the Byzantine Greeks, the Arabs, and now by the Turks. There was a difference, however, between the first conquerers and the last. The first came and went, but the last one stayed. It is this last one that will cause immeasurable damage to the Armenian civilization. It is now time for the people to wander around in search of a new homeland in quest for a fresh start.

CHAPTER SIXTEEN

THE SEARCH FOR A NEW HOMELAND

The Seljuk domination of Western Asia proved to be brief. A great coalition of other Turkic tribes coupled with the emergence of fanatic Moslem movements ultimately pushed the Seljuks to central Anatolia. The emergence of the Seljuks was only one phase of the great migrations of the Turks which brought into Western Asia a conglomeration of other Turkish tribes, the Danishmends, Khwarizmiens, Ghaznevids, Kipchaks, Petzenegs, Kharakhamids, and later the more destructive Ottomans, the half-savage and inarticulate nomads who moved toward western territories to fill the political vacuum, caused by the decadence of the Arab rule and the decline of the Byzantine power.

The emergence of the Turks was a turning point in the history of man, for the struggle between the Turks and the west laid the groundwork for a unity of European states to forge a military movement, in the name of religion, known as the Crusade. For the next two hundred years this adventure for religious supremacy, promulgated by the Pope himself, will bring together men from every nation in Europe, ferociously bent upon exterminating the Moslems, to gain control of the holy places of the Christian faith. The effect of this campaign will shape subsequent history. The Crusades will bring the newly emerging nations of Europe into direct contact with the more civilized world of the Middle East, and for the Armenians it will introduce a new era in which the survivors of the Seljuk holocaust will have the opportunity to design a new destiny for their nation in a strange land seven hundred miles away from their ancestral homeland.

THE BATTLE OF MANZIKERT

After conquering Armenia the Seljuk warriors proceeded west towards the Byzantine territory. The Byzantine rulers in Constantinople were alarmed by the increasing power of the Moslem hordes. Emperor Romanus IV Diogenes mobilized a powerful army and advanced towards Armenia to stop the Turks. In a decisive battle fought in Manzikert, near Lake Van, Armenia, in 1071, the Byzantines were defeated and the Emperor was taken prisoner. This battle in Armenia will have a far-reaching consequence for the fate of Byzantium and the subsequent history of western Europe. It will mark the beginning of the end of a period which was inaugurated by Constantine the Great seven hundred years earlier, imposing a pattern of Turkish influence in Asia Minor and threatening to change the face of the eastern Mediterranean. When the Byzantine Greeks failed to stop the Turks at Manzikert, the hegemony of Byzantium began to crumble and the rulers in Constantinople were forced to surrender the last remnants of their eastern territories.

The Seljuk victory in Armenia allowed the Turks to penetrate into the very heartland of Byzantine territory swarming across Asia Minor and forcing the Christians to move out. Political disintegration followed rapidly. The Byzantine towns and villages in Anatolia were abandoned and the Turks moved in with astounding rapidity. They integrated their forces into one organic unity and established a political entity known as the Sultanate of Iconium, immediately to the east of the Byzantine frontiers with Konya as their capital. For the next two centuries the Seljuk Sultans will rule this country of the Turks. In 1308 they will be taken over by their cousins, the Ottoman Turks, who will deliver the death blow to the Byzantine Empire.

Invasions into the Byzantine territory were common occurrences throughout the history of this Empire. Invaders came and went; they occupied the Byzantine towns awhile, but eventually were driven away when the rulers in Constantinople recovered their strength and chased the intruders out of the country. This intrusion by the Turks was different, however. The battle in Armenia was a shattering disaster for the fortunes of Byzantium. It marked the process of disintegration of the Byzantine power and made the Turks the permanent residents of the Byzantine territory in Asia Minor.

TURKS CAPTURE JERUSALEM

The victory in Armenia encouraged the Turks to proceed south and capture the Holy Lands from the Arabs. The Roman knights and princes in the west were alarmed by the increasing power of the Turkish infidels, and the growing incompetence of the Byzantine Greeks to protect the Christian strongholds in the east. The Byzantine power was disintegrating rapidly at home and abroad. At home there was a seemingly endless conflict for power between the imperial palace and the great landed aristocratic magnates, who vied with one another in accumulating material wealth usually at the expense of the state. In foreign affairs the decline of the Byzantine power promoted the newly emerging city republics of Italy to compete with Byzantium in international commerce, encouraged by the Pope himself, whose policies towards Byzantium widened the schism between the western and eastern divisions of the Christian Church. At a time when the Turks were spreading their influence in the Middle East and conquering the holy places of the Christian faith the ecclesiastical leaders of Christianity in Rome and Constantinople were debating whether the Holy Spirit proceeded from the Father or from both the Father and the Son.

The Turkish victory in Armenia laid the groundwork for the Christians in Europe to forge a holy war against the Turks to rescue the sacred places of Christianity from the evil tyranny of the Moslem hordes. The result was a religious militarism that will bring a European presence in the Middle East in an attempt to dismember the lands previously occupied by Byzantium.

A NEW HOMELAND

While the Seljuk holocaust attempted to destroy the civilization of this ancient people, Armenians had enough resilience to preserve their vitality. They made their way to the southern corner of Asia Minor, the region of Cilicia. Cilicia was a country of unusual topography with impregnable and rugged mountains and a climate desperately hot in the summer and severely cold in the winter. On the west side stood Mount Isauria and Cilician Trachea. On the northern side were the fertile plains of Lycaonia. The east side of the country was bordered by the Gulf of Satalia with sheltered harbors and a peerless coastline of the Mediterranean. Separated from the central Anatolian pla-

teau by the mountain ranges of the Anti-Taurus, Cilicia formed
a barrier between Anatolia and northern Syria. The famous
defile of the Cilician Gates made communication with northern
Asia Minor possible while the Gulf of Issus connected the central regions with northern Syria.

Historically Cilicia was a Hittite territory with a preponder-
ant Luwian population. After Alexander the Great the country
was ruled by the Seleucids and the Egyptian Ptolemies and after
the demise of the Roman Empire the Byzantine Greeks ruled
the country until it was taken over by the Arabs in the Ninth
century. One of the principal cities of Cilicia was Tarsus, the
birthplace of St. Paul.

The Armenian migration into Cilicia began during the
reign of the Armenian Emperor Tchimishkik of Byzantium who
reconquered the territory from the Arabs in 973. Subsequent
rulers of Byzantium favored the Armenian migration into Cilicia
to populate the area with Christian elements ostensibly to create
a buffer zone between Byzantium and the Islamic east. The Seljuk terror brought a deportation of Armenians from Greater
Armenia. Thousands of Armenians, the survivors of the holocaust, were forced to embark to the shores of the Mediterranean.

At first the development of a political system in Cilicia was
spurred by contacts with the Greeks, Jews, and the Arabs, who
had made Cilicia their home within the jurisdiction of the Byzantine Empire. Political organization for Armenians did not materialize, however, until the conclusion of the turbulent process
of settlement and the appointment of an Armenian noble, Ashin
as the Byzantine Governor of the Cilician Gates. Gradually other Armenian nobles migrated to Cilicia and assumed the title
Ishkhan, or prince. They consolidated their family's position,
acquired hereditary status, and established independent baronies under a Byzantine mandate.

A movement of political independence was organized by
an Armenian prince by the name of Roupen in 1080 who began
a military campaign principally to avenge the assassination of
King Gagik II. There was no love lost between the Byzantine
Greeks and the Armenians. Centuries of religious harassment,
culminated in treachery, had created a serious political cleavage between the Empire of Byzantium and the survivors of the

Armenian holocaust. The Armenians blamed the Greeks for
their national sufferings and political misfortunes.

Roupen's military activities produced some concrete results. The Armenian forces seized the fortress of Partzerpert
located on a tributary of the Pyramus River and Roupen declared northern Cilicia independent from Byzantine rule. Constantin I succeeded his father, Roupen, in 1095 and ruled until
1099. His principal objective was to push the frontiers of Cilicia
and annex more Byzantine lands to the Armenian territory.
The territorial expansion brought important commercial centers
under Armenian jurisdiction allowing the Armenian princes to
collect taxes on commercial traffic.

The Armenian independence in Cilicia was not what the
Byzantines had in mind. While the land became heavily populated and urbanized by Armenians, the Byzantine Greeks
wanted to maintain their control over this strategically important
region in their southern flank. The Greeks welcomed the Armenians as traders and mercenary soldiers and wanted to use
them as tools to insulate Byzantium from Islamic incursions.
They intended to have the Armenians as independent settlers.
As Armenians in Cilicia became increasingly powerful, the
Greeks resented Armenia's rise to prominence. Cilicia began to
flourish and before long the country became a prosperous little
state, partly by its control of the strategic commercial routes and
partly by the indomitable will of the people to survive and continue the process of their political experience. Commercial traffic began to pour goods in the sheltered harbors of the Gulf of
Alexandretta and caravan trade passing through Cilicia began
to distribute goods to the coastal cities of Syria and Palestine.

Just as the plains of Mount Ararat had stimulated commerce in Greater Armenia, the renewed contacts with the neighboring countries helped to galvanize the Armenian productive
energy to conduct international trade in the new homeland.
The land route from Syria to Asia Minor passed through Cilicia
and the coastal cities on the Mediterranean became   ports of
call for international commerce. The access to the sea made
Cilicia an important intermediary between Europe and the
Middle East exposing the country to the tides of political movements.

A PERIOD OF RECONSTRUCTION

When the Armenians began to migrate to Cilicia they found
the country in need of repair. Most of the castles and citadels

were destroyed by the Arabs, the towns were abandoned, and the villages had become uninhabitable. The seemingly endless bloody strife left many farms desolate. The Armenians found the Greeks, Arabs, and Jews living in dilapidated shacks under the walls of ruined castles and conducting a nomadic life with no political or social organization. During the turbulent period in which Cilicia changed hands between the Moslems and the Byzantines, the administrative system of the province collapsed and the population was driven away as slaves.

Under the leadership of their princes the Armenians made the cities in Cilicia great cities in the Near East. Seaports were reopened, castles were built, churches were erected, canals were dug to provide water for farming, the land was cultivated, and commercial activity began to flourish. Soon there were orchards in river valleys and sheep and cattle pastured on the adjacent steppes. An abundant forest growth on the mountain slopes provided timber for building. Private enterprise began to develop. Armenian merchants pooled their resources to make international commerce possible. Many became wealthy and their fortunes rivaled those of the aristocratic families of Byzantium. Silver deposits in the Taurus Mountains were mined to mint coins for currency.

While the Armenians lost their homeland on the plains of Mount Ararat, the elements of their civilization along with the heritage of their national glory were not lost. They preserved their social and cultural institutions and brought their religious concepts to the new soil. The Catholicos, the spiritual leader of the people, transferred his ecclesiastical See from Greater Armenia to Cilicia. In time the transplanted Armenian culture, blended and harmonized with the culture of the west, promoted the coalescence into a strong organization of political structure. As Greater Armenia was a corridor of passage between east and west, Cilicia also became a corridor of passage between Asia Minor and Europe. It was then that the Europeans came marching in on their way to the Holy Land.

THE MARCH OF THE CRUSADERS

Alexius I Comnenus rose to power in Constantinople in 1081 and immediately began to revitalize the Byzantine military and economic resources. For the next one hundred years his son,

John II and grandson, Michael I, will rule the Empire during one of the most trying periods of Byzantine history. The Armenians gained complete control of Cilicia during the reign of Alexius I. The Byzantine Emperor could not contain the Armenian expansion in Cilicia because of more serious external problems that threatened the very existence of his Empire. The Crusade fervor had gained momentum in Europe and armies were being mobilized by the kings and princes of the Holy Roman Empire to liberate the Holy Land of Christianity from the Moslem rule.

The military operation of the Crusade began in 1096 and ended in 1291 when the last Crusader was driven out to the sea by the more powerful and fanatic forces of Islam. For almost two hundred years men from Europe and the Levant fought for control of sacred places where Christ lived and died and Mohammed rose to heaven. Nothing was achieved and nothing was gained. The religious military movement attempted to change the face of the Middle East but came to be taken as one of the darkest ventures of the political history of Medieval Europe, reflecting the ferocious barbarism of the times, conducted in the name of religion. Men fought and prayed to kill men and sought God's help to save their souls and to kill more. Perhaps the period is best characterized by a Latin inscription on a mosque, which was once a church in Palestine, carved by an unknown Crusader of centuries past, exhorting to the men in the future, "To men who pass along this street, I beg you to pray for my soul".

For little Armenia the march of the Crusaders gave a breathing space for the people and an opportunity to build a political organization that will endure for three hundred years.

THE FIRST CRUSADE

To restore the fortunes of Byzantium, after the debacle of Manzikert, Emperor Alexius I appealed to Pope Urban II urging him to help drive the Turks out of Asia Minor. In 1095 at a Council at Clermont, Pope Urban II, the most ardent advocate of the Christian cause, called on Christians everywhere to rally to help the Eastern Church in its plight against the Turks and liberate the Holy Land from Moslem occupation.

The Pope's sermon was the galvanizing force which helped create a wave of enthusiasm throughout Europe. The first Crusade was organized by a monk, Peter the Hermit, whose fiery sermons moved men to take the cross. The army that he mobilized, however, was a motley group of poor peasants and undisciplined derelicts, who were the victims of a severe economic depression then prevailing in Europe. Earlier the political strife in the European continent had wrought havoc, accompanied with the spread of epidemics against which men stood powerless. The rich had become richer and the poor had become poorer by the exploitation by the rich. It was the poor who were mostly driven to take the cross for the Crusade. They were promised that their souls would travel straight to heaven with a Papal commitment of absolution and remission of their sins. For many, joining the Crusades was a relief from their depressed economic condition. Not all were moved by spiritual motives, however. There were many who came along to organize raiding parties for plunder.

A force of 35,000 headed by Peter the Hermit crossed the Byzantine territory and reached Constantinople. Emperor Alexius I was disappointed to see the quality of the fighting force that European monarchs had managed to put together. He warned the leaders of the group not to proceed further towards the Turkish territory until they received reinforcements from Europe. Ignoring the Emperor's advice, the Crusaders advanced towards Nicaea which was then part of the Seljuk Sultanate. With inhuman barbarism, they attacked the Turkish villages, raided, plundered, and pillaged, and initiated a pitiless massacre of men, women, and children. Soon a large Turkish garrison, headed by the Turkish Sultan arrived from the east, attacked the Christian soldiers, slaughtered most of them and gave freedom only to those who were willing to abjure their Christian faith. The Christian force of 35,000 was decimated with little loss to the Turkish army. A few survivors were saved by the Byzantine troops who placed them on a boat and shipped them back to Europe.

The news of Peter the Hermit's catastrophic defeat reached Europe during the summer of 1096. An angry wave of enthusiasm began to spread in France, Germany, and Italy. Religious zealots took the cross for the Crusade. Armies and commando units began to mobilize with no cohesive unity of leadership.

The resulting military force had no supreme commander. Each
state had its own separate unit headed by a commanding
prince. This was not uncommon in Medieval Europe. The
emerging nations of Europe rarely expressed their desire for
unanimity and throughout history the European leaders found
themselves ready to embrace schismatic movements. While the
Church attempted to bind the various nationalities together under the supreme spiritual leadership of the Pope, the so-called
Holy Roman Empire had many centrifugal forces that produced
a history of squabbles among the various Christian nations. The
Pope had no power to unite the Christian faithful into a single
corporate entity.

The leaders of this Crusade were Godfrey of Bouillion, the
Duke of Lower Lorraine, a gracious and charming prince, who
somehow had blackmailed the local Jews in his duchy to finance the operation of his crusading movement, Godfrey's
brother, Baldwin, a ruthless man and an opportunist, who used
the Crusade for his own purposes, and Behemund of Taranto, a
violent man who spread horror as he advanced with his army
towards Constantinople.

The leaders of the First Crusade congregated in Constantinople with their private armies in the summer of 1096 on their
way to the Holy Land. This was more than Emperor Alexius I
expected from Europe. His original intent, when he made the
appeal for military aid, was to expell the Turks from Asia Minor. He never anticipated that his appeal to the Pope would
evoke such a wave of enthusiasm for the leaders of Europe to
mobilize a crusading army to liberate the Holy Land. Byzantium did not particularly cherish the idea of having European
troops on its soil. The leaders of Constantinople had always
claimed to have the exclusive responsibiity of liberating the
Holy Land themselves, without foreign intervention, since the
Holy Land was regarded as the former provinces of Byzantium.
They claimed to have the possession of a divine power to protect and defend Christendom in the east.

The Pope on his part had another motive in promoting the
organization of such a large undertaking. Besides liberating the
Holy Land he also looked to Constantinople as another city to
be liberated. He wished to bring Byzantium under the Roman
Catholic fold. As the schism between the two churches widened, the papacy in Rome began to press its claim to universal

Christian leadership, asserting that all Christian churches in the world should be subject to Rome's spiritual primacy.

This was too much for the Byzantine Emperor to swallow, but being a man skilled in international diplomacy, the Emperor went along and played the part of hosting this impressive cavalcade of European leaders in his capital. He was, however, able to exact a commitment of sorts from the leaders of the Crusade that former Byzantine colonies, when recaptured by the Crusaders, should be returned to Byzantium. In return, the Emperor promised to supply the Christian soldiers with war materiel and supply.

Hostility soon developed between the Byzantines and Europeans. There was a wide difference of culture between the two. Byzantium was old and civilized, the European nations were newly organized and immensely uncivilized. Upon their arrival in Constantinople the adventurous Crusaders were lured by Byzantium's unlimited wealth. While their primary purpose was to fight the Moslems, they were also interested in raiding and plundering the Byzantine towns and villages.

During the reign of Alexius I Comnenus, Byzantium had become enormously prosperous. Armenian and Jewish merchants were actively engaged to sell Byzantine products to the newly emerging nations around the Mediterranean Sea. There were special trading concessions made to Venetian and Genoese shipping concerns to carry Byzantine goods to the west.

The prosperity of Byzantium, however, was only the veneer covering up serious political and economic problems facing the nation. Byzantium's continued reliance on Italian shipping companies eventually made the Byzantine Greeks lose their dominance in international trade, making the Byzantine currency weaker in the world market. Politically the Empire was in a state of exhaustion. The deterioration of the Byzantine authority in the Balkans and the collapse of the Byzantine power in Western Asia had seriously impaired the government in Constantinople. The government failed to maintain a coherent body of administrators of Greek race. Most of the highest positions in government were held by Armenians and non-Greeks. Politically the Empire was surrounded by enemies. In the west there were the Normans and the Franks, in the north there were the Petzenegs and in the east there were the Seljuks who had by now occupied a large territorial area long believed to be the

source of Byzantine strength.   Militarily the Byzantine forces
were well equipped and organized but the army was generally
composed of foreign mercenaries whose loyalty to the imperial
throne was questionable.   The blood of the military had become diluted with that of aliens, which gradually sapped the
vitality of the imperial leadership.

Faced with these problems at home and abroad Emperor
Alexius was eager to see the European Crusaders leave Byzantium and get on with the work of crusading towards Jerusalem,
which was nearly one thousand miles away.

THE CRUSADERS IN ARMENIAN CILICIA

The Crusaders' first task was to capture the city of Nicaea from
the Seljuk Turks.   Sultan Kilij-Arslan of the Seljuks was away on
a military expedition to fight the Danishment Turks for the over-
lordship of Greater Armenia.   The Crusaders surrounded the
city.   The Turks fought ferociously but were forced to retreat
and leave the city to the tender mercies of the Christian troops.
To celebrate their victory the Crusaders went on a rampage.
They cut the heads of thousands of Turks, sacked the city, and
mercilessly put Turkish babies on pikes in front of the principal
buildings of the city.   The journey south proved to be more
treacherous.   The inhospitable climate and the terrain of Anatolia made the movement of the Christian soldiers a formidable
task.   The Anatolian winters were blistery cold and the summers
were stifling hot, humid, and dusty.

Leaving Nicaea behind, the crusading army began to
march towards Armenian Cilicia.   There was an estimated force
of l00,000 troops that needed to be moved as rapidly as possible.   They moved mostly on foot.   Mules and oxcarts were used
to carry the war supplies.   Soon it became a monstrous task of
logistics to feed an army of l00,000 in a territory believed to be
barren and devoid of any plantation.   The task of feeding the
troops had become more difficult by the defeated Turks, who
during their retreat had destroyed the warehouses containing
the food supplies and contaminated the reservoirs of water.
The soldiers began to eat grass roots and chewed bushes to
squeeze moisture to satisfy their thirst.   Thousands died of
starvation.   Horses and mules became weak and were abandoned along the way.   Some leaders were willing to abort the

entire mission. Conditions became worse as they continued to march towards the Armenian territory. The mountain peaks and the difficult terrain made their march increasingly difficult. After weeks of traveling, the army finally reached Armenian Cilicia. The newly established Armenian principality had everything to offer to the suffering soldiers. The Armenians in Cilicia had an abundant supply of food with gardens, streams, and rivers. The cellars were full of wine, the orchards were full of fruits, and the warehouses were full of farm products. It was as if the Crusaders had entered through the gates of paradise.

The arrival of the Crusaders in Armenian Cilicia was the turning point for the entire Christian mission. Armenians took the Crusaders into their homes, gave them clothing, food, and shelter. The Armenian Prince Constantin I immediately began preparations to help the Christian soldiers. He gave them provisions of war, horses, arms, and troops. The Armenian contribution was so significant that centuries later Pope Gregory XIII will declare that "no nation came more readily to the aid of the Crusaders than the Armenians". Had the Armenians failed to provide help, the subsequent history of the Crusade might have been entirely different.

In appreciation of the Armenian help the leaders of the First Crusade bestowed the title of Baron on Constantin I. This immediate alliance and friendship between the Armenians and the Europeans brought cultural fusion and intermarriages. A leader of the Crusade married Constantin's daughter, and Baldwin, the brother of Geoffrey of Bouillion, married Constantin's niece. The Crusaders stayed in Cilicia for a long time. Strategically located, the Armenian principality offered a fortified base of operation to the Crusaders to launch raids at will against the Turks in Anatolia and make preparations for their march towards the Holy Land.

THE ATTACK ON ANTIOCH

The Armenian prince Toros I succeeded Constantin I in 1099 and ruled Cilicia until 1129. With the help of Baldwin's Crusaders Toros was able to drive the Greeks and Turks out of northern Cilicia. He made the city of Sis the capital of Cilicia and initiated a vigorous campaign to build churches, castles, and monasteries. He encouraged the Armenians in the northeast to migrate to Cilicia and in time introduced a system of government to rule the newly acquired homeland of his people.

Meanwhile proceeding east towards the Euphrates, Baldwin and his crusading army reached Edesa and with the help of Prince Toros I, liberated the city and massacred most of the Turkish inhabitants. Baldwin declared himself the King of Edesa, thus becoming the first Crusader to establish a kingdom in the east.

After receiving ammunition and provisions for war from the Armenians, the crusading armies proceeded south towards Antioch. To the Christians, Antioch was one of the most important centers in the east. Founded by the successor of Alexander the Great, Antioch had been a target for invasion for 2,000 years. Successive waves of military forces of Persians, Armenians, Greeks, Romans, Arabs, and Turks, had taken the city. Now it was the turn of the Crusaders. For the Seljuk Turks who were the new rulers of the city Antioch was a strategic location for their military operation against the Christians.

The leaders of the Crusade waited before the walls of Antioch for new reinforcements from Armenian Cilicia. Their plan was to surround the city, cut the Turkish lines of communication and eventually climb over the walls and storm the city. They waited before the walls for three months. By Christmas time they ran out of ammunition and supplies. Many died of famine. Others sought refuge among the native peoples of Syria. A group of Flemish Crusaders resorted to cannibalism. They began to collect abandoned Turkish corpses, boiled them in water and ate them. Others chased live Turkish babies, killed them, boiled them in a pot, and ate them for supper.

By the middle of January 1098 the Crusaders found themselves in the most desperate situation. The long siege of Antioch had demoralized the troops and frequent attempts to occupy the city proved fruitless. To break the deadlock, Behemund, a leader of the Crusade, initiated secret contacts with the leading Armenian general of the Turkish army inside the city walls. Through his intelligence network he learned that the Armenian general wanted to exact vengeance from his Turkish rulers because his wife had been raped by his superiors. Through his contacts, Behemund persuaded the Armenian general to betray his masters. During the night, when the Turks were asleep, the Armenian opened the great gates of Antioch and allowed the Crusaders to pour into the city. As soon as the Crusaders entered the city the Armenian inhabitants of Antioch joined the Christians and began a wholesale massacre of the Turks. No one was spared. Men, women, and children were decapitated and their bodies tossed over the cliffs. In a few hours the streets were full of Turkish bodies and blood flowed in torrents. While seeking help from Jesus and crossing themselves constantly, the Christian soldiers burned mosques, mutilated the bodies of young women, and cut the throats of the old. As in the case of Edesa, the leaders of the Crusades refused to hand over Antioch to Byzantium and began to rule the city as an independent Christian state.

THE MARCH TOWARD JERUSALEM

The Christian conquests in the south of the Armenian territory resulted in a permanent settlement. With two kingdoms behind them, the Crusaders felt secure in their newly acquired territory. They swept into Palestine from Syria after occupying Tripoli, Beirut, Tyre, Acre, and Jaffa, and proceeded south towards their final destination, Jerusalem. They reached Bethlehem and placed their flag over the Church of the Nativity. From there they could see Jerusalem in the distance. Within a few days the Crusaders' war cry echoed at the gate of Jerusalem, but strong fortifications erected by the Arabs earlier, prevented them from entering the city. The Christians began to fight and attempted to climb over the walls but failed to storm Jerusalem. The situation of the Moslems inside the city, however, gradually became hopeless. They were cut off from food and water supply and were exposed to Christian assault on all sides.

After several weeks of siege the Crusaders finally tore down the gates of Jerusalem and poured into the streets. The Moslem residents ran towards the Dome of the Rock, the holiest place of Islam in Jerusalem, and took shelter inside the sacred Mosque of al-Aqsa. The Crusaders chased the Moslems and began massacring men, women, and children indiscriminately. The Armenians in the city provided the Crusaders with food and shelter. The Jewish inhabitants, however, did not fare well. They were chased by the Christian soldiers to their synagogues and were burned alive when the synagogues were set on fire. The Crusaders sacked the Jewish temples and desecrated

the graves of the prophets. The streets of Jerusalem were littered with dead bodies. The entire city was given over to plunder and rampages. The odors emitted by unburied corpses
compelled the Crusaders to withdraw to the Christian section of
the city for a while. After completing their wholesale butchery,
the Crusaders went to the Church of the Holy Sepulchre to give
thanks to God for their triumphant victory. The year was 1099.
After years of struggle, the cross finally supplanted the crescent
in Jerusalem. The Crusaders elected Geoffrey of Bouillion as
the King of Jerusalem and the defender of the Holy Sepulchre.
Geoffrey ruled the Holy City until 1100. Upon his death his
brother Baldwin I, the King of Edesa, became King of Jerusalem and ruled the city for eighteen years with his Armenian wife
as the Queen.

CULTURAL DIFFUSION

The first Crusaders were mostly Normans and French. Their
contacts with the Armenians offered the Armenians the opportunity to develop and refine their conceptions about the world
in the west. This was the second time that the Armenians were
coming in contact with the men from Europe. The first was
during the period of the Roman occupation of Armenia. The
Crusaders showed an appreciation of statecraft by making interracial marriages with the daughters of Armenian nobles. A new
progeny of Armenian children were born, and the descendants
of these mixed marriages came to be known as *Poulains*.

The amicable relationship between Armenians and the
Europeans had a beneficial effect on both cultures. The Crusaders spoke French and the Armenians acquired French words
in their vocabulary. In the area of art, science, and intellect,
however, the uncultured Crusaders had much to learn and very
little to offer. They came to a country where the people were
already rich in memories of an enduring civilization which extended over 1,500 years of recorded history.

While the newcomers were able to establish themselves as
a military force, they were gradually assimilated to the patterns
of Armenia's culture and elements of its civilization. Geographically located, Cilicia represented the meeting point between east
and west. The Armenians were adopted to act as intermediaries to transmit Greco-Roman-Moslem culture. The Armenian

architects and craftsmen traveled around the Mediterranean world to help the Christians build their churches and castles. Most of the Crusaders were unable to read or write and very few had the basic skills of farming and agriculture. Some were half-savage barbarians who satisfied their appetite by boiling live Moslems for their supper, baptised their babies with saliva, ate wolf meat, and drank their own urine. Unlike the Roman soldiers of centuries past, the Franks and Normans of the Crusade had no exposure to Greco-Roman culture. They were brought up as Christians but seemed to have no feelings for conventional morality and decency. While in Cilicia they learned how to bathe and how to stay clean and acquired new tastes in food. The Armenians were known as the culinary experts of the Middle East. Most of the Crusaders had not seen or eaten some of the fruits that Armenians had the expertise to grow and cultivate. Plums, peaches, even grapes were novelties to some of the Europeans. Armenian merchants began to export apricots and a type of onion called scallion, which acquired its name from Ascalon, a city in Palestine. The Armenian merchants became instrumental in introducing the Arabic *zukkar* to the Crusaders which delighted the western palate and came to be known as sugar in the west. Sugar replaced honey which had been used as the principal sweetener for European foods.

The Armenians helped the Crusaders reclaim land for cultivation by the establishment of irrigation systems. As a result great stocks of food supply were accumulated, making the Christian occupied lands self-sufficient territories. Trade began to flourish and the Armenian seaports brought goods from Europe.

DISSENSION WITH THE CRUSADERS

The territorial expansion of Armenian Cilicia was accompanied by an increase in military power. Cilicia was changing rapidly into an organized state in which members of the Armenian nobility began the process to revitalize the nation's resources for a more cohesive and urbanized society.

Toros I died in 1129 and was succeeded by his brother, Levon I, who reigned over the Armenian principality until 1137. Levon extended the Armenian territory further by annexing large Byzantine land tracts to Armenian Cilicia. As Armenians

proceeded with their task of consolidation to establish a semblance of political equilibrium, relations with their European
allies became uneasy. The Crusaders began to interfere in the
internal affairs of the Armenian government. They wanted the
Armenians to vacate some strongholds around the Gulf of Alexandretta and the Fort of Savouantikar. In 1136 Raymond de
Poitiers, the Prince of Antioch, ordered Levon to surrender the
fort but Levon refused. Raymond then lured Levon into a trap
and held him prisoner for two months. The Armenian prince
gained his freedom after agreeing to surrender the fort.

After gaining his freedom Levon I marshalled a powerful
army in Cilicia and attacked Raymond's forces, recaptured the
lost territories and proceeded south to attack Antioch. The hostilities between the Armenians and the Crusaders were ended
by a mutual alliance in 1137 signed primarily to launch a
combined attack against the Byzantine Emperor, John II Comnenus, who had begun to press the Crusaders to hand Antioch
over to Byzantium as originally promised by the leaders of the
First Crusade.

In order to proceed to Antioch the Byzantines needed to
pass through the Armenian territory. Although Cilicia had
been the effective limit of Byzantine control, the Byzantines regarded the possession of Cilicia vital to Byzantium's security.
Aided by the Turks, the Greeks invaded Cilicia and took the
Plain of Adana and the Gulf of Alexandretta. Prince Levon surrendered himself to the Byzantines who dragged him in chains
to Constantinople along with his son, Roupen. Levon died in
prison in 1141 and Roupen was murdered a few years later. With
the conquest of Cilicia the way to Antioch was now cleared.
John II Comnenus occupied Antioch and forced Raymond de
Poitiers to pledge allegiance to Constantinople. For the next
eight years Cilicia remained under Byzantine rule. One of Levon's sons, Toros II, who was held captive in Constantinople
with his father, fled the Byzantine capital on board a Venetian
vessel headed for Cyprus. From Cyprus Toros proceeded to
Antioch and with the help of Raymond de Poitiers reconquered
Cilicia and threw the Greeks out of the Armenian territory.

THE SECOND CRUSADE

Emperor John II Comnenus died in 1142 and his son, Manuel I
succeeded him to the throne. Meanwhile in Europe the Chris-

tian leaders were alarmed by the increasing power of the Turks in the Middle East. The Turks had already taken Aleppo from the Crusaders and Edesa from the Armenians and were threatening to march on Jerusalem. Christianity was in trouble in the east. Pope Eugenius III made an appeal to kings and princes to organize another Crusade to help their brothers in the east. A new Crusade was hastily mobilized by Conrad III, the King of Germany and Louis VII, the King of France. With their private armies the two leaders proceeded towards the Levant in 1147. They arrived in Constantinople but their march towards Jerusalem became a nightmare. Before reaching Armenian Cilicia the Seljuk Turks were successful in decimating a large portion of the Crusading force. The roads were hazardous and the troops were always short of food and water. Icy winds, storms, and seemingly incessant Turkish onslaught delayed their march. Thousands died on the road and the survivors finally reached Antioch in late spring 1148.

After spending several months in the north, the army of the Second Crusade finally made its way to Jerusalem. In a conference held with King Baldwin III of Jerusalem, Kings Conrad, and Louis made a decision to attack Damascus where Moslem ruler, Nur-ed-Din, had become increasingly powerful, threatening to take over Jerusalem and drive the Crusaders to the sea. In a battle fought near Damascus Nur-ed-Din's Turkish army annihilated the Crusaders by killing most of them and forcing the survivors to retreat to Jerusalem. The heavy defeat inflicted on the Christians was a catastrophic blunder by the leaders of the Second Crusade. To avoid further disgrace and embarrassment King Conrad left the Holy Land and returned home by way of Constantinople. King Louis of France followed him a few months later. The Christians in the west blamed the Byzantines for their misfortunes. Some thought that perhaps a new Crusade should be organized, but this time to attack Byzantium itself and bring Constantinople under European control.

THE CONQUEST OF CYPRUS

The debacle of the Second Crusade changed the complexion and the prospects of the entire movement. It helped the Turkish leader, Nur-ed-Din, strengthen his position in the east. He had by now captured most of northern Syria and was able to unite the forces of Islam to organize a unified attack against the Christians in the east. The Fatamid Caliphate of Egypt had weakened and a dynastic war had created a chaotic stalemate in Cairo. Amid chaos and anarchy a Crusade leader by the name of Reynold of Chatillon attempted to exploit the resentment felt by Armenians towards the Byzantine Greeks, and decided to invade the Island of Cyprus. This was an unusual turn of events. Cyprus had nothing to do with the struggle with Moslems. Its inhabitants were mostly Christians and the island technically was part of the Byzantine Empire. The adventurous Reynold wanted to build a stronghold against the Byzantines and establish an independent kingdom in Cyprus to promote his political aggrandizement.

In 1158 a Crusade ship carrying Latin and Armenian troops landed in Cyprus, and immediately began to rampage. The Armenians, together with the Europeans, indiscriminately slaughtered the Greek inhabitants of the island. This was an Armenian response to Greek atrocities in the past. The murder of thousands of Armenians by the Greeks in Ani, a hundred years earlier, was still fresh in their minds. The news of the Armenian rampage in Cyprus reached Constantinople and Emperor Manuel was infuriated. He sought revenge by invading Armenian Cilicia with a force of 50,000.

Toros' brother Stepane mobilized a disciplined force and began to chase the Byzantine troops out of the country. The Armenian troops were so powerful that the Byzantine governor of Tarsus had to resort to coercion. He invited Stepane to a feast on a pretense to sign a peace treaty. During the festivities he ordered his aides to assassinate the Armenian prince. After hearing the news of his brother's murder, Toros II ordered a wholesale massacre of Greeks in Cilicia. An all-out war between Byzantium and Cilicia was averted, however, by the personal mediation of the King of Jerusalem.

THE RISE OF A NEW POWER IN EGYPT

The unwieldy Caliphate of the Fatamids in Egypt was in a desperate political situation. The young Caliph was engaged in passionate homosexual affairs and had left the reign of the government in the hands of a powerful Armenian Vizier. The Fatamids had risen to power in 909 as a Shiite challenge to the religious leadership of the Abbasids in Baghdad. For two hundred years they controlled Egypt and North Africa. At the time of the administration of the Armenian Vizier the Fatamids had brought Egypt to a new height of prosperity and splendor. With his compulsive authority, the Armenian had pushed himself to a status comparable in dignity to that of the Caliph himself. While he proved to be an effective leader, forces beyond his control prevented him to continue his reign. He was murdered by his mistress and was succeeded by his son, who in turn was murdered after ruling the country for only fifteen months.

Successive murders and assassinations left Egypt powerless and prey to all-powerful Nur-ed-Din in Syria. In 1164 Nur-ed-Din sent an army to Egypt under the command of a Syrian Kurd. The Kurdish general took his nephew along with him, a young man named Saladin, who was destined to become the most dedicated warrior for Islam and the greatest foe of the Crusaders.

The Syrian army advanced towards Egypt in 1167, crossed the Nile, and occupied Egypt. The Fatamid rule crumbled away and Saladin became the absolute ruler of Egypt at the age of 31. As a paragon of chivalry, Saladin was held in high esteem by friends and foe alike. He devoted himself to the banishment of the Shiite movement in Egypt and attempted to stimulate a new wave of Islamic nationalism bent on driving the Europeans to the sea. With Saladin in Egypt the balance of power in the east was now shifted towards Egypt.

Armenians, however, were not affected by the developments in the Arab world. They were preoccupied with their own struggle for political leadership. Toros II abdicated in 1169 in favor of his son, Roupen, a minor, with Baille Thomas acting as regent. Toros' brother, Mleh, assisted by the Turks, invaded Cilicia and seized the principality for himself. Baille Thomas failed to make a show of force. He secretly transported Roupen to Hrumgla, where the See of the Catholicos was located, and placed him, perhaps unwisely, under the care of Catholicos Nerses Shnorhali. Despite precautions taken by church leaders, Roupen was found dead shortly thereafter.

Mleh ruled Cilicia as a vassal of the Seljuk Turks, but he proved to be unable to retain power. He was assassinated by his own men in Sis in 1175. Stepane's son, Roupen was elected head of the Armenian government, and ruled the country in relative calm until 1187. Meanwhile in the south the focus of attention was directed towards Egypt whose leader, Saladin, after consolidating his power prepared to mobilize a force to invade Palestine and bring Jerusalem within the Islamic fold. In 1174 Nur-ed-Din died in Syria and Saladin became the absolute ruler of the Islamic Empire.

ANARCHY IN BYZANTIUM

While Byzantium was regarded as the most important and seemingly the most powerful Christian state in the world, the Crusaders never trusted the Byzantine emperors. They found it fashionable to blame the Byzantine Greeks for their misfortunes and defeats. Promises were made in Constantinople, but they were not often delivered. To effectively direct the Crusade movement the Latins felt it would have been more facile for the Crusaders if they somehow were able to take Byzantium under their wing and run the Empire the way they saw fit. This was an ambitious plan originally conceived by Pope Urban II, when he promoted the movement of the Crusade one hundred years earlier.

The opportunity for a Latin takeover came when Emperor Manuel I Comnenus died in 1180 leaving his twelve year old son to succeed him with his pro-Latin mother, Empress Mary of Antioch, taking over the regency. Resentment against the Latinophile segment of Byzantium soon followed. The people, supported by the Orthodox Church, began preparations to overthrow the pro-Latin regime.

A cousin of Manuel, Andronicus Comnenus, the Governor of Pontus, a man with great charm and elegant manners, made plans to advance towards Constantinople with an organized army under his command. He reached Constantinople in 1182 and began a wholesale butchery of foreigners in the capital. After taking over the reign of the government Andronicus ordered the execution of Empress Mary. He eradicated corruption and attempted to inject a new spirit into the aging and debilitated Empire.

His method of governing, however, proved to be ruthless and brutal. He terrorized the people and ordered the execution of the important members of the Greek nobility. He ordered Armenians living in Constantinople to abandon their language and religious practices and ordered the destruction of Armenian Churches.

The people of Constantinople rose in revolt. An enraged mob attacked the imperial palace, captured Andronicus and literally tore him to pieces. They broke his teeth with hammers, and after cutting off one of his hands, they tied him to the back of a sick camel and paraded in the streets of Constantinople. They put his head in a pot of boiling water and plucked out an eye from its socket. The emperor finally died a hideous death when a soldier plunged a sword into his intestines. His tragic death marked the beginning of the end. From this point on Byzantium will cease to be a world power. Andronicus was succeeded by a man who proved to be feeble and incompetent, making Byzantium an open target for the Crusaders. The Latins will now be ready to invade Constantinople but new developments in the south postponed their march on Constantinople.

THE THIRD CRUSADE

The collapse of the Byzantine power helped Saladin consolidate his power in the Islamic east. With no effective Byzantine force threatening his authority, Saladin began to expand his rule to territories previously owned by the Byzantines. Before long his Empire stretched from Egypt in the south to the Euphrates in the north. In the process of consolidating his power he eliminated all his rivals in the Islamic Empire.

In 1187 Saladin won a brilliant victory against the superior forces of Christianity and captured Jerusalem with ease. The crescent replaced the cross and the prestige of Islam was on the rise once again. Unlike any other Moslem warrior, however, Saladin, in winning his battles, acted with justice and humanity and proved to be one of the most noble adversaries of Christianity and the greatest champion for the Islamic cause.

When news of the Moslem conquest of Jerusalem reached Europe, Pope Urban III died of a heart seizure. People everywhere greeted the news with horror and despair. The new Pope, Gregory VIII, immediately issued an appeal for a new Crusade to liberate Jerusalem. German Emperor Frederick Barbarossa responded and began preparations to lead a third Crusade. A vigorous man for his age of seventy, Barbarossa took the cross in the spring of 1188 and began marching towards the Holy Lands with an organized army of 150,000 men.

As the army of the Third Crusade began their march towards the Armenian territory, the political situation in Cilicia had improved considerably. This was the first time in many decades that the Armenians found themselves living in a period of political tranquility. Prince Roupen had abdicated in 1187 in favor of his son, Levon II. A skilled diplomat and a brilliant ruler, Levon vied for an Armenian kingship. His most ambitious objective was to establish an Armenian kingdom in Cilicia and restore the Cilician territory to its original extent. As the king of Armenia he wanted to find a new basis for leadership and act as a broker between Byzantium and the Latin principalities in the east.

Levon headed a delegation of Armenian nobility to welcome Barbarossa to the Armenian soil. As in the past, the Armenians provided the Crusaders with ammunition, food, and supplies. The Pope had written to Levon and the Armenian Catholicos, Grigor IV, urging them to help Barbarossa's army. At a meeting held with the Armenian prince, Barbarossa promised Levon II a royal crown. That promise was not destined to be delivered, however. While swimming in a river in Cilicia, Barbarossa was drowned and all hopes of an Armenian kingship were drowned with him.

With Barbarossa's death the mission of the Third Crusade was doomed to fail. The German Emperor's death came as a shock to the Crusade army. With their leader dead, the great Crusade came to a halt in the Armenian territory. To continue their march and to boost the morale of the troops, the leaders of the Crusade decided to place Barbarossa's body in a casket full of vinegar and carry it with them during their march toward the Holy Land.

ARMENIAN DELEGATION IN CONSTANTINOPLE

The Byzantine Emperor sent word to Armenian Cilicia that Levon's ambition for a crown could be achieved if the Armenians accepted the Greek Orthodox faith. A delegation of Armenian clergy arrived in Constantinople to discuss the religious issue. The talks, however, became unproductive and fruitless. The head of the Armenian delegation upon his return home submitted the following report to Levon - "We found the Greeks ignorant, rude, and dull, obstinate like the Jews. We were grieved in our spiritual good will, and returned home confused and disappointed".

Levon, unable to find a political accommodation with the Byzantines turned his attention to Rome. The Pope welcomed the idea of an Armenian kingdom in Cilicia to serve as a base of operation for the crusading movement in the Near East. It was understood in western circles that Byzantium's days were numbered. The west wanted Byzantium to be replaced with Latin rule to prevent the Turks from entering Europe through the Bosporus. To get the royal crown Levon appealed to the German Emperor, Henry VI, who had succeeded Barbarossa. He sent ambassadors to the Pope and the Pope sent a legation to Cilicia to discuss political and religious issues.

Conditions were now set for the Latins to place a royal crown on Baron Levon. The Armenians had waited long enough. Levon began his rule as a prince but ended it as one of the greatest kings in the history of his people.

CHAPTER SEVENTEEN

THE KINGDOM OF CILICIA

Prince Levon realized that the establishment of an Armenian monarchy was necessary to legitimize the Armenian presence in Cilicia and ensure the continuity of the political process. From the inception of the Cilician principality the Armenian lords were able to successfully maintain the political stability of the region while playing host for the Crusaders and defending their hordes from Moslem and Byzantine incursions. A new epoch is about to be inaugurated for these transplanted Armenians, an epoch that will mark the most critical test for the nation to survive as a politically independent entity. The monarchy will place the Armenian people in the family of nations and enable Cilicia to act as an intermediary between the Byzantine east and the Latin west. For the next 177 years the Armenian kings had to reckon with the policies of powerful states, some near, some far away, and provide a political direction for their people; a direction that will play a decisive role for the very survival of the nation.

A KINGDOM FINALLY

When Prince Levon was struggling with the problem of establishing a monarchy on the Armenian soil, the Third Crusade was already on its way for a fresh attempt to take control of the holy places in the east. Armenia's alliance with the leaders of the Crusade enabled Levon to achieve his goal to establish a kingship in Cilicia. Levon gradually began to identify himself as the protector of Christianity in the east, and the champion for the Christian cause against the Moslem infidels.

The Third Crusade created new principalities and kingdoms on the eastern shore of the Mediterranean, one of them was the Kingdom of Cyprus, established by King Richard the Lionhearted, the King of England, who occupied the island and installed a Frenchman by the name of Guy de Lusignan as the first occupant of the throne. The occupation of Cyprus caused political dissension between Byzantium and the Latin west. The Byzantines viewed the Crusade as a threat to their Empire, while the Latins viewed the Turkish presence in Asia Minor as a threat to Christianity. The Greeks accepted the Turkish state as a temporary nuisance and refused to organize a military coalition with the Latins to contain the Moslem challenge around the periphery of their Empire. Their arrogant behavior was partly due to religious and ideological differences. As fanatics in Christian orthodoxy the Byzantine emperors refused to accept the doctrines of the Roman Catholic Church and rejected the primacy of the Pope. The pages of subsequent history would have been written differently had the Greeks chosen to pursue a policy of cohesive unity with the rest of the Christian world. Their miscalculations had become apparent. The Turkish wars against Christian strongholds had been more than short term military adventures. The Seljuks had already gained the heartland of Asia Minor and were threatening to cross the Bosporus and enter Europe. The Pope and the Latin leaders were concerned about such an eventuality. It had become obvious by now that Byzantium had outgrown its political framework and the religious issue had consumed the resources of the Empire. Decay and corruption had destroyed the fabric of the society and the transformation of Byzantium from a world power into a regional force had encouraged the Moslems to consolidate their own resources and establish zones of influence on the fringes of the Christian world.

It was, therefore, in the interest of Rome and western states to establish Christian outposts in the east as buffer states to insulate the Christian world from Arab and Turkish encroachments. The political breakdown of Byzantium had made the Greeks unreliable partners in Church's universal struggle against Islam. The Armenians, on the other hand, while maintaining the independence of their Christian faith, had proved to be more de-

pendable allies. As a shrewd statesman, Levon had already begun to strengthen Armenia's political institutions and had won
the good will and support of both the Crusaders and the
crowned heads of Europe.

Conditions were now ripe for Rome to send a crown to
Levon. In a ceremony held on January 6, 1199 in the Cathedral
of Tarsus, Cardinal Conrad of Wittelsbach, the Archbishop of
Mainz, acting as the Legate of the Pope, placed a royal crown
on Prince Levon II in the presence of Catholicos Grigor, bishops, feudal barons, and a great number of knights and foreign
dignitaries. After years of wandering around the outer edges of
their ancestral homeland and continuously grappling with the
task of holding their people together, the Armenian leaders
were finally able to establish a monarchy on the Cilician soil
and reorganize the institutions of their government under the
centralized authority of a king. Prince Levon II will be King
Levon I and his descendants will rule Cilicia for the next 177
years.

ECONOMIC BOOM AND PROSPERITY

The newly established kingdom had to protect itself from a restless world and attempt to preserve its identity as an independent
Christian Kingdom. But the Papal coronation of the Armenian
king had strings attached. The Pope's ulterior motive in sending a crown to Cilicia, was to force the Armenians to accept the
doctrines of the Papacy. Immediately after the coronation ceremonies the Pope's representative in Cilicia advised the newly
minted King and the Armenian Church leaders to accept the
Pope's primacy and begin to celebrate the religious holidays on
the same days as the Roman Church. The differences between
the Armenian Church and the Roman Catholic Church were
dogmatic and quite irreconcilable. The most important issue
that separated the two churches had something to do with the
nature of the Holy Ghost. In 325 the Nicaean Council had
decreed that the Holy Ghost proceeded from the Father. This
was a universally accepted dogma of the Christian world until
the Roman Catholic Church sometime later decided to amend
the dogma and add the words "and the Son", *Filoque*. According to the Roman Catholics, therefore, the Holy Ghost proceeded from the Father and the Son. But the Armenians and the

rest of the Christian world rejected this amended concept. They continued to adhere to the original creed of the Nicaean Council.

Putting aside such religious issues King Levon turned his attention to issues more germane to the administration of his Kingdom. He cultivated a wide range of alliances with the powers surrounding Cilicia. Soon the Caliph of Baghdad and Emperor Alexius III Angelus recognized the Armenian Kingdom and sent diplomatic missions to Cilicia. Levon married the daughter of Amaury de Lusignan, the King of Cyprus. The marriage helped him seal amicable relationships with the Latin principalities of the east.

The almost immediate result of the establishment of the Armenian Kingdom was the regimentation of the Armenian society and the establishment of a political organization based on a system of a centralized government for which the political experience of the Armenian people had furnished the precedent.

King Levon fostered a luxuriant court life based on European traditions and accepted the Latin and French languages as the official languages of the State. He modified the ancient Armenian feudal system and bestowed European titles on the feudal lords. He consolidated various regions of Cilicia and brought the feudal baronies under his jurisdiction with a centralized government in the capital city of Sis. Levon established a supreme court and wrote a constitution separating the church from the state with the Armenian Catholicos empowered to hold his own tribunal on ecclesiastical matters. The king organized trading posts and encouraged commerce to flow through Cilicia linking Europe with Asia. International trade began to flourish and the seaports in Cilicia were reopened to funnel goods. Caravans began to move European goods through Armenian ports, and bring oriental products such as spices, perfumes, soaps, gems, silk, and rugs to Cilicia for exportation to the merchant houses of Venice, Genoa, Pisa, Sicily, and Montpellier. Coastal cities of Armenia were used to transport people between Europe and the Near East. The Christian pilgrims used the seaports of Cilicia on their way to the Holy Land.

The international trading activity made Cilicia prosperous with a share of the revenue going to the nation's treasury. The establishment of a monetary economy in Cilicia and the plentiful circulation of coinage, contributed to this enormous econom-

ic growth. Levon minted coins in gold, silver, and copper, and
instituted a system of credit notes. The Armenian merchants
began to issue letters of credit and lend money at interest. They
acted as distributing agents offering clearing house facilities to
European merchant bankers. The king introduced a standard-
ized system of weights and measures to promote economic unity with the rest of the world. City republics of Italy established
consular offices in Cilicia and Latin bankers opened branch offices in Sis, Tarsus, and Adana.

This was indeed a great period of economic boom and
prosperity marking a new phase of political and economic
achievements paralleling that of the Kingdom of Ani. The period also marked the Armenian commercial supremacy promoted and organized by the King himself who will go down in
history as Levon the Magnificent. As the architect of a new
epoch Levon successfully welded Cilicia into a strong state and
helped his nation move towards the center of the political spectrum between Byzantium and Latin Europe. The spectrum of
international politics will soon be changed, however, by a new
tide from Europe threatening to shake the very foundation of
the Byzantine Empire.

THE FOURTH CRUSADE

Frustrated with the ineptitude of Byzantium's government and
its reluctance to help the Latins to take over the Holy Land, the
Roman Catholic Church decided to organize another Crusade,
this time to invade Byzantium itself and bring the Church of the
east under Rome's superintendence. This was the original intent of Pope Urban II during the organization of the First Crusade. It was Innocent III who, after occupying the Papal throne
in 1198, finally made Urban's dream come true. A gifted politician and expert in military affairs, Innocent became a dedicated
protagonist of Urban's doctrine of making the Papal supremacy
accepted throughout the Christian world.

To attain his goal the Pope began to marshall the resources under his command and organize the Fourth Crusade
without the military assistance from the kings of Europe. The
military campaign without the help of the royal families required a great deal of money. Negotiations were made with the
Doge in Venice to help finance the operation. The Doge, a

cunning old man by the name of Enrico Dandolo, agreed to transport the Crusaders to the east using the Venetian merchant vessels. To legitimize the operation a suggestion was made to bring along the Byzantine Prince, Alexius Angelus, who earlier had fled from Constantinople and sought refuge in Europe after his father, the Emperor, had been deposed and thrown into jail. The Doge's plan was to capture Constantinople, install Alexius on the Byzantine throne under a Latin mandate, with the understanding that after having access to the Byzantium's treasury, Alexius will reimburse him the entire cost of financing the Crusade. The idea suited the schemes of Pope Innocent III, who in turn was promised that Alexius, after occupying the imperial throne, would bring the Byzantine Church under the supremacy of the Roman Catholic Church and end the schism between the two principal divisions of the Christian world.

In the summer of 1202 a large flotilla of Crusaders sailed from the lagoon of Venice headed for Constantinople. The ships dropped anchor within the proximity of the Byzantine capital and the Crusaders set up tents under the walls of the Byzantine capital. The ruling Emperor, threatened by this formidable army from Europe, fled the capital, taking with him most of the treasures of the empire and seeking refuge with the Seljuk Sultan of Iconium. With no leadership in the Byzantine Empire the Greek aristocrats allowed the Latins to enter the city and install Alexius Angelus on the Byzantine throne.

The puppet Emperor soon discovered, however, that the imperial treasury was completely empty. In order to honor his commitment to the Doge he began to impose oppressive taxes on the people of the Empire. He proved unable to hold power. The people eventually rose in revolt, seized control of the government, captured Alexius, and after strangling him to death, placed a nobleman on the Byzantine throne.

The revolt prompted the Latins to initiate a wholesale massacre. In April, 1204, 20,000 Venetian troops poured in the city and began to slaughter men, women, and children. They pillaged the city mercilessly and took the precious relics from the imperial palace, churches, and monasteries. French priests brought their mules and let them urinate on the holy altars of the Byzantine churches. The Venetians raped nuns on the street and crushed the skulls of Greek infants against the pavement. The Latins sacked palaces, monasteries, and libraries.

They tortured the members of the upper class by dismemberment and carried away their treasures to Venice as plunder.
They tortured the head of the Byzantine Church and placed a
prostitute on the Patriarchal throne in Hagia Sophia. Before
concluding their savage orgy they set fire to the art treasures
which for centuries had adorned the glory of Byzantium.

For Latins this was a striking military accomplishment no
matter how bestial and savage the assault may have been. But
for Byzantines it marked the end of the Greek rule and the beginning of an era in which immediate decisions had to be made
for the survival of the Byzantine civilization. The Latins placed
a Frenchman, Baldwin of Flanders, on the Byzantine throne.
Baldwin received the formal submission of the Byzantine
princes, but there were many who chose to flee rather than to
submit to the Latin rule.

When they occupied Constantinople the Latins expected
that the removal of the Byzantine Emperor and the installation
of the Frenchman on the throne would mean the end of Byzantium as a political entity. They had miscalculated the Byzantine
zeal to survive. Most of the Byzantine princes fled the capital,
joined the deposed Emperor, set up shop in Nicaea, and organized a government in exile. The Europeans soon realized that
real power rested on the people who had little interest in the
unification of the Church and regarded the Latin occupation of
their capital as an insult to their dignity. It soon became apparent that eight hundred years of Byzantine tradition could not be
wiped out by a cruel assault into the heartland of Byzantium.

Commercially, the military occupation of Constantinople
suited the Venetians well. The reign allowed them to monopo-
lize the entire eastern trade and establish new commercial colonies. They failed to preserve a continuity in commerce,
however, since most of the merchants regarded their enigmatic
rule of Byzantium as an interim situation. The Latin occupation
brought economic absolutism as the Venetians failed to maintain a system of banking.

The Latin presence in Constantinople placed the Armenians in a rather tenuous position. As a skilled diplomat King
Levon wanted to stay aloof and continue to maintain an amicable relationship with both antagonists in their struggle for the
legitimacy of power in the north of the Cilician borders. A con-
cord with the Latins and a partnership with the Greeks were

achieved when Levon signed a commercial treaty with the Venetians in Constantinople, gave his niece in marriage to the newly crowned Byzantine Emperor in Nicaea, and wedded his daughter Rita to John Brienne, the King of Jerusalem; thus establishing a multifaceted alliance with the powers surrounding Cilicia.

KING HETOUM I

Before he died, King Levon designated his younger daughter, Zabel, to be the successor to his throne. He died in 1219 and since Zabel was only an infant, Baron Constantin of the Hetoumian dynasty was appointed as her guardian. Seven years later, in 1226, when Zabel was 12 years old, Constantin arranged a marriage of Zabel to his son, Hetoum. Hetoum was the scion of a wealthy family, strikingly handsome with intellectual capacity on the order of a genius. His ability to grasp international politics will chart the future direction of the Armenian people. He was destined to have one of the most picturesque careers in the history of Armenia with a flair for heroic adventure. He will rule Cilicia for forty years. But during the first twenty seven years Hetoum will share the throne with his wife, Zabel.

By now Cilicia had grown into a powerful state by exploiting its strategic position between the Latins and Byzantium. In the political turbulence that followed the occupation of Constantinople, the Armenians searched for a power strong enough to guarantee the integrity of their borders and secure a political autonomy for Cilicia. But all these considerations were soon put aside because the Near East was about to experience a tragedy on a colossal scale making the period one of the bloodiest in the history of man.

THE RISE OF THE MONGOLS

The ferocious Mongols came on the horizon of man's history in the Thirteenth century. Their country in central Asia was a land of hills and mountains with treeless steppes and a flat wilderness broken only by mountain ranges. Nomadic in character the Mongols lived as hunters and stock raisers. They hunted animals and lived a wandering life and constantly changed their habitat in search of food. By the turn of the millennium they were forced to establish a new pattern of life and began to move west along the historical route of caravan trade as the steppes of Asia failed to support the growing population of these nomads.

The Mongols regarded themselves as the chosen people sent by god to punish men for their sins. Their religion was based on the universal forces of nature. They revered the open sky as the source of supernatural qualities, perhaps because living in tents as nomads they looked to the sky for their guidance and considered it as the arbiter of their action. They called the sky *Tengri*, their god, and worshipped it in open air with services conducted by a powerful priestly class called the *Shamans*.

JENGIS KHAN

Mongolia emerged in the pages of history as the country of Jengis Khan, a man with immense military prowess and administrative ability. He was able to unite the various Turkic and Mongolian tribes in central Asia and formed an integral force with an army powerful enough to conquer the neighboring lands during the early years of the Thirteenth century. In 1206, at the age of twenty seven, he was named as the Great Khan or the universal ruler of his people with a claim of hereditary descent from the ancient Khans of Mongolia. During the next twenty one years Jengis will build the largest and the most powerful empire the world has ever known. He destroyed kingdoms and shook the foundation of the ancient world. His followers butchered millions of people wholesale in the most hideous manner and his military campaigns inflicted immense sufferings on the human race, spreading death and destruction with a paralyzing effect on much of the known world. Jengis Khan was a symbol of savage barbarism destined to destroy man's civilization.

As the Scythians of almost two millennia ago, the Mongols began to pour down from the steppes of Asia proceeding towards their more civilized neighbors, bent on plunder and destruction rather than control or possession. They were daring horsemen, who traveled with their wives and children using their bows and lances as their principal weapons. They took care of their prisoners of war by boiling them to death. They levelled cities to the ground and slaughtered farmers to convert their fields into pastures for their horses. As the archenemy of

Islam the Mongols slaughtered millions of Moslems and destroyed everything Islamic with merciless brutality. They destroyed mosques and killed governors of the Islamic provinces by pouring molten gold down their throat.

Proceeding west the Mongols entered Persia and conquered the entire territory bordering the Caspian Sea. In a town called Merv the Jengis hordes massacred 700,000 men, women, and children. The only survivor was an insignificant Turkish tribe whose members fled westward and entered Asia Minor. The world will hear from these nomads a century later as they will take over Asia Minor, coalesce into a Sultanate, assume the name of Ottoman, and design a new destiny for the future of mankind.

MONGOLS ENTER GREATER ARMENIA

Jengis Khan died in 1227 at the age of sixty and was succeeded by one of his four sons, Ogedei. The new Khan inherited the Empire of his father which by now stretched from Korea on the Pacific across the land masses of Asia, to Germany in central Europe. Ogedei built the capital city of Karakorum which will be the center of power in world affairs for the next half century.

In 1230 the Mongol hordes entered Greater Armenia, destroyed what was left of the Armenian towns and villages, and slaughtered thousands of Armenian men, women, and children. They entered Ani, the old capital city of Armenia in 1239, ransacked it and levelled buildings to the ground. A Nestorian priest by the name of Simeon, acting on behalf of the suffering Armenians, traveled to Karakorum and made an emotional appeal to Ogedei to leave the Armenians alone. The Great Khan was touched. He ordered his regional commanders to protect the Armenians and their properties and appointed Simeon as the Governor of Greater Armenia. A period of reconstruction followed in Armenia with peace and tranquility guaranteed by the Mongolian governors. Simeon built churches, monasteries, and hospitals and encouraged the Armenian King of Cilicia to forge a policy of accommodation with the Mongols. Cilicia needed a shield to protect itself from its dangerous foes the Moslems who were incessantly threatening to destroy the little kingdom. Ogedei died and his grandson, Mongke became the Great Khan in 1251.

KING HETOUM TRAVELS TO MONGOLIA

At the time of Ogedei's death, the Near East was in a state of anarchy. Constantinople was still in the hands of the Latins and the Byzantine power of the exiled government in Nicaea had been diminished to the point of extinction. The Crusading principalities, a group of clumsy little states along the coast of the eastern Mediterranean, had lost the will to defend themselves and had been maneuvered by the Moslems into a state of impotence.

But the greatest danger facing Christianity was the Mongol power which was then threatening to extend its influence over Christian Europe. The Mongols had already entered Asia Minor and a series of striking military achievements have made them subjugate states and kingdoms allowing them to gain control of the routes leading into the heartland of Europe. The world was in a turmoil and the Mongols had successfully moved in the direction of being the only great power of the known world.

Such were the affairs of the world when King Hetoum of Armenia decided to take the initiative to travel to Karakorum and seal a pact of alliance with the Great Khan. This was indeed a bold approach and one that will guarantee to secure Armenia's territorial integrity, insulate the country from Islamic terror, help Christianity in general, and allow the Crusaders to prolong their presence in the Middle East. Hetoum's proposed alliance with the Mongols was principally inspired by an indication of a common interest between the Mongols and the Christians. They were both bent to destroy Islam. This unity of purpose played some part in the rise of speculation in western circles that Mongols were about to adopt the Christian faith thus stimulating feverish missionary activity in central Asia. There was a growing influence of Nestorian Christians in Mongolia. Some of the wives of the Mongolian Khans were Christian and there were Christian monasteries, including one founded by the Armenians, and missionary centers scattered all over Mongolia. Since the days of Jengis Khan the Mongols had adopted a policy of tolerance toward Christianity and Mongol leaders had occasionally shown an increasing tendency to favor the Christian faith and help the Crusaders free the Holy Lands from Moslem domination.

Hetoum began his journey in early 1254 with a small group of Armenian dignitaries. He traveled in disguise through Seljuk territory. Moving into the Caucasus the Armenian delegation was offered supplies of beaver furs and food. They rode for weeks over the interminable steppes of Asia, and saw miles and miles of land littered with human bones. Hetoum arrived at the first Mongolian outpost after reaching the outer limits of the civilized world. He showed his credentials to the frontier guards and explained the purpose of his journey. The Mongol governor of the region gave the Armenian delegation guides and horses and an abundant supply of food. But as they continued their journey across the Gobi Desert their food supply was exhausted and they were forced to live on salt and melted snow for the remainder of their journey. They reached Karakorum in September after traveling 3,500 miles and an Armenian monk, who had earlier founded a monastery in Mongolia, escorted King Hetoum to the tent where the Great Khan held court.

After greeting King Hetoum courteously, Mongke motioned the Armenian King to sit next to him on the couch which was covered with gold cloth, silk, and tapestries embroidered with precious stones. They signed a treaty of alliance and friendship and the Great Khan gave Hetoum a letter of enfranchisement for Christian churches everywhere. Mongke pledged not to invade the land of Armenia and promised to give military aid to Hetoum in the event Cilicia was attacked by the Moslems.

This was a diplomatic breakthrough of the first order. King Hetoum's *rapprochement* towards the Mongols gave rise to an aura of great expectations, religious as well as political. His alliance helped stop the tide of the Mongolian invasion of Europe. At the time of Hetoum's journey the Mongolian hordes were already at the borders of Italy and the conviction of the inevitability of a Mongol hegemony was creeping throughout Europe. Had Italy suffered the fate of Western Asia there would have been a strong possibility that the civilized period that began with the Italian Renaissance would have been postponed.

Hetoum's alliance with the Mongols shaped subsequent history. It introduced a period of political reorganization in which Armenia became a dominant partner in the coalition of states bent to protect the holy places of Christianity. There was a seemingly endless and futile warfare among the Christian principalities of the east, and while Rome wished to stop this bickering, it found itself powerless as various attempts of unity failed to materialize. As a political force, Christianity in the east stood on the threshold of extinction. This political malaise was largely corrected by Hetoum's visionary policies which ultimately made him one of the greatest statesmen of his period.

But if Hetoum's policy saved Christian Europe from Mongolian invasion, it became detrimental to the very survival of his own kingdom. His alliance with the Mongols will ultimately expose Armenia to the savage fury of another group of people who were now emerging as a powerful force in the Valley of the Nile to assert their influence on the history of Armenia.

A CULTURAL REAWAKENING

The establishment of peace enabled King Hetoum to foster a cultural reawakening accompanied by a great economic boom and prosperity. This was the second time that the political tranquility in Cilicia stamped a creative mold on the cultural life of the people. The first flowering of intellectual culture in the Cilician period occurred during the reign of King Levon I from 1186 to 1219. Both periods identified as the Silver Age of Armenian Cilicia will have a potent influence on the political orientation of the Cilician leaders. Works of literature, poetry, philosophy, history, law, and rhetoric produced a wealth of treasures and conceived a new framework of thought immensely influenced by the influx of Crusaders and the transplantation of foreign elements in the Armenian soil. It was the blending of this foreign element that made possible the transformation of the Armenian person into a more cosmopolitan individual without discarding the traditional beliefs of the ancient past.

As in the past, it was the clergy who were primarily responsible to spearhead the cultural movement. Armenian priests began to build schools, seminaries, libraries, community halls, and academies to provide educational facilities to the people in general and to the children of the aristocratic elite in particular. Armenian linguists added two more characters to the Armenian alphabet to meet the phonetic requirements of foreign words. King Hetoum encouraged the construction of secular establishments along with religious buildings and it was in these establishments that the new schools of thought, rhetoric, and philosophy were developed. Armenian scholars extended their horizon of knowledge and wrote one of the brilliant pages in the history of Armenia.

This great age produced a new style in historiography, and gifted writers used the technique of reportage as modern day correspondents to report contemporary events. A notable example was Grigor of Akner, who wrote the history of the Mongol invasion of Greater Armenia. His book entitled *History of the Nation of the Archers* is a valuable chronicle of the conquests of the Mongols. The writer Gomidas, who accompanied King Hetoum to Mongolia, acted as a free lance journalist and wrote a book on his return describing in detail the king's adventurous journey and impressions on Mongolia in the form of vignettes. His book gave detailed description of the Mongolian court life and conditions of life in central Asia. Armenian historians recognized the need to go beyond the confines of the Armenian society and write about events in other countries. Interest in others brought new perspectives to the greatness of this Silver Age.

Madteos Ourhayetsi, a historian of some renown, wrote about the history of Armenian Cilicia covering two centuries of the political experience of the Armenian people. His book reveals a wide range of activity of Armenians away from their ancestral homeland. Stepanos Orpelian wrote about the political and social struggle of Armenia, the disintegration of the Mongolian power in the Near East and the emergence of the Memluks and their oppressive policies towards the Armenians. Historiography brought a new interest in geography. The pre-eminent geographer of the day was Vartan Aykegtsi who wrote about the inhabited world and drew its map using latitudes and longitudes based on reports from travelers. His book became an important source of geographical information of the period.

The period was also rich in the growth of philosophy. Clergy and laymen turned to philosophy and scholarship to explain their thoughts on the social and political condition of the period and the role of the individual in it. The struggle of the Armenian Church to preserve its autonomous entity prompted gifted scholars to write about doctrinal issues. Chief among them was Nerses Lambronatsi, the Bishop of Tarsus, who prepared a lengthy and academic treatise about theology, the doctrines of the Armenian Church, divinity, and the nature of Jesus Christ.

The growth of science was stimulated by royal patronage and by the influx of foreign elements. Armenians began to show interest in astronomy and broadened their knowledge of mathematics. Hovhannes Erzngatsi wrote an astronomical treatise on celestial movements. His works formed the body of knowledge which later supplied information about scientific research and the development of science. A noted linguist, he translated parts of Thomas Aquinas' theology into Armenian. Blessed with an encyclopedic mind of accumulated knowledge, Erzngatsi developed new techniques in political oratory. An outstanding oracle himself, he taught politicians and members of the aristocracy the mastery of public speaking.

Armenian scientists also excelled in the science of medicine, foremost among them was Mekhitar Heratsi, a prominent physician who wrote a book entitled *The Malarials' Comfort*. Centers of anatomy were opened in Cilicia and advanced surgical procedures were performed using opium as anesthetic. New techniques in diagnostic medicine were developed and clinics for medical care were opened generally sponsored by members of the royal family. Most towns had private practitioners as well as physicians paid by the state. The science of pharmacology was developed based on rudimentary chemistry using a variety of herbs as sources of drugs and medicines.

In the field of art the period opened a new world of opportunity to artists and architects. New palaces and citadels were built in the old Armenian tradition, and artists were commissioned for works of art funded by the patronage of the royal family or members of the aristocracy. The chief representative of this period was Toros Roslin who became renowned for his manuscript illuminations and elegant paintings.

The development of law and jurisprudence affected the political experience of the people as the state constitution, framed by King Levon earlier, moved to provide social equality and regulations for the administration of the government. The interpretation of the law and the constitution was made possible by a prominent legal scholar, Mekhitar Koch, who wrote the first juridical book in the Armenian language. The book provided the framework in developing Armenia's legal institutions and standards of conduct advocating an impartial justice for all, and stability of law and order. Until the publication of this book the administration of the law was in the hands of the local lords whose capricious and compulsive rulings at times disrupted the community's life and gave rise to social and political disorder.

The giant and cultural patron saint of this period whose intellectual pursuits guided the destiny of this Cilician community in its formative years, was Nerses IV Shnorhali, the Catholicos and the grandson of the influential writer, Grigor Magistros. Shnorhali was a true representative of the Silver Age. His voice led the Armenian nation and his eloquence and courage became a source of inspiration to clergy and laymen alike.

He had an indomitable faith in the sanctity of the Church and the stubborn tenacity to preserve the heritage of his ancient race. He fought vehemently to maintain the independence of the Armenian Church and kept the pro-Greek and the pro-Latin elements away from the hierarchy of the church administration. His works reflected a profound humanism in the form of philosophical dialogue.

He earned the title Shnorhali, meaning Gracious, by the purity of his life and the eloquence of his speech. To be understood by everyone Nerses Shnorhali wrote in the Armenian vernacular. He is immortalized by his work of twenty-four verses written in prose corresponding to the twenty four hours of the day. It is called *Havadov Khosdovanim* (Faithfully, I Confess), which until today is sung in the Armenian liturgy.

THE REORGANIZATION OF THE NEAR EAST

Mongke of Mongolia confided to King Hetoum during their summit in Karakorum that he was planning to mount a great military expedition against the Assassins in Persia and the Moslem Caliphate of Baghdad and that he had assigned his brother Hulagu to carry on this military campaign.

Hulagu became a great conqueror and one of the most ferocious Mongol generals. Within a short period of time he changed the face of Western Asia and established the il-Khan Mongolian dynasty in Persia with a hereditary descent that will continue for the next eighty years. Through intimidation and skillful mastery of military techniques Hulagu made Mongolia a dominant power in Western Asia and the Near East.

Hulagu marched towards Persia, exterminated the Assassins, butchered babies in their cradles, made pyramids out of human skulls, and proceeded towards Baghdad, spreading death and terror. There was some speculation among the Christian leaders that it was King Hetoum who urged Mongke to send Hulagu to overthrow the Caliph in Baghdad and restore the Holy Land to the Christians.

The military campaigns of the Crusaders had generally been a failure. While several Christian strongholds had been established along the narrow strip of the Syrian coast, Jerusalem, the center of the Christian faith, continued to be under the occupation of the followers of Mohammed. At the time of Hulagu's march towards Baghdad there was every indication that the Mongols will eventually help the Christian cause. Hulagu's wife was a Nestorian Christian and most of the principal generals of the Mongolian army had already adopted the Christian faith.

It was agreed in Karakorum that the Mongolian military campaign against the Islamic states in the east would be a joint enterprise with the Armenians. In accordance with this agreement, therefore, King Hetoum had supplied a contingent of 16,000 Armenian troops to bolster Hulagu's military strength. In 1258 the Mongols entered Baghdad and terrorized, destroyed, and plundered. Hulagu's hordes slaughtered the inhabitants and obliterated Islam's cultural achievements of five centuries. An estimated 800,000 people of Baghdad were massacred. The Caliph rushed to offer an unconditional surrender, but Hulagu had no taste for negotiation. The Caliph and all the members of the Abbasid court were put to death.

Christians everywhere rejoiced at the destruction of Baghdad and the demise of the Abbasid Caliphate. The way was now clear for Hulagu to proceed south and take the Holy Land from the Moslems. After destroying Baghdad, the joint Mongolian and Armenian forces advanced towards Aleppo. The Mongols captured the Moslem governor of the region, cut off pieces of flesh from his body, thrust them into his mouth and forced him to eat. In 1260 the Mongol forces entered Aleppo, massacred the inhabitants, put 80,000 women and children to the sword, destroyed buildings, and looted the treasures. King Hetoum gratefully accepted some of the booty and carried it to Cilicia.

Western Asia had now been reorganized, the Abbasids were destroyed, and the principal institutions of the Islamic faith were shattered. It is now time to turn to Egypt where a major power is about to emerge into the light of history to place its mark on the subsequent pages of the history of man.

THE RISE OF THE MEMLUKS

It was in 1250 that a new Moslem power emerged around the banks of the Nile. They were the Memluks, the former slaves to the Sultans of Egypt. These slaves, after dismantling the power of their masters, established a political party in Egypt, laid the foundation of an organized empire, chased the Crusaders out of the Near East, checked the advance of the Mongols, and in the process became one of the most dominant powers in the eastern Mediterranean. For the next 267 years this medieval dynasty of former slaves will rule the world of Islam and preserve the continuity of the religious and political institutions of the Arabs. For little Armenia their rise will bring the most critical test for the viability of the people to survive as a politically independent entity. If the Mongols were violent and brutal, the Memluks were bloodthirsty and savage. Their atrocities tended to overshadow the cultural achievements of the Arab Caliphs. Most of their leaders were illiterate. Some could not even speak Arabic. One was insane and another was an incompetent drunkard. Most of the Memluk Sultans were homosexual and maintained a harem of young boys. One blinded an alchemist and cut out his tongue for his failure to turn copper into gold. Another had his physician beheaded because he could not relieve the Sultan from an incurable illness. But in spite of their peculiarities and lack of cultural pursuits, the Memluks' rise was spectacular. Within a single generation they rose from servitude to empire building, absorbed the culture of the Moslems, successfully coalesced into a military oligarchy, and toppled the decadent rule of the Arabs. They maintained a political stability in the turbulent world of the Near East and indirectly influenced the formation of modern Europe.

The Memluks were a conglomeration of races and peoples predominantly Turkic in ethnicity. They were originally brought to Egypt as slaves by the Arab emirs. Paradoxically their rise to power was mainly due to the presence of an Arme-

nian woman, the wife of one of Saladin's descendants who had
inherited the Islamic throne after a series of dynastic struggles.
After Saladin's death in Damascus in 1193, his brother Melik-el-
Aadil became the ruler, followed by his son, Melik-el-Kamil,
who in turn was followed by his son, Melik-el-Salih Ayyoub. Saladin's dynasty came to be known as the Ayyoubids. They all
proved to be courteous, generous, benevolent, cultured, and
highly religious rulers.

At the time when Saladin was waging war against the Crusaders his army included a core of 500 bodyguards called Memluks, which meant slaves in Arabic. The Memluks were
ferocious men, mostly Qipchuk Turks in origin, sold by their
parents when they were ten or twelve years old. Cut from their
ethnic background these young men were trained by Saladin's
army officers in strict and regimented Moslem discipline. They
were taught to be dedicated fighters loyal only to their masters.
They grew from boyhood to manhood with no feeling towards
their ethnic background, bound only to their masters and to nobody else.

When el-Salih Ayyoub rose to power in Egypt, he married
an Armenian woman with an adopted name of Shajar-ad-Durr,
which in Arabic meant Branch of Pearl. To protect his bride
and her household, Ayyoub gathered 1,000 Memluks as palace
guards, headed by a powerful slave called Baybars. By then the
Memluks had already acquired enormous power over the administration of the government. It was at this time that another
wave of Crusaders from Europe came to the shores of Egypt to
destroy the last vestiges of Saladin's Empire.

AN ARMENIAN WOMAN ON THE ISLAMIC THRONE

El-Salih-Ayyoub was at the sunset of his life. While fighting the
Crusaders in 1249 he died of tuberculosis in the arms of his Armenian wife, who immediately took charge of the military operation and continued to fight. The brilliant Armenian Sultana
connived with the Memluks of her palace, kept the death of the
Sultan secret in order to give herself time to consolidate her
power, and allow her stepson, Turanshah to return to Egypt and
assume his father's throne. Turanshah, in assuming the reign of
the Empire, proved to be an incompetent fool. His reign lasted
only a few months. He began to quarrel with his stepmother.

To solve the family feud the Armenian Sultana ordered her favorite Memluk, Baybars, to kill Turanshah. Turanshah's death in 1250 marked the end of the Ayyoubid Dynasty and the beginning of a new era in which the Memluk oligarchy will rule the world of Islam until the occupation of Egypt by the Ottoman Turks in 1517.

The Memluks after killing Turanshah declared the Armenian woman as the Queen of Egypt. She became the first woman ruler in a world in which women were considered inferior to men. While the Armenian woman's spectacular rise to power was a significant development in a society in which the Moslems regarded people of non-Moslem origin with suspicion, it failed to stir controversy or jolt Moslem sensibilities. As the Queen of Egypt the Armenian woman ran the government with unusual courage, and with the help of her loyal Memluks, was able to quell revolts and make Cairo an important center for Islamic culture. To strengthen her power in the administration of the government she ordered her Memluks to arrest all Ayyoubid sympathizers and strangle them to death. She increased the number of Memluks to consolidate her power and skillfully played one Memluk general against another. The Memluks intrigued by the Armenian Sultana, became a close knit brotherhood, consolidated their hold on the government, and gradually rose to become army commanders and governors. When the Armenian woman died the Memluks took over the reign of the government. Thus began the Memluk rule.

With brutal power unmatched in the annals of Moslem history, the Memluks began to rule Egypt. They were concerned only with military affairs and left the administration of their Empire to the Christians, Armenians, and Jews living in Egypt. They failed to maintain the continuity of sensible and orderly succession. In most cases a popular general rose to power only to be toppled by a stronger general shortly thereafter.

MEMLUKS STOP THE MONGOLS

News of the Mongolian terror in northern Syria reached Damascus but the people were so terrified that they simply surrendered the city to the Mongols and fled to Egypt. The Armenian contingent under the command of King Hetoum entered Da-

mascus triumphantly. Christians everywhere were now elated
about the prospect of Christian victory and the demise of Islamic power. Hulagu began preparations to invade Egypt to crush
the Memluk power. The course of history is about to be
changed, however, and Hulagu will not be able to proceed further. While in Syria he learned that his brother, the Great Khan
Mongke, had died in Karakorum and he had to rush home to
attend the funeral. Hulagu took with him the bulk of Mongolian forces and left only a small regiment under the command
of a Nestorian general.

Hulagu's departure forced the Mongols to abandon their
military campaign against the Memluks. One may only specu-
late that had Mongke not died at that point in time, there would
have been no question that Hulagu would have destroyed the
Memluks, decimating the Moslem power in the east. Mongke's
death will eventually cause the disintegration of the Mongolian
Empire. The unity of the Empire will crumble away as dynastic
squabbles for succession will force the Mongols to dismantle
their Empire and create separate il-Khanates. Hulagu will acquire the Persian il-Khanate and will rule it as an autonomous
entity with the Great Khan in Karakorum acting as the titular
head of the Mongols.

The Memluk who emerged as a prominent leader after a
bloody process of political succession was Qutuz. He was
elected the Sultan of Egypt and immediately began preparations
to consolidate his power and assume   control of the Islamic
world. His principal objective was to check the advance of the
Mongols and secure the frontiers of his newly established Islamic Kingdom. When news of Hulagu's departure reached Cairo
Qutuz appointed Baybars to organize an army to attack the
Mongols in Syria. Baybars marched east with unusual rapidity
and in 1260 met the Mongol army in Ain Jalut, a town to the
south of Damascus. The Memluks attacked the Mongols, savagely slaughtered most of the forces, captured the Mongolian
commander and decapitated him. The remaining Mongolian
forces fled north. This was a decisive victory for the Memluks
and one that will make this battle a turning point in the history
of man.

With the defeat at Ain Jalut the Mongol advance to the
west was forever stopped and the Memluks emerged as the
greatest Islamic power on earth. The battle of Ain Jalut encour-

aged the Memluks to proceed north to clear the Mongol troops out of the Near East. King Hetoum of Armenia was forced to retreat with considerable damage to his power and prestige. His hopes to recover the holy places from the Moslems had now evaporated. He returned home a defeated man to face a disillusioned nation. He had been away from his country for a long time. While international trade had made Cilicia somewhat prosperous, politically the country had lost the benefit of a strong leadership. His wife, Queen Zabel, had died and various constables had assumed the reign of the government in King Hetoum's absence. When his grandiose plans to help the Mongols capture the Holy Land failed, he was forced to reorient his policy, and substitute international interests with national issues. New developments in the Near East forced King Hetoum to concentrate his attention on Cilicia. His pro-Mongol policy incurred the hostility of the Memluks who now began to blame the Armenians for all the injuries inflicted on Islam.

GREEKS RECOVER CONSTANTINOPLE

While the Memluks were rising in importance and the Mongols were crushing Islamic power, the political balance within Byzantium had shifted. The Byzantine Emperor, Michael VIII Paleologus, in Nicaea was able to harness enough military strength in 1261 to recover Constantinople and chase the Latins out of Byzantium. After settling down in the old palace and reorganizing the government, he began the difficult task of rebuilding the country which had been devastated by the Latins. The nation's treasury was stolen and the Venetians had carried Byzantium's wealth to Venice as plunder.

The return of the Byzantine Greeks to Constantinople was celebrated with great triumph. A new epoch is about to begin in the history of Byzantium with a link to its legendary past. For the next 200 years a new dynasty, Paleologus, will rule Byzantium. This will be the last and the longest in the history of this once proud nation. While Michael's victory will bring a new rhythm of life, the political forces surrounding the Empire will gradually weaken the fabric of the society, making the country an easy target for exploitation by others. The Empire was crippled and reduced in size. Paleologus will begin to rule an empire confined only to Constantinople, a small section of Anatolia, and the Balkans, with his military resources seriously depleted. There were new players now in the political rearrangement of Asia Minor and the Near East. His first task was to placate the most powerful players of all, the Memluks of Egypt. He sent ambassadors to Cairo and sealed an accord of friendship with the Memluks.

With the dismissal of the Latins from Constantinople the situation for the Crusaders in the east became precarious and the entire Christian mission was placed in jeopardy. The Greeks condemned the Crusaders as savage barbarians and sided with the Moslem Memluks to take revenge for what the Latins had done to Constantinople. The situation for Cilicia was different. For the first time in many decades the Armenian Kingdom felt insecure as the Mongol power in Asia Minor began to fade away. Hulagu died in 1265 and the Mongols left the Memluks alone, allowing them to expand their Empire and pursue their territorial aggrandizement unobstructed.

Baybars, once the senior Memluk to the Armenian Queen, anxious to take over the Memluk rule, usurped the throne by conspiring to murder Qutuz immediately after the latter's successful victory over the Mongols. Baybars was a Qipchuk Turk. He was a born leader with extraordinary courage. With the Mongols out of the way, Baybars' principal objective was to crush the remaining strongholds of the Crusaders. He organized a powerful military unit and in 1263, occupied Karek and demolished most of the churches in the city of Nazareth. He marched towards Jaffa, Antioch, Cæsarea, Tyre, Tripoli, and Beirut, occupied the cities, butchered most of the inhabitants, and carried young boys and girls as slaves to Egypt. Proceeding north Baybars attacked Armenian Cilicia in 1267. The Armenian troops defending the capital were promised their freedom in return for the Castle of Sis. The Armenians did not know, however, that Baybars' promises carried little credence. As soon as the Armenians surrendered the castle, Baybars ordered every one of them to be beheaded. His chief leutenant, Qalaoon, was even more ruthless. Qalaoon gathered thousands of Armenians and cut them in half at their waist. 40,000 Armenian men, women, and children were shipped to the slave markets of the Islamic world.

King Hetoum after witnessing his country's devastation by the Memluks undertook a trip to Tabriz to seek help from his old friend the Mongol Khan, but events were moving at a rapid pace. His two sons, Toros and Levon, could not stop the Memluk onslaught in their father's absence. Toros died in battle and Levon was taken prisoner. The Memluks set fire to the Cathedral of Sis and plundered centuries old treasures. The Armenians were left helpless. The Christian principalities along the Syrian Coast had fallen into anarchy. Antioch, the principal city on the Mediterranean shore, with the largest Christian population, had been destroyed. Baybars' forces had laid the city to waste. After occupying the city the Memluks had begun a systematic program of wholesale massacre of every Christian man and woman. The palaces and churches of Antioch were destroyed, and bishops, priests, and deacons were butchered at the altar of their churches.

KING LEVON II

Hetoum's son, Levon II ascended the Armenian throne and ruled the country until 1289. A wise and cultured man, Levon's first task was to reorganize the country's military strength. Armenia's military power had been shattered beyond recognition. In 1275 when Baybars attempted to attack Cilicia again, King Levon, with his uncle General Sembad, organized a counter offensive and retaliated by attacking the Memluks in the rear. Sembad lured the enemy into a mountain pass and launched a decisive battle in which the Moslems were decimated and the survivors were chased away. This was a tremendous victory for little Cilicia and one that brought renewed hope for a Christian uprising against the Moslems. The Armenian victory also elated the Mongolians whose Khan sent a precious sword as a gift to King Levon II.

Baybars' death in 1277 brought a breathing spell for the Armenians. But trouble was not over. Qalaoon, after succeeding Baybars, immediately began to marshall a new force and in 1283 marched towards Cilicia. He crushed the resistance of the Armenian troops, overran Cilicia and to symbolize his victory, he buried thousands of Armenians in a large ditch up to their necks. Unable to free themselves from the ditch, they all died a few days later.

In 1289 Qalaoon attacked Tripoli, a large Christian outpost, butchered all male inhabitants and carried women and children off as slaves. All principalities of the Crusaders had now been destroyed with the exception of Acre. The Armenians, afraid of their own fate, sent a deputation to Qalaoon imploring peace. The request was granted in exchange for a number of fortresses around the periphery of Cilicia. For the next eleven years there will be peace and tranquility in Cilicia, and Armenians once again will begin to rebuild the country.

THE FALL OF THE CRUSADERS

Qalaoon died in 1290 and his successor Sultan Khalil immediately began preparations to launch an all out attack on Acre and deliver the final blow to the last stronghold of the Crusaders in the east. The military preparations rapidly grew into an Islamic Holy War to drive the Crusaders out to the sea once and for all. On March 3, 1291 the Memluk forces stormed Acre and after a siege of a few months, destroyed it completely. Khalil's forces razed the city to the ground. They sacked, raided, and killed, and converted most of the churches into mosques. The fall of Acre marked the end of the Crusaders and the Levantine Franks disappeared from the pages of history. The Knights of Acre fled to Cyprus and eventually settled on the Island of Rhodes in the Aegean Sea. For almost 300 years the Crusaders fought to protect the holy places of the Christian faith, but at the end they failed to achieve their objectives. In 1291 the holy places of Christianity were still in Moslem hands as they were 300 years earlier. The era of the Crusaders drew to an end. What will remain of this ill-fated movement will be some ruined castles, citadels, and fortifications and the painful memory of a miscalculated Christian adventure.

Armenian Cilicia was now the only Christian state south of Byzantium. To avoid bloodshed major cities in Cilicia surrendered to the Memluks. But Hrumgla, the residence of the Armenian Catholicos, proved to be a formidable obstacle. This city which served as the most important religious center for Armenian Cilicia since 1151, was a strongly fortified place on the Euphrates. Monks and priests under the command of the Catholicos, heroically fought to defend the city. The Memluks employed heavy siege machinery to batter down the walls of the city. It took the Moslems thirty three days to force the priests to surrender. After breaking the walls down, the Memluks poured in, slaughtered all the priests and monks, destroyed the precious relics of the Cathedral and took Catholicos Stepan IV into captivity.

ARMENIANS RETALIATE

Discouraged by the continued atrocities of the Memluks, King Hetoum II abdicated the throne in 1293 in favor of his brother, Toros, and retired to a monastery. His retirement did not last long. Toros pleaded Hetoum to return to the throne and make a fresh appeal to the Mongols for help. Hetoum II undertook a trip to Mongolia to renew the old treaty of alliance that his grandfather had sealed earlier. Hetoum's renewed alliance with the Mongols provided the stimulus to the Great Khan to organize a joint enterprise with the Armenians and attack Memluk strongholds in the Near East. In 1299 il-Khan Ghazar, with the help of Armenian troops, revived the Mongol war against Islam. The combined Armenian and Mongol troops invaded Damascus and took the city from the Memluks. They ransacked the city and killed thousands of Moslems in retaliation for the Memluk's savagery in Cilicia. The victory gave Hetoum the opportunity to restore all Armenian territories previously taken by the Memluks. The occupation of Damascus by the Mongol and Armenian coalition forces lasted a year. The Memluks reorganized their forces again and chased the alien troops out of the city.

King Hetoum II abdicated the throne, this time in favor of his nephew Levon III, a young lad of sixteen who ruled Armenia from 1303 until 1307. At a time when Armenia needed a more resolute leader, the youthful king, faced with a rapidly changing and restless world, was not militarily equipped to stop the Memluk encroachments on the Armenian territory. He was unable to win the support of the people. A significant new factor in foreign affairs left the Armenians completely unprotected. Their old ally, the Mongols, had an abrupt change of heart. Shortly after their last battle with the Memluks they decided to accept the faith of Islam and seal a political and religious treaty of collaboration with the Memluks.

Events in the Near East played into the Moslem's hands. Rising to the height of their power the Memluks began to press hard against the last vestiges of the Christian presence in the east. Confronted with the coalition of two great Islamic powers, the Mongols and the Memluks, Armenia was now left alone. The Crusaders were long gone, Byzantium had become militarily impotent, and the Roman Pope was not too anxious to send an army to help a group of Christians in the east who for centuries had refused to accept his primacy in the Christian world. The Memluks, allied with the Mongols, were well prepared to undertake a full scale campaign against the Cilician Armenians. Levon III pleaded his uncle, Hetoum II, to come out of retirement and help him prepare the country against Islam's coordinated enterprise.

The trouble began with the Mongol general when he demanded to erect a mosque in the heart of the capital city of Sis. The Armenians prevented the construction. Infuriated, the Mongol general invited Hetoum, King Levon, and forty Armenian noblemen to his tent, in the pretense to discuss some political issues. When the guests were well inside the tent the Mongols ambushed the guests, took out their swords, and slaughtered every one of them shouting, *Allah Akbar, Allah Akbar.*

A PERIOD OF ANARCHY

Oshin, the fourth brother of Hetoum assumed the throne in 1308 as the King of Cilicia. His reign coincided with a period of savage anarchy and the disintegration of Armenia's political and religious institutions. The irrational passion of Moslem fanaticism continued to exact extraordinary pressure on the Armenians forcing them to accept the faith of Mohammed and renounce Christianity.

The political problems of Armenia were aggravated by yet another difficulty from the west. Rome expressed its willingness to help Cilicia if only the Armenians agreed to convert their faith into Roman Catholicism. Cilicia was bankrupt and economically hard hit by seemingly incessant military assaults. The west had ceased to use the Cilician ports for commercial traffic. The Armenian farmhouses and vineyards were destroyed beyond recovery and the loss of revenue from international trade had impoverished the people to the point of deprivation. While they continued to preserve their sense of ethnic unity, political, military, and religious pressure from east, west, and south, had diminished their spirit in their struggle for survival.

Oshin died in 1320 and his son, Levon IV succeeded him at the age of ten with the Count of Gorigos assuming the title of regency. The introduction of this foreign element into Armenia's political organization created yet another problem for the little kingdom. A man of considerable talent but despotic, ruthless, and brutal, Gorigos persuaded the young king to accept the Catholic doctrine. He became the *de facto* ruler of Armenia and threatened to kill members of the aristocracy, priests, monks, and all those who refused to renounce their Armenian faith. Earlier an Armenian priest, with the help of Dominican monks had established a religious movement called Unitor, the objective of which was to convert the Armenian brand of Christianity into Catholicism. The pro-Latin elements were prepared to abandon their Armenian traditions with a pledge to recognize the Pope's claim as the spiritual leader of Christians everywhere. They believed that the only way to save Armenia from the menace of Islam was through the union with Rome.

Catholicos Hagop II, a wise and humble Patriarch, made an emotional appeal for the traditional Armenian sentiment to keep the Armenian Church independent. Soon the country was divided into two opposite, hostile religious factions, one was the Latin Party headed by the King and the other, the Nationalist Party, headed by the Catholicos. The Nationalists were resolved to defend their country's ancestral heritage. The independence of their Church was the only element left to rekindle their passion for liberty which in the past was won at a cost of immeasurable human sacrifice. They issued a manifesto to reject Catholic interference in their Christian life. King Levon deposed the Catholicos and ordered the closing of all Armenian churches. This religious struggle came to an end in 1342 when the Nationalists assassinated the King and crushed the pro-Latin movement.

ARMENIANS RULED BY FOREIGN KINGS

Levon IV did not have any male issue. Before he died he had chosen his cousin, Guy de Lousignan, as his successor. A Frenchman living in the Greek Islands, Lousignan accepted the throne, assumed the name Constantin II and ruled Cilicia until

1344. The Catholics once again emerged from obscurity and began to assert their influence publicly. Soon the country was infiltrated with Catholic clergy. There were Catholic bishops, priests, monks, teachers, and miracle workers everywhere. As they gained converts and built their religious centers they came into open political conflict with the Armenian Church and convulsed the country with religious strife once again.

The new King removed Armenian traditions and suspended the state constitution. He surrounded himself with French associates and exalted Latin practices and court rules. As a member of the French royal family he received considerable help from Paris. Constantin's dislike toward the Armenians was vented by removing Armenian national monuments and substituting them with statues of the Pope. He sent representatives to Avignon, France, which was then the seat of the Roman Pope, to draw up the terms of church unity. The Armenian Nationalists, while powerful enough to organize the assassination of Constantin's predecessor some years back, were now at the threshold of a political breakdown. They found themselves voiceless and leaderless in the affairs of the Armenian government and simply stood by while the French functionaries made a travesty of government.

The people of Cilicia gradually gained power and rose in revolt without the benefit of political leadership. They organized mob demonstrations against the king's Catholic policy and the oppressive rule of the foreigners. King Constantin was assassinated and his entire regiment of 300 Frank knights were slaughtered one by one. The only survivor was a small band of Armenian Catholic sympathizers who covertly continued their pro-Latin movement and renounced the traditions of the Armenian Apostolic doctrines. This pro-Latin Armenian party bequeathed a legacy of ill-will among the Armenian people and promoted the formation of the Armenian Catholic Church which until today continues to exist, in small number, and accepts the Pope as the universal leader of the Christian Church.

Immediately after Constantin's death, the Armenian nobles in 1344 elected another Constantin to occupy Cilicia's throne. He was Constantin III, another monarch of French origin. His reign gave promise of an able ruler but was marred in 1347 by the devastating spread of an epidemic, the Black Death, which annihilated most of the population of Armenian Cilicia. Constantin III died in 1363 with no heir and the Armenian nobles elected another Frenchman, Constantin IV.

Meanwhile in Europe another Crusade expedition was being organized by Pierre I, the King of Cyprus, who sailed from Venice in 1365 with an organized army and a flotilla of eighty ships. He landed at Alexandria, Egypt, and after taking the city from the Memluks by surprise, killed thousands of Moslems. The Crusaders stripped the city of its wealth, loaded the treasures on their ships and sailed away. The Memluks were outraged by this latest act of piracy by Christian Europe. The Sultan gave immediate orders to arrest all Franks in the Memluk Empire, and began preparations to wipe out the only surviving Christian enclave in the east, Armenian Cilicia. While in Venice, Pierre I was offered the crown of Armenian Cilicia. He returned to Cyprus in 1368 to incorporate the Cilician Kingdom with his Kingdom of Cyprus, but his plan never came to fruition. A group of Armenian Nationalists fearing that Pierre will force the Armenians to accept the Catholic doctrines, assassinated him while he was on his way to Cilicia.

King Constantin's reign also ended in revolt. He was assassinated in 1373 during a palace revolution. After a year of political unrest the Armenian nobles concurred in the selection of another Frenchman, Levon de Lousignan of Cyprus, to accept the Armenian crown. Raised and educated in Cyprus, a man of aristocratic lineage, and administrative ability, Levon became one of the most erudite kings in the history of Armenia, but his reign lasted not quite a year. He will be destined to be the last king of Cilicia and the last King of the Armenian people. He was coronated as King Levon V with pomp and music, festivities, and church bells, but the jubilation did not last long. The Memluks were at the doorstep. They organized a powerful army to deliver the final blow to the Armenian Kingdom.

THE END OF THE KINGDOM

The successive reign of European elements in Cilicia had irritated the Memluks of Egypt who were afraid that Armenia's link with the west would spur yet another Christian movement in the east. They were careful to avoid the mistakes of the past and were prepared to maintain their political and military supremacy in the Islamic east. Melik Ashraf Shaman, at the head of a powerful Memluk army marched towards Armenian Cilicia, and surrounded the capital city of Sis. Cilicia was now in the grip of impending doom. Shaman positioned his army in front of the main gate of Sis and ordered his troops to batter the walls down, smashing the Armenian forces with heavy casualties. King Levon V took refuge with his family in the impregnable fortress of Sis. The Memluks used heavy siege machinery to destroy the gates of the fortress. The Armenians fought with great courage, but the Memluks never stopped their heavy bombardment. When they ran out of ammunition for their catapults the Moslems used Armenian corpses as missiles. The Moslem army engineers continued to mine the towers of the fortress while the Imams chanted *Allah-Akbar*, urging the troops to fight to destroy the enemies of Mohammed. By now wave upon wave of Moslem troops were gathered around the fortress. King Levon, with no military resources at his disposal, finally capitulated on April 13, 1375, and ordered the gates of the fortress to be lowered. The Moslems poured in and began an orgy of systematic killing. They brought the buildings down stone by stone. Shaman gave orders to destroy farms, cut down trees, raze villages to the ground, dismantle the irrigation systems, preventing the Armenians from ever building their country again. The Moslems disembowelled live some 25,000 Armenian men, women, and children, leaving their bodies on the streets to rot. The remnant of the Armenian troops who survived the ordeal were forced to parade in the streets of Sis, each carrying the severed head of a murdered comrade hung around his neck.

The King, the Queen, and their children, Catholicos Boghos I, Armenian barons, dignitaries, and noblemen, were taken captive to Aleppo in the most humiliating manner. From Aleppo they were taken to Cairo where great preparations were made to welcome the victorious Memluk army. The Egyptian capital was decorated with carpets, and draperies. The people of Cairo turned out to greet the Sultan and the Armenian captives. Amid cheers of *Allah-Akbar* the sultan proclaimed "this is our greatest moment of victory. The Armenians are finally destroyed". Indeed they were.

Levon's wife and children died while in captivity. In 1382 the Memluk Sultan allowed King Levon V to leave Cairo for Europe. Levon died on November 29, 1393 in Tournelle,

France. His tomb today is in the Basilica of St. Denis in a suburb near Paris. Armenians everywhere, while visiting Paris, take a short taxi ride to St. Denis to pay homage to their last King and think back to the day when they once had a kingdom. The epitaph carved on Levon's tomb reads "Here lies the most noble and excellent Prince, Levon de Lousignan Fifth, the Latin King of the Kingdom of Armenia, who rendered his soul to God on the 29th day of November, in the year of Grace, 1393. Pray for him".

With the destruction of the Cilician Kingdom the political history of Armenia will now come to an end, and this ancient and proud people will be thrown into the abyss of obscurity. As a political entity, Cilicia, which was once the cockpit of the Christian movement in the east, will cease to exist. Perhaps a leader with enough energy and political prowess could have saved the country from political extinction. While as a people the Armenians had enormous recuperative powers, their political experience had shown that even their most powerful rulers were often helpless against the repressive regimes of the great powers of the day.

The Armenians will abandon Cilicia and scatter all over the world. The survivors will be carried away to be sold as slaves in the markets of the Islamic world. Some will continue to cling to their soil, live a squalid life awhile and later occupy mountain fastnesses. For the next five centuries they will live in self contained communities with no political unity or leadership. The two thousand year old Armenian civilization will now be transformed into a rural existence and the people will wander around the fringes of their ancestral homeland. While the men of the Renaissance were about to emerge in Europe to shape the destiny of the western civilization, the Armenians will be doomed to succumb into the age of darkness and shut themselves off from their great past with no reason to dream for greater tomorrows.

CHAPTER EIGHTEEN

THE AGE OF DARKNESS

At a time when the western world was coming out of the Middle Ages and entering the illuminated period of the Renaissance, the advanced civilization of Armenia was falling into the abyss of darkness through a rapid process of deterioration caused by the collapse of the Cilician Kingdom. During the next five centuries the urban civilization of the Armenians will be transformed into a rural existence in which the individual struggle for survival will be more critical than the need to restore national unity. There will be some timid attempts to rebuild Armenia's political organization but powers surrounding the national homeland will prevent the emergence of a territorial state. Most of the Armenians will be reduced to the status of nomads, leading a wandering existence and leaving their country in a state of anarchy. They will be confronted with an age of darkness in which the preservation of the heritage of nostalgic memories will be their only guide for their struggle for survival. Their land will cease to be a country. It will be transformed into a corridor of passage between east and west. Western Asia Minor will be studded with Armenian communities governed by an imperialistic system of oppressive powers. A new wave of warrior hordes bent on terror and destruction will herald a change in the character of the east, topple the political barriers of the old empires, and establish a new order with an eye for world domination.

THE RISE OF THE OTTOMAN TURKS

Originated in Mongolia, and fired with a passion for plunder, the Turks gradually worked their way into central Asia and settled around the town of Merv. They emerged into the light of history when they accepted Islam as their religion and took upon themselves the task to uphold the Moslem faith by destroying the non-Moslem elements in the areas surrounding their adopted land. Earlier they were identified with the Huns and the Finns who also were lured to the western territories to escape the increasing aridity of central Asia.

A period of wandering followed around the early part of the Thirteenth century when Mongolian troops terrorized Merv and exterminated most of the Turks. A group of survivors headed by one Suleyman Shah fled west to safer territories. Suleyman drowned in the Euphrates River while crossing Armenia but his followers continued their migratory movement led by his son, Ertugrul. They sought asylum from their cousins, the Seljuks, and gradually spread into the heartland of Asia Minor and finally settled in semi-autonomous communities.

Ertugrul died and his son, Osman, rose to power as the leader of these Turkomen nomads. He expanded his territory and when the Seljuk power collapsed around 1300, founded a political unity and established a dynasty whose supremacy will dominate the pages of history creating the largest and most enduring empire in the history of Islam. Osman's followers will come to be known as the Osmanlees, or Ottomans, and their empire will be called the Ottoman Empire.

The Ottomans were warlike and predatory with no sophistication in culture and tradition. They became the staunch protagonists of Islamic doctrines with no tolerance for non-Moslem races. They gained the reputation of savage barbarism prompting others to call them Ghazis, the holy warriors of the faith. They were led by Sultans whose atrocities tended to overshadow their military prowess. Most of the Sultans applied heinous brutality in administering the lives of their subjects with no regard for human life. One of them is reported to have killed 35,000 men by his own hand. Another ordered the massacre of half a million Armenians. An early Sultan instructed his men to strangle his orphan nephews while listening to their cries from an adjoining room. Some were corrupt and others were debauched thugs. It soon became their practice, upon rising to power, to kill all their brothers and other pretenders to the throne to assure that there will be no struggle for succession within the royal family. One of them had his nineteen brothers strangled by mutes and their bodies tossed out into the street for the people to see. Another ordered the Moslem jurists to codify the practice of fratricide by declaring that "the son to whom Allah grants the Sultanate may lawfully put his brothers to death".

Most of the Sultans led a promiscuous life with harems full of wives and innumerable concubines, and practiced bizarre and imaginative sexual perversions. One of them required the services of three concubines in a single night enabling him to sire more than one hundred children who were later slaughtered when one of them rose to power. The harems of another was so huge that it required the services of 3,000 eunuchs to manage the administration of the household. One of the Sultans drowned six pregnant concubines to prevent them to give birth to pretenders to the throne and another had the habit of sending his scouts to the public baths every night to bring beautiful women for his pleasure. A number of them were homosexual and once a Sultan ordered the decapitation of a Christian aristocrat's entire family when the man refused to turn over his handsome teenage son for Sultan's pleasure.

EXPANSION INTO BYZANTINE TERRITORY

Upon rising to power Osman immediately initiated a military campaign which resulted in the expansion of his territory towards the Byzantine Empire. Through successful raids and invasions he gained control of large chunks of Byzantine territory in Anatolia and around the Black Sea. His conquests were effective and speedy primarily because of the inability of the Byzantines to launch a counter attack. His successes won him the loyalty of his people and within a few years he was able to secure possession of major centers of the Byzantine Empire. In 1326 his troops captured Bursa and made it their capital. Nicaea followed in 1329 and Nicodemia in 1337. But it was in 1356 that the Ottomans gained a decisive victory over Byzantium when they reached the Sea of Marmara, crossed the Dardanelles and secured a bridgehead on the European continent. In 1362 the Turks made themselves the masters of Thrace and Macedonia and moved their capital to Adrianople. Within a few generations the Ottomans became the overlords of most of the Byzantine territories in Asia Minor and Europe. The area left for Byzantium was the city of Constantinople and a parcel of land in the Hellenic peninsula.

Prostrate Byzantium simply watched in frustration and fear. The emperors abandoned all efforts to regain their territories and accepted the *fait accompli* of the Turkish rise to power. Having lost all its vitality the Empire was on the verge of collapse with no European potentate eager to mourn its demise. Internal quarrels and religious disunity prevented the Christians in the west to mount a unified resistance against the Turkish avalanche. Rome was not interested in helping Byzantium without receiving assurances from the Greeks to submit themselves to the Pope's supremacy. The schism between the two churches had become so well entrenched that neither side was willing to help the other. Taking advantage of this Christian sterility, the Turks gradually extended their territory from central Anatolia to Bulgaria and Serbia and laid the foundation of an empire that will stretch, within a few generations, from the Euphrates to the gates of Vienna, from the Black Sea to the eastern half of continental Europe, across north Africa to the Atlantic. To legitimize their conquests the Sultans began a program of forced migration of the Turks to the newly occupied territories.

As the Turks advanced towards the interior of Europe they faced relatively little resistance. Small principalities were willing to accept the Sultan as their ruler and agreed to pay tribute. So did John Paleologus, the Byzantine Emperor. He signed a treaty with the Sultan accepting him as his suzerain, making Byzantium a vassal state with an annual payment of tribute to the Ottomans.

ARMENIAN BOYS RECRUITED TO FIGHT FOR ISLAM

It was Sultan Murad I during the latter part of the Fourteenth century who transformed the Turkish army from mere plunderers into a regimented military organization. To bolster his army's strength Murad initiated a program to recruit young boys from Armenian and Greek families and developed them into a well trained, highly disciplined and coordinated militia and called it Janissaries, the new force in Turkish. Each Armenian family was required to give its brightest son to be enlisted as a Janissary for the services of the Sultan, similar to the conscription of the Memluks from the Caucasus centuries earlier. The Janissaries were brought up as Moslems imbued with an unquestioned loyalty to the Sultan and became members of a privileged military elite. As fighters by avocation they lived their lives with uncompromising devotion to the cause of Islam. In times of peace they kept order and guarded the imperial palaces. In times of war their ferocious brutality proved to be vital for the conduct of the war.

TAMERLANE AND THE TATARS

When Sultan Bayazid I rose to power he wanted to shift his attention from Europe to the east, to assure his hold on Asia Minor and prepare an all out attack on Constantinople to finish up the Byzantine Empire. Preparations to attack Constantinople were halted, however, in the spring of 1402 when the Turkish forces were threatened by a more barbarous and formidable power which will allow the Greek state to continue its life for another fifty years.

Around the middle of the Fourteenth century a tribe of Tatars appeared in the light of history to spread death and destruction in Asia, Russia, and the Near East. Originally they accompanied the Mongol army during its march to the west but finally settled around Samarkand during the declining years of the Mongolian power. Headed by a man called Tamerlane, the Tatars expanded their territory through successful raids and plunder. In time Tamerlane, who claimed descent from Jengis Khan, came to be regarded as the personification of evil for his savage barbarism and his ability to smash everything in his way. As he began to expand his Empire he exacted casualties of millions of people and within a few years subjugated lands from the great walls of China to western Russia and the Caspian Sea.

If the Mongols were brutal the Tatars were inhumanly barbaric. In 1370 Tamerlane's warrior hordes poured down into Iran, Mesopotamia, and Syria and then marched north, conquered Afganistan, slaughtered thousands and built towers using live human beings piled on top of each other with bodies cemented together with mortar. In Isfahan, after ravaging the land and massacring 70,000 men Tamerlane used the skulls of the corpses to build minarets. He did the same in Baghdad when in 1393 his forces took the town and used severed heads of the inhabitants to build towers with faces looking out. Tamerlane invaded Greater Armenia and put all the inhabitants of Van to the sword. 4,000 Armenians were buried alive in a plain which has since been called *Sev Hogher* (Black Ground). Children's skulls were crushed against pavements and their mothers, tied to the tail of wild horses were dragged in the streets until they died. Tamerlane left a carnage of terror in Armenia and made thousands of families homeless.

Having completed his conquests in Western Asia Tamerlane marched against the Ottomans in 1402, occupied the city of Ankara, captured Sultan Bayazid I, and, according to legend, ordered him to serve as his footstool for the rest of his life. Bayazid died in captivity and Tamerlane returned to Samarkand in 1405 where he died shortly thereafter. The Tatar Empire was left in shambles and the Ottoman Empire was thrown into a state of anarchy. The dynastic struggle for succession among the four sons of Sultan Bayazid I lasted a decade. In 1413 one of them, Mehmed, rose to power and became Sultan Mehmed I and gradually regained all the territories lost to the Tatars.

THE FALL OF CONSTANTINOPLE

If Sultan Bayazid failed to conquer Constantinople, his great grandson will be able to do it with ease. After reorganizing their army the Ottoman Sultans began to exact economic and military pressure on Byzantium and in 1422 began to move their forces to the walls of Constantinople. Alarmed, Emperor John VIII Paleologus decided to sail to Italy with the Patriarch of Constantinople and a retinue of 700 Greek bishops, theologians, and scholars, to negotiate a church unity and attempt to enlist western help to save his Empire from impending calamity. The Emperor and the Pope had agreed to summon an ecumenical council in Florence, under the sponsorship of the prominent Medici family, to discuss issues that had kept the two great churches of Christendom at loggerheads for six centuries. The principal point of the dispute was the origin and nature of the Holy Ghost. After ineffectual sermons and futile ecclesiastical maneuvers that lasted almost two years, a declaration of union was finally signed in 1439 with the Greeks accepting the supremacy of the Pope in return of a promise of military assistance from Rome. When the pact of unity was leaked to Constantinople the Greeks were infuriated. They refused to endorse the unification process and issued a manifesto of their own to reject the Council of Florence. The slogan "better the Sultan's turban than the Cardinal's hat" had already become fashionable in the capital of Byzantium. The brutal terror that the Latins inflicted on Constantinople during the Fourth Crusade was still fresh in their mind. The church unity evaporated, the Pope withdrew his support, and Europe abandoned all efforts to save Byzantium and left the Greeks to their own fate.

In 1451 Sultan Mehmed II rose to power and immediately began preparations to attack Constantinople. The Ottoman Empire was disturbed by palace intrigue and Mehmed needed to make a show of force to consolidate his position. After removing potential rivals Mehmed reorganized the Janissaries and marched towards Constantinople.

On the fifth of April 1453 the Sultan placed a formidable army immediately outside the walls of Constantinople. By employing European engineers, who were as anxious as the Turks to crush the Byzantine power, the Turks built heavy siege machinery with caliber cannons big enough to smash the walls. Emperor John VIII had been succeeded by his brother, Constantin IX Paleologus, who found himself unable to organize a military force powerful enough to launch a counterattack. The capital was hard hit by the results of continuous warfare. The palaces were in ruin and the Bubonic Plague of the Black Death had ravaged most of the population. The splendor and glory of Byzantium had vanished, the government was crippled and the military had become impotent with only 7,000 men, mostly non-Greek mercenaries, facing an enemy of 80,000 strong.

Having surrounded Constantinople by land and sea the Turkish combat forces began to hit the walls with cannons blazing. Scraping together several ships Mehmed launched a naval attack from the sea to batter the city walls down as his army intensified the bombardment from the land. The battle reached its climax on May 29, 1453.

The Sultan was ready for the final assault. During the night he walked around the camp and reminded his officers of the will of Prophet Mohammed who is claimed to have said "He who will conquer Konstantiniya and spend the emperor's treasures in God's behalf, will be the rightly guided one". Mehmed promised his men the freedom to pillage the city and rape the women, or the young men of their choice.

Inside the capital the situation had become hopeless. Cut off from food, water, and the outside world, the Greeks huddled together as the troops continued to defend the walls. The Emperor had organized a solemn procession with clergymen carrying the bones of their saints and offering prayer to the heavenly God. In Hagia Sophia, which had symbolized the glory of Byzantium for one thousand years, the Patriarch of the Byzantine Church conducted what was to be the last Christian service.

As the sun began to rise the Janissaries climbed up the walls with cries of *Allah-Akbar, Allah-Akbar.* The Byzantine forces on the other side, encouraged by cries of women and children, fought with great courage to chase the Turks down the walls. Emperor Constantin IX removing his royal insignia, threw himself into the Janissaries and began to swing his sword left and right. He was instantly killed and his body was never recovered. The Turks smashed one of the gates and placed the Ottoman flag over the wall. They poured into the city in an orgy of looting and devastation and began to massacre men, women, and children. Sultan Mehmed II, surrounded by his Janissaries, made a triumphal entry into Constantinople. He proceeded straight to the gate of Hagia Sophia, dismounted from his horse, took a handful of earth and sprinkled his turbaned head as an act of humiliation before God. He then entered the church and gave orders to turn Hagia Sophia into a mosque. A Moslem imam climbed up to the pulpit and recited the Islamic prayer. Outside the bodies of the victims were left unburied to be devoured later by savage dogs.

This was Islam's greatest victory over Christianity. With the fall of Constantinople the Byzantine Empire ceased to exist. For over 1,000 years it had preserved the cultural heritage of the Greco-Roman civilization and acted as the central power for the Christian faith in the east. All was gone. Only a remnant of this Empire will continue to exist in the mountains of Athos, Greece, where the emblem of Byzantium will fly over the monastery of the Greek monks who will to this day piously recite the names of the Byzantine emperors in their daily prayers.

With the Crusaders out of the Near East and the Byzantine Empire completely destroyed, Islam stood at the threshold of a triumphant era with immense possibilities for world domination. The conquest of Constantinople gave the Turks the control of the waterways, with the Bosporus as the bridgehead between

the Black Sea and the Mediterranean. Mehmed exploited the
prestige of his victory to dominate much of the eastern Mediterranean and place the remaining Byzantine possession under his
control. In 1456 Athens was taken and the Parthenon, the symbol of the Hellenic civilization, was converted into a Moslem
mosque. The victory of the Turks created a new world in
which Islam was the most powerful force and Christianity was
regarded as an anachronism tarnished with signs of potential
weakness.

ARMENIANS UNDER THE OTTOMAN RULE

Sultan Mehmed II immediately began to centralize his government. The most important issue of the moment was to provide a
new unity for his Empire and break the power of the non-
Moslem elements in the administration of the state. He made
Constantinople the capital of the Empire. The first order of the
day was to repopulate the city and initiate a vigorous program
of reconstruction. Located on both continents, Europe and
Asia, Constantinople provided the most important maritime
route between the Black Sea and the Mediterranean, and
eventually helped the Turks to make the Black Sea an Ottoman
lake. To build the city's economic organization Mehmed
moved thousands of Armenian families from Cilicia and Greater Armenia and forced them to settle in Constantinople. With
their reputation as good merchants and bankers the Armenians
began to participate in international trade. Using the old Armenian cities as way stations they began to import goods from Asia
and exported them to Europe.

Mehmed the Conqueror, as he was now called, demonstrated an unusual skill of statesmanship by granting a considerable degree of freedom to non-Moslems and made the
Armenians free to run their mercantile activity without much
interference from the state. To bring the disenfranchised into
the fold of the Ottoman society he adopted a system of *Millet*,
an autonomous self-government of ethnic communities and offered the church leaders the opportunity to run their respective
communities within the framework of the Ottoman Empire. He
summoned the Armenian Archbishop of Bursa in 1461 and
made him the Patriarch of the Armenian Church with religious
and secular powers to run the affairs of the Armenian communi-

ty in the capital and the provinces. Twenty years earlier the seat of the Supreme Catholicos had been transferred from Sis in Cilicia to Echmiadzin, the birthplace of the Armenian Christian faith. This transfer eventually created a division within the church with the emergence of two other Catholicates, one in Aghtamar in Lake Van and the other in Cilicia, which continues to this day in Antelias, Lebanon. While the Catholicos in Echmiadzin continued to act as the titular head of the Armenian Church, Mehmed decreed the overall authority for the Armenian people to reside in the Armenian Patriarchate of Constantinople. This was a clever political design. He wanted to focalize the power within the confines of the Ottoman capital and in his own back yard.

The Millet system, engineered to find a new basis of loyalty from non-Moslem elements, placed the ethnic minorities into religiously oriented groups with distinguishable features to separate them from the Moslems. The non-Moslems were required to use different dress codes. The Armenians were ordered to wear a bonnet of red, black, and yellow, with violet boots and slippers. The judicial system was separated. The Armenian community was governed by Armenian Church laws and the people were tried by their own clergymen. Turkish laws applied only to cases when the Armenian ecclesiastical laws were inadequate for a particular litigation. Each Armenian community was allowed to establish and maintain its own schools, hospitals, and institutions under the superintendence of the Armenian Patriarchate and within the purview of the Ottoman government. In the provinces the Armenians were allowed to live in their own separate quarters centered around the Armenian Church and led by the local clergy. The regimentation of their lives helped them to preserve their identity. In the villages the Armenians were mostly farmers, worked their land and paid taxes to the Sultan on a proportion of their farm products. In the cities they were the professionals and the merchants.

In spite of this seemingly organic unity, the gulf remained wide between the Armenians and the Turks and the government failed to weld them into a unified society. There were wide differences in culture and traditions. At times the laws of the Armenian Millet were in conflict with Turkish laws. The testimony of an Armenian involving a Turk carried no weight and was not acceptable in the court of law.

This fragmentation caused by the Ottoman policy and diversity of culture will never be mended, and in time will become a source of irritation to the Turks, who will begin to resent the existence of segregated Armenian enclaves in their midst. Some Sultans tried to force the amalgamation of the two communities with no success. Some Turkish governors in the interior tried to impose harsh measures to fuse the Armenians and Turks together. They prohibited the use of any language other than Turkish. In these districts the Armenians could speak Armenian at the risk of having their tongues cut off.

ARMENIA TORN APART

While the Ottomans had successfully conquered southeastern Europe, the eastern provinces of Anatolia and Greater Armenia were still in the hands of the Persians, who were immensely wealthy and militarily powerful. Around the end of the Fifteenth century, after a series of murders and dynastic intrigues, a new Persian dynasty, the Safavids, headed by one Ismail, liberated Persia from foreign domination and coalesced the various tribal groups into a national unity. Ismail established a regime with traditional Shiite doctrines and decreed fanatic Moslem fundamentalist ideas and programs. The Ottoman Turks opposed the Safavids not only because they represented a political threat to their territorial integrity, but also as Sunni Moslems, the Turks regarded the Shiites as heretics and religiously unacceptable.

Soon Ismail's followers enlarged their territories, occupied Baghdad, slaughtered thousands of Sunni Moslems, and destroyed Sunni mosques and religious establishments.

The destruction of Baghdad infuriated the Ottoman Turks. Sultan Salim I, after rising to power in 1512, reorganized the Ottoman's military structure, beefed up the ranks of the Janissaries, and with a sizable army marched against the Safavids. He took Greater Armenia with ease, chased the Shiites to the mountains, and crushed the Safavid power. Salim then diverted his attention to the Memluks in the south who had continued to pose a threat to Turkey's policy of aggrandizement. He ordered the Ottoman forces to invade Armenian Cilicia, and in 1515 with hardly any resistance from the Memluks, occupied Cilicia and immediately began to establish lines of communication with the capital.

With the Safavids out of the way, at least temporarily, Salim I then invaded Syria and took Aleppo, followed by Damascus a few months later. The swift victory of the Ottomans over the Memluks was facilitated by the Armenians living in Syria and Palestine. Their participation in the fight between the two Moslem powers was publicized as an act of revenge for the Memluk attacks on territories inhabited by Armenians. In January 1517 the Ottomans crossed the Sinai, entered Egypt and crushed the Memluk power in Cairo. To commemorate their victory they butchered 25,000 people and put thousands of Memluk army officers to the sword. The Memluk power was annihilated and the dynasty as a political force came to an end. The Sultan of the Ottomans took his place in line of the Moslem tradition, as the "Servant and Protector of the Islamic Faith". The Turks took control of the entire Arab world and became the principal custodian of the holy places of the Prophet. The power of Islam shifted from the valley of the Nile to the city on the Bosporus, leaving the Arab world in a state of oblivion. The Sultan brought the Caliphate to Constantinople and established his hegemony over the Islamic world. He was now ready to pursue his plan for world domination. He will soon tell his Vizier that he will someday ride to Rome and feed his horse on the altar of St. Peter's Basilica.

SULEYMAN THE MAGNIFICENT

Salim I will not be able to achieve his goal but his son will come very close. Salim died in 1520 and was succeeded by his son Suleyman I, whose reign will mark the most glorious period of the Ottoman Empire. With virtually no opposition, Suleyman enlarged his Empire far beyond what he inherited from his predecessors. He pushed the frontiers of his Empire to the heart of Europe and consolidated the various regions of the provinces to form an organic unity. With a flurry of bold strikes he successfully pulverized the forces of his foes and made his reign the zenith of the Ottoman Empire. Suleyman will be regarded as one of Turkey's great military leaders prompting his contemporaries to bestow the epitaph "Magnificent" upon him.

Suleyman accomplished his first objective by annexing Hungary to the Ottoman Empire. He occupied the twin cities of Buda and Pest and burned them to the ground. He rewarded his men with gold bullion taken from the Hungarian treasury and ordered centuries old treasures to be transported to Constantinople. Suleyman's military success and spectacular conquests in Europe were partially due to the religious upheaval caused by the movement of the Reformation. The Protestants, in attempting to reform the archaic practices of the Catholic Church, regarded the Pope and not the Turks as their foe. The spread of ill will towards Rome had changed the fabric of the Christian community, making it impotent to organize a unified force to check the Turkish advance. While the Catholics were still immensely powerful, the hold of Rome on Christian Europe had weakened considerably. The Christian despots had begun to rule their great fiefdoms as private kingdoms with no central figure powerful enough to lead the march against the Turks.

Suleyman consolidated his forces in Hungary and made the country the center of his European military operation. His annexation of Hungary, however, brought the Turks into direct conflict with the Hapsburgs of Austria. His next project was an all out assault on Vienna, the center of the Hapsburg military establishment and the gateway to western Europe. Vienna proved a formidable obstacle, however, and forever destroyed Suleyman's will to continue his thrust into the interior of Europe. The Hapsburgs marshalled all their resources and successfully stopped Suleyman's army at the gates of Vienna. This was a decisive victory for Christian Europe. The Ottoman defeat at Vienna was a turning point forcing the Turks to retreat. The Ottomans will never be able to penetrate Europe beyond this point and gradually succumb into a long period of decline.

While the Turks were fighting in Europe the Safavids in Persia occupied Armenia and disrupted the political balance of power in the eastern region. After returning from Europe Suleyman decided to turn his attention to Persia, crush Safavid's power base and secure the eastern approaches to Turkey. He invaded Armenia and after annexing the Erzerum and Van regions to Turkey, proceeded south, chased the Shiites out of Baghdad, and reinstituted the Sunni rule. To preserve the continuity of their political system the Safavids sued for peace. Under a peace accord signed by Turkey and Persia, Armenia became dissected into two parts. The western region came under the Ottoman rule and the eastern section remained under the Safavid control. From this point on Armenia will become a political football between the Turks and the Persians. The Ottoman influence in Armenia will soon vanish by the rise of a powerful Safavid who will design a new destiny for the people on the plains of Mount Ararat.

ARMENIANS UNDER SHAH ABBAS

The Safavid Shah Abbas rose to power in 1587 and immediately began to mobilize his forces to attack the Ottoman military strongholds in eastern Anatolia. He recaptured the major portion of Armenia in 1603, taking Kars and Ardahan and pushing the Turks to the borders of Lake Van. He ordered his men to massacre Sunni Turks, kill their leaders by boiling them in oil, and blind their children by pouring vinegar in their eyes. To make the Armenian territory a wasteland and useless to the Turks, Shah Abbas obliterated the towns and villages and ordered the mass deportation of thousands of Armenian families to Persia. Crossing the Arax River most of the Armenian women and children perished. The survivors managed to reach Persia and settled in a town called New Juffa, near the capital city of Isfahan. The Armenian refugees in Persia immediately began to build their new community and in time converted New Juffa into one of the most important centers of international commerce. In deporting the Armenians to Persia the Shah's political maneuver was to legitimize his occupation of Armenia by removing the Armenians from their ancestral homeland and at the same time exploiting the Armenian business acumen to restore Persia's rapidly deteriorating economic structure.

Within a generation the Armenian refugees in New Juffa took control of major businesses in Persia and began to manufacture and export goods. They developed new techniques in the production of silk and within a short period of time assumed the monopoly of the entire silk and textile industry of Persia. Armenian merchants began to develop new trading posts throughout Persia and territories bordering the Safavid Empire. They organized a system of banking and established favorable relations with the merchant houses in Europe and Asia. To enhance the mercantile activity Shah Abbas granted extraordinary privileges to the Armenian merchants and added new roads to the existing system of international trade. New commercial contacts brought the exotic products of the east, such as ivory, spices, and precious stones, for resale in the European markets. New Juffa served as an intermediary to funnel trade between the east and the Mediterranean world.

This commercial activity made the Armenians in Persia enormously prosperous. Within a few generations these former refugees began to live in luxuriant estates with summer houses on the Caspian Sea. Economic prosperity brought new vigor which will soon be galvanized into a political movement to attempt to lay the foundation of a kingship on the Armenian soil. A new power in the north, however, will soon change the political spectrum posing a threat to the territorial integrity of both the Ottomans and the Persians and design a new destiny for the Armenian people.

THE RISE OF THE CZARS

While the power of the Ottomans began to recede, the Russians in the north began to organize an empire of their own. Soon after the fall of Constantinople the Russians began to act as the successors to the Byzantines to perpetuate Byzantium's religious heritage within the framework of Christian Orthodoxy. It began in 1480 when Ivan III liberated Russia from the Tatars, coalesced the Russian principalities and formed a political organization. He married Sophia Paleologus, the niece of the last Byzantine Emperor, adopted the Byzantine insignia of the double headed eagle, and assumed the title of Czar, which was a Slavonic equivalent of the word Cæsar.

Ivan became a self ordained and self designated legal heir to Byzantium and turned Moscow into another Rome. If Byzantium was the link between the world of ancient times and the new world emerging from the Middle Ages, Russia provided the liaison between the Slavic east and the amorphous states of the European continent.

The Turks in the south never considered the Russians as a threat to their policy of territorial expansion. Political conditions began to change considerably, however, when Ivan's grandson, Ivan the Terrible, rose to power in 1547, and developed an ambitious program to transform the Grand Duchy of

Muscovy into an empire with a design to install a political structure reminiscent of that of Byzantium of the past.

The origin of the Russians as a people was not too spectacular. Before the rise of the Romanov dynasty in the early Seventeenth century they were regarded as a bizarre conglomerate of people led by autocrats with perverse and savage disposition. For the Armenians, however, the rise of this northern power, savage or otherwise, will bring new opportunities offering a fresh approach to formulate a new direction in their struggle for survival. If other people regarded the Russians as savage barbarians, the Armenians considered them as their uncle and sought to build their fortunes under the Russian tutelage not necessarily because of their abundant love towards the Russians, but because there was no other power at the time which was willing to protect the Christian minorities. Their first contact with the Russians began when Armenian merchants in New Juffa established commercial ties in the north, and through special privileges granted by the Czar, took control of the entire silk and textile industry in the Russian provinces. The vast regions of the Russian continent had been devastated by Tamerlane's raids, and acute shortages of the basic commodities brought Russia to the brink of economic anarchy and deprivation. Russia's resources were impaired and the Czars began to look outside to establish a semblance of economic order.

Politically it will be Peter the Great in 1696 who will bring a new vitality, reorganize Russia's archaic system of government, modernize the army by adopting western customs, and through a revival accompanied by a military renaissance, raise Russia to the status of a primary power. A man with impeccable qualities of leadership, Peter's first goal was to extend his frontiers to the south and acquire territories from the Ottomans with an eye towards the warmer waters of the Mediterranean. He began his expansion by breaking the old political barriers and in the process became one of the great constructive statesmen in the history of his people.

His career also marked the beginning of a new era for the Armenians. He will be the first of many Czars who will direct Russia's interest towards the Caucasus and assume the role of protector of the Armenian interests. This was not exactly a demonstration of charitable sentiments towards the Armenians. The Czar's ulterior motive was to use Armenia for his own purposes. He wanted to use Armenia as a point of entry and enlist native cooperation of the Christians to fight the Persians and the Turks. By now eastern Anatolia had become a hotbed of secessionist feelings and people everywhere had begun to organize nationalistic movements. Christians looked to Russia for guidance and support.

AN ATTEMPT TO ESTABLISH AN ARMENIAN KINGSHIP

While the Armenians in Persia were being treated reasonably well by their Safavid masters the Armenians in Armenia proper suffered considerably. The churches were in ruin and the clergy were in prison. Around the end of the Seventeenth century they began to nurture sentiments to establish an independent political structure and extricate themselves from Persian oppression. At a national conference held in 1678 in Echmiadzin the Armenian noblemen decided to appeal to the western powers to secure a territorial independence and lay the foundation for a kingship on the Armenian soil. The council decided to send Catholicos Hagop IV to Europe with a delegation of Armenian aristocrats to discuss the issue of political recognition with the foreign potentates.

The Catholicos became ill on the way to Europe and died in Constantinople. A member of the mission, a nineteen-year-old nationalist by the name of Israel Ori, the scion of a noble family, took over the leadership of the delegation and continued the journey. Ori went to Rome and promised Pope Innocent XII that Armenia would be willing to accept the Catholic doctrines and recognize Pope's primacy if Rome helped his people to gain their independence. His idea for church unification, however, was promptly rejected by the newly elected Catholicos in Echmiadzin. Ori then proceeded to Russia to discuss the issue of independence with Peter the Great. While the great Czar was sympathetic to the Armenian cause, he showed no interest in any direct military confrontation with the Persians. His plan then was to transform the Black Sea into a Russian lake. Disillusioned and dismayed, Israel Ori returned home a broken man and died in 1711. Legend has it that his name was an anagram of "il sera roi", he will be a king. He failed to become one, but the spirit of independence will not die. His people will continue their struggle for freedom.

THE MALIKS OF KARABAGH

Shortly after Ori's adventurous mission the Armenian warriors, known as the Maliks, in the mountainous region of Karabagh organized an uprising under the leadership of David Beg to free the region from the Turkish domination. Through guerrilla warfare and with a remarkable demonstration of ferocious fighting, the Maliks managed to gain their freedom by chasing the Turks to eastern Anatolia. They immediately established a system of government, built churches, and reorganized the traditional Armenian institutions. They fought stoutly to legitimize their political organization and held the Turks and the Persians in check. Their independence will be short-lived, however. They were not strong enough militarily to maintain their autonomy and found themselves repudiated by foreign powers. Angered by this unexpected show of force and the rise of Armenian nationalism in the east, the Turks enlisted the cooperation of the native Kurds, invaded Karabagh and crushed the Armenian Maliks. David Beg died in 1730 and the Turks annexed the region to the Ottoman Empire.

Meanwhile in Persia the Safavid rule was coming to an end. Internal weakness and dynastic quarrels had turned the reign of Shah Husayn into a period of political anarchy. Taking advantage of this political deterioration, an Afgan tribe in the north invaded Persia in 1723 and forced Husayn to surrender. On the way to Persia the Afgans invaded Armenia, ravaged the countryside and butchered thousands of Armenian men, women, and children. Turmoil in the south encouraged Peter the Great to move his army into the Caucasus. The Turks, alarmed by this Russian military build up in Western Asia, began to move their forces towards Armenia and the eastern provinces. Both sides knew that the territorial spoils left by the Safavids were too great to wait too long. The Russians occupied the southern region of the Caucasus and the Turks took the Armenian towns of Kars, Ardahan, Erevan, and Nakhichevan. The territorial dispute was resolved by a peace agreement in 1724 in which Armenia, Georgia, and Azerbeijan came under the Ottoman control and the lower provinces of the Caspian Sea went to the Russians.

CATHERINE THE GREAT AND THE ARMENIANS

If Peter the Great wished to transform a backward nation into a civilized society, Catherine the Great wished to revive the glories of Byzantium, conquer Constantinople, and install her

grandson, Constantine on the throne of a new Byzantium.
While she will not be able to achieve her goal, she will, nevertheless expand the borders of her Empire at the expense of the
Ottomans. Shortly after occupying the throne in 1762 Catherine
pushed the frontiers of Russia to include the Crimea, Poland,
and the Ukraine. In the Caucasus she met Turkish resistance.
The Ottomans prevented Catherine to establish a permanent
foothold in Western Asia. Under a treaty signed at Katchuk Kai-
mardji in 1774 Russia agreed to give up its hold of the eastern
strip of Armenia, and the Sultan agreed to allow the Russians to
establish a sort of protectorate over the Armenians and other
Christian minorities in the Ottoman Empire. It is this treaty that
will set the tone of relationship between Russia and Turkey that
will continue until World War I.

By the beginning of the Nineteenth century it had become
abundantly clear that the Ottoman Empire was on the verge of
political decay and the decadent rule of the Sultans was coming
to an end. People in the west had begun to refer to Turkey as
the "sick man of Europe" and Christian monarchs were getting
ready to witness the dismemberment of the Ottoman hegemony. The Russians were the first to exploit the Turkish political
sterility, and one by one began to secure control of the Ottoman possessions around the periphery of their Empire.

Through a series of military victories the Czars inflicted
humiliating defeat after defeat on Turkey and occupied the territories of the Caucasus. Russia's imperialistic policy did not sit
well, however, with the kings of England and France. They
wanted to preserve the balance of power, keep the existing borders intact, and maintain the *status quo* on the continent. In
April 1828 Czar Nicholas I declared war on Turkey and the Russian forces immediately began their advance towards eastern
Anatolia. With the help of local Armenian guerrilla units the
Russians occupied Kars, Erzerum, Erevan, and Nakhichevan
and found themselves in Western Armenia on the way to the
heart of the Ottoman Empire. The Armenians joyfully accepted
the Russian military adventure and fought fiercely to help the
Russians liberate their country from Turkish oppression. Terrified, the Sultan appealed to the western states. In a peace treaty
signed in 1829 Russia was allowed to keep Eastern Armenia but
was forced to return Western Armenia to Turkey. After gaining
control of the western Armenian provinces the Turks took re-

venge by massacring thousands of Armenian men, women, and children and sending 90,000 Armenians into exile. On the way north most of these Armenian refugees died of starvation, and others perished in the mountains of the Caucasus.

THE CRIMEAN WAR

There was frantic military and political activity among the ambitious European monarchs to exploit the disintegration of the Ottoman Empire and pick up spoils with a passion to pre-empt one another in their struggle for takeover. The Sultan, however, was determined not to surrender an inch of ground.

The Crimean War, between Russia on one side and France and England on the other, was ostensibly fought for this particular purpose. It began in October 1853 when Turkey declared war on Russia and the Ottoman forces crossed the Danube to chase the Russians out of the principalities of Moldavia and Wachovia. To protect their Ottoman friends, England and France declared war on Russia, but instead of attacking Russia in eastern Europe, which would have been a logical strategy, they chose to send their fleets to the Crimea to destroy the Russian naval base and prevent Russia from attacking Turkey from the north. When the European armada began to cross the Dardanelles on the way to the Crimea, the Turkish forces in Armenia began to advance against the Russian troops in the southern Caucasus.

The war in the Crimea was indecisive and no party was powerful enough to claim victory. To change the course of the war Russia invaded Armenia and with the help of Armenian volunteers attacked the Ottoman forces and occupied the Armenian province of Kars. The entire eastern region of the Ottoman Empire was now in jeopardy. The situation changed almost overnight, however, when Czar Nicholas I died in 1855 and the western allies used the occasion to sue for peace.

In a conference held in Paris in 1856 none of the issues for which the war had started were resolved. Both sides had suffered severe losses and neither side was bold enough to demand much from the other. The parties simply agreed to withdraw their forces from areas taken during the war. Accordingly Russia left Western Armenia and the allied forces abandoned the Crimea. Once again the integrity of the Ottoman

Empire was preserved without much loss of prestige. However, the Crimean War will forever change the character of the Ottoman rule. In the course of succeeding decades the Empire will be transformed from an autocratic rule into a constitutional monarchy and the political reform will disturb the traditional stability of the state, accelerate its fragmentation, and ultimately lead to the breakdown of the Empire half a century later.

ARMENIANS SCATTERED AROUND THE WORLD

Armenians began to scatter around the world immediately after the fall of the Cilician Kingdom. Some migrated voluntarily and others were exiled forcibly. Thousands of Armenian families left their homeland, but the majority remained within the proximity of Greater Armenia. The people who chose to settle in other countries did so to flee from the merciless oppression of Armenia's rulers. Their migration to foreign lands, however, did not guarantee immediate social stability. They too suffered persecution and oppression, at least during the initial phases of their settlement, and rarely did they enjoy periods of peace and tranquility. They were the homeless refugees and were regarded as easy targets for persecution. They were the first to be blamed and were used as scapegoats to correct an injustice on foreign soil. In most cases they were able to maintain their separate identity with no desire to participate in the social stratification of the host country. As migrants from a distant land they were bound together by a sense of destiny with a mission to maintain the fundamental tenets of their tradition.

From Greater Armenia and Cilicia the Armenians migrated to places as remote as India, China, Singapore, and western Europe. Some converted, intermarried, and chose to forget their heritage but others built churches, schools, and continued to transmit their traditions from one generation to the next. When the Kingdom of Ani was destroyed the Armenians migrated to Poland and in the course of time lost their identity as a people. The same was the case for the Armenians who migrated to India and the Far East. People went and settled in other countries but made no effort to come home even when conditions in the homeland had become favorable. Their sentimental attachment to the motherland had no political intonation. They regarded Armenia as a country of their dreams but preferred to stay abroad and look at it from afar.

ARMENIANS AS MERCHANTS

The settlement of Armenians in foreign lands brought a profound change in the economic development of the host countries. In choosing their livelihood the Armenian migrants were versatile enough to engage in an occupation which was generally despised by the community at large. If commerce was not regarded as a valued activity by the local inhabitants, the Armenians became merchants and tradesmen and successfully exploited that activity to the fullest, making themselves and the country prosperous.

From the status of homeless refugees they graduated to become successful businessmen and acquired the reputation as honest and trustworthy entrepreneurs in domestic and foreign trade. In Venice the Armenians established merchant and banking houses as early as 1497. Their colony consisted of sea captains, shipowners, and engineers. Among the prominent members were Kevork Theodosian whose family controlled large tracts of real estate for over 120 years, Aslan Barsek, the proprietor of large cotton mills, David and Mardiros, the manufacturers of fine leather goods, and Manoog, an industrialist who became the owner of sugar refineries in Italy. Most of these Armenians, however, intermarried with Italians and in the course of time lost their national identity.

In the north of Europe the Armenian migrants settled in the Netherlands as early as the Thirteenth century. In 1478 an Armenian colony was established in Bruges and merchants began to sell pearls and diamonds in Amsterdam. They were granted special privileges and concessions by both the Ottomans and the Dutch to export-import diamonds and precious stones between Europe and the east. In the Middle East Armenians established large commercial enterprises stretching their mercantile activity to China, India, Ceylon, Siam, Java, and the Philippines. They became enormously wealthy and lived opulent lives with palaces and summer villas on the Caspian Sea and the Mediterranean.

In the middle of the Eighteenth century the Armenian merchants from New Juffa established merchant houses in Russia and India. Notable among them were Aghazar, who ran a successful cotton and silk operation in Moscow, and Petros Voskanian who later became associated with The East India Company. When Persian rulers began to impose unreasonable taxation on the Armenian merchants in New Juffa, Armenians began to leave Persia and settled in India. An Armenian woman, Mariam Zamani, was crowned as the Queen of India. She encouraged the new Armenian settlers to build churches in Agra, Delhi, Calcutta, Surat, Bombay, and Madras. The Armenians built trading posts and by the middle of the Sixteenth century took over the entire mercantile activity of India. It was the Armenian merchants in India who later helped the English and the Dutch to secure a foothold on the Indian subcontinent. With their successful contacts with the Moghuls of India the Armenians helped the British East India Company to establish its operation in India with long sea routes to Europe. In return the British allowed the Armenians to use the English ships to transport goods from east to west. A group of Armenians from India established commercial enterprises in Hong Kong, Singapore, and Malaysia. An Armenian financier, Sir Catchick Paul Chafer, represented the colony of Hong Kong during the coronation ceremonies of the British monarch in London.

The Armenians came to North America as early as 1623 when a group of Armenian businessmen was invited by the Governor of Virginia to establish a silkworm breeding operation. Large scale Armenian immigration to the New World, however, did not start until the 1850's.

ARMENIANS IN ASIA MINOR

The largest concentration of Armenians remained around the periphery of the Armenian heartland. In large metropolitan areas, such as Baku on the Caspian Sea, Smyrna and Constantinople in the west, the Armenians were the leading businessmen and the financiers for the Ottomans and the Persians. They developed an important network of commercial activities and in most cases managed to control entire industries exclusively.

The most important center for the Armenian social, cultural, political, and religious life was Constantinople. Armenians settled in Constantinople after the fall of Cilicia to flee from Tamerlane's persecution and Memluk oppression. Their settlement in the Ottoman capital was encouraged by the Sultans who wanted to use the business acumen and the commercial expertise of the Armenians to build an economic order for the Turkish Empire. In the course of time the Armenians acquired important positions as merchants, financiers, bankers, industrialists, ship owners, architects, and engineers. Most of the administrators of the Ottoman government were Armenians. The wealthy Armenians were called Amiras and their fortunes rivaled that of the Turkish pashas. Trade and wealth were concentrated in the hands of the Amiras whose merchant houses supplied goods needed by the entire country. They held a privileged position in the Ottoman Empire and lived luxuriously on estates and villas in the suburbs of the capital. During the reign of Sultan Abdul-Mejid the Armenian Amiras controlled the entire financial operation of the Ottoman government. The Crimean War was financed primarily by the Armenian bankers in Constantinople and the Sultan found it more convenient to borrow from the Armenians than from the western states.

Among the prominent families in Constantinople were the Duzians who acted as the superintendent of the Imperial Mint, and the Bezjians who ran a successful silk business. A member of the family, Hovhannes, became a protege of the Sultan in 1824 and acted as the financial adviser to the Sublime Porte[1]. He built churches, hospitals, and schools for the Armenian community in Constantinople. Another prominent family was the Dadians who were entrusted to be the custodians of the gun powder for the Ottoman army. As manufacturers of explosives they exerted a considerable influence over the conduct of the military operation of the Empire.

Caesarea, in the heart of Asia Minor, was another important center for Armenian business and commercial life. After the fall of the Bagratuni Kingdom of Ani a large number of Armenians settled in Caesarea and in time took over the entire commercial activity of the region. Rugs produced by Armenian weavers in Caesarea were well known throughout Europe. A

---

[1] The head of the Ottoman government was the Grand Vizier appointed by the Sultan. In 1694 the Grand Vizier acquired an official residence which came to be known as Pasha Kapisi, the Pasha's Gate or more commonly, bab-i-Ali, the Sublime Porte. From this point on the Sublime Porte had become the effective center of the Ottoman government.

prominent member of this community was Kevork, the owner of large tracts of real estate who acted as the commercial attaché between Turkey and the city republics of Italy. The Gemushians, Funduklians, Manoogians, and Selians of Cæsarea rose to prominence in business as the manufacturers of weapons, cutlery, rugs, leather goods, and textiles.

Among the Armenian merchant houses the most visible were the Gulbenkians who exerted considerable influence over the business and financial affairs in the Middle East and Europe until modern times. They rose to prominence immediately after the Crimean War, when the brothers, Serope and Sarkis Gulbenkian opened branch offices in major cities of the Ottoman Empire and Persia. Gullabi Gulbenkian opened a large commercial enterprise in New York City in 1890 and Calouste, Sarkis Gulbenkian's son, became an oil magnate of international repute controlling major interests in the production of petroleum in the Middle East. In the east most of the oil production in Baku was in the hands of Armenian aristocrats whose families earlier had controlled the commercial traffic passing through Azerbeijan and Tiflis.

While the Armenians in Constantinople were prosperous businessmen and professionals, those in the provinces were mostly small businessmen and farmers. The affluence and the privileged economic status of the Armenians in major cities failed to provide economic benefit to the Armenians in the provinces, almost two and one-half million in number. The wealthy regarded the downtrodden in the provinces backward and uneducated and had a contemptuous attitude towards the poor. But it will be this group in the provinces whose claim for social and political justice will eventually lead the people to organize revolutionary movements to secure rights for themselves.

CULTURAL ACTIVITY

The passion of Armenians to preserve their national identity in countries away from home resulted in the growth of literary scholarship. While the Armenian scholars could not enjoy the patronage of kings and royalty, since they no longer had kings or royalty, they were nevertheless able to lay the foundation of a highly cosmopolitan cultural movement in the diaspora.

The principal expression of literature in the Middle Ages was the development of folk songs and lyric poetry recited by troubadours known as *Ashoughs* or *Gusans*. They sang in the vernacular using a language which was an amalgam of Armenian, Turkish, Persian, Arabic, and Georgian. They composed music and sang songs expressing the pleasures and pain of love and to arouse the nationalistic sentiments of the people. Their music was vibrant with philosophical intonations chronicling the events of the day. The most prominent of these Gusans were Frik, Naghash Hovnatan, Ashough Tchivani, and Sayat Nova.

The Armenians in Europe were the first to develop patterns for intellectual activity. The first Armenian book was printed in Venice in 1512 and the first Bible in Armenian was published in Amsterdam in 1660. In 1715 Mekhitar Sebasdatsi established a Benedictine order in Saint Lazarus, an island in the lagoon of Venice. Sponsored by the Doges of Venice, Mekhitar's monastery became a center for immense cultural and intellectual activity. In 1773 a number of these monks separated from the main group, moved to Trieste and eventually settled in Vienna, establishing another order of the Mekhitarists. Both monasteries served and continue to serve as important strongholds for the Armenian culture in the diaspora dedicated to scholarship and the preservation of the Armenian traditions. The monks wrote and published books and periodicals and helped develop the modern Armenian language.

Constantinople was the center of a great surge of creative energy. In the field of arts and sciences it was mainly the Armenians who provided the stimulus to the Turks to develop an Ottoman cultural heritage. In 1868 Hagop Vartovian organized the first Turkish theater and Armenian intellectuals began to introduce new ideas emerging in Europe as a result of the French Revolution. Armenian scholars began to translate western works and introduced them to the Turks.

The Armenian intellectuals began to write history, philosophy, law, and politics. This new renaissance was stimulated by the emergence of modern language, referred to as *Ashkharapar*, the language of the country. As a result the Armenian literature became popularized and writers began to translate the old classics and made them accessible to the public. This was indeed a great age of intellectual vitality. New schools of thought began to replace the free-lance literary style of the troubadours expressed in a language easily understood by the people.

The person who pioneered the use of the modern Armenian language was Khatchadour Abovian who in 1840 wrote a book called *Verk Hayastani* (The Wounds of Armenia) inaugurating a new era in the Armenian literature. Until then the Armenian language was the language of the elite and the clergy. Abovian wrote in the vernacular and moved beyond the traditional norm in which the church had dominated the cultural life of the people. The isolation of the Armenians in small enclaves throughout Western Asia and Asia Minor had stimulated the growth of several dozen dialects with no basis of linguistic uniformity. Abovian's work initiated an era in which the use of the common people's language will gradually eradicate the dialectal differences in the Armenian culture. With his work Abovian laid the goundwork for the struggle for political self-determination. He rekindled the desire of a new social order that will drive the Armenians to fight for their freedom in the succeeding decades.

Abovian's work was a reflection of a new cultural movement in which new thoughts of nationalism will make the Armenians conscious of their ancestral heritage. He wrote about the suffering of his people under foreign domination and his affection for his country and the people. His work will make a deep mark on the subsequent development of Armenian thought heralding the dawn of a new era in which men of letters will depart from the aloofness of traditional ecclesiastical writing and bring the Armenian literature to a simpler and more human level.

With the creation of the people's language a new group of Armenian writers and poets emerged marking the period as one of the golden periods in the history of the Armenian culture. Mekhitarist monk, Father Alishan wrote patriotic poems. Some of the notable writers were Terzian, Yervant Odian, Arpiarian, novelist Dzarents, Bishop Servantsiants, who became an author on Armenian folklore, humorist Hagop Baronian, music composer Gomidas Vartabed, dramatist Sundukian, who made a decisive contribution to the Armenian theater and a poet extraordinaire, Bedros Tourian, who at the age of twenty-one wrote some of the finest poems in the history of Armenian literature. In the mid-1800's Tigran Chukajian wrote a grand opera,

Arshak II and later in the century Armen Tigranian wrote the opera *Anoush*.

THE BEGINNING OF POLITICAL REFORMS

Pressured by foreign powers in the mid-1860's the Sultans reluctantly granted personal liberty, equality, and freedom of speech to their citizens. The foreign powers were particularly concerned about the treatment of the Christian minorities in the Ottoman Empire. The Turks had proved to be less tolerant about their Christian subjects in the recent past. They had massacred thousands of Greeks in Constantinople in 1821 and had put to death the Christians in Lebanon in 1856.

A new intellectual circle was formed by Turkish intellectuals and a society called the Young Ottoman came into existence, and began to foment new ideas of Turkish nationalism. The activities of the society gave rise to a constitution in 1876 and the installation of a representative parliament in the Ottoman Empire. Encouraged by this atmosphere of openness, the Armenians in Constantinople drafted a constitution in 1863 which was promptly ratified by the Turkish government.

This was truly a period of affluence and prosperity for the Armenians. All they needed now was a benevolent Sultan. They thought they had one when a young Ottoman prince, Abdul Hamid rose to power in 1876. Legend had it that his mother was Armenian which may have prompted the Turks to call him by an Armenian name, Bedros. Shortly after Sultan Abdul Hamid's ascension to the Ottoman throne, the Grand Vizier called on the Armenian Patriarch to assure him that under the reign of the new Sultan, the Armenians will be treated fairly with personal liberty and equality before the law. He assured the Patriarch that a sweeping range of affirmative measures will be instituted by the government for the welfare of the Armenian people. The Armenians were elated by the prospect of a new future. The Patriarch made a declaration to his people that a new era had been inaugurated for the Armenian people. Events will soon reveal that both of them were mistaken.

CHAPTER NINETEEN

THE STRUGGLE FOR INDEPENDENCE

Among the thirty-five Sultans of the House of Osman the first ten were the empire builders, but the last twenty-five contributed much to the decline and the eventual demise of the Ottoman Empire. They were all autocratic despots who ruled the Empire with an iron fist. Some converted the personal tyranny into benevolent Sultanates and introduced social and political reforms, particularly during the period known as the *Tenzimet*, in the mid-Nineteenth century, but others were totalitarian tyrants and ruled their Empire with violence and oppression.

Sultan Abdul Hamid II belongs to the last group. About his reign there is little good to be said, except that his incompetent and destructive policies hastened the end of the Empire and brought the collapse of Osman's dynasty, never to rise again. He repudiated the reforms, sent his enemies into exile, established a police state and for thirty-three years ran the affairs of the Empire with the most fearsome absolutism through conspiracy, tyranny, and ruthless brutality. For the Armenians in his Empire this presumably half Armenian will prove to be one of the most inhuman and barbaric rulers whose heinous conduct against the unfortunate Armenians will earn him the epithet as the curse of the Armenian people.

Tradition represents Abdul Hamid as a man dominated by fear. He rose to power through palace intrigue when his brother, the Sultan, was adjudicated as mentally incompetent and the reformists selected him as the ruler most amenable to continue the political reforms instituted by his grandfather. At the beginning of his reign there was a rash of conspiratorial activities in the ranks of his closest associates, with one of them even attempting to organize a *coup d'etat* against him. It may have been this abortive attempt on his life that made Abdul Hamid a pathologically paranoid person to the point that he trusted nobody except a boyhood friend, an Armenian banker by the name of Hagop Pasha. He installed devious programs to forestall any conspiracy against the throne, and made his palace a virtual fortress, rarely venturing outside his residence.

Abdul Hamid was perpetually obsessed about the safety of his life. He surrounded himself with thousands of guards, secret police, and intelligence officers. He ordered the construction of guard houses and a second wall around his palace to secure maximum safety. He centralized the power of the Empire around the throne and transferred most of the functions of the government from the Sublime Porte to the palace. He referred to his ministers as parasites and delegated his authority on the basis of treacherous machinations of playing one against the other. He instructed his subordinates to submit daily reports, gathered through the most sophisticated network of spies, about the personal and official activities of the Viziers, deputies, and provincial governors. He designed an elaborate system of censorship in which almost every letter, newspaper, communications media, and printed material, entering or leaving the empire were censored by trusted employees. The constitution that he allowed the country to have awhile proved to be a veneer covering up a decayed bureaucracy and a corrupt administration infested with financial, economic, and political problems. He dismantled the political structure of the reformists, suspended the constitution, sent the Parliament home, and borrowing a phrase from a French philosopher, told an associate that excessive liberty was as dangerous as the lack of it.

Sultan Abdul Hamid II formulated his domestic and foreign policies on the basis of Islamic fundamentalism to propagate the Islamic supremacy throughout the Empire. It is this policy that will incubate a period of revolt, foment nationalistic uprisings in the outer fringes of his Empire, and convulse the capital and the provinces with political strife.

THE BULGARIAN ATROCITIES

With great energy and skill the Turks consolidated their holdings in eastern Europe, and strengthened their defenses against the possible encroachments of foreign powers. Over the years they had successfully established zones of influence and made eastern Europe the center of gravity of their power with commercial and political links with the capital. The Sultan was aware of the strategic importance of the European territory and took steps to protect the weak points and maintain the Turkish hegemony. Unlike central Anatolia, however, where the Islamic Turks were the dominant majority, eastern Europe was Christian, studded with various nationalities and ethnic groups with no cultural or linguistic unity with the corporate body of the Ottomans. The Christians continued their way of life, paid their taxes and seldom considered the Turkish presence detrimental to their society. The masses lived as peasants along the Danube, and the artisans and professionals lived in the cities with Ottoman governors taking no part in the administration of the local authorities.

During the centuries of Ottoman domination the Turks were careful to win the cooperation of the local nationalities and cultivate amicable relationships with the Christian leaders, concerning themselves only with the defense of the region and the preservation of the economic resources from which they derived a considerable amount of revenue.

Things began to change, however, in the middle of the Nineteenth century, when the Turkish administrators initiated oppressive measures for the collection of taxes and the conduct of religious affairs. The Orthodox Christian majority of the region had always been sympathetic towards the Russian Church and regarded the Czar as the principal heir to the Byzantine tradition. Local communities around the outer ridges of the Ottoman Empire were successful on occasion in breaking away from Ottoman rule with the help of Russian intelligence, but all attempts of insurrection were put down quickly by Turkish forces.

In the summer of 1875 the Christian peasants of Bosnia and Herzegovina rose against their Moslem masters and caused an upheaval that will introduce an international dispute which will come to be known as the Eastern Question. The peasants armed with forks and sticks successfully chased the Turks out of their community, seized control of the local government, and declared themselves independent from Ottoman rule. This uprising encouraged the neighboring Bulgars to organize their own rebellion the following year, but their attempt to gain independence was swiftly crushed with savage brutality. The Turks, as resolute foes of political reform, slaughtered 15,000 men, women, and children, destroyed sixty villages, burned churches, and raped monks and nuns. Thousands of bodies were later discovered in a churchyard piled on top of each other, three feet deep. Some were mutilated beyond recognition, others were flayed alive, impaled or dismembered with severed penises of men inserted in the mouths of women.

This bloody repression caused universal horror and indignation. The foreign press reported the gory details, called the massacre the most heinous of the century and the Turks one of the most savage barbarians on earth. The incident led to a cry of outrage throughout Europe, and inflamed a widespread sentiment of Turkophobia prompting the foreign powers to hold a conference to discuss the Turkish savagery.

The conference was held in Constantinople in July 1876 but produced nothing but confusion. Ostensibly convened to discuss political reforms in the Ottoman dominions in Europe, the conference instead became a forum for Turkish propaganda. The foreign delegates returned home with hollow promises from the Sultan that political reforms will soon be instituted and the newly framed constitution proclaimed with much pomp and publicity, will guarantee protection of the rights and liberties of all Ottoman subjects regardless of race and religious creed. Events will soon reveal that the constitution, while it promulgated the theories of the French philosophers and political thinkers and established a constitutional monarchy, was only a sham. It will soon be repudiated by Abdul Hamid and all promises of reform will remain on paper.

The Parliament will be dissolved and the great age of enlightenment will come to an end. The entire constitutional process was only a political maneuver, designed to deceive Europe as a token gesture to show the world that Turkey meant business in protecting the rights of its citizens. Oppression and tyranny returned in their original form and Sultan Abdul Hamid assumed his old role as the master of the apparatus of brutal despotism. Deceived and betrayed the Christians in Europe now looked to Russia to help them gain their freedom from Turkish oppression.

THE RUSSO-TURKISH WAR

On April 24, 1877 Czar Alexander II, the Czar Liberator, who had earlier emancipated the Russian serfs, declared a full scale war against Turkey. Discredited among the great powers and with a military organization hopelessy bankrupt, the Sultan was not prepared to defend his frontiers. The Russians, far superior in military strength, gained large territories immediately and within a short period of time reached the outskirts of Constantinople. In the east the Czar's forces invaded Western Armenia and won for themselves a considerable degree of Armenian participation. Earlier the Turks had begun to wage a vicious campaign against the Armenian minorities in the villages and towns of Western Armenia. Sporadic raids on Armenian peasants and properties had left the Armenian communities in the east in a desperate situation. Insurrections were put down ruthlessly and anti-Turkish sentiments had spread among the Armenian communities. For Armenians everywhere the reign of Sultan Abdul Hamid had become a reign of terror. Armenian peasants were robbed and killed, the churches were destroyed, and oppressive taxes had impoverished the communities. While the privileged Armenians in Constantinople prayed for Ottoman victory in the war against Russia, the Armenians in the provinces wanted a Russian deliverance.

Armenian guerrilla units, armed by Russia, began to help the Czar's army to liberate Western Armenia from Turkey's oppressive domination. Within weeks the Russian forces occupied Erzerum, Kars, and Ardahan, and took most of the Armenian towns and villages. In the west the Russians marched down the coast of the Black Sea and freed Christian territories, chased the Turks out, and restored stability. With most of Western Armenia under Russian occupation, the Russians now concentrated their attack on smashing the Turkish forces around the capital. The Turks suffered heavy casualties. The Russian dream of taking over Constantinople was now within reach.

Abdul Hamid panicked and appealed to Queen Victoria to arrange an armistice. The Queen ordered the British warships to sail to the Sea of Marmara and anchor within a short range of the Russian command headquarters. Threatened by the prospect of British participation in the war, the Czar decided to halt the military campaign within ten miles of Constantinople.

Under an armistice agreement signed on January 31, 1878, Bulgaria, Montenegro, Romania, Serbia, Bosnia, Herzegovina, became independent states, but the territories in Western Armenia were left in limbo. The agreement virtually eliminated Turkish power in Europe. The Armenian leaders were offended by the blatant display of favoritism towards the Europeans, and discrimination against the Armenians. While at the beginning they were sympathetic towards an Ottoman victory, they now began to press for political autonomy for their own provinces in Western Armenia. The victorious Russians were welcomed by the Armenians as their liberators. The Armenian leaders sent a delegation headed by the Armenian Patriarch, to the Russian army headquarters in Adrianople to plead the case for an Armenian autonomy. The Russians, while sympathetic towards the Armenian cause, did not particularly favor the creation of an Armenian state in their southern flank.

The armistice agreement in Adrianople led to a peace treaty signed on March 3, 1878 at San Stefano, a suburb of Constantinople. Turkey was told to guarantee the security of the Armenians in the eastern provinces and the Sultan promised to institute social and political reforms. The issue of an autonomous Armenia was left in abeyance.

The bilateral agreement between Russia and Turkey at San Stefano did not sit well with the major powers in Europe. Russia's military expedition, while ostensibly organized to protect the Christian elements from Turkish oppression, gave the Czar the opportunity to expand his borders at the expense of the Ottoman Empire, leaving very little for the other powers. The British Prime Minister Benjamin Disraeli, protested vehemently. He attacked the Treaty of San Stefano and proposed instead an international conference in Berlin to discuss the territorial disputes. The Russian occupation of Western Armenia was regarded as a threat to England's commercial interests. As a corridor between east and west Armenia, under an Ottoman rule, had served as an important link for commercial traffic between India and Great Britain. Disraeli did not want to disturb this particular zone of influence and allow Russia to occupy the territory.

To protect the British interests in the region Disraeli entered into a secret accord with Abdul Hamid a few days before the opening of the Berlin conference, agreeing to protect the

Ottoman territories in the east and fight alongside Turkey, if necessary, to restore the Ottoman jurisdiction over Western Armenia. In return, the Sultan promised to guarantee the security of the Armenians. To prevent Russia to penetrate further down and gain access to the warm waters of the Mediterranean, Disraeli persuaded Abdul Hamid to turn over to him the Island of Cyprus to be used as a British military base in close proximity to Asia Minor.

THE CONGRESS OF BERLIN

The Congress of Berlin opened on June 13, 1878 under German Chancellor Bismarck's chairmanship with six powers attending. The conference was ostensibly organized to institute a new management system over the affairs of Europe. The atrocities of the Turks and the emergence of new nationalities had created the necessity to prepare a new blueprint for the management of Europe. This was the first major great power conference since the Congress of Vienna in 1815 convened immediately after the conclusion of the Napoleonic Wars.

The world order had broken down since 1815 and the blueprint of the Congress of Vienna had somewhat become obsolete. Europe needed a new concert of power to subdue the emergence of minor powers and repress change which had become visibly dangerous in eastern Europe. Without upsetting the *status quo* the Great Powers in Berlin made a scrupulous search for new alternatives to help the nationalities in the Balkans but no help was extended to the Armenians.

The Congress nullified the Treaty of San Stefano and reinstated Turkey's presence in Europe with territorial adjustments in favor of the major powers. Bismarck solidified his hold on Prussia, Austria-Hungary extended its rule in the Balkans, the European segment of the Ottoman Empire was granted a new lease on life, and Russia enlarged its presence in the Balkans.

The principal beneficiaries of this conference were the Serbs, Greeks, and other Christian groups in the Balkans who were offered the opportunity to gain political self-determination, blessed by the great powers, who were unanimous in their proclamation that the Balkans must be ruled by the Balkan people only.

No such declaration was made for the Armenians, however. They were dismayed and frustrated to be left under the care of the Turkish oppressors. The Congress which pompously ordained itself as the instrument of peace and honor, offered no peace or honor to the unfortunate Armenian masses in Western Armenia.   An Armenian delegation to the Berlin Congress headed by venerable ex-Patriarch Archbishop Khrimian Hairig filed its grievances and pleaded the Armenian case. The Armenian delegates requested from the great powers the designation of a Christian governor over the six eastern provinces inhabited by Armenians, and the implementation of measures towards the creation of an Armenian autonomous entity on their legally defined and historically documented ancestral homeland. But the great powers regarded the Armenian issue irrelevant and allowed only the insertion of a paragraph in the Berlin Treaty, identified as Article 61, requesting the Sultan to institute political reforms and protect the lives and properties of the Armenians in the provinces.

On the eve of his historic mission to Berlin Archbishop Khrimian, who could not speak a foreign language, was asked "How are you going to communicate with the foreign diplomats, Your Eminence?" "I will weep," was his reply. Weep he did, but came home empty handed.

In a sermon delivered at the Armenian Cathedral of Constantinople upon his return, Khrimian cried from the pulpit "People of Armenia, people of Armenia, arm yourselves. Use your intellect and muscle. Man must toil himself in order to be saved. Take a gun as a gift to your friend." In order to gain their political freedom the Armenians wanted to imitate the revolutionary movement of the people in the Balkans. "Freedom cannot be achieved without blood. Freedom will not be given to you as a gift," Khrimian declared. His sermon was the beginning of a new consciousness in which the concept of nationalism will acquire a new significance and a revolutionary movement against the Turkish power will soon come to be regarded as the only means of achieving the establishment of a political organization for the Armenians.

THE STEPS TO REVOLUTION

Until the beginniing of the Nineteenth century the Armenians were considered as the most loyal subjects of the Ottoman Empire and were referred to as the *Millet-i-Sadika*. The Turks looked at the Armenians for the formulation of their national, political, and economic policies, accepting them as advisors to the Sultan and the Sublime Porte. The amicable relationship between the Armenians and the Turks benefited both, making the former richer and the latter well informed.

Historically and traditionally the Turks were uninterested in the affairs of commerce and finance and considered these professions as the degrading activities of the infidel. The Empire's economic growth and its continued relationship with the west increased the importance of the non-Turkish merchant class, the Armenians, the Greeks, and the Jews, who had the appropriate instinct and the business acumen to build the economic and financial structure on which the Sultans and the Sublime Porte relied heavily. Among the three groups the Armenians were considered the most trustworthy, free from any suspicion of treasonable act against the state. The Jews, while good merchants, were discriminated in Europe and failed to receive favorable treatment from the European merchant houses. Their community declined as they gradually began to migrate to other countries for better opportunities. The Greeks, while skilled in maritime commerce, began to lose their special privileges after their insurrection against the Ottoman rule during the first quarter of the Nineteenth century. The Armenians gradually moved into areas previously held by both and played a decisive role in the economic and industrial development of the Ottoman Empire. The Ottoman treasury was kept solvent primarily because of the Armenian bankers. At times of financial difficulties it was the Armenian bankers in Constantinople who usually rescued the Empire from economic collapse.

The change of attitude began when the dynastic process of selecting Sultans produced inept rulers, causing the breakdown of the imperial system and the deterioration of instruments of sovereignty in the Ottoman regime. The army, deprived of the power of the Janissaries, had become an ineffective tool for the administration of the Empire. Financially bankrupt and economically depressed the Turks began to blame the Armenians for their misfortune. It was not within the realm of coincidence that while the Turks, in general, were becoming poorer, the Armenians were becoming richer, making the Turks subservient to the Armenian financial interests. Resentment soon caused tension and the Turks began to look at the Armenians with increasing suspicion and considered them as elements disloyal to the Ottoman cause.

No matter how closely the Armenians and the Turks lived in the past, there was always a distinction between the two, not only in the context of religion, race, and culture, but also in the area of social orientation, which was the basis of the corporate identity of the two nations. The Armenians, as the first Christian nation in the world, were concerned about the preservation of their cultural and religious heritage. For them the struggle to preserve their national identity was an on-going process reinforced and renewed in every passing generation. For the Turks, having already demonstrated their passion to crush anything non-Islamic, the presence of infidels in the community of Islam was regarded with hostility and resentment.

The occupation of Eastern Armenia by Russia in 1828 and the creation of an Armenian territory within the framework of the Russian Empire, generated yet another conflict between the Turks and the Armenians. The Turks considered this Armenian enclave in their eastern border as an obstacle for their expansionist policies, which called for the eventual unification of all Turkish speaking peoples in Western Asia. Unlike the distant European provinces of the Ottoman Empire, Eastern Armenia was situated in the heart of the Ottoman territory, preventing the Turks in Asia Minor to unite with their cousins in the east.

The hostility against the Armenians grew considerably, immediately after the Russo-Turkish War. The Turks sought vengeance on the Armenians for their participation in the war as allies to Russia. Turks, Kurds, and Circassians began to pillage Armenian villages, and robbed and killed Armenian farmers. These were prearranged and prepaid Turkish attacks against the helpless Armenian population, systematically organized not only to generate anti-Armenian sentiments, but also as a population control to thin out the Armenian population in the provinces to produce a demographic change in favor of the Moslems.

Abdul Hamid's treaty obligations to protect the Armenian lives and properties proved to be hollow. The Sultan was ill-disposed to any European request or demand. He had no intention to implement the provisions of Article 61 of the Berlin Treaty with regard to the Armenian Question. Foreign consuls

were occasionally dispatched to the interior to report on the
Turkish atrocities against the Armenians and the great powers
sent a collective memorandum to the Sultan in 1880 demanding
the implementation of reforms in the Armenian provinces.
They received nothing but evasive answers as the Sultan's forces
continued to terrorize the Armenian communities. The major
powers, themselves, in spite of their promises to the Armenian
people in the Congress of Berlin, were not in unison with regard
to the Armenian Question. It became increasingly difficult for
the great powers to forge a consensus over steps to force the
Sultan to implement reforms in the Armenian communities.
Germany's Bismarck voiced reservations and even opposition in
managing the Ottoman affairs and advised his European colleagues to leave the Sultan alone. Most of them did, particularly the Russians who had some serious internal problems within
their borders.

AN ARMENIAN DICTATOR IN RUSSIA

The Russians had been snubbed and humiliated by the great
powers in the Congress of Berlin. They had lost 100,000 men in
the war against Turkey and at the end all they received was
only a parcel of land in Bulgaria with no access to the warm waters of the Mediterranean as they expected. They had come
within a few miles of fulfilling their centuries old dream of freeing Constantinople from Turkish rule, but the Czar had been
forced to stop to avoid British military intervention.

It was this particular issue that made Czar Alexander II
lose his popularity at home and damage his prestige abroad.
The Russian nobility blamed the Czar for his indecision. Russian terrorists increased their subversive activities to topple the
government. Losing all control, Alexander II declared a state
of emergency and appointed an Armenian general, Loris Melikov, in charge of the administration of the Empire with unlimited power and authority. This was a bizarre situation and quite
unprecedented in Russia's political experience. The Czar, the
all-powerful ruler of the Russian Empire, withdrew himself to
the background and allowed the Armenian general to establish
a virtual dictatorship in the land. Upon rising to power Loris
Melikov introduced administrative changes and began to reconcile the Czar's political reforms with the need for strong leader-

ship.   He restored order and took the necessary steps for parliamentary elections and with shrewd statesmanship, won the hearts of the Russian liberals. Russia had outgrown its imperial framework and the time was ripe for the development of a new order based on democratic processes, individual freedom and liberty, and the principles of government by consent. Melikov worked rapidly to put his political reforms into execution with a goal to change the structure of the imperial system. The Russians accepted the Armenian general as the principal architect for a new destiny, but his power was cut short by the assassination of the Czar in 1881. The successor, Alexander III assumed the reign of the government, abolished all political reforms, and reinstituted strict autocratic rule.

Meanwhile the Turkish terror in Western Armenia continued with no sign of reprieve. Thousands of Armenian villagers were killed and the Armenian Patriarchate found itself powerless to stop the terror.

THE ARMENIAN REVOLUTIONARY MOVEMENT

It became abundantly clear to the Armenian community leaders that Sultan Abdul Hamid had no intention to carry out the demands of the foreign powers prescribed in treaty accords of San Stefano, Cyprus, and Berlin. The foreign powers and their ambassadors in Constantinople continued their pressure on the Sublime Porte. They were powerless, however, in forcing the Sultan to stop the injustices inflicted on the impoverished Armenians. The people continued to suffer from cruel exactions at the hands of Moslem elements. With no hope from abroad the Armenians took the matter into their own hands and began to organize their own political basis to defend themselves against the Turkish oppression.

The idea of organizing a revolutionary movement was not new to the Armenians in Turkey. The seeds of the revolution were sown on the mountaintop of Cilicia in an enclave called Zeitun many years earlier.

After the Ottomans conquered Armenian Cilicia, the Sultans had left the courageous Armenian mountaineers of Zeitun alone and never wanted to interfere in their internal affairs. Zeitun was the last remnant of the Cilician Kingdom and the Armenian inhabitants wanted to preserve its independence with the tacit approval of the Sultan and his ministers. For centuries the Armenians in Zeitun lived happily without much intrusion from the Ottoman government. The trouble began immediately after the Crimean War, when the Turkish government took some lands away from the Armenians to settle Moslem Tatars, who had fled the Russian territory and sought asylum with the Ottomans. A few years later the Turks imposed heavy and unreasonable taxation on the Zeitun Armenians. At first the Armenians protested peacefully. They sent a delegation to the Sublime Porte to plead the government to leave them alone. When the Turks continued their pressure the Armenians drew up a petition and presented it to the French Emperor Napoleon III in Paris. The Armenians told the French that if their case was not heard, they will be ready to bear arms to fight for their freedom. When France transmitted the Armenian petition to the Turkish government, the Sultan took it as a declaration of war against his authority. He immediately began preparations to crush Zeitun and annihilate the Armenian mountaineers once and for all.

In the summer of 1862 a Turkish force of 40,000 men marched against Zeitun but was completely decimated by an Armenian force of 5,000. This spectacular victory inspired Armenians everywhere and gave a renewed impetus to their nationalistic zeal. The Armenians felt that the liberation from Turkish oppression may now be within their reach. The Armenian victory and the humiliating defeat of the Turks encouraged other Armenian towns to rise against the Ottoman Empire. Earlier 20,000 Armenians in Van had rebelled against the Turkish authority followed by Mush in 1863. To protect their lives, properties, and honor, the Armenians in Van organized a revolutionary society in 1872 and called it the Union for Salvation, making Van the logical center for the Armenian revolutionary movement. Later the Armenians in Erzerum founded a secret order and called it the Protectors of the Fatherland. Its objective was to arm the people to defend themselves against the Turks and the Kurds.

By the middle of the Nineteenth century revolutionary ideas began to appear in Armenian literature. Khrimian Hairig, the chief Armenian delegate to the Congress of Berlin, headed the list of writers who began to stir the spirit of freedom in the Armenian people. A man with remarkable qualities, Hairig became the first to galvanize the passion of Armenian nationalism and began to educate his people through sermons, books, and publications. His revolutionary motto, "Let us stop crying and let us start fighting" became the revolution's slogan. He established the first printing press in Western Armenia and began to publish a journal, the *Eagle of Vaspouragan* in 1855. He shook the conscience of the Armenian people and planted the seeds of freedom and liberty in the Armenian soil. As a priest, revolutionary, Patriarch, and later Catholicos, Khrimian shifted the nation's direction from the Dark Ages to the dawn of a new age that was struggling to establish a political structure for the people. He told his countrymen to walk in serenity and self respect but carry a gun to fight for individual liberty and political self-determination. He was as earthy as the plains of Armenia and as majestic as the mountains surrounding them.

Khrimian's gallantry and passion for justice brought a new vision to the people of his country. He came at a time when national values had decayed and the people faced great questions of their destiny. This was a time when the oppressive rule of the Sultan had created a jungle of fear and terror in which the very survival of the Armenian people was in jeopardy. He was the first to cultivate the resources of the spirit of the revolution and offered a beacon of hope to those who wanted to fight to stay alive. This was a time when sentiments of freedom and liberty were everywhere in the world. The Russian Czar had liberated the serfs, the American President had emancipated the slaves, and revolutions for freedom had ignited all over Europe. While Khrimian's revolutionary ideas were later imperfectly formulated by the leaders of the movement, he at least proposed a direction from which there was no turning back.

Khrimian was followed by three distinguished revolutionary writers, Mikael Nalbandian, Kamar Katiba, and Raffi, who helped formulate the theoretical foundation from which the Armenian nationalism emerged. They began to write about nationalism in their journals and publications. Nalbandian published the journal *Hissussapayl*, in Moscow, Katiba, a nationalist poet, encouraged insurrection to gain freedom, and Raffi, a prolific writer, wrote about the organization of the revolutionary movement. He invited his countrymen to fight a holy war to defend the fatherland the way Vartan the Great did on the field of Avarair 1,400 years earlier.

New publications stirred revolutionary ideas. *Massis*, published in Constantinople advocated the amalgamation of the ideas of the old and the new generations of Armenians to remove the cleavage between the two. *Mujak*, published in Tiflis for the Armenians in the Caucasus, brought to the forefront a new group of intellectual elite. A monthly publication called *Arakelian Mamoul*, published in Smyrna, offered the works of the European thinkers. Founded by Madteos Mamourian, the journal introduced western literature to the Armenians and published articles about history, philosophy, economics, and politics. Mamourian brought a new sense of patriotism from the New World. He translated the biographies of George Washington and Benjamin Franklin and wrote about the American democratic principles and Jefferson's noble ideas of freedom and liberty. All of these made a decisive contribution to the revolutionary movement and heightened the interest of the Armenian intellectuals in liberty and freedom.

THE REVOLUTIONARY PARTIES

During the second half of the Nineteenth century a growing number of Armenian students began to travel to Europe to study in European schools and colleges. Europe opened a whole new world to them, and the Armenian students became intoxicated by the spirit of liberty and freedom, enlightenment and progress. The ideas of August Comte, Victor Hugo, and Montesqueu provided the framework for the Armenian political thought and the basis for the revolutionary parties. The students returned home and formed the core of the Armenian intelligentsia. They founded societies, associations, literary clubs, opened schools and began publishing newspapers. The Armenians demanded political freedom from their Turkish rulers. They demanded a political self-determination over the land which was historically theirs. But the Turks claimed that Western Armenia was all theirs and the Armenians were only guests of the Turkish rulers.

Educating the Armenian masses was the first prerequisite for the revolutionary movement. But education in itself was not enough to generate the momentum for a revolutionary undertaking. The people needed political parties and parties needed arms and money.

The first political party was the Armenagan Party founded in Van in 1885 with branches in Bitlis, Mush, Trabizond, Constantinople, Persia, Russia, and the United States. In August 1887 a group of seven Armenian students headed by Avedis Nazarbegian formed the Hunchakian Party in Geneva, Switzerland. Its purpose was to establish a political independence in Western Armenia and free the Armenian people from Turkish oppression. They advocated a guerrilla war against the Ottoman rule and immediately began to recruit members. Within a short period of time thousands of Armenians joined their ranks. In time the guerrilla units assumed control of areas where the Armenians were the largest single community.

The Hunchaks' first revolutionary act was a public demonstration in Constantinople on Sunday, July 13, 1890 in the heart of the Turkish capital. Their aim was to make the people and the Sublime Porte aware of the terrible condition of the Armenians living in the provinces. The demonstration began as a peaceful manifestation but resulted in a terrible bloodshed in which many Armenians were brutally beaten to death.

Another revolutionary party called the Dashnaks came into existence in 1890 founded by Mikaelian, Zorian, and Zavarian in Tiflis with an aim to liberate Western Armenia from Turkish oppression. Both parties began to publish periodicals to disseminate ideas of nationalism. But the severity of the censorship in Turkey forced them to publish the newspapers in exile and smuggle them into the Armenian provinces.

In formulating their revolutionary ideas the young intellectuals became wrapped up in the political ideologies of the late Nineteenth century. They imitated the western thinkers and borrowed ideas from Europe which often confused the Armenian masses. The Hunchaks embraced the Marxist concept of socialism while the Dashnaks adhered to the ideas of the Russian revolutionaries of the day. For the Armenian people living in the provinces the idea of world socialism espoused by the Hunchaks was poorly understood. International socialism impeded the development of a vigorous revolutionary movement and encouraged the formation of splinter groups in an effort to postulate a more applicable definition for the new nationalism of the Armenian people. The idea of Armenia belonging to the Armenians was by no means easy to understand by a people so long subjugated by political and religious oppression. But the

quest for political self-determination helped them to recover
their sense of nationhood which had been dormant during the
Age of Darkness.

Concomitant with the development of the Armenian nationalism the Nineteenth century also brought a new age of enlightenment, when a group of European Armenologists began
to study the history of this ancient race. It was during the first
quarter of the Nineteenth century that a European archeologist
discovered the civilization of the Urartians in the Lake Van region of Western Armenia, and linked the Urartians to the formative period of the Armenian people during the Sixth century
B.C. The interest in Armenology shed new light on the history
of the people and accelerated the emergence of a national self-
awareness.

As the Balkans were for the Balkan people, Armenia was
for the Armenian people. For Armenians the identification of
Eastern Armenia and Western Armenia as Russian Armenia
and Turkish Armenia, respectively, became offensive. The Armenians declared that they were there centuries before the
emergence of the Russians and the Turks. But if the Russians
annexed Eastern Armenia in 1828 and allowed the Armenians
to have a semblance of a political organization, the case for
Western Armenia was different. Western Armenia had been a
part of the Ottoman Empire since 1514 with no political autonomy. The majority of the Armenians lived in the six provinces of
Van, Bitlis, Erzerum, Diyarbekir, Sivas, and Kharpert. By the
mid-Nineteenth century there were approximately three million
Armenians living in these provinces. The aim of the revolutionaries was to create a territorial entity in Western Armenia, but
Sultan Abdul Hamid never accepted the concept of an Armenian homeland on the Turkish soil. Abandoning distant provinces in the Balkans was one thing but dissecting the corporate
body of the Ottoman Empire was another. "I would sooner allow to sever my head from my body than to permit the formation of a separate Armenia. I would not accept the concept of a
nation within my nation," he once told a foreign diplomat. But
the Armenian revolutionaries never accepted their political aspirations as unattainable fantasies. "The Armenian is no longer
imploring. He now demands with gun in hand", they proclaimed.

ARMED REBELLION

With guns smuggled from Russia and Persia, the Hunchaks organized a rebellion in Sassoun, in the summer 1894, to fight the Turks and the Kurds who had been encouraged by the Ottoman government to plunder the Armenian villages. The rebellion was put down ruthlessly. The Turks slaughtered 3,000 Armenian men, women, and children. The women were mutilated and the children were tossed against rocks. The Turks put Armenian priests to the sword after taking their eyes out of their sockets. The massacre, reminiscent of the one in Bulgaria, immediately drew international attention. The foreign powers sent their consuls to the scene to report on the incident. They urged Abdul Hamid to institute political reforms and bring the Turkish murderers to justice. Western protests were met with evasive answers. The Sublime Porte blamed the Armenians for the insurrection and called the report of the foreign consuls imaginary and full of falsehoods.

It was around this time that Sultan Abdul Hamid founded a Pan-Islamic movement to unify the Moslem peoples in western and central Asia. This was a movement primarily formed to ignite Moslem hatred against the Christian people. The Sultan also formed a military unit, called *Hamidiye*, after his name, composed of barbaric Kurds and other predatory Moslem elements.

In organizing the Pan-Islamic movement Abdul Hamid's ultimate goal was to extend the Ottoman power across the entire length of Islamic Asia. In the world of Nineteenth century imperialism, major European powers had already staked out their claims in Europe, Asia, Africa, and the Americas. The Sultan's aim was to incorporate the Turkish speaking regions of Asia into the House of the Osmanlees and purify the community of Islam by driving out the non-Moslem elements or forcing them to accept the Islamic faith. His goal was to achieve the creation of a homogeneous Islamic empire under a sovereign Caliph just like the Abbasids had accomplished centuries earlier.

With this Pan-Islamic movement Abdul Hamid was able to galvanize the loyalty of the Moslem peoples towards the Ottoman cause and strengthen his efforts to repress the non-Islamic elements of his Empire. He did not have much luck in other territories of his Empire. In Europe he had lost most of the Balkans and the Hellenic peninsula. In Africa, Tunis was lost to the French and Egypt to the British. In the Levant, Lebanon had gained an autonomous status. In the east, most of the southern territories of the Caucasus were in the hands of the Russians. His government was bankrupt and its economic order was in shambles. Uncontrolled borrowing from the west had impoverished his country, forcing him to use most of the State's revenue to service the foreign debt. He realized that sooner or later Turkey had to abandon the territories in Christian Europe and shift the Ottoman's center of gravity to Anatolia. Anatolia was closer to the Islamic east, but little Armenia was in the way. His instruction to the Hamidiye units was to stamp out the Armenian presence and his orders to the Orthodox Moslem mullahs were to force the Armenians to accept the Islamic faith.

TURKS MASSACRE ARMENIANS

On September 30, 1895 the Hunchaks organized a mass rally at Bab Ali in Constantinople. Thousands of Armenians gathered at the Armenian Cathedral and began to march towards the palace to present the Sultan with a petition about the reign of terror in the provinces. This was supposed to be a peaceful demonstration but when the demonstrators approached the palace gates, fighting broke out between the Turkish gendarmes and the Armenians. The guards at the palace were ordered to shoot. Many died and thousands were wounded. The Armenians were prevented to present their petition to the Sultan. There followed ten days of systematic slaughter of the Armenians in the streets of Constantinople. The Turks bayoneted men and women to death and tossed the children against the pavement, crushing their skulls. The public demonstration was a failure. The Armenian revolutionaries failed to serve the Armenian cause. On the contrary they generated savage anti-Armenian sentiment among the Turkish people. For almost twenty years since the Congress of Berlin, the Armenian revolutionaries wanted to imitate the Balkan example by which the Bulgars and Serbs gained their freedom primarily because of the outpouring of sympathy generated as a result of the Bulgarian atrocities of 1876. But the desire to attract the sympathy of others distracted the Armenian revolutionaries from working out their political fate on their own. If they thought that by means of insurrections and ill-conceived demonstrations they will draw the attention of the foreign powers who would then intervene to help them gain their freedom, they were totally mistaken, naive, and misguided. By 1895 Europe had long forgotten the Berlin Congress and its proclamation for the rights of the Armenian people. The misjudgments of the Armenian revolutionaries catapulted their forces into dangerous adventures, resulting in a wholesale massacre of thousands of defenseless Armenians. The demonstrations at Bab Ali brought heinous reprisals against the Armenian masses all around Turkey. Sultan Abdul Hamid was outraged. He ordered the crackdown of the Armenian merchant houses in Constantinople and instructed the Hamidiye terrorists to initiate a systematic massacre of the Armenians in the provinces.

It began in Trabizond when the Turks attacked the Armenian quarter and murdered 1,000 Armenians within a few days. Next came Erzinjan where 1,200 Armenians were butchered, followed by Bitlis. In Erzerum the Armenian shopowners were bayoneted to death. Thousands of Armenians in Diyarbekir were put to the sword. The town of Arapgir was set on fire and 300 Armenians perished and young Armenian boys were covered by brushweed and burned to death. Thousands of Armenian girls were carried off to the harems of the Moslem pashas. Infants were piled on top of each other, their heads crushed by boulders and rocks. In one village 500 Armenian women were thrown into a ravine. They were all found dead a few days later. Armenian girls were raped in churches by Turkish troops while mullahs read verses from the Koran. In Sivas 5,000 Armenian men, women, and children were slaughtered. The survivors gathered the mangled bodies of the dead, and buried them in a wide trench. In the villages thousands of Armenians were cut in half at their waist.

The Turkish mob was xenophobic throughout the country. The massacre was planned as a systematic extermination of the people conducted by the Sultan's army and police with orders coming directly from the Sultan himself. The chief organizer of the holocaust was the Sultan's principal adviser, Shakir Pasha whose *modus operandum* was to gather all uneducated Moslems in a big mosque, tell them that the Armenians wanted to crush the Islamic faith and order them to get out and kill them in the name of Mohammed, the Prophet. After the meeting at the mosque a bugle call would order the troops to begin their attack, followed by the Kurds who would then loot and plunder the Armenian houses and shops and chase the fugitives to the mountains to finish them off.

One of the worst scenes occurred in Urfa. The Turkish official in charge of the extermination program ordered the Moslem mob to go to the Armenian quarter, plunder the houses and shops and kill all Armenian men above a certain age. He then told them to bring the children in front of the mosque, tie their hands and feet and force them to lie down on their backs. The Turkish official then methodically cut the throats of the children one by one while reciting verses from the Koran. The children's parents ran to the Armenian church seeking sanctuary. They closed the doors and windows and knelt down to pray. The Turkish mob surrounded the church, broke down the doors and began their orgy of slaughter. A mullah rose to the pulpit and shouted to the crowd wailing with terror, "Prove to us that your Jesus is a greater prophet than Mohammed". They then poured kerosene around the church and burned the people alive.

The massacres precipitated an outrage throughout the world. The European press reported the gory details. The Armenians in the diaspora made a dramatic appeal for help. The great powers urged the Sultan to stop the bloodshed, but Abdul Hamid remained untroubled. He became concerned only when the western press urged the foreign powers to send troops to topple him down. He then began a vicious campaign to exploit the western press, blame the Armenians for the dreadful events in an effort to generate anti-Armenian sentiment. While there was a universal disgust about everything Turkish and the entire public opinion in the west was against him, Abdul Hamid found a political activist, Theodore Herzle, the founder of Zionism, who agreed to discredit the Armenians in the western press and make vociferous speeches against them. In return the Sultan promised the Zionists a Jewish homeland in Palestine, which was then under Turkish jurisdiction.

The Armenian revolutionaries were bitterly disappointed over the outcome of their revolution and the lack of direct action by western powers. While the Turkish threat had become very real, it failed to diminish the revolutionary fervor. On the contrary, it gave the Armenians a new momentum to organize more demonstrations and strikes. In August 1896 young Dashnak revolutionaries seized the Ottoman Central Bank in the heart of Constantinople and demanded the cessation of the reign of terror in the provinces. They were ready to blow up the bank, they declared. The foreign ambassadors intervened and the revolutionaries released the hostages with no damage to the bank. The Turkish reprisal was severe. For two consecutive days religious fanatics ran through the Armenian quarter and butchered 6,000 Armenians leaving their bodies on the street for the wild dogs to devour.

The massacres were now over. Western Armenia was devastated. Thirteen towns, hundreds of villages, and twenty districts were destroyed. 300,000 Armenians had lost their lives. 80,000 Armenians had fled to Europe and America and thousands were left homeless. In a speech to his people the British Prime Minister, Gladstone, who was then at the twilight of his life, branded the Ottoman Empire as a "disgrace to civilization", called the Turks the "curse of mankind" and the Sultan, "Abdul the Assassin". The French press called Abdul Hamid the Red Sultan and a minister referred to him as the "scum of the earth". But these were only words. No foreign power cared to come forward to help the unfortunate Armenians, the way they had in the Balkans twenty years earlier.

The Armenian revolution had failed. The Turks seemed to have broken the organized resistance of the Armenian revolutionaries. The revolutionary leader who started it all, Khrimian Hairig, was now on the throne of the Armenian Church as the Catholicos of all Armenians. One of the survivors of the massacre, Der Sarkis, a village priest, had fled to Echmiadzin and wished to have an audience with the Catholicos. "I had a family of twenty, Your Eminence", he said, "and the Turks slaughtered them all, my children, grandchildren, they burned my house and my church".

"And you came to see me," Khrimian said.

"I just wanted to see you, Your Eminence, and receive your blessing", the priest said. After a moment of silence the Catholicos said, "How many children did you say you lost, Der Sarkis"?

"Twenty, Your Eminence".

"You lost twenty, but I lost 20,000, I lost 20 times 20,000. Whose sorrow is greater, Der Sarkis, yours or mine?"

"Yours, Your Eminence, yours." the priest replied.

"Please come forward, Der Sarkis", the Catholicos said "place your hand on my head and pray for me. Give me your blessing so that I may have the strength to bear my sorrow."

The Supreme Catholicos of all Armenians bowed his head before a village priest, who, tears in his eyes, whispered a prayer.

CHAPTER TWENTY

THE YOUNG TURKS

While disgraced in the eyes of the civilized world, Sultan Abdul Hamid II remained undisturbed. He continued his reign with no difficulty. The Armenian massacres, however, had somehow damaged Turkey's relationship with the west and tarnished the Ottomans' ability to govern their dwindling Empire. The great powers, with the exception of Germany and Russia, discontinued their courtship with the Sublime Porte and gradually began to withdraw their investments from Constantinople. The German case was different. For many years Bismarck's political design was to act as the arbiter in international disputes and as an "honest broker" assist the countries to maintain a political stability in the continent. It was because of his skilled diplomacy in the Congress of Berlin that the Bulgars and Serbs had gained their independence and the major powers had placed their claims on the European territories of the Ottoman Empire. Bismarck's grandiose plans failed to include, however, any consideration for the unfortunate Armenians and his political intransigence prevented the others to organize a collective front against the Ottoman Turks.

Bismarck was not in power during the Armenian massacres. He had been dismissed in 1890 by Kaiser Wilhelm II who had ascended the imperial throne two years earlier. The Kaiser did not care to interfere in Turkey's internal affairs and considered the Armenian massacre as a healthy process of thinning out unnecessary elements from the human race. Unlike Bismarck, however, the Kaiser wanted to discontinue the arbiter's role and play a more dominant role in Germany's relationship with Turkey with an eye on Ottoman territories in the event the Turkish power finally crumbled. He wanted to extend Germany's influence and power throughout Europe and the Middle East and fill the political vacuum caused by the shrinkage of British and French influence over the Ottoman affairs.

Abdul Hamid favored the German participation, not only to bolster his political standing at home and abroad, but also to receive desperately needed financial aid to repair his country's economic organization which had been seriously weakened by the withdrawal of foreign investments and the departure of the Armenian financiers.

Turkey needed to modernize its military apparatus, and the country needed roads, railroads, and communications network to help the Ottoman society enter the Twentieth century. Beginning in the decade of the 1880's the Germans, at the invitation of the Sultan, began to help the Turkish army to modernize itself with new arms and equipment. Kaiser launched an ambitious economic program to help the Sultan to build the country. His first undertaking was to finance the construction of the Baghdad Railway to link Baghdad with Berlin and extend the German influence over the Persian Gulf. The Sultan, in turn, granted extraordinary concessions to German banks which eventually brought an influx of German financiers in every field of commercial activity. Merchant houses began to operate steamship service between Hamburg and Constantinople and Germany began to export its manufactured goods to Turkey.

The Russian policy towards the Ottomans had a different political coloration. The construction of the Trans-Siberian Railroad and the Russo-Japanese War forced the Czar to change his policy towards the Ottomans, to seek *rapprochement* with Turkey, and direct Russia's attention to the Far East. The Czar, while outwardly condemning the Turkish atrocities against the Armenians, refused to support the zealous pursuit of the Armenian nationalists to have an autonomous Armenia in the south of his border. The Czar had his own problems in Eastern Armenia. His awkward handling of the Armenian quest for freedom had alienated the Armenians who did not particularly cherish the idea that the Czar had assumed the title, "King of Armenia". The Czar had flagrantly prevented the Armenians to exercise their rights of political self-determination in their own homeland.   There were sporadic demonstrations against the Czar in Eastern Armenia and the Church of Russia had occasionally imitated their Byzantine predecessors by badgering the Armenian Church leaders to accept the Russian Orthodoxy and place their Church under a Russian superintendence.   There were also some harsher measures.   In 1903 Russia had confiscated most of the Armenian Church properties and closed down schools and libraries in Eastern Armenia, and in 1905, when the Turkish Azeris massacred thousands of Armenians in Baku, which was then under Russian domination, the Czar failed to stop the bloodshed and bring the murderers to justice.

Meanwhile trouble was brewing in Macedonia and events in the Balkans will once again change the course of subsequent history.

THE TURKS REVOLT

Abdul Hamid's policies in the Balkans had alienated not only Christian but also the Moslem elements in Macedonia.   The Christians wanted freedom and the Moslems wanted security of life and property.   During the closing years of the Nineteenth century groups of Christian bandits began to attack Turkish villages and the Turkish troops fought to maintain order.   A Christian insurrection in Salonika in 1903 was brutally suppressed by Ottoman forces, causing an outrage in Europe and subsequently forcing the Sultan to appoint an inspector-general to govern the region.   The inspector hastened to propose political reforms to satisfy both Christian and Turkish constituencies, but the Sultan ignored them all and let Macedonia elapse into chaos and anarchy.

Abdul Hamid's reactionary policies in the Balkans ignited the fuel of the Turkish revolutionary movement.   The center of agitation was no longer among the Armenian or Christian elements but among the Turks themselves, who began to form a revolutionary group to bring about political reforms and organize a *coup d'etat* against the Sultan.   A growing number of Turkish intellectuals educated in Europe, began to nurture sentiments for equality, liberty, and the rule of law.   Abdul Hamid's oppressive regime and his Pan-Islamic policies, supported by Moslem radicals, had intensified the interest of thoughtful Moslems to form political groups and formulate appropriate policies to put an end to Sultan's absolutist rule and his destructive handling of the Empire's domestic and international affairs. As in the case of the Armenian university students, the age of enlightenment and reason in Europe had also opened doors of opportunity for the Turks, and encouraged them to apply the theories of the European thinkers to their own country and help the people to take advantage of the fruits of the civilized world. They began to discuss the rights of the people and their inherent right for liberty to bring about a much needed humanism to an otherwise backward and medieval society. Their home base was Macedonia and their publication was called *La Jeune Turquie* thus prompting people to refer to them as the Young Turks.

The publication of this journal, which was regularly smuggled into Turkey, encouraged a group of political exiles to form an organization called the Committee of Union and Progress. Their spectacular rise into political activism helped them to spread their influence throughout the Ottoman Empire, enticing Turkish students to organize secret political cells and infiltrate the ranks of the military. Soon sporadic revolts against Sultan's arbitrary rule began to erupt in Salonika spearheaded by a relatively unknown young army officer by the name of Enver. Enver organized a successful mutiny, separated himself from the army and taking with him a large contingent of loyal soldiers, arms, and equipment, went to the hills and proclaimed a revolution against the Sultan. The objective of the revolution was the restoration of the Constitution of 1876 and the revival of the Parliament which had been dissolved by Abdul Hamid some thirty years earlier.

Enver's revolution gained momentum encouraging other army corps to join the ranks. Soon the entire army in Macedonia openly opposed the Sultan and defied his orders. Abdul Hamid sent a military expedition to crush the rebels but the commander of his army was shot to death by the revolutionaries. When the chain reaction of the revolt spread to the army units scattered around the capital the Sultan had nowhere to turn for support.

In July 1908, Enver, strengthened by a series of victories against the Sultan's forces, sent a telegram to Abdul Hamid in the name of the Committee of Union and Progress, demanding the restoration of the Constitution and upon his refusal threatening to march on Constantinople to topple him down. Panicked and terrified but supported by the Council of Ministers and the Moslem hierarchy, Abdul Hamid finally gave in. He ordered his palace staff to send a telegram to Macedonia advising the revolutionaries that the Sultan had acceded to their demands.

The long years of despotism were now over. The Constitution was back and elections for a new Parliament were ordered. The people began to celebrate the victory in great triumph. A jubilant procession of Turks, Moslems, Armenians, Greeks, and Jews, marched on the streets and embraced each other. The oppressive regime of the Sultan was now over and the people were finally free. The censors were chased and beaten, and the spy rings were disbanded. Enver proclaimed that all citizens of the Ottoman Empire were now brothers and sisters, and to dramatize his sympathy towards the Armenians, he declared a special memorial day for the victims of the Armenian massacres, and headed a joint congregation of Armenian prelates and Turkish mullahs, prayed with them with hands outstretched to heaven, calling on Almighty God to save the nation from any more massacres. A new age of liberty and freedom, inspired with the common brotherhood of man, had been inaugurated. The dictatorship was dead, the Sultan's coterie was removed from the government, but the Sultan was still alive and well.

While most people rejoiced at the passing of Abdul Hamid's autocratic regime, others wept in witnessing the demise of the Sultan's power. The successful rebellion in Constantinople precipitated an immediate reaction and unleashed a wave of outbreaks in the provinces where the pro-Sultan sympathizers began to attack non-Turkish elements, loot and plunder their homes. The Young Turks, while able military men, proved to be immature and incompetent rulers. They were immediately confronted with a political turmoil and their revolutionary muscle was not strong enough to suppress uprisings which were being organized in support of the Sultan. Taking advantage of this political malaise, the Turks in Adana massacred 20,000 Armenians and burned 200 villages in Cilicia. This was a logical continuation of the anti-Armenian feelings which were still prevalent throughout Turkey.

Abdul Hamid was still in the palace ruling the Empire as a figurehead under the dictate of the Revolutionary Committee. The Sultan's diminished power did not sit well with the Moslem

fundamentalists who opposed all liberal reforms and demanded
the restoration of the autocratic monarchy. In April 1909 they
staged a counter-rebellion against the Young Turk Revolutionary Committee and organized a march in Constantinople. A
large crowd of Moslem extremists gathered in front of the Parliament and shouted "Down with the Committee", "Down with
the Constitution". It soon became evident that it was Abdul Hamid who had instigated and financed the counter-revolutionary
movement.

The Committee acted swiftly. It dispatched a military unit
to Constantinople headed by a young army officer, Mustafa Kemal. The army marched into the capital and surrounded the
Sultan's palace. A decision was made to depose Abdul Hamid
and send him into exile. Late that night Sultan Abdul Hamid
II, the omnipotent ruler of the Ottoman Empire, accompanied
by his two sons and favorite concubines, was taken to the railroad station to live in obscurity in a rented house of a wealthy
Jew in Salonika. While boarding the train, holding the hand of
his twelve year old son, the Sultan muttered in despair, "This is
kismet. May God punish the evildoers". An Armenian porter
carrying the luggage murmured under his breath, "May He do
so, Padishah, May He do so". The Sultan boarded the train
and fainted in the arms of his chief eunuch.

PRELUDE TO THE HOLOCAUST

The Sultan was gone but the oppressive gods and the demons
of racism were still around. The counter-revolution of 1909 was
followed by a proclamation of martial law, which allowed the
ruling party to institute oppressive measures limiting the activities of clubs, associations, and societies, to consolidate its power
and forestall outbreaks against the regime. The leaders of the
Turkish Revolution were temperamentally unfit to preserve the
constitutional guarantees and institute political reforms. Soon
they formed a military oligarchy and began to rule the Empire
by a junta of three pashas, Enver, Jemal, and Talaat, and transformed Abdul Hamid's repressive regime into a dictatorship of
a triumvirate.

Enver Pasha, the youngest of the three, was the son of a
porter. An impulsive, reckless, and flamboyant man in his twen-
ties, Enver acted as the Napoleon Bonaparte of Turkey and saw

himself as the symbol of the Turkish Revolution. He assumed the title of Minister of War. The second in rank was Jemal Pasha, a competent military man with an unpleasant and ruthless disposition, who became the Military Governor of Constantinople. The third was a civilian, Talaat Pasha, a former post office clerk and a fanatic nationalist, who became the Minister of the Interior. The financial genius of the clique was Javid, a former Jew but a converted Moslem. Javid was not a member of the Triumvirate but he was a powerful member of the ruling party. He was appointed as the Minister of Finance.

After years of working towards constitutional reforms, the return of military despotism proved once more that there were some things in the realities of life of these Turkomen nomads that will remain unchanged. The noble ideas of the European renaissance carried by the Turkish revolutionaries who at first pretended to be *avant-garde* thinkers, had made no impact on the fabric of their society. The Revolution of 1908 failed to restore freedom and liberty and arrested the development of democratic principles. The constitutional government came to an end and the affairs of the Empire continued to be conducted through plots, counterplots, repression, violence, and brutality.

There was an understanding between the Dashnaks and the Young Turks during the formative years of the Turkish Revolution that the rights and properties of the Armenian people would be protected at all times, and the directors of the Committee of Union and Progress would allow the Armenians to promote the organization of a political self-determination in the six provinces of Western Armenia. Hopes quickly vanished, however, and Armenians began to face new difficulties from the new regime which surpassed the magnitude of Abdul Hamid's reign of terror.

The new junta prohibited the formation of political groups and sent opposition leaders into exile. The age of brotherhood, proclaimed by Enver Pasha at the dawn of the Revolution, had now been transformed into an age of terror. In a speech in August 1910 Talaat Pasha declared that "equality among the various non-Moslem peoples of the Empire is an unrealizable ideal. For the Revolutionary Committee to succeed in its objectives the Turks must "Turkicize" the non-Moslem minorities, religiously and culturally, to form a homogeneous society". The junta began to formulate a policy of Turkification of non-Moslem elements, with renewed ferocity and ruthlessness, which made Sultan Abdul Hamid's policies seem more tolerant and gentle. Differences of religion and race began to surface once again and the old animosities between Armenians and Turks began to appear. For the Turks, loyalty to the state was measured with the yardstick of the religious faith. For them a fellow Moslem was a brother bound by the teachings of the Prophet, but an Armenian Christian was an alien, a pollutant in the community of Islam, no matter how tolerant the Turks pretended to be. The Armenian, in turn, while he supported the government's policies and remained loyal to the sovereign of the state, refused to consider himself an Ottoman or a Turk.

It was this racist sentiment that laid the foundation of a new doctrine, Pan-Turkism, which was a permutation of Abdul Hamid's Pan-Islamism. If Pan-Islamism was bad for the Armenians, Pan-Turkism was even worse and more potent. Pan-Turkism was ethnic and less universal. It called for the unification of all Turkish speaking peoples from the Aegean Sea to the Walls of China, and the blending of the Turkish race into the embroidery of a single society, based on kinship and a renewed loyalty to its ancestral past. The Young Turks professed that the corporate body of the Turkish state, which then included Western Armenia, was limited only to those who had accepted the Islamic faith, and the amalgamation of all non-Islamic Ottoman elements into one unity under the umbrella of Turkish nationalism, was an unattainable illusion. It will be this policy that will serve as the principal rationale to exterminate the Armenian race and remove the Armenian presence from their ancestral homeland.

Politically the ruling party was in trouble in governing the Empire. The inept policies and deteriorated military organization made the Turks lose virtually all Ottoman territories in continental Europe. In a war with Italy during 1911-1912 Turkey lost Libya and most of the Island of Rhodes, which had been the prize possession of Suleyman the Magnificent centuries earlier. The Balkan states formed an alliance and chased the Turks out of the Balkans during the Balkan Wars of 1912-1913. Turkey lost its center of gravity in Europe and the leaders decided to retrench towards central Anatolia.

The Armenians continued to suffer in the provinces. They appealed to the great powers for help. The western powers applied enormous pressure on the Turkish government to leave the Armenians alone and institute political reforms. The Armenians in the diaspora appealed to their respective governments for help. Suddenly out of nowhere, and contrary to its pronouncements, the ruling party finally gave in and made a provisional arrangement in favor of the Armenians. Under an accord made on February 14, 1914, it was agreed to grant the six provinces of Western Armenia self-autonomous administrative powers, governed by European inspectors-general, designated by the Turkish ruling party with the advice and consent of the major powers. The governor was to secure the protection of the lives and properties of the Armenians and the preservation of interracial harmony in the region. It was the understanding between Turkey and the European powers that this would be the first phase for the Armenians to eventually gain their political self-determination and form a territorial entity on their ancestral soil. The so-called Armenian Question, which had become an irritating international issue since 1878, was about to be resolved and a new dawn of consciousness was about to emerge on the horizon of the plains of Mount Ararat. The Armenians suddenly found themselves on the eve of a great day with the faint outline of their country, free from oppression and political turbulence. After years of revolution, bloodshed, and massacre, the Armenians, fortified with the strength of faith in the decency of man, were now ready to build the walls of their ancestral home. Europe had finally come to help and show some compassion towards an unfortunate nation.

In April 1914 two European administrators, a Dutch and a Norwegian, were on the way to their assigned posts in Western Armenia to prepare the Armenians to achieve their dream of self-determination. An unrelated incident 1,600 miles away shook the entire world and forever changed the course of subsequent history. On June 28, 1914 the heir to the Austrian throne, the Archduke Franz Ferdinand, while riding through the streets of Sarajevo, was assassinated.

CHAPTER TWENTY-ONE

THE WAR TO END ALL WARS

The assassination of Archduke Ferdinand was a turning point in the history of the world, for the struggle among the great powers ignited a major war which will come to be known as World War I. The war will shatter the political stability of Europe, force the United States to participate in an international conflict, create new molds of nationalities, and lay the groundwork for the establishment of political philosophies that will have a profound effect on the pages of subsequent history.

For the Ottomans, who had become ineffective to grapple to maintain the integrity of their Empire, World War I will bring the final disintegration of their system of government and give them the opportunity to fulfill their objectives of solving the Armenian Question once and for all. Under the pretense of the war, the Turks will initiate a systematic extermination of the Armenian people and shake the very foundation of this ancient race.

THE START OF WORLD WAR I

The heir to the Austrian throne was assassinated by a student terrorist, a member of a secret Serbian organization which protested against Austria's annexation of Bosnia and Herzegovina. The organization's primary goal was to create a Pan-Serb nationalist state under the auspices of the Russian government, with the tacit approval of the imperial family. The hold of the Czars on the Serbian people in the southern part of Europe had strengthened in the early part of the century, expanding Russia's role as the principal guardian of Serbian interest. The imperial family frequently sent delegates to Serbia to organize and direct covert espionage operations in an attempt to free the country from Austrian hegemony. By 1914 the country had been infiltrated by Russian agents and a sophisticated intelligence network dominated the political life of the region. While the Serbians had revolted several times against Austria on their own without foreign intervention, this time it was well understood by the political sages of the day that Ferdinand's assassination was engineered by Russian intelligence.

The assassination triggered an immediate reaction. On July 28, 1914 Austria declared war on Serbia and four days later Germany, as the principal ally to Austria, declared war on Russia. The French declared war on Germany and Austria, and when the German army invaded Belgium on August 4, 1914 jeopardizing the British interest on the continent, England entered the war alongside Russia and France. Thus began World War I. As the fighting began, the participants declared that this will be a "war to end all wars."

Turkey's attitude was not immediately clear. While the Triumvirate of Enver, Talaat, and Jemal had solidified its position and consolidated its power in the administration of the Empire, the ruling party was reluctant to participate in any military confrontation. The Turkish leaders wanted to stay aloof from the international conflict. They were still experiencing political intrigues at home and their embarrassing defeats in the Balkans a year or so earlier had seriously tarnished their credibility to preserve the integrity of their Empire. Ever since the ouster of Sultan Abdul Hamid in 1909 the governors in the provinces had increased their political power, ruling their regions as private fiefdoms to the detriment of the central government in Constantinople. But Enver Pasha appeared to be the all-powerful ruler with plans of his own. In an effort to placate his German masters Enver on August 2, 1914 entered into a secret accord with Germany, promising the Germans to bring Turkey alongside the Central Powers in exchange of a commitment from the Kaiser to safeguard the integrity of the Ottoman interests in Europe and the Middle East. Earlier in the spring of 1914, the Germans had dispatched an important military mission to Constantinople to train the Turkish army and modernize the military organization. By the summer of 1914 a German general had already been installed as the Chief Inspector-General of the Turkish army and German military personnel were in virtual control of Turkey's military power.

Enver's alliance with Germany was kept secret, however. Not even his partners in the Triumvirate were aware of his political machination. While the Germans had considerably increased their influence on Turkey's political and military life, the public in general did not particularly share Enver's foolish honeymoon with the Germans. The people largely favored England and France as powers more akin in assuring the longevity of their Empire. The members of the ruling party went along with Enver, however, when he finally disclosed his secret accord. They ratified the alliance but wanted to wait for a change in the public opinion before they decided to enter the war alongside Germany.

The change was made possible fortuitously by England itself when the British government at the outbreak of the war refused to turn over two warships that were being built for the Turkish navy in the English shipyards. The building of these ships had some emotional implications. With the deterioration of the military power caused by the disastrous wars in the Balkans, the ruling party, in order to bolster the public's interest in the affairs of the Empire, organized a successful fundraising campaign from schoolchildren across the land to finance the construction of the warships in England. When England refused to turn over the ships, the Turks became indignant and expressed their anger against Great Britain. The event prompted violent public uproar and demonstrations throughout the capital. The Turkish government accused England of shameless piracy. The incident opened the way for the Triumvirate to publicize Enver's secret German accord.

Taking advantage of the political malaise and in an effort to push Turkey to his corner, the German Kaiser ordered two German warships to be delivered to Turkey. The German ships entered the Sea of Marmara in August of 1914 and the ruling party immediately commissioned the admiral of the ships as the Commander-in-Chief of the Turkish navy.

With the installation of the German navy commander and a German army inspector-general the Turkish military power was now virtually in the hands of the Germans. Pressure was now mounting for Turkey to enter the war. England and

France fought in the thick of diplomatic battle to prevent Turkey to enter the war. With the public opinion in favor of the Germans and the Turkish economy and military power completely dominated by German interests, the way was now open for the Triumvirate to enter the war against the alliance of England, France, and Russia. But not everybody was in favor of this. There were some percipient Turks, among them Mustafa Kemal, the military commander who had been instrumental in ousting Abdul-Hamid; and Javid, a prominent member of the constellation of political stars, who argued vehemently for Turkey to stay neutral. The Balkan wars, they said, had devastated the Turkish economy and militarily the country was unprepared for an international confrontation on such a large scale. But reckless and hot headed Enver Pasha had already made up his mind.

On October 28, 1914 the German admiral in Constantinople led a Turkish squadron into the Black Sea to hit Russian targets and provoke Russia to declare war on Turkey. On November 2, 1914 Russia declared war on Turkey as expected, followed by England and France three days later. Turkey began to mobilize its armed forces and took its place as a principal participant of World War I alongside the Central Powers of Germany and Austria.

To run the military campaign effectively the Turkish Triumvirate decided to divide its power. Enver took the command of all military operations in Eastern Anatolia, Jemal took control of Syria and Palestine, while Talaat ran the administration of the government from the capital. To strengthen the Turkish military organization two German generals joined the Turkish high command. Von Seeckt became Chief of the Ottoman General Staff, and General von Falkanhayn became the Commander of the Ottoman forces in Palestine. Other German officers were placed in strategic departments, such as intelligence, railroads, munitions, coal, and fortresses.

Kaiser's intention was to use Turkey to fight the Russians in the Caucasus and the British in Egypt to divert the attention of both powers from the European theater. No arrangements were made for any Turkish military engagement in the Balkans or eastern Europe, possibly because of the existence of anti-Turkish sentiment in the region. By then the Germans had already taken Bulgaria and concentrated their attack on smashing the Allied naval power in the waters surrounding the Balkans. The Russians, on the other hand, wanted to use the opportunity to exploit the pro-Russian elements in eastern Europe and expand the periphery of their Empire by fusing the Balkans into the Russian hegemony. The Czar's primary objective, however, was to gain territories in eastern Anatolia at the expense of the Ottoman Empire by taking advantage of Turkey's deteriorating military power and the lack of leadership in the region. The Czar knew very well that he could count on the loyalty of the Armenians in Anatolia who will be more than willing to help the Russians in exchange of a commitment to establish an independent Armenian state on the plains of Mount Ararat.

This display of Russian interest in the Armenian cause was dramatized by a personal visit of Czar Nicholas II to the Caucasus. The Czar spoke with the Armenian leaders and the Catholicos and reiterated his intention to convert the six provinces of Turkey into an Armenian autonomous republic under a Russian suzerainty. To the Armenians Nicholas II appeared as a great liberator. 150,000 Armenian volunteers joined the Russian army immediately ready to fight the Turks and help the Czar achieve his objectives. Armenians all over the world joined volunteer groups to fight alongside the Russians against the Turks. Young men from the United States and Europe converged on Tiflis in response to the appeal of the Armenian revolutionary parties to recruit in the volunteer army. Students quit their schools and Armenian girls from Kars disguised themselves as men in an attempt to enlist in the Armenian army.

THE WAR IN THE EAST

The war began badly for Turkey. The emergence of Arab nationalism promoted by the British, helped the Allied military campaign in the Middle East. Jemal lost decisive battles in Syria and Palestine and Enver lost half of his forces in eastern Anatolia.

With inadequate military resources Enver organized a military campaign with headquarters in Erzerum to fight the Russians in the east and stop their penetration into Anatolia. He knew that he could count on the loyalty of the Moslem elements in the Caucasus to help him fight the Russians. Enver's long-term ambition was to liberate the Turkish speaking peoples of the Caucasus and central Asia from the Russian yoke and establish a Turkish Moslem hegemony across the Asian continent.

In November 1914 the Russians penetrated the eastern borders of Turkey and within a few days chased the Turks out of the area. Enver was unable to launch a counterattack and lost the strength of his men in a faulty deployment, allowing the Russians to advance towards Ardahan, Kars, and Erzerum. In desperation Enver ordered the Moslem elements in the region to harass the Russians by guerrilla war, but it was not enough. By January 1915 the Russians had mobilized a formidable army and successfully decimated seventy-five percent of the Turkish forces in eastern Anatolia. Enver's defeat against the well equipped Russian forces inflamed the Moslem terrorists who began to attack the Armenian communities in the east. And the Armenians emboldened by the Russian advance began to organize local rebellions and revolts against the Turks.

THE ALLIES IN GALLIPOLI

While eastern Anatolia was being devastated the situation in the west was quite different. Encouraged by his victories in the east the Czar wanted the British to crush the Turkish power in the Straits of Bosporus to allow the Russians to have access to the warm waters of the Mediterranean. A military campaign organized by Winston Churchill, the First Lord of the Admiralty, failed to achieve that objective. Churchill's plan was to invade the Gallipoli peninsula on the western side of the Dardanelles to secure the straits for the Allies. His squadron began to attack the Turkish forces, expecting to capture Constantinople from the west, but the waterway was mined and the British lost three battleships within a few days. Turkish troops led by Mustafa Kemal gained strategic control points on the peninsula, and chased the Allied forces from the Bosporus. This was a decisive victory for the Turks and a humiliating defeat for the British. Some 500,000 Allied soldiers died in the peninsula in ten months of battle. The Germans promptly rewarded their Turkish friends by sending more warships and lending Turkey a considerable amount of money to strengthen its forces.

The Turkish victory in the west did not help the deteriorating military situation in the east. The Russians, with the help of the Armenian volunteers, had already gained a large chunk of

Turkish real estate and the entire Lake Van region was placed in jeopardy. The Russians had finally broken the organized resistance of the Moslem elements and were on their way to march across the length of Anatolia to capture Constantinople from the east. With the failure of the British in the Straits of Bosporus, the capture of the Turkish capital from the east suddenly became the Czar's primary goal. To help the Russians, the Armenian guerrilla units led a series of armed forays into the Turkish heartland to chase the Turks out of the Armenian provinces. Humiliated and demoralized, Enver Pasha returned to Constantinople and blamed the Armenians for his catastrophic defeat. Turkey's defeat in the east could have been prevented he claimed, if the Armenians did not collaborate with the Russians. The victory in Gallipoli and the defeat in the east offered the Turks an excellent opportunity to solve this nagging Armenian Question once and for all.

THE DECISION TO EXTERMINATE THE ARMENIANS

At the outbreak of World Wark I the Triumvirate had given specific orders to Moslem elements and Turkish troops to attack the Armenian villages in Western Armenia. These orders were issued during the week of October 29, 1914 in anticipation of the Turkish entry into the war. The leaders of Turkey felt that the Armenian communities in the east would block the Turkish advance towards the Caucasus in the event the Czar decided to forge a military campaign in the east against Turkey.

It was during this week in the latter part of October that Enver designated a Turkish intellectual, Dr. Shakir, as his special envoy and placed him in charge of a special task force, ostensibly to organize the wholesale massacre of the Armenian people. The Turks regarded the Armenian presence on their soil as a violation of their sovereignty and an obstacle to their political ambitions. Militarily the Armenian provinces were considered indispensable to Turkey's defense structure. The long background of Turkish oppression abetted by years of Turkish terror made the Armenians favor the Russians against the Turks. For the members of the ruling party the only reasonable solution to the problem was the expulsion and the wholesale extermination of the Armenian people. As the Turks continued to lose ground in the east this solution seemed to be the most appropriate and one that eventually took precedence over any other issue. For the Turks, England and Russia were far away but the Armenians were on their land, living like a cancerous organism in the Turkish body. This was an unjust assessment of the Armenians' immeasurable contribution to the Ottoman cause.

From time immemorial the Armenians had been the major contributors to Turkey's national life. They were the builders of the new order and at times of crisis it was the Armenian bankers who financed the Turkish wars and saved the country from economic chaos. Their significant contributions in art, medicine, science, and industry, helped the Turks chart a new destiny for their nation. During the early months of this particular war it was the Armenian engineers who became actively involved in building Turkey's roads and military installations. Armenian women sewed uniforms for the Turkish army, Armenian merchants offered their services free of charge, and Armenian farmers supplied food to the Turkish troops. No matter what the Armenians did or promised to do, however, it was commonly understood that they were not in the general scheme of the Turkish nationalist grand design of building a Pan-Turkish empire from the Aegean Sea to central Asia. Soon armed hostility towards the Armenians became a commonplace Ottoman policy and not a day passed without the Armenians in one province or another being subjected to Turkish terror.

In a meeting held in February 1915 the ruling party planned to organize a massive program to exterminate the Armenians living in Turkey. Talaat told his associates that the elimination of the Armenians would assure the effective preservation of the Turkish hegemony in Western Asia. It was during this meeting that the actual plan of the Genocide was drafted and procedures for its implementation were instituted. Some raised the issue as to the logistics of carrying on such a mass murder. It may be necessary, Talaat suggested to carry on the evacuation and extermination simultaneously to expedite the execution of the plan.

The participants of the meeting represented various branches of the Turkish government. They were told that the program of Genocide would include the participation of the local Moslem groups, the Kurds and the Circassian Turks, and the cooperation of the mullahs to incite the Moslem fanatics to kill the Armenian infidels.

Not all the participants at the meeting were in favor of this program. Javid, the Jew turned Turk, opposed vehemently such a drastic action. He proposed instead to use the Armenians for hard labor to build roads and help the military fight the war. "The Armenians could not be trusted", Talaat said, "and their revolutionary groups would sabotage the Turkish military efforts. Their continued presence on the Turkish soil constitutes a potential danger to us." "If you proceed with this heinous act," Javid retorted, "history will never forgive the Turks and you will forever stain your reputation."

Talaat then issued a detailed list of the number of Armenians living in Turkey.

Constantinople 150,000, Ismit 72,000, Edirne 8,000, Dardanelles 20,000, Bursa 35,000, Bandirma 9,000, Balikesir 6,000, Afion Karahisar 10,000, Ismir 11,000, Kastemuni 10,000, Ankara 22,000, Caesarea 47,000, Yazzed 46,000, Konya 25,000, Kilis 12,000, Urfa 33,000, Aintab 30,000, Antioch 12,000, Sivas 55,000 Tokat 30,000, Amasya 30,000, Shabin-Karahisar 40,000, Gurun 28,000, Divrigi 24,000 Derende 18,000, Erzerum 78,000, Erzinjan 25,000 Bayburt 19,000, Pasen 10,000, Tercan 12,000, Kemah 7,000, Kizi 20,000, Hnus 21,000, Ispir 3,000, Bayazid 20,000, Kharpert 65,000, Egin 34,000, Arabgir 29,000, Chmisgezek 17,000, Charsencak 23,000, Malatya 36,000, Diyarbekir 60,000, Palu 30,000, Argana 12,000, Chinkush 13,000, Mardin 19,000, Bitlis 40,000, Gizan 29,000, Mush 80,000, Bulanik 19,000, Siirt 18,000, Manazgirt 10,000, Ginc 3,000, Van 90,000, Lim-Ktuts 13,000, Archesh 10,000, Alcayaz 10,000, Hekkiari 12,000 Aghtamar 62,000, Adana-Marsin-Tarsus 79,000, Dortyol-Osmaniye-Sis, 18,000, Marash 28,000, Zeitun 28,000, Firnuz 13,000, Trabizond 35,000, Samsun 30,000, Tomarza 5,000, Everek 10,000, Severek 9,000, Meden 15,000.

The program was now ready to be implemented. Deportation schedules were established and extermination camps were set up. Thousands of local government employees were called on duty. On February 28, 1915, the Central Committee of the Young Turks, known as the Jemiyet, sent the following telegram to the provincial governors:

"The Jemiyet has decided to free the fatherland from the covetousness of this accursed race and to bear upon their shoulders the stigma that malign the Ottoman history. Unable to forget the disgrace and bitterness of the past, filled with vengeful episodes, Jemiyet, hopeful of its future, has decided to exterminate all Armenians living in Turkey, without allowing a single one to remain alive, and to this regard, has given the government extensive authority".

Talaat's representatives were dispatched to major Armenian centers in Anatolia and Cilicia to discuss with local Turkish leaders the program of deportation and extermination. The program called for the removal of the Armenian masses to the south, away from the watchful eye of the foreign diplomats and in the process execute the plan of extermination. In the spring 1915 the full force of the Turkish terror was ready to be put into action.

The government dismissed all Armenian government employees and isolated the Armenian combat officers, taking their arms away from them and forcing them to work as pack animals to carry the military equipment for the Turkish army. The Turks began a massive search of arms in the Armenian provinces. Guns were seized and their owners were put in jail. The Armenians in the villages were beaten and those in jail were tortured. This was only the beginning.

CHAPTER TWENTY-TWO

THE GENOCIDE

The plan to exterminate the Armenian people was implemented in the most swift and systematic manner. It was the German military advisors in Turkey who acted as the principal collaborators with the Turks to put the plan into action. The plan satisfied the German extremist policies which called for the removal of those who were in the way. It was a German political leader who at the outbreak of the war declared, "Let no one say every people has a right to existence. They may live only as long as they do not stand in the way of a mightier one". It was this policy that the Turks adopted, since it also fitted their own tradition of genocide, which they had acquired from their Asiatic ancestors. During the meeting of the Jemiyet in which Javid argued against the policy of extermination, it was Talaat who shouted at him, "If the Armenians stand in our way, to spare them would be folly".

In the spring 1915 the Armenians in Turkey stood in the shadow of a national catastrophe. It began on April 24, 1915 when 235 Armenian leaders, intellectuals, writers, lawyers, educators, and the Armenian members of the Turkish Parliament, were taken from their homes in Constantinople and shot to death. A few days later 365 were arrested, taken to a remote place and slaughtered. During the same week five thousand Armenian merchants and professionals in Constantinople were taken from their homes and murdered.

In the provinces a program of massive deportation and extermination was put into action. Armenian men were arrested for no reason at all, taken to extermination camps, beaten severely, and their mutilated bodies thrown into the street. In the villages Armenian homes and farms were attacked and children were beaten to death. The Turks confiscated Armenian properties, dragged the people out of their homes, and put them in extermination camps. The mullahs posted signs on church doors. The sign read "This village will be purged of Armenians. This land is ours". In each community the procedure was to isolate men from women and children. The men were ordered to come to the government house. From there they were taken to an open field and shot to death. The women and children were ordered to march towards the Syrian desert. Thousands upon thousands of Armenian women, children, and old men began to march accompanied by Turkish gendarmes. On the way to the south, passing through Turkish villages, they were beaten, robbed, and raped by local Turks and Kurds. Infants were taken away by Moslem families and young girls were raped and then hanged. The gendarmes whipped the marchers regularly and killed those who could not continue to walk.

Concomitant with the deportation of Armenians from the villages a program of resettlement was initiated, organized by one Dr. Nazim, the head of the Turkish Refugee Organization. As the Armenians were being forced to leave their homes, the Turkish refugees who had fled the European territory during the early months of the war were moved to settle on Armenian properties. Within a few weeks Mush and the surrounding 100 villages were emptied of Armenians and Turkish refugees were settled in the Armenian communities. Violent acts against the Armenians culminated in the mass murder of the Armenian farmers around Mush. As the Turks began to attack, farmers began to hide their children in haystacks. The children were soon discovered, however, taken to a nearby shed and burned alive. Around 50,000 Armenians in Mush were massacred during the early weeks of the Genocide. Only a few thousand were able to flee.

In Marsin around 1,000 were stripped naked and flogged. Young lads were taken to an open field, raped, and ordered to dig their own graves. In nearby Adana the Armenian stores were looted and the shopowners were taken to an open field and shot. In Kharpert 13,000 Armenians were butchered. This historical city was a center of Armenian cultural activities and the American missionaries had established an American school, the Euphrates College. Most of the professors were Armenian, educated in the United States and England. In July the Turks arrested the Armenian professors and after torturing them brutally, killed them all.

In Trabizond the Turkish troops patrolling the streets seized hundreds of Armenian boys, threw them to the ground and ordered them to eat animal excrement. During the night they had arrested thousands of Armenian men and set the churches on fire. The burned bodies of the priests were thrown into the streets and the Turkish mobs were instructed to spit at them. A few days later the leaders of the Armenian community were taken to extermination camps, beaten savagely, and their skulls smashed with an axe. 53,000 Armenians in Trabizond and the surrounding areas were massacred during the early months of the Genocide. Thousands were thrown into the Deyirmeni River. The women were thrown into the river after their breasts were sliced off.

As winter snow began to melt and the first rain of spring brought warm weather, the Armenian leaders in Trabizond made arrangements with shipowners to take the Armenian refugees to safety. A Turkish ship captain, after accepting a large sum of money promised to transport some several hundred Armenians through the Black Sea to the Russian territory. Hundreds of refugees, with hardly anything on their back, gathered at the pier. They began to board the ship and the captain crammed them in like cattle. There was no room to take all of them. There was a young lad of seven holding his mother's hand standing at the pier. His name was Aram Garentz. Mother and son were being left behind with hundreds of other refugees. The mother pleaded with the captain, kissed his hands, and gave him her wedding band, to at least take the boy to safety. The captain agreed. The boy in bidding goodbye hugged his mother, squeezed her legs with tears streaming down his face. "I will take another ship, my son," the mother said, "I will join you soon. Don't worry. But if I don't, never forget that you are the son of a proud people". As the boy went up the ladder, he turned around and saw his mother weeping like a child.

The ship never made it to safety. After sailing for a few hours the Turkish captain ordered his crew to dump all the passengers into the sea. Very few survived. Among the survivors was the young lad, who was rescued by a Russian battleship and taken to the Crimea. The boy's mother was ordered to march with countless other refugees towards the Syrian desert. She never made it.

In Divrigi, in the vilayet of Sivas, 400 Armenian peasants were lined up in front of their church and executed. Turks ransacked their homes and ordered the survivors to move out. They were all taken to an open field and shot to death. In one of the shacks they found a pregnant woman hidden underneath a hay stack. They pulled her out, ordered her to spread her legs and shot a bullet through the abdomen. In nearby Gurun hundreds of Armenian women were ordered to strip from the waist up. A mullah began to slice off their nipples and another one meticulously put the nipples on a string while reciting verses from the Koran. In Derende the Turks took several hundred infants to an open field, cut off their hands and feet and left them there for the wild dogs to finish them off. The body of an infant boy was dragged back to town a day later and his parents saw the wild animal devouring their son's body in front of their eyes.

On a Sunday morning when the Armenians were attending church services in Amasya, the Turkish troops entered the church, raped the women, and savagely beat the old men and children. After locking the doors and windows they set the church on fire, burning the people alive. The priest tried to escape from a rear door. He was promptly captured, taken to a mullah who stuffed the priest's mouth with pages of the Bible and then cut off his head.

Old men and women in Tomarza were ordered to go to their church. The Turks closed the doors and ordered the men to relieve themselves. They then ordered the women to clean the floor.

In a well-to-do Armenian neighborhood in Samsun Turkish troops entered Armenian homes and demanded money and jewels. They ordered the men and women to strip naked. The men were taken to an open field and shot to death and the women beaten brutally.

During the early months of the Genocide the Armenians in Constantinople were left alone, but when Enver continued to suffer defeat after defeat in the east and continued to blame the Armenians, the Turks went on a rampage. Turkish gangs combed the streets of the Armenian quarter. They began to beat the Armenians and plunder and burn their shops and homes. Hundreds were beaten to death and thousands were injured severely. The injured were taken to stables and hung on hooks like butchered cattle, while still alive. In June 1915 twenty leaders of the Hunchak Party were hanged in Constantinople, and Archbishop Zaven, the Armenian Patriarch was deported together with several dozen clergy.

In Kigi, in the Vilayet of Erzerum, Turkish gangs chased the Armenians through the narrow streets of the town. The Armenians ran to their church and closed the doors. The gangs set the church on fire and forced other Armenians to push themselves inside the burning church. Those who stumbled were cut in half.

The massacre continued with unabated fury. The order from the capital called for the systematic destruction of all Armenian communities in Anatolia and Cilicia. It was Talaat's order that Turkey should be cleared of all Armenians. He knew he could rely on the fanatic network of mullahs and Moslem fundamentalists to inflame the Turks against the Armenians. Thousands of Armenians in all cities and towns were rounded up by Moslem fanatics, taken to an open field, and butchered. Piles of dead bodies were left in the field to the delight of vultures and wild animals. Rewards were given to those who butchered the greatest number of Armenians. A mullah offered the local fanatics good rewards if they would deliver to him the penises of young Armenian boys.

The advance of the Russian army into Anatolia offered the Turks excellent opportunity to massacre more. The eastern region was quite remote from foreign diplomats and the Turks had no difficulty in accomplishing their plans. In a matter of months Anatolia and Cilicia became a scene of one of the most heinous crimes committed in the history of man. The news of the terror traveled abroad but no help arrived, not even from the United States, since it continued to keep its diplomatic relationship with Turkey and maintained its neutrality during the early years of World War I. The American missionaries living in Turkey tried to do all they could to help the stricken people, but they had no funds nor the facility to transport masses of people to safety. Some were fortunate to emigrate to the United States and people of means bribed their way into Europe. American missionaries and European diplomats were not allowed to wander around the Armenian communities lest they witness the persecution and the slaughter of the people. Occasionally some American ministers managed to go around. An American minister in Aintab, while riding in the outskirts of the town came across a field filled with corpses. Unable to watch the horrifying scene, he instructed his companion to see if there were people left alive. These were newly slaughtered Armenians, and there were some severely wounded, but still alive, thrown on top of the dead. There was also a baby trying to suck the breast of the dead mother. The Turks rushed to the scene and ordered the American to move on.

In Everek 200 Armenians were taken to a barn. The Turks locked the doors and set the barn on fire. In another village nearby, a group of Armenian women was taken to a meadow with their children. The children were put to the sword and their mothers were ordered to bury them. The bodies of the children were taken to a large pit and the women were forced to spread dirt over them. The women began to cry and wail. The Turks ordered them to stop crying. Those who continued were shot to death. As the women continued to throw dirt around, one of them heard a voice from the pile of the dead children, "Mommy, Mommy, I am still alive". but the Turk gendarme ordered her to continue shoveling.

There were many Turks who earlier had established friendly relationships with the Armenians. They were forbidden, however, to help the stricken people. The government had made it clear that any Turk discovered helping or protecting the Armenians would be punished by death. Most of those friendly Turks also fell into a kind of hysteria which made the entire Turkish population terrorize the Armenians. There is the story of an Armenian priest who managed to crawl out of a heap of dead bodies in a mass grave. Bloodied and wounded with one leg severely smashed, the priest walked in darkness and reached the home of an old childhood Turkish friend. The Turk gave the Armenian something to eat, but turned him over to the Turkish authorities who promptly took the priest back to the mass grave and crushed his skull.

THE EXTERMINATION CAMPS

In planning the mass extermination of the Armenian people, Talaat and his colleagues decided to achieve their objectives in several stages. The first was to isolate the men from the women and children, and transfer the men to the newly built extermination camps, and the second was to force old men, women, and children to march in a southerly direction towards the Syrian desert hundreds of miles away.

The extermination camps were situated in large areas with hundreds of primitively constructed barracks within the proximity of the Armenian communities. By the spring of 1915 Anatolia and Cilicia were studded with hundreds of these camps, each designed to accommodate several thousand prisoners. The Armenian men taken to these camps were destined to die within a few days of their arrival. Their death was not painless. They were first taken to torture chambers. The Turks tortured them using heinous and imaginative methods. Shooting, drowning, and hanging were the simplest methods. Using wild dogs was another. The victims were tied to a pole and the dogs were ordered to tear them apart. Other methods included burying the people alive, burning them alive, amputating their feet and arms, gouging their eyes out, and leaving them in an open field to die.

Others were placed in isolation booths, one and one half foot by one and one half foot in size, standing up for several days, with no food or water. Many died within a few days. The survivors were then taken to extermination chambers, beaten to death or hanged upside down. The Turks were careful not to kill them all. For each group of 300 they left around twenty able bodied men to be used as a labor force to bury the dead. These men carried the bodies of the dead from the extermination chambers to a large field. They were ordered to dig large pits and throw the corpses into the pits. Shovels were provided to cover the dead with dirt. Often a new batch of twenty men were used to bury the new arrivals if the first group had proved to be ineffective to carry on the task expeditiously. Speed was important and bullets were hardly used. Swords, beating, and hanging were thought to be more economical. Sometimes women and children were brought to these camps if the local authorities considered these people unfit to travel by foot. A pregnant woman gave birth to a baby boy upon arrival at one of these camps. The Turkish guard wanted the baby for himself. The woman held the baby tightly in her arms and refused to let him loose. The guard hit her, the woman fought ferociously, howling like a wild beast. The guard attacked her, jumped on top of the woman, smashed her to the ground, slit her open with his knife and shoved the screaming baby inside her belly and left the mutilated bodies on the ground.

In camps in the Vilayet of Sivas 175,000 were exterminated, 92,000 perished in the Vilayet of Erzerum. Around 145,000 Armenians were murdered in the Vilayet of Kharpert. In the Vilayet of Diyarbekir, 85,000 men were slaughtered. In the extermination camps in Bitlis and the surrounding areas 90,000 were murdered. In the Vilayet of Van 70,000 were killed. 60,000 were massacred in Cilicia. 50,000 were butchered in Trabizond and the surrounding villages. 50,000 perished in the extermination camps in the Vilayet of Bursa. 87,000 were murdered in the Vilayet of Angora. In the extermination camps of Konya 15,000 men were massacred. One third of the population of Gurun perished in extermination camps after the people were savagely beaten. Most of their bodies were dismembered and left in the field to the delight of wild animals. Sis, the old capital of Cilicia, claimed 8,000 lives. 25,000 Armenian refugees from Erzinjan were taken to the Kamakh Gorge of the Euphrates River. The Turks tied their hands behind their back and pushed them into the river. The same fate awaited the Armenians in Erzerum. They were ordered to march towards the Kamakh Gorge. The women were taken away and raped in public and the men were shot to death. The bodies were then thrown into the river.

In the villages near Derende, 300 Armenian farmers were taken to a barn. The Turks locked the barn and burned the people alive. In another village near Hnus, 500 villagers were driven like cattle to their slaughter.

In Egin the Turks drove hundreds of old men to a nearby forest, broke their arms and legs with axes and left their mutilated bodies in the open field. In towns around the Euphrates River groups of Armenian men were taken to the bank of the river and were ordered to walk on water: "Be Jesus, go ahead, walk to the other side" they were told. Most of them drowned. The survivors, who were able to swim to the other side were captured and their skulls axed before they were able to get out of the water. In Mayyafarigin, where Tigranakert, the capital of Tigran the Great was once located, 2,000 Armenians were crushed to death.

The mass murders and the systematic destruction of the Armenian communities were committed in secrecy under the protection of the wartime censorship. When sporadic news about the mass executions and deportation of the Armenian people arrived at foreign consulates the diplomats were puzzled over the astonishing docility of the Armenians to obediently comply with the orders of a handful of Turkish officers and guards. The diplomats were told that thousands of Armenians were being forced to march, without protest, supervised only by a handful of Turkish military personnel. For the Armenians this was not unusual. Turkish terror had been inflicted upon these people for so long that they dared not resist or attack back, because experience had shown that the murder of one Turk led to the annihilation of the entire community. In some cases a couple of Turkish policemen was enough to butcher an entire district of Armenians. The people found themselves powerless. In walking to their slaughter they only relied on their religious faith, as in the past, and sought the mercy of God. There were exceptions, however. Some people rose in revolt and broke down the Turkish power.

THE REBELLION AT VAN

From time immemorial the city of Van had been one of the centers of the Armenian civilization. It was here that the Urartians built their kingdom and the old Urartian citadel stood guard for 2,500 years over the Armenian district, now occupied by the Turks. It was also in Van that the Armenian political parties began their activities. Since the mid-Nineteenth century, several generations of revolutionaries had strengthened the spirit of nationalism in Van and hardened the determination of the people to fight for their freedom and political self-determination.

At the outbreak of World War I, there were around 197,000 Armenians living in the Vilayet of Van, with 90,000 in the city proper and the rest in the surrounding towns and villages. Among the villages Lim-ktuts, Archech, Alcayaz, Hakkiari, and Aghtamar were the most prominent.

In the fall of 1914 when the Russian forces began to invade Turkey and crush Enver's undisciplined forces in the east, the Armenian revolutionaries in Van, began to send signals to the Russian army command that they would be more than willing to help the Russians if the Russians chose to advance towards Van. The Russians had already deployed regiments full of Armenian volunteers to help their military campaign in Anatolia, with the intention of opening a corridor through the length of Turkey to attack Constantinople from the east.

As the war began to rage, it became vitally important for Turkey to defend its eastern flank to stop the Russians from penetrating central Anatolia. To suppress the Armenian nationalist movement in Van and to prevent the Armenians from collaborating with the Russians, Enver placed his brother-in-law, Jevdet Bey, as the Governor of Van, with instructions to get rid of the Armenian population as expeditiously as possible. Jevdet was a fanatic anti-Armenian. His savagery and brutality were well known in the Armenian community. He began his terror against the Armenians in the villages in the winter of 1915. Hundreds of Armenian peasants were taken to the field and shot to death. When the villagers rushed to the scene and buried the dead, Jevdet ordered his troops to exhume the bodies and lay them in the open field for the wild beasts to devour. His troops then drove women and children to the snow-capped mountains around Van. Most of them perished on the way up. The Turks arrested the village priests, cut off their ears and nose, gouged out their eyes and left them in the open field to die. The mouths of infant girls were stuffed with horse excrement. Penises of infant boys were severed and sent to the local mullah for collection. By 1915 fifty-five thousand Armenian peasants in the villages surrounding Van were slaughtered and thousands were left homeless.

In Van proper, Moslem minarets poured out messages of venom against the Armenians. Mullahs inflamed their fellow Moslems to free the Turkish fatherland of this undesirable race The Armenian shops were ordered closed. Posters appeared in the Armenian quarter ordering the Armenians to leave the city. American missionaries and foreign diplomats stationed in Van tried to intervene with Jevdet Bey in behalf of the Armenians but the Turks had already made up their mind.

In the spring of 1915 Jevdet issued an order to evacuate the Armenian district of Van and instructed the Armenian community leaders to surrender themselves to the Turkish authorities. The Armenians were fast in their response. There will be no evacuation, they told Jevdet. This was their country. This was their homeland. They will stay in their ancestral home and defend their lives and properties with guns if necessary.

The Armenians began to prepare to fight. A force of 1,000 was organized within a matter of days, under the leadership of Aram Manougian, a courageous young revolutionary from the Caucasus. Armenian shopowners, farmers, businessmen, doctors, lawyers, teachers, and priests, formed committees for the defense of Van and within a few days, built barricades around the entire Armenian quarter with eighty defense positions at various strategic locations. The Armenians found themselves in the front line of a military confrontation. They flocked to the Armenian cathedral and the bishop celebrated mass. An overflowing crowd of people stood and prayed, crying to the God of their forefathers to have mercy on them and save the people from this calamity.

Enraged by this military insurrection against the Turkish authority, Jevdet organized "Butcher Batallions" of 10,000 strong, to invade the Armenian quarter and massacre the people. The Turkish forces encircled the Armenian quarter with cannons and heavy artillery. They seized the German and British consulates which were adjacent to the Armenian district and used them as their military base.

The Turks began their bombardment on April 20, 1915 aimed at Armenian defense positions. The Armenians responded with hand grenades and killed hundreds of Turkish troops within a few hours. Peasants with pick axes and spades attacked the Turks and occupied an important Turkish outpost located immediately outside the Armenian quarter. Encouraged by their success the Armenians began to dig tunnels and passageways underneath the streets of the barricaded area. These dugouts allowed the Armenians to have access to the Turkish military camp on the other side of the Armenian quarter. Using the tunnels, the Armenians dynamited military installations, killing dozens of Turkish troops and seizing a considerable quantity of weapons.

While the Armenians were militarily successful, fatigue and exhaustion began to take their toll and their food supply began to run out. As the fighting continued the Armenian peasants in the neighboring villages began to flee the Turkish massacres and entered the Armenian quarter in Van. This overcrowding condition made the military operation extremely difficult. By now there were about 60,000 Armenians behind the barricades surrounded by Turkish troops. Soon famine struck and some people died of starvation. But rescue was on the way. On May 16 Russian troops from the east began to advance towards Van. The Turkish army was compelled to retreat and Jevdet fled Van, leaving the city to the Armenians.

The news of the Turkish withdrawal reached the Armenian quarter. Men, women, and children began to cheer. The battle was over. The Armenians had won. A group of Dashnak revolutionaries began to sing the battle hymn of their party, "*Haratch, Nahadag Tseghi Anmahner*" - "Forward, you immortals of an oppressed people". They sang in military formation, tapping out the rhythm with their guns. This was their song of hope, this was their song of the future, and their song of inspiration against the Turkish oppression. The Armenians poured out of their quarter, brought down the barricades and occupied Turkish outposts. They brought the Turkish flag down and mounted the Armenian flag on top of the government buildings. For the first time in one thousand years the Armenian flag began to fly on the old Urartian citadel of Van.

On May 18, 1915 the Armenian volunteers headed by General Dro entered Van with the Russian army. The people embraced the Armenian troops in joy and the military procession entered Van triumphantly.

An Armenian govenment was immediately established and Aram Manougian became the head of the Armenian Free Republic of Van. This marked the end of centuries of Turkish domination. The Turkish people fled west with their troops and within weeks thousands of Armenians from other areas flocked into Van. As Armenians were being massacred in other parts of Anatolia, the survivors after hearing the news about the emergence of an Armenian independent state, began to flee to Van for safety. Armenian military men, revolutionary and intellectual leaders flocked into Van to organize a military operation and a political system.

The Republic was short lived. On July 21, 1915 the Russian command ordered the evacuation of Van. The Turks had strengthened their forces in Anatolia and were on the way towards Van at a rapid pace. The Russian army, which had acted as the protector for the newly formed Armenian Republic, began to retreat. By now there were about 200,000 Armenians gathered in Van. With their dream irrevocably shattered they all began to follow the Russian troops, in a mass exodus, towards the Caucasus. Men, women, and children marched for hundreds of miles of arid land and mountain passes under the scorching sun. 40,000 of them were massacred by the Kurds and many died of starvation. The survivors, wretched and emaciated, reached Erevan to face famine and epidemic. A British army officer, while traveling through this region described the condition of these Armenians. "It seemed impossible that humanity could be reduced to such extremes and live. To most death brought a speedier relief from their sufferings".

MUSSA DAGH

Mussa Dagh was another outpost where Armenians fought rather than give up. The Armenian community of Mussa Dagh consisted of six villages clustered near Alexandretta, which was once a seaport of the Cilician Kingdom. In July 1915 the courageous Armenian mountaineers of Mussa Dagh defied Turkish deportation orders, left their villages in the valley and climbed up the impregnable mountains carrying with them guns, ammunition, food, and supplies. Within a few days they built barricades, and fortifications and dug trenches to defend themselves against a possible Turkish onslaught. A Turkish force of 3,000 began to climb up the mountain and set up camp within a few miles of the Armenian camp. During the dead of night, Armenian guerrilla units crept behind the Turkish line and in a surprise attack decimated most of them and chased the rest down the mountain. By dawn the mountains were cleared of Turkish troops.

While the Armenians were victorious, their situation was hopeless. They were trapped on the mountain top with no communication with the outside world. Soon their supplies ran out. Women and children began to suffer of starvation and exhaustion. Winter was upon them and their chances of survival on top of the snow-capped mountain were minimal. The Armenian high command decided to devise a plan for their escape. Swimmers were posted in Alexandretta harbor carrying signs: "Christians in distress. Rescue", to hail any passing vessel. They waited for several days but no vessel was in sight. On the other side of the mountain the Turks had reorganized their troops and were on their way up to attack the Armenians, this time with heavy equipment and cannons, to finish them off. Suddenly on Sunday, September 12, 1915 the Armenian swimmers in the harbor sighted a battleship. It was a French vessel. The captain had seen the distress flags and was on his way to save the people. The swimmers swam up to the ship and told the captain of their plight. The captain immediately sent messages to the French admiral to dispatch other vessels to rescue the Armenians. The entire community of 4,000 came down the mountains and boarded the vessels. They were all taken to safety to Port Said, Egypt.

THE DEATH MARCHES

The Armenian massacre was accompanied with a massive program of deportation. When the order to exterminate the Armenians was issued in February 1915 it was anticipated that most of the Armenians would die during their march on the way south. The Turks were right. Most of them died.

With most of the men in extermination camps or already murdered, the Turks now ordered old men, women, and children to leave their homes and assemble into a convoy and begin to march in a southerly direction. The reason for this evacuation, the people were told, was to keep them away from the war zones, even though most of the Armenian communities were quite far from the war zones. The Armenians were told that at the end of the war they will all be allowed to return home and resume their normal life. In the meantime their properties will be in safe hands, and they will be rented out with the rental income placed in a special trust fund to be given to them with accrued interest upon their return. While Armenians took this as a sadistic joke, there were some naive Americans who accepted the Turkish explanation. A retired U. S. Admiral wrote sometime later that the "Armenians in 1915 were moved from inhospitable regions where they were not welcome and could not actually prosper, to most delightful and fertile parts of Syria, where the climate is as benign as in Florida and California, whither New York millionaires journey every year for health and recreation. All this was done," the Admiral wrote, "at great expense of money and effort by the Turks."

An endless caravan of refugees began to move towards
Syria. They walked with whatever pitiful belongings they could
manage to carry with them. They passed through devastated
towns where the corpses of their fellow Armenians were left on
the roads. They were the haggard refugees of an impoverished
nation with nothing to eat and hardly anything on their back.

A group of 10,000 women and children were driven to the
Euphrates River and were forced to cross the river. Women
holding their children above their heads attempted to swim.
They cried for help but the Turkish police accompanying them
on a raft began to whip the women and put most of the children
to the sword. Thousands were drowned with parts of human
body floating in the water. The muddy water of the Euphrates
turned red with blood.

The refugees from the Vilayet of Sivas were divided into
groups of several hundred. Occasionally some people were tak-
en out of the group and were never seen again. Of the 9,000
Armenians who were ordered to march from Gurun, 5,000 disappeared during the first few weeks of their march. The survivors continued their march. Old men died from exhaustion
and children starved to death. Some were left on the road and
later shot to death.

The roads to Syria soon became filled with an endless
stream of hunger stricken and emaciated people.

The marchers from Arabgir were ordered to take their
clothes off and walk naked to the edge of a ravine. They were
then roped together and thrown into the ravine. For the marchers from Cilicia the stench of the corpses on the road was so
powerful that many fainted and were left on the road. The old
and the sick were thrown into a ditch and the rest marched aimlessly with no food or water.

When the Armenian refugees from Diyarbekir began to
march, a group of able bodied men was given shovels and ordered to dig a large trench at the foot of a hill. It took the men
three days to dig a trench one hundred feet long, six feet wide,
and four feet deep. They were then taken to the top of the hill
and slaughtered. The following day the Turks brought five
hundred Armenian women and children to the edge of the
trench, roped them together and threw them into the trench.
They poured kerosene over their bodies and burned them alive.
Another group of refugees was taken to the trench and ordered

to cover the bodies with dirt and on the third day of this operation, while the men were spreading dirt over the bodies, they saw some people still moving in the trench and some burned infants attempting to crawl over the heap of corpses. They heard noises of groaning and sobbing coming from underneath the pile of bodies. Looking at this horrifying scene an Armenian lad of eighteen became hysterical. Howling like a wild beast, he took his shovel, ran to one of the Turkish soldiers standing by and smashed his skull with the shovel. The killing provoked a merciless reprisal. About three hundred Armenians were taken out of the convoy and cut in half right on the spot. The rest crying and wailing resumed their march towards the desert.

Refugees from Malatya were panic stricken when they saw wild dogs tearing the people's bodies as they were marching through one of the villages. Earlier 2,000 Armenian women and children were butchered and their mangled bodies were left on the road. Refugees from Aintab were taken to Birecik, on the bank of the Euphrates River. They were ordered to jump down into the river from a precipice one hundred feet high. Those who resisted were beaten savagely and thrown down into the river half alive.

A woman from Mersin was so far advanced in pregnancy that she was unable to keep up with the rest of the refugees. The Turkish officer whipped her to move but the woman became horrified and stayed motionless. The Turk then pushed her to the ground, pulled her dress up, slashed her belly with his knife, grabbed the premature fetus from the woman, cut the umbilical cord and smashed the fetus against the pavement. He then turned to the woman and said "Now walk".

Most of the marchers from Gizan never made it to the Syrian desert. On the third week of their march the refugees were taken in groups of 300 to the edge of a large trench and murdered. Around 500 families from the city of Gurun were taken to Papert. At the city limits they were forced to march over bodies of people who had recently been slaughtered. In Erzinjan the Turks took 500 boys in their teens, tied them together and pushed them into the river.

The Turks destroyed the Holy Apostles' Monastery, one of the ancient monasteries of the Christian world, slaughtered the priests and tore the dean's body into pieces and threw the pieces to the beasts to devour.

An Armenian mother took her four children to the woods near the village of Taronig and dug a hole in the ground to hide the children. When one hole was not large enough to hide all four of them she dug another hole for her older daughter and placed the three children in the first hole. After camouflaging the holes with leaves she ran to the village to help others do the same. The plan did not succeed. The Turks discovered the first hole and pulled the three children out. One of them, a three year old, began to call his older sister, "Kouyrig, kouyrig", in the other hole, but his older brother held the boy's mouth tightly, whispering in his ear, "Don't call Kouyrig, they will kill her too". The sister survived the massacre.

In the village of Vartenis the Turks entered Armenian houses, dragged the girls in the courtyard and raped them. They took boys in their teens tied them to the tree and flayed them alive. They slit their skin with razors and peeled it away with pliers.

Hundreds of Armenian women were taken to their church in Tarsus and burned alive. A group of Kurds were then ordered to take the bodies out to a field and pull the gold teeth from the women's mouths. They were then ordered to slash open the bellies to look for hidden jewels.

A group of Armenians from Shabin-Karahisar was assigned as mobile grave diggers. They were kept busy by burying Armenian refugees killed on the road. Each morning the men were taken to a large trench to wait until horse drawn carts with corpses would arrive. Their job was to carry the bodies from the cart and throw them into the trench. They were told not to cover the dead with dirt until the trenches were full to the top. The carts carried around twenty bodies at a time. They were mostly women and children piled on top of each other, bound tightly with a rope. Most of the victims showed signs of brutality. Some were burned. Others had their limbs missing. Some were decapitated, and still others had their eyes gouged out. The diggers were occasionally whipped and flogged by their Turkish masters and some were tortured savagely and their bodies thrown into the same ditch along with others. This mobile unit of grave diggers marched along with the rest of the refugees, ready to dig new trenches on a moment's notice. At each stop they were taken to a place where a suitable location for mass burial could be found and were ordered to dig. After finishing the job, a newly murdered number of Armenians would arrive and the diggers were ordered to dump them into the trench. They were told to look for any valuables hidden on the body of the victim first. Fingers were severed to take rings off and mouths were slashed open to pull out gold teeth.

The Armenian revolutionaries attempted to save some lives, but the Turkish reaction to any revolutionary act was brutal and massive. For every Turk killed hundreds of Armenians were slaughtered after they were savagely tortured. On the road from Adana a group of Dashnak revolutionaries killed five Turkish soldiers to save the lives of women and children who were being tortured. The Turkish reprisal was bestial. Bellies of Armenian women were slit open and wild dogs were fetched to pull their intestines out while the women were still gasping for their last breath.

These defenseless remnants of the Armenian people, wounded and beaten, moved from one town to the next under the scorching sun. By the time they reached the desert, hundreds of thousands were murdered, and others died of starvation, exhaustion, and disease. Passing through Turkish villages screams and cries of Armenians could be heard from the death marches. Women holding their babies high above their heads cried for water. They offered their wedding rings for a drop of water. But no one was allowed to approach them.

The terror stricken refugees from Kharpert, on the fifth week of their march, came across a large trench in which there were hundreds of dead bodies piled on top of each other. The stench of the decomposed bodies permeated the air. The bodies were bloated with swarms of flies hovering over them. Not all of them appeared to be dead, however. While the corpses were packed closely, there were some who were still moving. They saw an old woman, half hidden on top of the bodies lifting her arm pointing to an infant lying next to her. She moaned aimlessly to no one in particular *Okne, Khentrem.* "Help, please". Nobody dared to approach her. A moment later she was gone. The infant began to whimper. An impatient Turk struck the unruly baby with his rifle butt, cracking the skull, and ordered the marchers to move on.

In Hekkiari a band of Moslem Kurds attacked a group of Armenian women, tore off their clothes and thrust their fingers into the women's sexual organs to look for jewelry. The women were so emaciated that they had no strength to resist. After finishing their search the Kurds mangled the women's bodies and threw them into a cesspool of human waste.

In June as the refugees from Bularik continued their march, the weather became unbearably hot. Water was scarce. The refugees tried to bribe the Turkish officers accompanying them to bring them some water. A woman gave her wedding band to a Turk who promptly brought a large bottle of cold water. This was incredible. The people were shaken at this unprecedented gesture of charity. When they saw the bottle filled with water, the woman and the people around her reached for the bottle. They had not had a drink of water for many days. As they were about to grab the bottle, the Turk intentionally dropped the bottle, spilling the water. The people became hysterical. They bent down to lick the water from the ground. The woman yelled and screamed and demanded her ring back. The Turk slapped her and pushed her away. The woman then became wild, bent down, took the broken bottle and thrust it into the Turk's face, twisting the broken end of the bottle ferociously against his face. Then with a fast stroke she thrusted the broken bottle into the Turk's throat, killing him instantly. The Turkish reprisal was heinous. Hundreds of Armenians were shot to death with parts of their bodies scattered around the countryside to be preyed upon by wild animals, and the woman's body was mutilated beyond recognition.

THE DESERTS OF SYRIA

About half of the population of the Armenians in Turkey was exterminated during the early months of the Genocide and by the end of October Anatolia and Cilicia were cleared of Armenians, and their communities were completely obliterated. The survivors were driven to the deserts of Syria. This particular desert was chosen as the most logical location to place a punctuation mark to their existence. When the original plan of the Genocide was hatched in February, it was anticipated that the survivors, if they were fortunate enough to survive, would die of starvation, exhaustion, and disease after they reached the desert. The Turks were right.

Upon reaching Syria the refugees were taken to Jarabluss, Rakka, Ras-el-Ain, Meskane, and Der-el-Zor, the principal towns of the desert around the Euphrates River. Soon the epidemic of cholera and typhus spread among the survivors. Many died within a few weeks, and thousands committed suicide by throwing themselves into the river.

The Turkish terror continued unabated. Refugees were beaten constantly. Hundreds of Armenian children in the desert were dragged by their feet, stabbed with knives and thrown into a well half alive. When the well became full to the top other refugees were brought to press the bodies deeper into the well to make room for others.

In Rakka the Turks took a group of Armenian children, tied them up and poured sand down their throat until they died. In Jarabluss Turkish troops on horseback would prowl among the refugee camps, select Armenian girls, tie their necks to the tail of the horse and ride the horse, dragging the girls behind them.

It was only after the Armenian refugees reached the Syrian desert that the American missionaries began to witness the grim reality of the Turkish atrocities. Here in the desert of Der-el-Zor, these wretched people, emaciated, hungry, and exhausted, moved around like images of horror. On their first Sunday when the refugees were all together, the American missionaries organized a prayer gathering. Around 5,000 refugees knelt down on the sand and chanted their prayer of despair: *Der Voghormia*, "Lord have mercy on us". They mourned the passing of their loved ones and the extermination of the people.

"May God help this tormented people", cried an American minister watching them pray. "God, who is God?", responded an Armenian priest standing by. "There is no God. There is no Jesus. Otherwise this wouldn't have happened to us. Perhaps that pagan priest was right when we were fighting to accept the Christian faith. 'If you accept Jesus,' he said, 'the Armenian nation will forever be cursed'. Perhaps this suffering is our reward for accepting Jesus".

A group of Turkish officers approached to disperse the crowd. The Armenian priest walked towards them and began to shout. "The Armenian nation will never die, you murderers.

The Armenian nation will never die, you bastards. We have endured these sufferings before. We shall survive. It is you, murderers, it is you, filthy Turks, that will die before we do. You are the curse of the human race. You will someday pay dearly for your crimes". When one of the Turks raised his gun to shoot him, the priest screamed, "Lord Jesus, help me".

Thousands upon thousands of Armenian refugees were now gathered around the banks of the Euphrates. They lived in open air, stripped of their clothing, herded together like cattle. Der-el-Zor had become the city of misery and suffering. It was the last stop for the survivors of a destroyed nation. As the refugees began to wander around for food and water, the town soon became littered with heaps of decomposed bodies. On the third week of their arrival in Der-el-Zor, a group of American missionaries came to the refugee camps in horse drawn carts. The sight of the Americans provoked mass weeping and wailing. Beating their heads to the ground the Armenians pleaded for some water and food. They hugged the Americans, kissed their hands, kissed their feet and screamed at the top of their lungs, "America, America, God bless America, you are our only hope".

THE SURVIVORS

The American missionaries in Der-el-Zor helped several thousand refugees to emigrate to the United States through a complicated travel arrangement. The refugees were taken first to Aleppo, and after staying there for several months they were issued certificates allowing them to travel to Beirut. In Beirut the Armenians were given travel visas to board whatever ship or freighter they would find in the harbor. The ships, funded by the American mission, carried the refugees through the Mediterranean to the French port of Marseilles. The refugees stayed in Marseilles for several months, finally reaching America a year or so later.

The Armenian Genocide generated horror throughout the world. Representatives of the American government reporting on the Armenian holocaust wrote "the traveler in Western Armenia is seldom free from the evidence of the most colossal crime of all ages."

Civilized people everywhere condemned the Turks and urged their governments to demand restitution. Anti-Turkish sentiment became public matter, fomented by news from the Middle East where thousands of refugees were starving to death. An American Committee for Armenian Relief was organized in the United States headed by former President William Howard Taft and former Supreme Court Justice Charles Evans Hughes. President Woodrow Wilson declared two days in October 1916 as "Armenia Days" and urged the American people to help the "starving Armenians". In a national fund raising drive millions of dollars were raised to help the stricken refugees in the desert of Der-el-Zor. Fund raising drives were organized at police and fire stations throughout the United States to collect food and clothing for the Armenian refugees. Principals of public schools urged teachers to place cups at their desks to encourage students to contribute pennies and nickels for the refugees. In Great Britain a British Armenian Committee was organized to help the stricken Armenians and the Prime Minister declared that "His Majesty's government will never forget its responsibilities towards this martyred race". In France a group of French intellectuals headed by Anatole France organized fund raising drives to help the Armenians.

This tremendous outpouring of sympathy was not enough, however, to help the people in the deserts of northern Syria. The Arabs, in revolt against the Turks themselves, helped the Armenians by allowing them to settle in their communities. Several thousand reached Lebanon, Palestine, and Egypt and others settled in the Sudan and Ethiopia. In their zeal to help the refugees, many Arab sheiks and Bedouin tribesmen snatched children from dying parents and placed them in the homes of Moslem families. Hundreds of Armenian children, mostly orphans left on the road, were distributed among the Bedouin families. They were later absorbed in the Moslem religion and forever lost their Armenian identity. Among the children taken by the Arabs was the three year old brother of a little girl named Zabel.

THE SAGA OF A LITTLE GIRL

Zabel was from Everek. She had walked with her mother, sisters, and brother, taking them fifty seven days to reach Der-el-

Zor. When the deportation call was issued in April her father had cemented all the family treasures in a hole on the floor of their home in Everek. Two days later the father was taken away by the Turkish police. On the way to Der-el-Zor Zabel's mother and one of the sisters died of starvation. The other sister, a beautiful girl of seven was lost in the crowd of thousands of refugee marchers.

At the age of twelve Zabel was now alone with her three year old brother, Garbis, on the bank of the Euphrates with nothing to eat and no place to stay. She had assumed the role of mother to take care of her little brother. Every day she would go around Bedouin villages, collect some orange peels and grass roots and feed her brother. Her determination to survive and to support her brother had captured the heart of the refugees around her. But there was something else that made her the darling of the refugees. Every morning Zabel would sit down on the sand with her little brother and teach him the Armenian alphabet by writing the Armenian characters on the sand. Perhaps it was her courage that was so touching. She would take her brother's finger and help him write the Armenian letters on the sand at a time when both of them had nothing to eat and their physical survival was in jeopardy.

Every morning Zabel would place her little brother at a specific corner near one of the makeshift tents in the refugee camp and walk around all day to find some food for both of them. In the evening, before sunset, she would return to that corner and find her brother safe, playing in the sand with other children. As the days went by it became increasingly difficult for her to find food. One day Zabel placed her brother in the usual corner. When she returned a few hours later, her brother was gone. She became hysterical. She ran around, asked people, but nobody knew the child's whereabouts. She became frantic. She finally met someone who told her that the child was seen in the arms of an Arab Bedouin. The ghastly reality hit her. She fell face down on the sand and cried. With her parents and sisters gone and her brother abducted, Zabel moaned: "They are all gone. I am all alone".

Ten years later, after settling in Aleppo, Zabel met an American minister from Minneapolis. She told him about her plight and about her lost brother. The minister agreed to go with her to Der-el-Zor to look for her little brother. Leaving on an easterly route the couple headed towards Der-el-Zor traveling through the width of the Syrian desert. Two days later they reached the first outpost not too far from the Euphrates. They went straight to the main well in the center of the village to wash up and talk to the natives. Soon people began to gather around the strangers. Zabel told them that they wanted to see the village sheik. The couple was taken to a mud house where the sheik lived and Zabel told him the purpose of the trip. The sheik assured them that they will be free to inquire about any Armenian children in the village and if they found any, they will be allowed to take them home with them.

They went from village to village, from Bedouin sheik to Bedouin sheik. In each village they asked that all the Bedouins be brought together and children lined up with their parents. Zabel and the minister would then go through the line to see if they could identify Armenian faces and possibly find Garbis. But there was no trace of any Armenian children.

Two months later, as they were about to give up their search, they reached a village located about fifty miles east of Der-el-Zor. Here again they went through the lines but saw no trace of any children that were of Armenian origin. Suddenly Zabel saw a boy about twelve or thirteen years of age, who looked like an Armenian. He was tall with dark and bushy hair. Zabel approached the boy. The boy became confused in the presence of the stranger. Haltingly he answered some questions about his parents who were standing nearby. Zabel looked at the boy closely. The boy's Moslem parents began to protest and the boy drew back. Zabel took the boy's face in her hands, looked at him and said. "You are my brother, your name is Garbis. You are my brother". "No, No, No, the boy screamed, I am Moslem, go away. I am Moslem and these are my parents". "No" Zabel said, "you are Armenian, and you are my brother. Let me tell you about the place where you came from". As the sheik and the Bedouins listened attentively, Zabel told the boy about this little village where they once lived. She told him about his mother who used to take him by his hand every morning to the well in the center of the village. She told him about the tall mountains surrounding the village. "Do you remember, do you remember this village". "No, no", the boy yelled. "Leave me alone. I don't remember. I am Moslem. My name is Ahmed". The boy's parents began to protest and started to move the boy away. As Zabel was about to give up the questioning she suddenly remembered something. She told the boy to sit down on the sand with her. She held the boy's index finger and began to write the Armenian Alphabet on the sand. Suddenly the boy's eyes lit up. He stood up and looked around him. He looked at his Moslem parents and looked at Zabel. He looked again. Suddenly he cried. He hugged Zabel and screamed at the top of his lungs, "Oh kouyrig, kouyrig. You are my sister, you are my kouyrig".

As the trio began its journey back to Aleppo, the American minister with tears in his eyes murmured to no one in particular, "This is the triumph of conscience and the power of Christian God". And then he recited a verse of one of G. K. Chesterton's poems:

> "'To an open house in the evening
> Home shall men come,
> To an older place than Eden
> And a taller town than Rome
> To the end of the way of the wandering star
> To the things that cannot be and that are,
> To the place where God was homeless
> And all men are at home.'

"Faith will someday rise through the tears of the Armenian people, and they too will come home."

The Genocide was now over. One and one half million Armenians were massacred, 200,000 managed to escape to the Caucasus and 200,000 were forcibly Islamicized. The survivors, 400,000, lived for many years in the blazing hot desert land of northern Syria in wretched shacks and squalor. April 24th, the start of the Genocide, became a national day of mourning for all Armenians around the world and Der-el-Zor came to commemorate the suffering of the Armenian people.

Zabel, now a resident of New York, visited Der-el-Zor in 1956, forty one years after the massacre. She went to the clearing where thousands of Armenians were brutally slaughtered. It was a vast clearing of hard sand with pebbles, not far from the river. She dared not walk on the sand lest she desecrate the memory of the dead. She knelt down, crossed her face, murmured "Oh, you martyred people of a tormented race, let the breeze of your spirit touch my face, and the memory of your heroism warm my heart". She took a handful of sand, touched it to her face, and kissed the sand with tears in her eyes.

Nineteen-fifteen marks the end of one period in the history of Armenia and the beginning of another. With catastrophic swiftness it ushered in a new era, marking the beginning of the diaspora and the death of Western Armenia. This was the year in which the Armenians forever lost their ancestral homeland, the place which gave them birth and induced them to create a legacy which asserted the principle that men, by right, ought to be free. For 3,000 years the Armenians survived the pendular oscillations of history, surrounded by great powers who found it expedient to oppress them, to torture them, and to massacre them. But it was the Turks who tried to place a final punctuation mark to their existence. The Genocide of 1915 proved to be the most savage interval, far more widespread and barbaric than any other episode in the history of these people.

Some people today tend to forget this particular event. For them it appears remote and buried in the distant past. Those who remember will never forget the grotesque bestiality of the crime and those who survived will never understand the reason why so many died a merciless death. Perhaps their only crime was the desire to live as free men on the soil of their ancestors. For the Turks the nurturing of that desire was punishable by death. Since Turkey was a nation built on stolen land its government could not allow the establishment of another political entity on the same land.

Until today the Turks refuse to accept their responsibility of having committed this mass slaughter and regard the story of the Genocide as a figment of the people's imagination. They blame the Armenians for their misfortune. Today there is not much indignation heaped on the Turks for what they have done because history belongs to the victor and victors generally refuse to accept the burden of a historical wrongdoing. The Turks today want to rewrite the past, but events in history cannot be rewritten in contradiction to recorded history and the collective memory of the participants.

The Armenian Genocide needs no confirmation. It has already been confirmed by an entire generation of people who lived in the period and whose existence has been irrevocably shaken. The imperishable evidence of this monumental monstrosity lies in the recesses of the collective mind of that genera-tion.   If the people of that generation accepted the appalling events of 1915 as a true example of the Turkish bestiality, it should not be too difficult for others to accept the credibility of the historians, even though the government of Turkey has waged a worldwide campaign to change the pages of history. When the oppressor says that the oppressed is the responsible party for the heinous deed of the oppressor, he offends not only the credence of history but desecrates the memory of the dead and insults the intelligence of civilized men everywhere.   To pretend that it didn't happen may give others the opportunity to do it again.   If the Turks have decided to forget the past, others should remember that "those who cannot remember the past are condemned to repeat it".   The Armenian Genocide of 1915 paved the way for others to give the practice of Genocide a uni-versality a quarter of a century later.

CHAPTER TWENTY-THREE

OUT OF ASHES A REPUBLIC

While the Armenians were being massacred, the war was raging on all fronts, with neither side claiming any decisive victory over the other. A new epoch is about to emerge, one which will mark the most critical test for the great powers to maintain their superiority and smaller nations to survive as independent entities. The rise of malignant nationalities and the zeal of the great powers to enlarge their empires led to the development of social and political ideologies which will eventually change the course of subsequent history. The aim of each nation was essentially different while the method of achieving it was basically the same.

For Germany World War I was a war to build a Germanic empire at the expense of Allied powers. Unlike the other European powers the Nineteenth century Germany had failed to build a colonial empire. Situated in the heart of Europe, Germany, since the days of Bismarck, had never been interested in establishing colonial regions around the world and its commercial groups rarely enjoyed sufficient political clout to influence national policy. Things began to change gradually at the turn of the century and a chain of circumstances led the German Kaiser to think about acquisition of land to accommodate the rapidly growing German industrial and commercial power. It was Kaiser's intent to exploit the same factors which had stimulated the growth of British and French economy earlier, placing both at the height of their power and enabling them to accumulate enormous capital wealth.

For England and France this was a war of defense and an opportunity to grab the spoils of the disintegrating Ottoman Empire. For Russia the war offered the opportunity to galvanize the spirit of patriotism and nationalism to fight for the defense of the Slavic peoples and protect the integrity of their nationhood. In accepting the consequences of leadership in the Slavic world, Russia nurtured renewed interest to gain control of eastern Europe through a war of conquest, take whatever territory left over from the Ottoman Empire, and push the Germans and Austrians to the west.

For the Turks the war gave them the opportunity for their pan-Turanic policy, contrived to play off Turkic tribes against Russia whenever possible, to expand their sphere of influence to the east and establish a Turkish hegemony from the Aegean Sea to the walls of China. The annihilation and the deportation of the Armenian people paved the way for the vigorous execution of that policy.

THE WAR GOES ON

Having failed to defeat the Turks in Gallipoli, the British now concentrated their forces in the Middle East. Exploiting the Arab nationalistic fervor against the Turks, the British won a considerable foothold in major centers of the Middle East, and began to push their forces towards Iraq and northern Syria. The Turks could do little but adjust their strategy of defense. For the Allies the Middle East proved to be a more appropriate battleground than the peninsula of Gallipoli. In choosing to advance towards northern Syria and Iraq, the Allies planned to make a rendezvous with the Russian army, which was then organizing to march back to Anatolia and reoccupy the Armenian provinces as it had successfully done in the early summer of 1915.

Anticipating total victory over the Central Powers, the Allies began to make arrangements to distribute the spoils of the Ottoman Empire among themselves with no consideration to the Armenian territorial claims. An agreement forged in April of 1915 provided a post-war settlement under which Russia would acquire the city of Constantinople, the western shores of the Bosporus, the Sea of Marmara, the Dardanelles, and a portion of Thrace; England would acquire Arabia and the Holy Land, and France would occupy Syria and Cilicia. This agreement, coined as the Constantinople Agreement, was later incorporated into a more comprehensive accord between Sir Mark Sykes of the British Foreign Office and George Picot, the former French Consul General of Beirut. Under the Sykes-Picot Accord France would acquire Lebanon, Syria, Cilicia, and the Armenian province of Sivas; England would take Iraq, the Persian Gulf, and Palestine, and Russia would annex the remaining Armenian provinces of Erzerum, Van, Bitlis, Trabizond, and Kharpert.

The Sykes-Picot Accord which was finalized in September of 1916 encouraged Czar Nicholas II to change his attitude towards the Armenians and abandon the traditional policy of supporting the Armenian cause, despite the fact that thousands of Armenian volunteers had sacrificed their lives for the Russian war effort. The Armenians were no longer part of Russia's grand scheme and the Czar had little patience for Armenians' aspiration for political self-determination. The Turks had emptied Western Armenia of Armenians and for all practical purposes the Armenians were finished, allowing the Czar to populate Western Armenia with Russians and Cossacks.

The Armenian volunteer units which made significant contributions to the Russian victory in late 1914 and the beginning of 1915 continued to harass the Turks by guerrilla war, but this time more ferociously. From its inception the Armenian group was considered as a separate entity run by Armenian commanders and generals and operating under the Russian military leadership. Immediately after the Genocide the Czar began to look at this group as a source of irritation and considered the Armenian military activity as a latent danger to his overall strategy. In December 1915 he ordered his military command to disband the Armenian unit and make the Armenian volunteers an integral part of the Russian military organization.

The situation in the western front was different. While the Russians had a formidable army in eastern Europe, faulty deployment of their military personnel had caused considerable damage to their offensive position. The Germans had money and manpower to shatter the Russians in battle on all fronts. The Russian weakness lay in their obsessive desire to win a single decisive victory to finish up the war as soon as possible and bring the soldiers home by Christmas. The lack of an effective strategy and the inept counsels of the Russian high command had transformed the war of conquest into a war of defense. After a series of disastrous defeats in Poland the Russians abandoned their plan to hit the German heartland and shifted their attention to the Caucasus to fight against the Turks, the weaker member of the Central Powers.

RUSSIANS OCCUPY WESTERN ARMENIA

With the Armenian soldiers now incorporated with the Russian army the Russians prepared to launch an all out offensive against the Turks. In January 1916 Grand Duke Nicholas, at the head of a combined force of 180,000 Armenian and Russian troops, came down the mountains of the Caucasus and began to march towards Western Armenia. The Turks were hardly in a position to block his advance. Enver and Jemal Pasha had transported most of their command units to the Middle East, where the British had organized a successful campaign threatening to smash the Turkish power with the help of the Arab natives. The Russians and Armenians routed the Turks and began to occupy the Armenian cities and provinces one by one. One division drove the Turks north to the Black Sea and another followed the highway from Sarkemish towards Erzerum. In the midst of unprecedented snowstorms and subzero temperatures, the Russians crossed the Arax River and crushed the Turkish infantry, and in February 1916 stormed the city of Erzerum. The occupation of Erzerum, which was regarded as one of the most fortified cities in Western Armenia, paved the way to the rest of the Armenian provinces. Continuing their march westward the Russians occupied Mush and on March 2, 1916 took the city of Bitlis. Meanwhile the Russian columns that were chasing the Turks towards the shores of the Black Sea captured the seaport city of Trabizond on April 18, 1916 and a few weeks later took the city of Erzinjan with ease.

By the fall 1916 most of the Western Armenian provinces were in Russian hands albeit with no Armenian inhabitants left to celebrate the occasion. To the Turks the Russian threat was very real. The Russians had struck into the heart of their Empire threatening to proceed west towards the capital of Constantinople. An estimated 60,000 Turks were killed, and a huge stock of military supplies had fallen into Russian hands. For the Armenians this was indeed great news. Their ancestral land was now in the hands of their friends. They fought and sacrificed their lives to achieve that goal. The man who made a significant contribution towards the attainment of that goal was an Armenian revolutionary, Andranik Ozanian.

GENERAL ANDRANIK

Andranik began his revolutionary career in the province of Sivas in 1888 when he was a young man of twenty-three. A man with exceptional qualities for guerrilla war, he rose to national prominence when he successfully organized commando units to put an end to the atrocities that the Kurds were inflicting upon the Armenians in the Taron region of Western Armenia. Around the turn of the century a Kurdish strongman, Bishara Khalil, had begun a savage campaign to terrorize the Armenian communities. He and his band had devastated Armenian villages and slaughtered thousands of Armenian men, women, and children. Khalil's activities were supported and financed by the Turkish government with orders to massacre the Armenians, plunder their homes and chase the survivors to the mountains. He had been honored by the Turkish government and Sultan Abdul Hamid decorated him with the Ottoman Empire's distinguished medal of honor, recognizing his unique contribution to the Turkish cause. Since terror was the most characteristic activity of the Moslem Kurds, Khalil and his men made it as savage and heinous as they could. They burned churches, butchered priests, raped Armenian women, ransacked Armenian villages, destroyed crops, and decapitated hundreds of young boys.

To put an end to this Kurdish terror Andranik mobilized a group of guerrilla fighters and went to the mountains. It took his men only a few days to ambush the Kurdish band. They captured Bishara Khalil and brought him to Andranik. "Are you the one who had masssacred the Armenian villagers for the last many years", Andranik asked. Khalil did not answer. He repeated the question, but the Kurd did not respond. Andranik then ordered his men to tie Khalil's arms behind him. He approached the Kurd, held his hair gently with his left hand and using a sword in his right hand separated Khalil's head from his body with one stroke. He then tore off the Sultan's distinguished medal from Khalil's chest and sent it to Sultan Abdul

Hamid with a polite note "Don't decorate people with this medal again, Your Majesty, it has a bad omen".

This act made Andranik the hero of his people and the Armenians began to call him General. No Kurd or Turk dared to approach the Armenian villages any more. In a daring attempt to stop Moslem encroachments on the Armenian communities, and insulate his people from Turkish attack, Andranik organized commando units and took thirty-eight Armenian villages under his command. He became the *de facto* military leader of the Armenian people in the provinces, and created a state within a state. His fame spread throughout Turkey and his organization became the single most powerful factor in Anatolia.

Andranik's men used sophisticated arms smuggled from the Caucasus or taken as booty from Ottoman military depots. While the Turkish method of ensuing order was harsh, Andranik's method of resisting the Turks was even harsher. He believed in armed resistance and had no patience with political compromise with the enemy. "Arms not ideas can win wars", he was fond to say. For him political aspiration without military support was useless. He told his people to carry guns to fight the Turks. While devoted to preserve the Armenian Christian institution, Andranik was fond of reciting the statement made by an Armenian novelist. "Oh, forefathers! If in the place of these monasteries which abound in our country you had built fortresses; in the place of these holy crosses which exhausted your wealth, you had brought weapons; instead of burning flagrant incense in our churches you had burned gun powder; our country would have been fortunate now. The Kurds would not have devastated our lands, they would not have slaughtered our men, and would not have raped our women".

Tall, handsome, inspiring, and charismatic, Andranik yearned for nothing but the people's acceptance of his revolutionary plans. While others tried to avoid conflict with the enemy he tried to seek it. At one time he sequestered himself and his men in an Armenian monastery and invited the enemy to attack him. He knew no fear. He would ride his horse through a hail of fire. With a quality of leadership unmatched by any of his contemporaries, Andranik was able to transform the national struggle into a war of independence and set the stage to free his people from Turkish oppression.

Throughout his military career Andranik relied on the indestructible will and the fighting spirit of his men. He punished those who broke their oath of allegiance to the national cause, and rewarded those who carried out his directives and fought to protect the defenseless people. His men fought a series of difficult campaigns, marching through dangerous terrain, scaling mountains, and crushing the Turkish enemy in battle. At times even the powerful Sultan Abdul Hamid II was concerned about Andranik's increasingly threatening military organization. Hamid sent emissaries with solicitous proposals to urge the Armenian strongman to stop the war against the Turks. Andranik's response was swift and simple "You stop your terror and I'll stop the war". He broke away from Armenian political parties, acted on his own, and trusted nobody.

A man with intuitive genius and lucidity of mind, it was Andranik who during the heyday of the brotherhood of 1909 between the Armenians and the Young Turks, warned his people about the new Turkish Pashas, Enver, Talaat, and Jemal. While others began to fraternize with the new Turkish leaders, Andranik continued his fight. In a meeting held with the Armenian party leaders shortly before the Genocide, a prominent Dashnak party leader told Andranik that the Turks will not terrorize the Armenians any more. "I will assure you, Andranik, no Armenian nose will bleed hereafter". Andranik yelled back "You don't trust the Turks, you don't trust the Turks. They will butcher your wife, they will rape your daughter, they will slaughter your newborn baby and make your country a slaughterhouse. The Turk is a Turk is a Turk. You don't trust the Turk". He gained the tremendous adulation of the Armenian people throughout the world when his prophecy proved to be accurate in 1915. The tormented and wretched Armenian refugees began to call him the Father of the Armenians and looked to him to lead them to their liberation.

A thundering revolutionary with a profound devotion to the Armenian cause, Andranik accepted no criticism about the conduct of his guerrilla war. He once scolded Leon Trotsky, a Russian newspaper reporter at the time, for failing to report his war activities correctly, and beat up Anastas Mikoyan, another reporter who later rose to become a prominent member of Stalin's Politburo, when Mikoyan's article in an Armenian newspaper was not to Andranik's liking.

In 1916 when the devastation of the Armenian land and
the Genocide of the people made the issue of the Armenian political independence secondary to the people's physical struggle
for existence, it was Andranik who refused to give up the fight
and joined the Russian army to conquer the Armenian homeland. He raised a well trained militia and marched with the
Russians to meet the Turks. The Armenian refugees who had
earlier fled the massacre and gone to Eastern Armenia, followed
Andranik's army, and as the Armenian troops occupied the old
Armenian towns, the refugees settled in them and began to rebuild their communities.

The occupation of Western Armenia was due not only to
the heroism of the Armenian troops but also Turkey's weakened
defense posture. By the winter of 1916 Turkey's military structure had deteriorated beyond the possibility of repair. The war
in the Arab lands had weakened the country's military strength
with enormous cost in manpower and resources. Financially
Turkey was bankrupt and the Germans, now deeply involved in
Europe, were unable to continue to help their junior war partner. They watched with apparent indifference the deterioration
of the Turkish power and let the Turks carry the brunt of the
war against the Russians in Anatolia.

With the entire territory of historic Armenia now under the
Russian jurisdiction the Czar began preparations to annex the
territory to the Russian Empire. He established a system of military governorships in the occupied territory with no Armenian
participation, and ordered his high command to make arrangements to populate the country with Russian colonists. Earlier, in
a meeting held in Echmiadzin, the Czar had promised the Armenian Catholicos that all the wishes of the Armenian people
will be fulfilled and once the western provinces were liberated
he would help the Armenian political leaders to create an independent state under a Russian suzerainty. Now that the western
provinces were liberated Nicholas II chose to ignore those
promises. He thought about the Armenian Question in terms of
the Russian policy his predecessors had developed for the Armenian affairs since the beginning of the Nineteenth century.
The Russians preferred an Armenia without Armenians and for
years tried to Russify Eastern Armenia, which had been under
their occupation since the first quarter of the Nineteenth century. They were concerned that one day the Armenians may

change their enemies and fight against the Russians instead to further their demands for political freedom.

The Armenians were infuriated about the latest change in Russian policy. For years they hailed the Czar as their liberator and sacrificed their lives for Russia's war efforts. With the denial of the Armenian rights the Russian liberator proved to be as treacherous as the Turks. But the Armenians need not worry. The Czar's days seemed to be numbered. An event in St. Petersburg in March 1917 changed the course of history, charted a new destiny for Russia, and offered a different prospect for the future of the Armenian people.

REVOLUTION IN RUSSIA

While the conquest of Western Armenia was a significant military accomplishment, the Russian people were not particularly happy nor impressed. The war had gone on too long with no apparent victory on the European front. If the Russians were able to crush the Turkish power in the south, they were unable to put a dent on the powerful German machine in the west. On the contrary, they suffered humiliating defeats and most of their forces were decimated. Soon difficulties arose between the people and the Czar's policy makers. The war, now in its third year, had seriously affected the economic well-being of the people, and the tremendous food shortage had prompted the opposition groups to organize mass demonstrations against the Czar and protest against the continuation of the war.

By the beginning of 1917 Russia had lost more men and territory than all the other war powers combined. Corruption in government, domestic economic problems, and inefficiencies in the Czar's military command, had caused public unrest and sporadic local revolts had affected the imperial bureaucracy's ability to run the Empire. The people's diminished affection towards the Czar forced the government to concentrate its resources more on police matters to ward off internal revolts, than on battles against the Germans. By the winter of 1917 public unrest had spread throughout the empire to the point that the people had begun to think less of how to win the war and more of how to topple the Czar. The incurable disease of the Czarevich, the heir apparent to the Romanov throne, had made Czarina Alexandra surround herself with sinister and unscrupulous characters, chief among them was Gregory Rasputin, a Russian Moujik from the Urals, who claimed to possess supernatural powers. In an attempt to cure the little boy Rasputin gradually began to dominate the affairs of the court.

By the end of February 1917 the shortage of food and fuel in Petrograd, as the capital was now called, had become acute. The country's farming system had been virtually paralyzed with fifteen million farmers recruited in the army. On March 8, 1917 the people waiting on line to buy bread in Petrograd, suddenly rose in revolt. Two days later thousands of workers went on strike. "Give us bread. Down with the war, down with the Czar", they shouted. The government found itself powerless to stop the riot. The Czar ordered the Cossack guards to open fire on the people and restore order. The guards refused; instead they joined the rebels and together they marched on the Duma where the people's representatives were holding an emergency session. A soviet (council) of workers and soldiers was established to organize a revolutionary movement to topple the government. The army garrison in Petrograd joined the rebel forces and took control of the major functions. The Czar's attempt to contain the revolution was frustrated by the formation of a provisional government composed of representatives of all parties. On March 14, 1917 Czar Nicholas II was forced to abdicate in favor of his brother, the Grand Duke Michael, who promptly gave up the throne, and the Romanov Dynasty, after ruling the Russian Empire for 300 years, came to an end.

The Provisional government elected Prince George Lvov, who immediately assumed the reign of the Empire with a coalition council representing the Constitutional Democrats and Socialist Revolutionaries, chief among them was Alexander Kerensky, the leader of the radical peasant party. Autocracy had failed and democracy had taken its place. Banners of liberty and freedom were everywhere in the capital. The revolutionaries had shaken Russia's national conscience. The Czarist bureaucrats disappeared and thousands of Soviets were organized in the Russian continent.

The Provisional government failed to provide, however, the appropriate environment for mutual tolerance among the various political groups. After living under a despotic system propelled by Czarist terror for many centuries, the people suddenly found themselves unprepared to accept the principles of democracy. Soon anarchy replaced law and order. People stopped paying rents and taxes, and the army in the battlefield degenerated into chaos. Soldiers went on strike demanding pay raises and allowances for their families. The Provisional government gradually lost its control and gave way to the authority of the Petrograd Soviet.

The most important issue facing the nation at the time was the conduct of the war, but instead of addressing the war issue the Soviets became more interested in the implementation of measures to consolidate their power and extend their influence throughout the Empire. While the leaders of the Provisional government were anxious to follow a traditional military policy to carry the war to victory, the Soviets were primarily interested in finding a proper path to legitimize the revolution and create a new social order. The adoption of their anti-war policies was facilitated by their successful exploitation of the people's sentiment regarding the war. The people were tired of the war which the Soviets claimed was forged by the imperialist policies of the Romanovs with no regard for the people's political aspirations and economic well-being.

The opposition party which concentrated its power in the organization of the Soviets was divided into two groups, the Mensheviks, who were the moderates, and the Bolsheviks, who were the extremists, headed by Lenin, and Leon Trotsky, the former newspaperman. The Bolsheviks advocated the cessation of hostilities and urged the government to negotiate for peace to carry out the policies of the Proletariat.

In the early summer 1917 the Bolsheviks rose in revolt and organized subversive activities to topple the Provisional government. To offset the Bolsheviks' dangerous opportunism and rally public support for the Provisional government, Alexander Kerensky, the Minister of War in the Provisional government, decided to launch an all out offensive against the Germans in June 1917, as a prelude to peace to force the Germans to come to the negotiating table. He ordered extensive military preparations in the war zones and reconstituted the army command with top officers. The offensive proved to be a total disaster. The morale of the military men was so low that after ten days of fighting most of the soldiers threw down their arms and deserted the army. The relentless German army systematically mowed down the Russian troops and occupied most of the territories gained by the Russians a year earlier. Kerensky had overestimated his position. While he proved to be a man with practical administrative ability, his political base was not strong enough to change the people's mood and mobilize the country's dwindling resources to fight the Germans.

The Russian defeat was a tremendous blow to the Provisional government. It led to the resignation of Prince Lvov on July 17, 1917, and the formation of a new government under the leadership of Alexander Kerensky. Kerensky began his role in a conciliatory manner attempting to gain the cooperation of all political factions to bring about a cohesive unity among the various participants of the revolution. The six month old revolution was in a chaotic state. No particular group controlled the processes of the government. Friction among the revolutionary zealots did not bring an individual powerful enough to assert a strong leadership. Each tried to make the other appear as a person incapable to lead the revolution to a successful conclusion. Elections for a new representative Duma were postponed, rival gangs roamed the streets and the country fell into a political anarchy.

NEW HOPE FOR ARMENIANS

News of the Russian Revolution reached the Caucasus and the Armenians were rejoiced by the prospect of a new world. They accepted the Revolution as the single most important event after the Genocide, destined to change the fortunes of the remnants of the Armenian people. The Armenian leaders immediately proclaimed their loyalty to the Provisional government and the people demonstrated in the streets, welcoming the new era of democracy and civil liberties. Soon Soviets of workers were established all around Transcaucasia, with the Armenian leaders playing a dominant role in the establishment of the new order. Chief among them were Alexander Khatisian, the Mayor of Tiflis, and the newly elected Chairman of the Soviet of Workers' Deputies in Baku, Stepan Shahumian.

While Western Armenia was emptied of Armenians there was a considerable number of Armenians living in Eastern Armenia. The masses of the Armenian peasants lived in the provinces of Erevan and Nakhichevan, and the merchants, professionals, and political leaders lived intermixed with the

Georgians and Azeris in such non-Armenian cities as Tiflis in Georgia and Baku in Azerbeijan. Tiflis was an important center for Armenian cultural and political activities and most of the oil refineries in Baku were in the hands of the Armenians. Among the Armenian political parties, the Dashnaks were the most predominant in the Caucasus, while the Ramgavar Party, founded in Cairo in 1908, was strong around the eastern Mediterranean, and the Hunchaks were mainly in Europe and the United States.

Kerensky's Provisional government was sympathetic towards the various nationalities in the Caucasus, and continued to accept the region as an integral part of the Russian Empire. To win their support Kerensky allowed the three groups, the Armenians, Georgians, and the Azeris, to form a political organization to run the administration of the region. In the provinces of Western Armenia still occupied by the Russians, Kerensky placed Armenian governors and administrators. Hopes were now high among the Armenians that the new regime will finally allow them to repatriate to Western Armenia and help them form an independent state. Around 150,000 Armenian refugees in Eastern Armenia began their migration back to Van, Bitlis, Erzerum, and Trabizond to rebuild their homes and communities. Armenian farmers returned to their land and scores of new communities emerged all over Western Armenia. Kerensky assured General Andranik that Russia will continue to hold the Armenian provinces under its protectorate and rejected the Czarist plan of populating the region with Russian colonists.

To counter the rapid disintegration of the Russian power in Europe, Kerensky decided to solidify his hold in Western Armenia by turning over the military command of the region to Armenian generals and transferring the Armenian troops fighting in Europe to the Caucasus. General Tovmas Nazarbekian, a highly decorated Armenian General of the Russian army, was appointed as the Supreme Commander of the Armenian forces in Western Armenia.

The French and English were also interested in strengthening their hold in Western Armenia. In the summer of 1917 they approved a plan drawn by General Andranik to mobilize a force of 30,000 Armenian troops supported and financed by the Allied governments. Under the plan Russia would supply the ammunition and supplies, England would provide the funding, and the United States would allocate $10 a month for the up-keep of the Armenian soldiers' family.

It was in the interest of the Allied Powers to have an Armenian military presence in the heart of the Ottoman Empire, to accelerate the war efforts and deliver the final blow to the Turkish military power. The Allies had become impatient. The war had gone on for three years with seventeen million people dead or wounded and no prospect for a quick settlement. While the pendulum had tilted towards them by America's entry into the war, domestic unrest made the British and French anxious to move faster to bring the war to a successful conclusion. Things were looking good for the Allies. By December 1917 the British had virtually decimated the Turkish forces in the Middle East. In March they captured Baghdad and in December General Sir Edmund Allenby, a brilliant military man, occupied the Holy City of Jerusalem, thus ending the 700-year Moslem rule and finally fulfilling the Crusaders' dream of liberating Christianity's holiest place from Moslem domination.

Turkey was far from being finished. To prevent the formation of an Armenian state, Enver Pasha appointed the competent Mustafa Kemal as the head of the Second Army to fight the Russians and drive the Armenian forces out of Eastern Anatolia.

ARMENIAN NATIONAL CONGRESS

Alarmed by the Turkish military build up and to cope with the rapidly changing political environment, the Armenians decided to hold a national congress in the fall of 1917. Delegates representing various Armenian cultural, social, religious, and political organizations, gathered in Tiflis on October 11, 1917 to formulate a comprehensive Armenian national policy. Around 200 delegates attended the conference with more than half representing the Dashnak Party. The Congress elected a National Assembly of 35 members to serve as the legislative body and a National Council composed of 15 members to act as its executive arm. The hopes of the Armenian people to finally achieve a political self-determination on their ancestral homeland seemed closer than ever. Events in Petrograd, however, irrevocably changed the direction of subsequent history.

THE RISE OF THE BOLSHEVIKS

Throughout the summer of 1917 the Bolsheviks, a minority since the beginning of the revolution, began to exact their influence in the Russian capital. Lenin made speeches promising peace to the war weary Russian masses and bread to the hungry and the destitute. He told the people that the evil was not the German power but Czarism and wanted to transform the imperialistic war into a social struggle, organize a revolution of the Proletariat, and establish a Communist system based on the doctrines of Karl Marx. The war so far had produced nothing but pain and suffering, Lenin told the people, but his revolution was professed to bring a new social order exclusively devoted to improve the people's lot.

Lenin's message appealed to the people who cared less about the political differences between the Bolsheviks and Mensheviks. For them the question was not whether the Bolshevik or the Menshevik theories were right but rather who would be fast enough to make the country's economy work better and launch an effective program of deliverance. The people were in despair. The bread lines were still long and food on the farms remained unharvested, while the revolutionaries were at each other's throat to gain control.

It was Lenin, above anybody else, who showed a remarkable skill to hypnotize the people with promises of a good life, turning the Russian masses into his loyal adherents in his struggle for leadership. He created a bastion of power at the Petrograd Soviet which enabled him to block the attempts of others and accelerate the downfall of his adversaries. His activities in the summer of 1917 generated a genuine reaction against the Provisional government. Bolshevik agitators began to organize mob riots against the government and on November 6, 1917, the eve of the convocation of the Congress of the Soviets, they occupied strategic military installations in the capital. The following day, on November 7, 1917 the Bolsheviks took over the control of the Russian government and erected a governmental structure called the Soviet of People's Commissars with Lenin as Chairman, Leon Trotsky as the Commissar for Foreign Affairs, and Joseph Stalin, the Commissar for Nationalities. Thus began the Bolshevik regime which will rule the Russian continent for the next 74 years.

The Bolsheviks began to repress other political parties and imprison their political rivals. Alexander Kerensky fled for safety but others were not that fortunate. Government ministers and opposition leaders were put in jail, newspapers were suppressed, private ownership was abolished, and the properties of the wealthy were confiscated. Democratic principles were repudiated and the dictatorship of the Proletariat was established on the Russian continent. Lenin dismantled what he inherited and installed a new system in its place.

The Bolshevik Revolution convulsed Petrograd and the provinces with political strife and led the country to a civil war. On one side were the members of the upper class who wanted to restore Czarism and on the other, were the leftists and pseudo-intellectuals, eager to embark on a political adventure and sacrifice the interests of the Empire to the establishment of a Marxist state.

The Allied powers refused to accept Lenin's dictatorship as the legitimate government of the Russian people. They were more concerned, however, with Lenin's attitude towards the war. They believed that Lenin had an impetuous desire to suspend all hostilities at any cost and sign a separate peace treaty with the Central Powers.

THE REACTION IN THE CAUCASUS

The reaction in Transcaucasia was mixed. The people were bewildered by the Bolshevik victory and adopted a "wait and see" policy before deciding to jump on the bandwagon. The Bolsheviks were a minority in the Caucasus. The Mensheviks had already dominated most of the processes of the local governments, but wanted to keep the region within the Russian jurisdiction no matter what kind of political coloration the new regime in Petrograd pretended to have.

Amid this uncertainty and political turmoil, the three nationalities of Transcaucasia, the Armenians, Georgians, and the Azeris, formed a Commissariat in Tiflis to govern the region as a separate entity, until Petrograd solidified its political structure and allowed the people to elect representatives for the general assembly.

The establishment of a separate Commissariat did not affect the activities of the Armenian political leaders. Their principal concern was the status of the Armenian provinces, occupied by the Russian army and governed by Armenian administrators. The Turks had begun to strengthen their position in Anatolia and there was growing speculation that Mustafa Kemal's Second Army was preparing to launch a campaign to invade Eastern Anatolia and chase the Russians and Armenians out.

Enver Pasha was fast to exploit the political malaise in the Russian capital and seize the opportunity to reoccupy Turkey's eastern provinces. The separation of the Transcaucasian district from the Russian suzerainty suited Enver's plan just fine. In an attempt to coax the politicians of the Caucasus, Enver formulated a policy of friendship towards the region and sent signals indicating his desire to sign an agreement of cease-fire between Transcaucasia and Turkey. Enver, still at war with Russia, wanted to isolate Transcaucasia and remove it from the Russian protection and later, when conditions improve, conquer the region and proceed east and unite the Turkish speaking races under a Turkish hegemony. Inept Transcaucasian intellectuals turned politicos gullibly fell into the Turkish trap. Under a truce agreement signed on December 18, 1917 in Erzinjan, by the delegates of Turkey and Transcaucasia, both sides agreed on the cessation of hostilities and status quo of the Armenian provinces.

Meanwhile in Petrograd Lenin was in the process of consolidating his power. The Russian Revolution had caused turmoil in the Russian military command and the disintegration of the Russian armies on all fronts. In an effort to disengage Russia from the war, Lenin ordered the Russian troops to abandon the Western Armenian territory and return home. Alarmed by this sudden change in Russia's policy, prominent Armenian Bolsheviks, among them Anastas Mikoyan and Stepan Shahumian, rushed to the Russian capital and appealed to Lenin and Stalin to rescind the order and keep the Russian troops in Western Armenia until an autonomous state was created and the integrity of its borders guaranteed and protected. They told the Bolshevik leaders that the removal of the Russian forces without securing the safety of the Armenian people would be catastrophic. The Armenian leaders felt that the evacuation of the Russian troops from Western Armenia would allow the Turks to occupy the land and massacre the rest of the Armenian people.

Notwithstanding the Armenian plea, Lenin and Stalin decided to proceed with the plan and leave the Armenian provinces to the tender loving care of the Turks. Lenin did not care about the Armenians. His objective was to repress the ethnic groups and make Communism an international movement extending over territorial boundaries and petty nationalism.

RUSSIA ABANDONS WESTERN ARMENIA

As the Russian troops began to pull out from the Armenian provinces the Armenian troops began to mobilize their forces to protect the region from Turkish onslaught. With promises of financial aid from the Allies, the Armenian political leadership began preparations to organize an Armenian militia of 20,000 men, with General Andranik acting as the Commander-in-Chief. A separate Armenian military corps was also organized headed by General Tovmas Nazarbekian with Dro Ganayan serving as the civilian commissar and Generals Silikian and Arashian as commanders of various divisions. Fear of sudden Turkish attack was the primary reason for breaking up the military command. General Arashian's regiment covered the area from Erevan to Erzinjan, Silikian's troops were assigned the region between Van and Alexandropol, and General Andranik's brigades covered the cities of Erzerum, Erzinjan, Khnus, and Van.

While the Armenian army was small in number it was exceptionally well disciplined and well equipped. Its strength lay primarily in the enormous quantities of provisions, ammunition, food, and clothing abandoned by the Russian troops. As the Russians completed their evacuation, they left to the Armenian forces 3,000 cannons, an equal number of machine guns, provisions for an army of 100,000, enough to last for several years, 16,000 horses, 110,000 rifles, and millions of cartridges. With this huge supply of military equipment the Armenian military command felt safe against the possibility of a Turkish attack. "When the savage beasts are ready to attack", Andranik said to his men, "the men who bear arms will have nothing to fear. It won't be long when the Armenians will stop wandering from place to place". "With this much ammunition", he said, "we can even conquer Constantinople".

The Turkish army on the other side was terribly disorganized, weak, and practically bankrupt. The war had impoverished the country. The absence of the Armenian farmers, who earlier provided food for the Turkish army, had caused a severe famine. There was a dangerous shortage in military equipment and towards the end of 1917 most of the Turkish soldiers had deserted the army and gone home. There were fewer than 30,000 Turkish soldiers in Eastern Anatolia, and the hold of the Turkish commanders on the military had weakened considerably with only a handful of officers forceful enough to assert their authority. The time was ripe, therefore, for the Armenians to finally solve the Armenian Question. But the Armenian leadership, composed of men with mediocre skill in political affairs, failed to seize the opportunity to capitalize on the potential Armenian military strength, which was, at the end of 1917, far greater than Turkey's military power in Eastern Anatolia.

The relationship between Turkey and Transcaucasia gradually began to deteriorate. During the first weeks of 1918 the Turks complained that the Armenian forces were violating the Erzinjan Agreement and were massacring Turks to avenge the Genocide. The trouble spot was the city of Erzinjan which had a considerable number of Armenian refugees. Since it was located on the border between Western Armenia and Turkey, the Armenians needed to fortify its defense lines to protect the community from Turkish attack. An Armenian strongman, Sebasdatsi Murad, had taken control of the city's defense positions, but his fortifications were not good enough. The Turks, scraping together whatever military equipment they could, began to make thrusts and on February 13, 1918 launched a full scale offensive on Erzinjan to crush the Armenian forces. Murad and his men fought with exceptional bravery but at the end they were overwhelmed by the Turkish power. The Turks surrounded the city and destroyed the fortifications. Murad began to withdraw his forces, and thousands of Armenian refugees followed him. In the ensuing route most of the refugees were captured and slaughtered. The survivors froze to death on the way east. Very few made it to Erzerum.

The Turks, under the command of Kiazim Karabekir, continued their march eastward. They captured town after town, village after village and took possession of the enormous supply of food and ammunition abandoned by the fleeing Armenian troops. Enver Pasha sent congratulatory telegrams to the Turkish commander ordering him to push the Turkish army to the borders of 1914 and, if successful, march on Baku and liberate the Turkic Azeris.

The sudden resurgence of the Turkish army and its ability to put the abandoned military supply to good use, forced the Armenians to fight a defensive war. The Turkish high command had skillfully immobolized the Armenian military organization and was prepared to strike the Armenian power and chase the survivors to the east.

Alarmed by this Turkish advance the leaders of the Transcaucasia Commissariat sent word to the Turks in February 1918 that they will be willing to negotiate a peace treaty. To give their Commissariat the semblance of a sovereign state the Armenian, Georgian, and Azeri political leaders arranged the convocation of a constituent assembly, coined as the Seim, on February 23, 1918, to create an independent regional government to forge its own destiny without the interference of the Russians in the north.

Enver was elated about the prospect of an independent political entity in the Caucasus. He believed that a treaty with Transcaucasia would further separate the region from Russia. Both parties agreed to hold a peace conference in Trabizond on March 2, 1918. In the meantime Enver continued his advance in Eastern Anatolia. He ordered the Turkish forces to move fast and grab as much territory in Western Armenia as possible to present the delegates of the peace conference with a *fait accompli*. By the end of February the Turkish forces were at the gates of Erzerum.

THE DEFENSE OF ERZERUM

After withdrawing his forces from Erzinjan, Sebasdatsi Murad and his soldiers retreated to Erzerum where General Andranik had stationed his troops. The Turks under the command of Vehib Pasha, were moving fast towards Erzerum to destroy the last vestiges of the Armenian power. By now the Turkish threat had become very real. Before reaching the gates of Erzerum the Turks had taken the city of Trabizond on the Black Sea with hardly any resistance. Trabizond was an important post. It allowed the Turks to gain control of huge amounts of military equipment abandoned by the Russian navy and convert the character of the war from the land to the sea.

The loss of Trabizond was a tremendous blow to the morale of the Armenian forces. The Armenian leaders in Tiflis became panicky and some even entertained the idea of abandoning Western Armenia altogether. They wanted to leave the Armenian provinces to the Turks and focalize the Armenian forces in Kars and Erevan to defend the heartland of Eastern Armenia. But General Andranik refused to listen to such nonsense. "If we cannot defend Western Armenia, we can never defend Eastern Armenia". He told the political leaders.

General Andranik was prepared to continue his fight and defend Western Armenia. He had been encouraged by a telegram which the Armenian National Council had received earlier from Boghos Nubar Pasha in Paris advising the Armenian leaders that if the Armenians defend the borders of Western Armenia, the Allied Powers will recognize its independence and protect it.

Boghos Nubar was one of the most pre-eminent Armenian statesmen of his time. An austere man with a privileged background, Boghos was the son of the former Armenian Prime Minister of Egypt and had been appointed by the Catholicos in 1912 to be the head of the Armenian delegation in Paris to represent Armenian interests in the west. A man with profound political wisdom, Boghos Nubar was able to form a network of important connections with European political leaders and diligently worked to publicize the Armenian case. He played a dominant role in the evolution of political events and contributed greatly to the formulation of the Armenian national policy at home and abroad. The significance of his telegram to the Armenian National Council lay in its timing. It was dispatched immediately after Boghos Nubar's meeting with the French Foreign Minister in the French capital. With the military conflict stretching on in the Middle East, the Allies wanted to use the Armenian forces to finish up the Turks and direct their attention back to Europe. The Allied unity had lost its balance by the rise of the Bolsheviks. It was the intent of the Allies, now that they had full U. S. participation in the war, to convert Western Armenia into a buffer zone between Turkey and Bolshevik Russia, neutralize the region, and proceed east to capture the oil rich land of the Caspian Sea. If for many years the Allies had made promises to the Armenians while looking for ways to avoid honoring them, this time they pretended to mean business, not necessarily to help the Armenian cause, but to further their own interest.

Boghos Nubar Pasha's telegram to the Armenian Council about the promise of the Allies was destined to fan political passions. It created a tremendous excitement among the Armenians. Armenian volunteers rallied around Andranik and hundreds of army officers enrolled in the military academy in Tiflis to start their training.

To defend Western Armenia it was imperative for the Armenians to defend the heartland of the country where the city of Erzerum was located. Erzerum, with its impregnable mountains, was the gateway to the east. General Andranik wanted to concentrate all his military might to defend the city at any cost. The Allies agreed with Andranik and considered the defense of Erzerum extremely vital to their own strategy. It was for that reason that two Allied military officers accompanied General Andranik to Erzerum to assess the military situation and help the Armenians if necessary.

When Andranik arrived in Erzerum in the middle of February, 1918, he found the city in utter chaos with 25,000 Armenian refugees living in squalor. The man in charge of the military organization was an unscrupulous person, Tigran Aghamalian. A treacherous Armenian, Aghamalian and his associates had embezzled thousands of rubles from the Erzerum treasury and carted away supplies of ammunition to the Caucasus and sold them for profit. Tigran was suspected to have been bribed by the Turks and had even agreed to deliver the city of Erzerum to the Turks for a large sum of money. Aghamalian was not alone. There were other political leaders in the city, each claiming to have the only authority to govern the city. To complicate the situation even more, the Russian general, who was still in command of the Russian forces in the area, was the brother-in-law of Vehib Pasha, the Turkish commander of the eastern army which at the time was positioned to attack Erzerum.

With the city thrown into anarchy, the Armenians had no framework of a defensive military organization. Each group followed its own commander with no cohesive unity to maintain a defensive strategy against the Turks. The successive series of Turkish victories in battle had seriously demoralized the spirit of the Armenian fighting men and even Andranik's charismatic personality could not galvanize the forces to defend the last bastion of Western Armenia. The combination of theft and political intrigue was too great for Andranik to bear. Deprived of the loyalty of the fighting men, he ordered his troops to retreat. The Armenians were doomed. The Turks struck from the west and the Kurds attacked from the north. Before dawn of February 27, 1918 Erzerum fell and Vehib Pasha's forces mowed down the Armenian refugees with machine guns.

The fall of Erzerum led the Turks into a new type of war. While Sebasdatsi Murad's forces continued to harass the Turks with guerrilla war, the road was now clear for the Turks to march towards the Caucasus. They had broken the backbone of the Armenian military resistance. The Armenians were on their own, with 20,000 refugees fleeing in an easterly direction. All hopes to establish an independent Armenian state vanished and Western Armenia was forever lost to the Turks.

Having failed to defeat the Turks in the field of battle, the Armenian leaders now sought to defeat them in the field of diplomacy. Their attention was now directed towards Tiflis where a group of Transcaucasian delegates was making last minute preparations to travel to Trabizond to negotiate a peace treaty with the Turks, scheduled to begin on March 3, 1918. On that very same day an event in a small town in Poland changed the course of subsequent history.

THE TREATY OF BREST-LITOVSK

Lenin's principal concern upon rising to power, was to end the war. Even before the eruption of the Russian Revolution in March, there was a serious political movement in Russia organized by various activists to force the Czarist government to reach a compromise settlement with Germany without the participation of the Allied Powers. Empress Alexandra, who was of German descent, had been in favor of a separate accord with Germany and an extremist group, called the Black Hundreds, proposed to break off relations with England and forge a peace treaty with the Central Powers.

Shortly after taking the reins of the government, Lenin sued for peace with a pathetic impatience to end the war, and requested an armistice with the Central Powers. The peace negotiations began on December 22, 1917 in the Polish fortress town of Brest-Litovsk where the German military command had its headquarters. On one side were the delegates of Germany, Austria-Hungary, Bulgaria, and the Ottoman Empire, and on the other side were the delegates of the Soviet Union. From the very start both sides maneuvered to prolong the proceedings. The Russians wanted to use the forum to promote a propaganda for their Communist Revolution, and the Central Powers wanted to exploit Russia's military weakness to continue the fight and grab as much territory as possible. While the talks were going on, the Central Powers signed a separate peace treaty with the Ukraine on February 9, 1918, thus separating the country from Russia and depriving the Russians of the vast granaries of the Ukraine.

To force Russia to conclude the peace agreement, Germany launched an all out offensive on February 18, 1918, thrusting its military might towards the Urals. Unable to resist the German attack Russia immediately capitulated. Chicherin, who had earlier replaced Trotsky as the Foreign Commissar, hurried to Brest-Litovsk and offered to sign a peace treaty with whatever terms placed in front of the Russian delegation. The Treaty which was signed on March 3, 1918 formally ended Russia's participation in the war. It called for the demobilization of all Russian forces, the evacuation of Poland, the Baltic states, Finland, and all Western Armenian provinces, including Kars, Ardahan, and Batum. The Treaty laid Russia's southern flank to German penetration and drastically reduced the size of the Russian Empire. With the signing of the Treaty, Russia lost one third of its population and farm lands, one half of its industrial power and most of its coal mines. "Let the Germans have what they want, Lenin told Trotsky, Our Communist Revolution will soon take over Western Europe through the uprising of the Proletariat".

CRISIS IN TRANSCAUCASIA

News of the Brest-Litovsk Treaty reached Transcaucasia at the time when the delegation was en route to Trabizond to begin the peace negotiations with Turkey. The people were shocked and the delegates were infuriated. They were unconcerned about the loss of the Russian territories in the north. Their concern was Russia's agreement to hand over the districts of Kars, Ardahan, and Batum to Turkey, territories which were under

Russian domination since 1878, and to surrender all the provinces of Western Armenia.

The Treaty shattered the political aspirations of the Armenian people, and placed Transcaucasia in turmoil. The leaders refused to accept the terms of the Treaty and sent telegrams to Petrograd and the major capitals of the world repudiating the Treaty. The Transcaucasian Seim immediately began preparations to formally separate itself from the Russian political sphere of influence.

The Soviet Empire was in the process of disintegration. One third of its territory was in the hands of the Germans and various regions had severed their ties with the central government. The Ukraine had become an appendage to Germany and Don Cossacks had formed an independent republic. Ethnic groups within the Empire proclaimed their supremacy over the central authority, anxious to choose their own destiny without the intrusion of the Bolshevik power. Even the transfer of the capital from Petrograd to Moscow, a city closer to the heartland of Russia, had not helped Lenin to control the flow of authority from the center to the periphery. The crisis in Transcaucasia was the latest in a series of political events that were destined to stain the legitimacy of the Bolshevik regime. The Armenians wanted to create a state, the Georgian Mensheviks were opposed to the Russian Bolsheviks, and the Azeris were suspicious of the Russian dominated central government. It was in this kind of political atmosphere that the delegates of Transcaucasia sat down in Trabizond to talk peace with Turkey.

THE CONFERENCE AT TRABIZOND

When a motley group of about one hundred Transcaucasian delegates arrived in Trabizond on March 12, 1918, a Turkish newspaperman, borrowing a phrase from antiquity, remarked in jest "If this is an army, it's small, if it's a delegation, it's too big". The reason for such a large group of delegates was the existence of mutual distrust among the three nationalities of Transcaucasia. The Armenians and the Azeris never trusted each other and both regarded the Georgians as unreliable and manipulative partners. While the Seim in Tiflis had given them a specific agenda for negotiation, it was far beyond the capacity of these delegates to engineer a united front vis-a-vis their Turkish counterparts. This was a group of malcontents with scores of bodyguards to protect them from each other and even the head of the delegation, a Georgian Menshevik, A. K. Chkhenkali, had difficulty at times to maintain order with his own men.

The most important issue on the agenda as the conference began its deliberations was the status of the Western Armenian provinces. But the Turkish delegate shocked the conferees when he told them that his country's high command had ordered the Transcaucasian Seim, while the delegates were en route, to begin the evacuation of Kars, Ardahan, and Batum in accordance with the terms of the Treaty of Brest-Litovsk. As long as Transcaucasia continued to maintain its political ties with Russia and considered itself an integral part of its Empire, then, the Turks argued, it must be subject to all the provisions of a treaty signed by Russia. If on the other hand the Seim declares itself independent from the Soviet Empire, the Turks would then agree to recognize its independence and accept Transcaucasia as a separate political entity and negotiate a peace treaty on that basis.

The Transcaucasian delegates considered the Turkish demands so preposterous that they discontinued the talks on March 26, 1918 and returned home. Taking advantage of the diplomatic stalemate the Turkish forces continued their advance through the Armenian provinces and towards the end of March 1918 reached the borders of 1914.

Dissension and interracial hostilities dominated the emergency session of the Transcaucasian Seim when it convened in Tiflis to discuss the Turkish proposal and formulate a united policy against the Turkish demands. The Azeri delegates, who were sympathetic to the Turkish cause, argued for an unconditional acceptance of the terms of Brest-Litovsk. The Georgians favored a complete separation from the Soviet Empire, while the Armenians, afraid to be left alone with their untrustworthy neighbors, wanted to maintain their political link with Russia, knowing full well that without the Russian shield the Armenians will be doomed.

The leaders of the three nationalities failed to organize a unified authority. This was not exactly their fault. The demographic mix of the people was not conducive to promote a coherent plan of action and the Seim had no centrifugal force to hold the groups together. The nationalities lived intermixed, with no demarcation lines to identify their geographic areas as strictly Georgian, strictly Armenian, or strictly Azeri. Most of the Armenian political leaders were domiciled in Tiflis, which had an Armenian mayor and a population of 400,000 Armenians. Baku had a large Armenian population, and Erevan had 400,000 Azeris and 700,000 Armenians, mostly refugees from the west. Each group refused to be dominated by the other. They were each motivated by their own self interests and political passions and appeared to take separate paths to achieve their goals. In addition, the nationalities had their own spectrum of political factions, each plotting to dominate the other. There were the Dashnaks, Hunchaks, Social Democrats, Populists, Kadets, Mensheviks, Bolsheviks, Conservatives, Democratic Reformers, Czarist Loyalists, Social Revolutionaries, and the Musavat Party for the Azeris, a group of Moslem fundamentalists organized to free Azerbeijan from non-Azeri rule.

For the Azeris the traditional enemy was the Christian infidels, particularly the Armenians, who had stubbornly continued to pursue the quest for political self-determination. The relationship between the Armenians and the Azeris was embedded in a legacy of hatred and their interracial feuds had become an integral part of their national subconscious. It was this relationship that eventually led both to declare open warfare against each other.

CLASH BETWEEN ARMENIANS AND AZERIS

In January 1918, the Armenian National Council in Tiflis, decided to form a separate political organization in Erevan to protect the region from Azeri encroachments. This action was prompted by the increasingly belligerent attitude of the Turkic Azeris towards the Armenians. Earlier Enver Pasha had dispatched his relative, Nuri Bey, to Baku to stimulate Islamic nationalism and propagate a policy to promote the Ottoman interests in Western Asia. Nuri had successfully organized a pan-Turkist group to attack the Armenian villagers and prepare the path for the Turkish forces to eventually walk over Eastern Armenia and occupy Baku. Nuri's Azeri terrorists had killed thousands of Armenian peasants and decimated Armenian villages. The Azeri Turks were regarded as ferocious as their Ottoman cousins. Both shared a common heritage. Even the least

percipient person knew that their Asiatic instinct to kill, terrorize, and plunder gave them immense pleasure.

The Armenian Council designated Aram Manougian, the
hero of Van, as the political leader of the Erevan province with
instructions to protect the Armenian community, and if necessary, countermand orders from the Transcaucasian Seim if
those orders were contrary to the interest of the Armenian people.

Aram acted swiftly. He had to grapple with staggering
problems of poverty, disease, shortage of food, Azeri attacks,
unsheltered refugees, and a treasury with no funds. He immediately took possession of stocks of supplies abandoned by the
Russian army, levied taxes, and mobilized an army of Armenian volunteers. The Azeri inhabitants of Erevan became concerned about the increased Armenian political power. They
began to riot and attack helpless Armenian refugees. Azeri
guerrilla units looted and plundered Armenian homes and
properties and Nuri Bey's organized militia took control of the
railway system and imposed an economic blockade, preventing
the shipment of food to the Armenian communities. The Armenian army headed by Dro and General Silikian attacked the
Azeri strongholds on March 7, 1918, and destroyed hundreds of
Moslem villages. The conflict spread to Baku and the interracial atrocities claimed thousands of lives from both sides.

Meanwhile in the west Turkey and Transcaucasia moved
to resume the peace talks in Trabizond.

TRANSCAUCASIA FIGHTS FOR INDEPENDENCE

The peace talks began in Trabizond, but the diplomatic proceedings were abruptly ruptured when the Turkish delegates
gave an ultimatum to their counterparts to honor the provisions
of Brest-Litovsk and drop the issue of the Armenian political
self-determination in the Ottoman Empire. It was unclear why
Turkey continued to raise such issues,. because by then those
issues had already become academic. By April 1918 most of the
Armenian provinces were taken over by the Turks and Vehib
Pasha's army was already at the outskirts of Batum. The delegates returned home and the Seim in Tiflis braced itself for war
against Turkey. Tiflis became the scene of feverish activity.
Each nationality positioned itself in relation to the other. The

real power was in the hands of poets and intellectuals, who had mediocre political experience at best.

The task facing the Transcaucasian leaders was formidable. They had limited resources, demoralized military units, and a political leadership embedded in mutual distrust. The Seim organized a defense line and assigned the Georgian troops to defend Batum, the symbol of the Georgian territorial unity, and General Nazarbekian's army of 6,000 Armenian troops to defend Kars, the gateway to Eastern Armenia. The Turks with the help of Moslem inhabitants besieged Batum, captured it without much resistance and took 3,000 Georgian soldiers as prisoners-of-war.

Faced with the imminent danger of Turkish takeover, the Transcaucasian Seim convened a special session in Tiflis and on April 22, 1918 declared Transcaucasia independent from Russia. It formed a federated republic with Akakii Chkhenkali, the chief delegate of the Trabizond conference, as the Head of State and a cabinet composed of Georgian, Armenian, and Azeri ministers. This was not exactly an enterprise of a common purpose. It was some sort of umbrella to protect the groups from the common enemy, with no clear desire to favor a political unification of the three nationalities. If the common umbrella depicted some semblance of unity, that unity began to crack almost immediately.

The Georgians were recognized as the leaders of the government in which the Armenian ministers were only ornaments of the least valuable kind with no significant role assigned to them. It was a ramshackle republic with a policy reassuringly Georgian in character. Political discord and dissension disrupted the processes of government to the point that the new leaders could not even agree upon the boundaries of the new state and identify the territory that it covered.

To stop the Turkish march into the Georgian territory Chkhenkali, the head of the newly formed state, sent a cable to Vehib Pasha that he was willing to accept the terms of Brest-Litovsk, and to appease the Turks further, he ordered General Nazarbekian to halt all hostilities and surrender Kars to the Turks. The Armenian leaders in Tiflis were infuriated. They were enraged at Chkhenkali's deceitful political maneuvers. They defied the order and pledged their commitment to defend Kars to the last Armenian, "And if we get defeated and die in the process", they told the Georgians, "at least we will die with weapons in our hands".

On April 24, 1918, the Turkish forces began to march towards Kars. The Armenian forces bombarded the enemy positions but they were pathetically outnumbered. The Turkish advance caused panic and the Armenian inhabitants of Kars began to flee towards Alexandropol. The Turkish siege lasted only a day. The Armenian troops retreated and the Turks entered the city. They burned the buildings and slaughtered thousands of Armenian men, women, and children. General Nazarbekian ordered his forces to move to Alexandropol, knowing full well that the Turks will head in that direction sooner or later.

The fall of Kars caused turmoil in Transcaucasia. Angry mobs in Tiflis marched towards the government building and demanded Chkhenkali's resignation. The Armenians were outraged about the treacherous act of the Georgians. With Batum and Kars now taken by the Turks and the Transcaucasian military structure virtually obliterated, peace with Turkey suddenly became the most desirable alternative.

THE CONFERENCE IN BATUM

Enver Pasha was pleased about the turn of events in Transcaucasia. His plan to incorporate the Moslems of the east into the Ottoman Empire was finally coming to fruition. Since the outbreak of the war he wanted to see Transcaucasia divorce itself from Mother Russia. He was the first to recognize, therefore, the Transcaucasian federation as a sovereign entity and made arrangements to exchange ambassadors. The region of its own volition no longer enjoyed the privileges of Russia's protective shield, making the region easy prey to Turkey's imperialistic ambitions. As a gesture of good will Enver proposed a peace conference to be held in Batum, this time in the presence of German observers to somehow legitimize the proceedings.

When the Batum conference convened on May 11, 1918, Chkhenkali, as the head of the Transcaucasian delegation, informed the conferees that his government was now ready to accept the provisions of Brest-Litovsk and turn over the disputed territories to Turkey as was the demand of the Turkish delegation since the days of Trabizond. The delegates were shocked when Turkey categorically rejected such proposals and considered them preposterous. "Current circumstances have changed our attitude", Turkey's chief delegate said. In addition to the territories of Brest-Litovsk, Turkey now demanded Alexandropol, Echmiadzin, parts of Erevan province, and the entire corridor of the Kars-Juffa Railway, to allow the Turks easy access to the Caspian Sea.

The Turkish demands and their arrogant attitude did not sit well with General Otto van Lossow, the chief German delegate attending the conference. Since the days of Brest-Litovsk, the Germans were concerned about Turkey's deliberate and aggressive expansionist activities in the Caucasus. They wanted the Turks to stop at the borders specified by Brest-Litovsk, leave the Caucasus alone, and concentrate their activities in the Middle East. The Germans wanted Transcaucasia for themselves to enable them to open a corridor through central Asia and attack India, the British Empire's prize possession in the east. Enver regarded this German plan of *drang nach osten* as a scheme to abort the imperialist objectives of the Young Turks. He no longer had interest in the Arab Middle East. He knew very well that the Turks would not be able to contain the Arab nationalism. With the loss of the European territories and the Middle East, Enver's imperialistic ambition was to reshape the Ottoman Empire to include the territory between the Black Sea and the Caspian Sea, with the hope of reaching central Asia, the ancestral heartland of the Turkish race. It was for this express purpose that he had dispatched his half brother, Nuri Bey, to Azerbeijan to mobilize a Moslem army and occupy Baku and its precious oil fields, so vital for the Turkish military operation.

The presence of the Armenian people, sandwiched between the Ottoman Turks and the Azeri Turks, was an irritant and an obstacle to Turkey's Pan-Turanian policies. Those stubborn people were always in the way. Massacres and deportations had not been sufficient to put them out of the way. "Our political position is very simple", a Turkish commander once told an Armenian political leader. "Our goal is to push the Armenians out of the way. The Ottomans had a great empire once, but we lost most of it. We lost the Balkans, we lost Africa, we lost the Arab lands, but now we must reshape our empire towards the east, and central Asia. Our blood, our religion, our language is there. Our heritage has been an irresistible magnetism. Our brothers are in Baku, Daghestan, Turkestan, Uzbekistan, Afghanistan. We must have access to them. And you Armenians are always standing in our way. You wanted to occupy Van, but in doing so you blocked our road to Persia. You wanted to occupy Nakhichevan and Zangezur, but you obstructed our way to Baku. You wanted to stay in Kars, but you blocked our way to Kazakh. You must give us room to expand, to advance our armies, otherwise we will have no other choice but to annihilate you to achieve our goal".

The Turkish attitude towards the Christian Armenians, however, had caused a serious political problem for the German Kaiser at home. The Genocide of 1915 had caused a public uproar in Christian Germany and Armenophile politicians and professors had waged a successful campaign throughout the country to put pressure on the government to urge its Turkish allies to leave the Armenians alone. Annoyed by this German political and diplomatic maneuver Enver ordered the Turkish army to invade Eastern Armenia, to occupy the country, and deliver the final blow to the surviving remnants of the Armenian people.

THE BATTLE OF SARDARABAD

By May of 1918 Western Armenia was obliterated and taken over by the Turks. The survivors of the Genocide, and the wretched refugees of the Turkish deportations, were now huddled in a small section of Eastern Armenia still left unoccupied. This tiny piece of land included Alexandropol, the Holy City of Echmiadzin, and the city of Erevan, and its immediate environs. It was the objective of the Turkish High Command to secure this area to push the army to Baku.

The Turks, far superior in potential strength, mobilized an army of 35,000 Turks, and began to advance towards Eastern Armenia. At daybreak of May 15, 1918, fired with passion of Moslem fanaticism, the Turks attacked Alexandropol and drove the Armenian troops out forcing them to retreat to Hamamlu (modern Spidak, later destroyed by the earthquake of 1988). The Turks marched on Hamamlu, occupied the city on May 22, 1918, and cut the communication lines between Erevan and Tiflis. They divided their forces into three regiments. They directed one towards Karakilise, the other towards Bash Abaran, twenty-five miles north of Erevan, and the third towards Sarda-rabad in the south.

The Armenian troops under the command of General Na-zarbekian numbered around 12,000, surrounded by 150,000 disease-stricken Armenian refugees, huddled with their starving children, scattered on a 15-mile stretch between Echmiadzin and Erevan. From the very start the Armenian troop deployment was hampered by the spread of a mysterious plague which had begun to rage in the refugee camps, killing men, women, and children by the thousands. No one knew the origin of the plague. While the more intelligent attributed the spread of the disease to the lack of sanitation, the Moslems attributed it to the hatred that Allah had nurtured towards the Armenians. The Armenians had offended Allah by killing Moslems, they de-clared, and Allah had now become vindictive by punishing them with this plague. At the time when the Armenians were mobilizing their forces against the Turks the plague had become so violent that it had claimed the lives of many army officers and troops.

The poorly equipped and ill-fed Armenian troops had reached their limit. Their morale was badly impaired. They looked more like skeletons than fighting men. While they were determined to fight, they found themselves in a desperate struggle for physical survival. The odds were too great. Only a miracle would now save Armenia. General Nazarbekian as-signed General Silikian to defend the city of Sardarabad, and Dro and his guerrilla units to defend Bash-Abaran. The strategy was to prevent the Turkish march towards Erevan.

The Turks moved towards Sardarabad and positioned their forces in the outskirts of the city. They were now ten min-utes away from Echmiadzin. Sardarabad soon became the last stand for the struggle of the Armenian people. Even the least percipient Armenian knew that an Armenian victory at Sardara-bad will offer the people the chance to survive as a nation, and an Armenian defeat would place a punctuation mark to their existence.

For the Turks the town of Sardarabad was not exactly a part of their grandiose plan to finish up the Armenians. It was merely a continuation of their successful military campaign that began in Erzinjan four months earlier. Their aim was to take

Erevan, the heartland of Armenia, but to accomplish this they needed to conquer Sardarabad first.

The Armenian military command advised Catholicos Kevork V to leave Echmiadzin for his own safety. But the Catholicos refused and ordered his priests and deacons to help the Armenian fighting men. General Silikian moved his headquarters to Echmiadzin to prepare for the defense. How fitting. Here was the earth's most sacred place for the Armenian people, a place that had seen so much suffering but so little peace, was now ready to witness the nation's epic struggle for survival.

The Turks began their attack on May 21, 1918 and sprayed hundreds of Armenian troops with machine guns. The Armenians counterattacked and refused to flee. Peasants, priests, doctors, teachers, and refugees fought in hand-to-hand combat and stopped the Turkish advance. The Turks reorganized their forces the following day and moved towards the Sardarabad railroad station, threatening to isolate the Armenian troops. The Armenians were in a desperate situation. They were now trapped by Turkish forces.

General Silikian made an emotional appeal to his people. He called upon men, women, and children to fight for their life in the same spirit as their ancestors fought against the Persians in the battle for religious freedom. "Fight in the name of the physical existence of this eternally tortured people. Fight in the name of violated justice. Fight for your honor and the integrity of your country. Fight the way your ancestors fought to defend their lives and properties. Fight to defend the honor of the Armenian women. Arise all Armenians. On to the Holy War!"

Silikian's strategy was to seal off the approaches towards Sardarabad, deprive the Turkish troops of military support from the north, and push them back toward Alexandropol. He ordered the evacuation of a section of the town to make room for his troops to mount a line of defense. On the other side, he placed cannons to prevent the enemy's advance southward. His dual strategy, defensive on one side and offensive on the other, helped maintain the integrity of his armed forces as a coordinated operation, supervised by able field commanders, Pirunian and Pashaian. Not knowing the scale of the Turkish attack, Silikian concentrated his forces on the defensive line, holding the troops on the offensive side to a minimum.

In the evening of May 22, 1918, the Armenian regiment moved toward the rear of the Turkish main force with artillery cannons positioned to attack the enemy from the rear. At daybreak the following day, the Armenians attacked the right and left flanks of the Turkish regiments. By mid morning a fierce battle was raging on. The Turks were getting hit by a barrage of artillery bombardments from the left and right. Cannons hit the enemy targets incessantly with no pause between bombardments as the Armenian troops ambushed the Turks from the left, immobilizing the enemy position.

The Turks by virtue of their military superiority never expected such Armenian counterattack. At first they hesitated to advance. But shells kept coming, killing them by the hundreds. There was no real front, only the thundering noise of the bombardment and the howling cries of the Turkish troops. Shortly after noon on May 23, 1918, the enemy began to advance, but unable to sustain the heavy bombardments, they immediately retreated. As the left flank of the Turkish army crumbled, the Armenian forces attacked from the right. The enemy could no longer withstand the heavy barrage of bombardments. They began to retreat and abandon their positions. Silikian's forces pursued the Turks along the Sardarabad railroad tracks as Dro's fighters drove them back towards Hamamlu. Colonel Pirunian telephoned Echmiadzin headquarters advising General Silikian that the Turks were on the run. The Turkish expedition had failed in disaster and the Armenians had saved the country and 750,000 Armenians around Erevan from certain death. "This is one of the proudest moments in the history of the Armenian people", General Silikian told his associates as they gathered to celebrate the victory. Like the Battle of Avarayr in the Fifth century, the Battle of Sardarabad came to symbolize the Armenian will to freedom, and General Silikian, whose brilliant strategy won the victory became one of the pivotal figures in the history of his people.

News of the Armenian victory at Sardarabad spread quickly. The people rushed to the battlefield carrying bread, food, and pitchers of water to the fighting men. Victory brought mass excitement and patriotic frenzy, encouraging the Armenian troops to proceed further and chase the enemy towards Alexandropol, Kars, and possibly beyond. The Turks were now threatened. There was fear that the momentum of the Armenian power will push the Turkish forces back to Erzerum. To stop the Armenian advance, the Turkish delegation in Batum immediately called for an emergency meeting with the Armenian delegates to sign a peace treaty and cease all hostilities. Having failed in battle, they now wanted to replace guns with diplomacy. The Armenian National Council in Tiflis, responding to the Turkish request, ordered General Nazarbekian to halt all hostilities and General Silikian, on instructions from Nazarbekian, stopped the chase to the chagrin of his fighting men.

THE COLLAPSE OF THE TRANSCAUCASIAN FEDERATION

While the Armenians were fighting the Turks in Sardarabad the Georgians and Azeris were preparing to move away from the Federation and choose a separate destiny for their own people. The Azeris were encouraged by the Turkish successes in the Caucasus and chose the Turks to provide them with the necessary direction to help them forge a political entity under an Ottoman suzerainty. The Georgian Mensheviks, who had no taste for any political accommodation with the Soviet Bolsheviks, sought another direction to protect themselves from the rapacious Turks. They knew that the Armenians were doomed and sooner or later the Turks will finish them off. In an attempt to disassociate themselves from the Armenians, the Georgians sought their fortunes with Germany, a powerful European state.

In mid May 1918, the Georgian National Council appealed for German protection and prepared to liquidate the Transcaucasian Federation. The Georgian leaders held a meeting with their Azeri counterparts to draw the boundaries of their respective countries with no regard for their Armenian partners. They believed that Armenia as a country would no longer exist and, therefore, there was no need for them to draw the map of Armenia. The Turks were on their way to Sardarabad at the time and all indications were that the remnants of the Armenian people in the district of Erevan will soon be exterminated.

In the afternoon of May 26, 1918, the Seim of the Transcaucasian Federation held its last session and voted to dissolve the Federation and allow the three nationalities to seek their own fortune. A few hours later the Georgian National Council declared Georgia as an independent republic and immediately signed an accord of mutual friendship with Germany. The following day the Moslem National Council met and formally declared Azerbeijan as an independent republic with Baku as its capital.

The Armenians were now left alone. Theirs was the only delegation left in Batum to negotiate peace with Turkey. This caused a problem of logistics. How could Turkey and Transcaucasia continue their negotiations if the Federation had been dissolved and Transcaucasia, as a political entity, was no longer in existence. Alexander Khatisian, the chief Armenian delegate in Batum, met with Khalil Bey, his Turkish counterpart, to seek a diplomatic clarification. It was then suggested that perhaps the Armenians should also declare themselves independent and form a republic, sanctioned by the Turks, for the express purpose of bringing the peace talks to a successful conclusion.

The Armenian National Council met in emergency session to lay the groundwork for an independent republic. In a state of turmoil and political uncertainty, with no help from the outside world, the Armenian leaders found themselves in the most ironic situation. They discovered that the only way for them to survive as a nation was to secure a peace treaty with their ancestral enemy.

On May 28, 1918 the Armenian National Council made a declaration of independence. An Armenian republic was born. After five centuries of struggle the Armenians finally achieved what they always wanted, freedom, independence and a republic. This was the first time since the fall of the Cilician Kingdom that a new political order was emerging on the plains of Mount Ararat. From the ashes of the ruins, from death and destruction, rose a new state, ready to participate as a sovereign member in the community of nations. With Western Armenia obliterated, Eastern Armenia now prepared to be the cockpit, ready to lead the nation to the horizon of a new destiny.

Was this truly the culmination of the political struggle of the Armenian people. Was this what the people aspired to, a tiny state covering only a fraction of their ancestral homeland. Was this piece of real estate worth the spilling of blood. For many this was better than nothing. When the infant was born, however, people wondered whether the baby was healthy enough to survive the travail of the future. Many, including the founders, knew that the baby was born sick.

Those fighting for the creation of an independent republic suddenly found themselves without the means to govern it.

CHAPTER TWENTY-FOUR

THE REPUBLIC OF ARMENIA

After a savage interval marked by the destruction of Western Armenia, the birth of the Republic of Armenia, no matter how accidental it may have been, offered hope for the prospect of a new future. The establishment of the Republic was not the result of a political revolution nor was it meant to be the greatest event of a spectacular epoch. It was merely the reflection of a new dimension of Turkish intransigence by which the leaders of Turkey manipulated to contain the Armenian anger in the aftermath of the Battle of Sardarabad by allowing the Armenians to have a state of their own, but refusing at the same time to grant them the opportunity to be the masters of their destiny. For the Turks, Armenia was meant to be a geographic nothing to serve only as a stepping stone for their advance to the East.

To keep the Armenians in their employ and legitimize the creation of the Republic the Turks hastened to conclude the peace treaty in Batum. Khalil Bey, as the chief Turkish delegate, forced Alexander Khatisian, Kachaznuni, and Mikayel Papajanian, the Armenian delegates representing the Armenian National Council, to sign the treaty on June 4, 1918, with terms that would have made the survival of the new Republic a miraculous event. The treaty was not exactly a document destined to forge eternal friendship between the two adversaries. It was merely a pact to legalize the relationship between the oppressor and the oppressed. It assumed the existence of an independent state but its maintainance was guaranteed by the Turks. It was like assigning the wolf to guard a herd of sheep.

The Batum Treaty allowed the Republic to have 4,400 square miles, encompassing parts of Nor Bayazid, Erevan, Echmiadzin, and Alexandropol. The Armenians agreed to cease all hostilities and promised to help Turkey in its war against the Allies. The Turks even made a preposterous suggestion for the Armenian troops to be incorporated with the Turkish army to drive the British out of Persia. The Armenians rejected the proposal but agreed to demobilize all their armed forces and allow the Ottoman troops to march through their territory unhindered. The agreement called for the entire communications network of Armenia to be placed under the Turkish control and the transportation of all supplies, in and out of Armenia, to be monitored by the Turks with weapons and armaments placed under Turkish supervision.

While it was the Armenian victory of Sardarabad that compelled the Turks to create the Armenian Republic, the Armenian delegates in Batum were in no position to demand much from the Turks. The Turks made it abundantly clear that the Armenians were required to sign the treaty with no power to abrogate, amend, nullify, or modify its terms. The Turks pledged to protect the integrity of the Armenian borders only if it served the Ottoman interests. They continued to pursue their imperialistic aggrandizement. For them the creation of the Armenian Republic was an interlude offering them the opportunity to stabilize the Armenian military threat temporarily, open an unobstructed corridor to the east, use the Armenians as pawns awhile but later discard them when their usefulness had vanished. Enver's sinister design was to use the pitifully helpless Armenian State as a graveyard and someday to bury the Armenians when the opportunity arose.

It was this Treaty, however, and nothing else that formed the organic part that created the Republic of Armenia.

THE FORMATION OF THE GOVERNMENT

After signing the declaration for independence, the Armenian National Council in Tiflis began preparations to form the new government. Since the Dashnaks represented the most predominant party in the Caucasus, they took upon themselves the responsibility to organize the political structure of the new State. Hovhannes Kachaznuni was called upon to form a coalition cabinet. It took him several weeks to put together a cabinet but with no coalition. The Armenian Social Revolutionaries and the Populist Party refused to participate and accepted no partnership with the Dashnaks, who were generally blamed by non-Dashnaks to be the cause for all the suffering of the Armenian people.

The cabinet was composed of five members with Kachaznuni as the Prime Minister and the Head of the State, Alexander Khatisian, the Minister of Foreign Affairs, Aram Manougian, the Minister of the Interior, Katchadour Karjikian, the Minister of Finance, and General Hovhannes Hakhverdian, the Minister of Military Affairs. The leaders were mostly revolutionaries, with the exception of Khatisian, the former mayor of Tiflis. The Dashnak Party that they represented was a party of revolution, ostensibly organized to help the people free themselves from the Turkish oppression. While the leaders were unprepared to transform the processes of the revolution into the processes of a government, there was no question about their sincerity and vigor to practice the doctrine of self-determination and initiate the processes of a government of popular consent, in spite of the fact that they had no tradition for democracy and the socialist ideology of the Dashnaks had little tolerance for democratic principles.

The first task of the cabinet was to move the government from Tiflis to Erevan. Unlike cosmopolitan Tiflis, Erevan was a backward city with no functional buildings to house the administrative departments of the new government. There were police stations, a prison cell, and old relics from the Czarist days, all in bad repair, neglected and scarred by years of revolution and war. It was a drab and impoverished city with masses of refugees and orphans cluttered around the main streets. As the capital of the new Republic, Erevan had little to offer in terms of accommodation for the members of the new government. It was a colorless and sad place, full of human suffering and immeasurable poverty, wrapped up with an epidemic that had already claimed thousands of lives.

The situation was the same in the countryside. The war and the Turkish invasions had devastated the villages and farms. The Turks had cut off the supply of food and the Civil War in Russia had prevented the shipment of food and clothing to Armenia. Everywhere there was an endless procession of refugees and dilapidated shacks. And yet this was the place, located on the eastern fringes of historic Armenia, destined to provide the forum for the regeneration of the Armenian spirit. When the leaders of the government began to settle in Erevan in July 1918, few had any confidence that they will be able to develop a political base strong enough to support governmental institutions to govern a sovereign state. Their immediate problem was the bankrupt economic condition of the state. The treasury was empty and the Allied refugee programs had been terminated by Turkish authorities. Most of the farmlands were destroyed and those which were still in operation, were taken over by the Turks who, using Armenian slave labor, cultivated the fields and distributed the crops to the Turkish villages, letting excess food products rot. Unsheltered refugees in search for food spread a Cholera epidemic in August 1918, followed by Typhus a few months later.

In addition to their economic problems, interracial conflicts convulsed the new state with social and political strife. There were as many non-Armenians in Armenia as Armenians. The Georgians and the Azeris, in the midst of organizing a political order of their own, did not particularly cherish the idea of having Armenian leaders rule the Georgian and Azeri communities of Armenia. From the very inception of the three republics, the ill-defined territories of Transcaucasia caused a conflict among the three groups, leading them at times into armed hostilities. The Georgians, already under German protection, claimed the Armenian provinces of Lori and Pambak and the Azeris, enjoying the paternal influence of the Turks, put their claims on the provinces of Zangezur and Karabagh.

Although the interracial conflict as a political issue was a new experience for the revolutionary Dashnaks, who were generally accustomed to solve their problems by revolution rather than diplomacy, the friction among the races was not new at all. Eastern Armenia was besieged for many centuries not only by the Mongols, the Turks, and the Russians, but also by its immediate neighbors who were always eager to occupy the fertile land of the plains of Mount Ararat and chase the Armenians out of the region. Compulsory migration of non-Armenian peoples into the Armenian territory had for a long time become the national policy of the Georgians and the Azeris and it was the vigorous implementation of that policy that had converted Eastern Armenia into a home of a melange of non-Armenian races, causing a serious demographic imbalance and political dislocation. It was not only the Turks and the Russians but also the Georgians and the Azeris who precipitated much of the misfortune of the Armenian people.

Faced with these problems Armenia needed imaginative leadership to establish a semblance of a political order. Prime Minister Kachaznuni prepared his political agenda and presented his programs of social reform to the legislative body. But first the government needed to gain recognition by other countries to legitimize its existence as a sovereign state. Armenian diplomatic envoys appealed to the Central Powers in Berlin and Vienna to establish diplomatic channels and seek solutions to the country's economic and political problems. But since the basis of the new state was the Treaty of Batum, no power, Central or Allied, was willing to accept the terms of the Treaty as they were imposed by the Turks. The Germans were disturbed that Turkey had signed a separate treaty at Batum without their consent and participation. They refused to recognize the legitimacy of the Treaty, and therefore, the existence of Armenia, and advised Turkey to withdraw its forces to the boundaries of Brest-Litovsk. Enver Pasha scoffed at the German suggestion and continued to strengthen his military position in Transcaucasia. His goal was to occupy Baku, take control of the oil fields, proceed south and drive the British out of Persia and Baghdad. The relations between the two war partners deteriorated, but when Turkey was faced with a German ultimatum, Enver capitulated and agreed to review the Batum Treaty and make it available to the Germans for ratification.

ARMENIAN DELEGATION IN CONSTANTINOPLE

An Armenian delegation composed of Avedis Aharonian, Mikayel Papajanian, and Foreign Minister Alexander Khatisian, hurried to Constantinople in June, 1918 to appeal to the Turks to revise the Treaty of Batum and, with the help of the Germans, possibly expand the territories of the new Republic. Earlier the Turks had agreed, somewhat reluctantly, to hold a joint conference in Constantinople, with the Central Powers and the Armenians, to review and finalize the Treaty arrangements. The Armenian delegates waited in the Turkish capital for four months but no calls were made to bring them to the conference table.   After the delegates arrived in Constantinople Enver changed his mind. His arrogance and insensibility did not allow any further discussion about the Treaty of Batum and he saw no justification to give the Armenians the opportunity to ventilate their feelings and seek political recognition of their State.

While the waiting game proved to be a meaningless diplomatic exercise, the Armenian delegates did gain some insight into the Ottoman's political temperament during their stay in the Turkish capital. Enver Pasha, concerned about his next move in the Caucasus, showed little sympathy towards the Armenian delegates and treated them with disdain.   "I solved the Armenian Question", he proudly declared, "I created the Republic of Armenia without sacrificing an inch of Turkish territory".   What astonished the Armenian delegates the most, however, was the unusual candor of Prince Vahid-ed-Din, the younger brother of infamous Sultan Abdul Hamid II and the heir apparent to the throne. During an audience held at the royal palace, the Prince expressed his dislike towards Talaat and Enver and told the Armenian delegates that he was a great admirer of the Armenian people and blamed the Young Turks for the suffering of the Armenians. "If Enver Pasha claims that he had created the State of Armenia out of charity, he is a liar, and you should not trust him", he told the delegates. "If that is the case, Your Excellency", Aharonian said, "will you please tell us, just what aim and objective you feel Enver had in mind in creating our State". The Prince did not respond. He simply lowered his eyelids, as was his custom, and was soon absorbed in meditation. A few weeks later the Sultan died and Vahid-ed-Din succeeded to the throne and began his rule as Sultan Mehmed VI. He will be destined to be the last Sultan of the Ottoman Empire and the last Turkish head of state responsible enough to admit the Turkish atrocities inflicted upon the Armenian people.

TURKS OCCUPY BAKU

As the war continued to rage the oil fields of Baku appeared to gain considerable importance in the world of geo-politics. With dwindling resources in Europe, Germany needed the oil wells more than ever before, and so did the Bolsheviks. Russia was confronted with a civil war and the loss of Transcaucasia on its southern flank was taken seriously by the Bolshevik hierarchy. For many centuries the Caucasus had been an important appendage to the Russian Empire and the creation of the three republics posed a threat to Russia's territorial integrity. There was nothing Lenin could do about two of the three republics, Georgia and Azerbeijan, since both had received the protective shield of the Central Powers. Armenia was left alone. Lenin not only refused to accept Armenia's independence, but urged others to do the same. He exploited the situation in Baku and persuaded the Germans to go along with him with regard to Armenia's sovereignty. Under an agreement made between Joseph Stalin and the Kaiser, Russia allowed the Germans to have access to the Baku oil fields on the condition that Germany will not recognize the Armenian Republic as a sovereign state.

Enver Pasha, in pursuit of his own grandiose scheme in the east, did not care for this Russo-German Agreement over Baku. He ordered his stepbrother, Nuri Bey, to launch an all out offensive to take over Baku. Islamic army units invaded Baku on August 5, 1918. Armenian revolutionaries tried to stop them but they were overwhelmed by the Turkish onslaught. In the ensuing route several hundred Armenian fighting men died, including Sebasdatsi Murad, the hero of Erzinjan. A British force from Baghdad headed by Major General Lionel Dunsterville was dispatched immediately to block the Turkish invasion, but after a feeble attempt, the British withdrew, abandoning Baku to the Turks. The victorious Turks entered the city on September 16, 1918 and began to plunder and massacre. They slaughtered 30,000 Armenians, looted Armenian homes and businesses, and left the bodies of hundreds of Armenian children piled up on top of each other on the streets. The survivors, around 35,000, fled to safety to Erevan, increasing the number of the refugee population in the Armenian capital. Among the survivors was Stepan Shahumian, the leader of the Baku Soviet, who managed to escape in a small vessel in the Caspian Sea. But the vessel was soon diverted to hostile camps. Shahumian and twenty five other Bolshevik commissars were shot to death. It was later discovered that it was the British who engineered the assassination plot, a fact that Joseph Stalin would never forget for the rest of his life.

THE END OF WORLD WAR I

The Turkish victory in Baku will prove to be short-lived. The international conflict was coming to an end. The Central Powers were losing the war and the British were advancing rapidly towards Anatolia.

By early October it became quite visible that Turkey was losing the war on all fronts. The War Cabinet of the Young Turks found itself in the most precarious situation as the Turkish forces continued to lose ground and the political apparatus began to disintegrate. Talaat Pasha had gone to Germany for consultation but upon his return he found the Turkish capital in a desperate situation. Unable to revive their discredited leadership, the Young Turks decided to give up the reign of the government. Talaat resigned from his post on October 8, 1918, and taking his two collaborators, Enver and Jemal with him, fled to Germany on a German warship. The capital was left in chaos and the Allies were seen at the gates of Constantinople. Sultan Mehmed invited Ahmed Izzet Pasha to form a new cabinet in an attempt to preserve what was left of Turkey. The Turks needed an immediate cease-fire to extricate themselves from the war with little or no penalties if possible. The Allied troops entered Constantinople and set up a military administration. The Ottoman Empire lay in ruins and Germany capitulated on November 11, 1918, ending World War I.

ARMISTICE AT MUDROS

The negotiations for an armistice between Turkey and the British Empire began in late October 1918 on board a British flagship anchored off the coast of Mudros. Turkey was represented by Rauf Bey, the chief Turkish delegate at Trabizond. Rauf's diplomatic skill gained for Turkey the most conciliatory terms, turning military defeat into some sort of political victory by wringing major concessions from the victorious Allies. The conference at Mudros lasted 36 hours and the armistice that was signed on October 30, 1918 gave the British access to the Dardanelles and Bosporus but failed to impose the complete demobilization of the Turkish forces. Turkey was allowed to keep Kars, Ardahan, and Batum and no provisions were made to turn over the Western Armenian provinces to the Armenians. In spite of the promises made to the Armenians, before, during, and after the period of the Genocide and World War I, the Allied Powers failed to force vanquished Turkey to abandon the six Armenian provinces in Anatolia and pave the way to the establishment of an independent Armenian state. Perhaps the most bizarre of the Treaty's terms was the provision that allowed the Turks to maintain forces on the Armenian border and Cilicia ostensibly to keep law and order, a decision that will prove to be detrimental to the Armenian cause.

The Agreement at Mudros freed the Armenian State from Turkish suzerainty, and Armenia ceased to be a subservient state to the Turks. The Turks were told to leave Armenia. But as they began to withdraw their forces, they made sure to massacre a few thousand Armenians on the way out just to keep the memory of their brutal savagery alive. They looted and plundered Armenian villages and took 8,000 Armenian youngsters to Erzerum for slave labor. As the Ottoman forces began to withdraw from the Caucasus most of the Turkish officers chose to stay behind and join the Azeri army. It will be this force that will later be galvanized to exert military pressure on the Armenian Republic.

GENERAL ANDRANIK MARCHES ON

General Andranik, the indomitable hero of the Armenian people, refused to accept the Armenian Republic and regarded the new State as an instrument of the Turkish policy. He considered the Batum Agreement a shameless document and condemned the Armenian politicians for their treachery in agreeing to sign such a humiliating document with the Turks.

Disgusted over the outcome of the revolutionary struggle, Andranik took his 3,000 man army and moved to Nakhichevan, together with 20,000 Armenian refugees who had decided to follow him for protection. His objective was to cross to northern Persia, meet the British forces, and mount an all out offensive against the Turks. The route to Persia was blocked, however, by the Azeris and the Turks, forcing him to retreat. After some indecisive skirmishes with the Moslems, Andranik moved to Zangezur and stayed there for the rest of the war.

The Armenians in Zangezur greeted Andranik with great enthusiasm and promised to provide his army with necessary supplies. Andranik's presence in Zangezur provoked a Moslem uprising. A combined force of Turkish and Azeri terrorists attacked Nakhichevan and massacred Armenian villagers and proceeded towards Goris, the capital of Zangezur, to crush Andranik's army. Andranik moved his forces to block the Turkish advance. He surrounded the Azeri villages and placed his men at strategic control points to protect the Armenian communities. The Turks retreated and directed their attention towards Karabagh to establish a zone of influence, chase the Armenians out, and annex the region to Azerbeijan, an internecine struggle that continues to this day.

KARABAGH

For centuries the region of Karabagh had been part of historic Armenia. This was a land of precipitous mountains, meticulously protected by impregnable heights, shielding the Armenian communities and preventing others to penetrate into the interior. Through the centuries the Armenians had been fascinated and inspired by this maze of defiant mountains. They had built their churches, trading centers, cultural institutions and a capital at Shushi, with clusters of villages scattered all around the valleys. Karabagh was rich in mineral resources and provided a natural separation of Armenia from the Moslem Azeris. Around 94 percent of the people were Armenian, the rest were Azeris and Turks.

When the Armenian Republic was formed in May 1918, it immediately became one of the principal objectives of Armenia's policy makers to incorporate Karabagh into Armenia. The hold of the Moslems on the region had weakened through the years but the Armenians in Erevan found it prudent to wait for an opportune time to finalize their plan to take over Karabagh and make it one of the provinces of the new State.

The relationship between the Armenians and the Azeris began to deteriorate rapidly when the Turks occupied Baku in September 1918 and forced the Armenian leadership to give up their territorial claims. Shortly after the Turkish occupation Nuri Bey, Enver's stepbrother, issued an ultimatum to the Armenian leaders in Karabagh to surrender the region to the Azeris. The Armenians scoffed at the Turkish order but when the news of the Armenian massacre of Baku reached Karabagh, the leaders, intimidated by the Azeri massacre, surrendered the capital of Shushi, withdrew to the interior, and immediately appealed to General Andranik for help. Andranik responded to the appeal but as he began to organize an offensive to free Karabagh from the Azeri domination, news reached his headquarters in Zangezur that the war was over and the Turks had capitulated, agreeing to withdraw their forces from Baku. But Andranik continued his preparation to invade Karabagh.

On November 29, 1918 Andranik began his forward march towards Shushi. He fought the Azeri terrorists and in a few days placed his army within 26 miles of Karabagh's capital. He consolidated his forces in the villages surrounding Shushi and prepared for an attack to free his countrymen and make the region an independent Armenian state. As his troops continued their march towards Shushi, the newly installed Commander-in-Chief of the British forces in Baku, Major General William M. Thomson, sent word to Andranik not to proceed further and abandon his military campaign. He informed Andranik that the war was over and any further hostility on the part of the Armenian revolutionaries may seriously endanger the Armenian cause in the peace conference that was scheduled to convene in Paris within a few weeks. Andranik complied with the British advice and moved his army back to Zangezur, a decision that irrevocably changed the course of subsequent history. The Armenians will never again find another opportunity to take over Karabagh militarily and to this day the region remains under the Azeri jurisdiction.

Major General Thomson, after conveniently removing Andranik's military threat and having the Armenian army retreat back to Zangezur, ruled in favor of the Azeris and announced that not only Karabagh but also Zangezur belonged to the Azeris despite the fact that the majority of the people in both provinces were Armenian. The Armenian leaders were infuriated by the British treachery. Andranik sent word to the British headquarters expressing his anger and demanding an explanation. There were violent demonstrations in Erevan against the British policy and the leaders of the Republic met with the British representatives and told them that by offering Karabagh to the Azeris the British broke a solemn covenant the consequences of which will affect the territorial integrity of the State of Armenia.

There had been many interracial conflicts between the Armenians and the Azeris but there had never been a situation in which the Azeris were granted a territory which had been undeniably part and parcel of Armenia's history, tradition, and culture. Karabagh was the place where Eastern Armenians nurtured their national character and gave shape to their patriotism. "You are robbing us of our soul", Armenia's Prime Minister told the British. "Karabagh represents our national conscience. For us it is as important as our Christian faith. You are making the Armenians your pawns to design your pro-Moslem policies in Western Asia". The British favored the Azeris ostensibly to please the Moslem subjects of the British Empire, who had become vociferous of late in their protests against the English lords, and to extract as much oil as possible from the Baku oil fields. The pitiful Armenians offered no natural resources to the British.

To make matters worse, Thomson appointed a fanatic Moslem, Dr. Khosrov Bek Sultanov, to be the Governor-General of the Karabagh region. Sultanov was Enver's friend and a wealthy landowner with a reputation of having played a major role in the Armenian massacres of Baku a few months earlier. Sultanov organized an Azeri army of 2,000 and marched on Karabagh to assume his post. On the way to Shushi, the capital, he ordered his troops to destroy Armenian villages. Several dozen villages were obliterated and around 600 Armenians were slaughtered.

Thomson's choice of Governor-General and the Karabagh massacre drew violent protests from the Armenian communities at home and abroad. Angry mobs in Erevan and Tiflis demonstrated against the British, and the officials of the U. S. Department of State stationed in the Caucasus accused the British for their ill-conceived policies in the region. They demanded that Sultanov be arrested and sent back to Baku. But Thomson refused to reverse his decision and continued to support the Azeri leader.

After consolidating his power in Shushi, Sultanov concentrated his attacks on smashing the Armenian guerrilla units with heavy casualties. He initiated a massive operation to terrorize the Armenian villages, confiscate Armenian properties, and strip away the privileges of the Armenian landlords.

After taking over Karabagh the Azeris decided to march on Zangezur and Nakhichevan to incorporate those two regions into the Republic of Azerbeijan. To help the Azeri troops the Baku government used its economic muscle by suspending all shipments of petroleum to Armenia. Turkish nationalists and former Ottoman army officers incited fanatic Moslems to attack the Armenian villages around Kars and Nakhichevan. Baku had become a veritable haven for Young Turk provocateurs and a hotbed for a pan-Turkish nationalist campaign. The entire region had become a breeding ground for Turkish operatives who continued to pursue Enver's nationalist movement through coercion and subversion, taking advantage of the ineptitude of the Allied Powers in the Caucasus.

Within the Armenian State the Azeri terrorists derailed trains, ambushed detachments of the Armenian army, and harassed Armenian communities around Erevan. In Azerbeijan proper there was overt discrimination against the Armenian inhabitants and there were around 250,000 of them still living under Azeri jurisdiction. The Armenians were not allowed to hold government employment and operate commercial enterprises. Bands of Azeri terrorists regularly robbed Armenians and plundered their homes. Members of the fanatic Musavat Moslem Party spread terror in the Armenian quarter of Baku and massacred thousands of Armenian villagers in the countryside. Moslem bandits molested Armenian women on the streets and young Armenian boys were sold to slavery. The British were powerless to stop the Azeri furor.

ANDRANIK LEAVES ARMENIA

As the Azeris continued their advance towards Zangezur the British High Command in Baku became concerned about General Andranik's safety. In March 1919 the British advised Andranik to move out of Zangezur. Andranik accepted the suggestion but was fearful about the fate of the Armenian refugees around him. There were by now around 30,000 Armenian refugees who were living under Andranik's shadow, clinging to him for protection. Andranik told the British that he would consider to leave Zangezur if arrangements were made to resettle the refugees in safer areas away from the murderous Azeris. The British promised but never fulfilled their promise.

Disappointed about the outcome of his revolution Andranik finally decided to leave the motherland. On March 25, 1919 he bade farewell to the Armenian refugees and the people in Zangezur and after a treacherous journey through the mountains, reached Echmiadzin. He was welcomed by a delegation from the Republic of Armenia headed by his old friend, General Dro. Upon reaching the Armenian soil the people gave him a tumultuous welcome. Crowds swarmed around his group and children waving the Armenian flag sang patriotic songs devoted to him. Andranik bid farewell to the Catholicos in Echmiadzin. "There was a time when the nation looked forward to a glorious day on the horizon", he told the Catholicos. "We had our military might and we could have crushed the Turks at a time when they were at their weakest point. But our inept politicians did not know how to take advantage of the opportunity. We had a sword in our hand but we did not know how to use it. Napoleon Bonaparte once said 'You can do anything you want with the sword, except sit on it.' It seems to me, Your Eminence, that our politicians have been sitting on that sword for a long time. For thirty years I fought to protect the lives, honor, and properties of my countrymen. I feel sad now that we did not accomplish what we aspired for. But I will not give up, Your Eminence, I will not give up. I will not fade away. I will go abroad, raise a new army and come back to finish up the job".

Andranik departed for Tiflis on April 27, 1919 never to return again. He journeyed to Paris and London and attempted to persuade the Allied Powers to help him raise an army to occupy Western Armenia. He sailed to America and was welcomed by a tumultuous crowd in the New York harbor. Armenians from coast to coast had come to New York to greet the nation's hero and give him a parade down Fifth Avenue. He settled in Fresno, California where he died on August 31, 1927. On his deathbed the great hero told his associates, "If this pain ends my life, don't leave my body in foreign lands. Take me to Armenia and bury me near the graves of the Armenian saints, not that I deserve to be buried there, but as a soldier I would like to guard the graves of our great men who lit the torch that kept our nation alive for centuries". His body was taken to Paris to be transported to Armenia, but by then the Armenian State had become sovietized and Stalin refused to have Andranik buried in Armenia. He was buried in Paris with the hope that someday his body will be returned to the Motherland. Thousands of Armenians from all over the world attended his funeral. One of his soldiers read the eulogy: "Rest, great hero, rest until that time when we come back to transfer your ashes to the country for which you fought for many years. Until that time your memory shall remain a monument in our hearts, a source of inspiration for the realization of our ideas". Andranik was the embodiment of Armenian nationalism and his heroism earned him the epithet as the Father of the Armenian people. For many he was the greatest Armenian hero of all times. Until the last day of his life this legendary figure lived with the hope of returning to the Plains of Mount Ararat to chase the murderous Turks out of his forefathers' ancestral homeland.

REPUBLIC'S FIRST YEAR

The end of World War I did not bring good tidings to the Armenians. The Armenians expected much but received little. They expected that the defeat of Turkey would allow the Allied Powers to enlarge the Armenian territory immediately, incorporate the six provinces of eastern Anatolia to the Armenian State, and make plans for the Armenian refugees to repatriate to their homeland. The state of the refugees continued to be desperate. The five months of Turkish rule had devastated the country. The disease-stricken refugees milled around from place to place aimlessly in search of food. If the summer months provided grass roots for them to chew, the snow covered fields of winter had nothing to offer. Thousands died of starvation and others died of epidemic. By January 1919 virtually the entire city of Erevan was stricken with typhus fever, killing a thousand a week.

To strengthen the organization of the government and cope with the economic problem, Kachaznuni formed a new cabinet in November 1918 enlarging the size of the first one by adding some non-Dashnak members who were now beginning to feel confident in the future of the new State. But the refugee problem had such a paralyzing effect on the government that by January 1919 the country had become a virtual graveyard with no political leadership capable enough to offer an effective program of running the country. There was also some political strife. The Minister of Welfare was assassinated by an Armenian nationalist who blamed the Minister for the fall of Kars in

April 1918. Two other ministers died of the Typhus epidemic in January 1919. One was the Controller of the State and the other was the invincible hero of the Van uprising, Aram Manougian, who as the Minister of the Interior was the *de facto* ruler of the Republic.

To solve the economic problems the leaders of Armenia appealed to the United States for help. The American Committee for Relief in the Near East began to raise funds in America to help the refugees. Tons of food and clothing were shipped to the poverty-stricken people. The American relief workers stationed in Armenia sent urgent messages to the U. S. to help the starving Armenians. They reported scenes of horror and tragedy and urged the Americans to help "for the sake of Christian civilization". America shipped tons of grain to Erevan and in March 1919 an American medical team took charge of Armenia's hospitals and orphanages. Legislation passed by the U. S. Congress appropriated $100 million to the Armenian refugees in Armenia and the Near East. President Woodrow Wilson appointed Herbert Hoover as the head of the relief organization to oversee the program of economic aid to Armenia. Reports arrived at Hoover's desk stating that the economic condition in Armenia had reached a proportion beyond belief.

The Azeris and Georgians had plenty of food but because of the interracial problems they refused to share their crops with the starving Armenians. The Azeris deliberately dumped tons of excess grain in the Caspian Sea and the Georgians demanded a share of any goods passing through their territory on the way to Armenia. In some cases clothing and food supply coming from the American relief organizations en route to Armenia were confiscated by the Georgian authorities and later sold to other people for profit. There were also some unscrupulous characters, chief among them was the Allied High Commissioner in Armenia, an American colonel, William N. Haskell, who embezzled and misappropriated funds and sold food and clothing earmarked to the Armenian refugees to the Azeris.

To control the traffic of goods to Armenia Hoover appointed a special envoy to supervise the shipment of goods without the interference of the Georgians and the Azeris. In May 1919 American vessels reached Batum and delivered millions of dollars worth of flour, beans, peas, and condensed milk, which went directly to the Armenian refugees in Armenia. In August four more vessels arrived delivering food and clothing. American aid made a tremendous impact on the life in Armenia providing the leaders with some means to deal with the economic crisis and give the country a semblance of political order.

Amid this chaos there were some accomplishments. A member of the Cabinet who was versed in economic matters began to develop a system of national currency. Foreign currencies gradually disappeared and payment in produce and exchange by barter were discontinued. Another minister undertook the task of organizing a judicial system and established civil, criminal, appellate, and supreme courts. The Education Minister opened educational institutions and a university in the capital. The government invited foreign engineers to come to Armenia, study the country's mineral deposits, build roads, and reconstruct the railroad system. An economic organization began to take shape with the establishment of revenue producing industries. Engineers, technicians, and craftsmen were in particular demand.

With the departure of the Turks from the Armenian territory, farm lands once more became productive and vineyards produced wines and the Armenian cognac became an important commodity for foreign export. There was also some expansion in the Republic's territory. In early 1919 the British authorities in Constantinople told the Ottoman military command to withdraw its forces from Kars and deliver the city to the Armenians. After deliberate delays and political maneuvers, the Turks were finally forced to get out of Kars, allowing 100,000 Armenian refugees to journey back to their homeland. In April 1919 the British appointed an Armenian as the Governor-General of Kars and the Armenian troops victoriously entered the city on April 24, 1919, exactly a year to the day after the Turkish occupation of Kars, making the province an integral part of the Republic of Armenia.

In the south, the British allowed the Armenian Republic to annex major parts of Nakhichevan to make room for the refugees to resettle in their homeland. Preparations were also made to reorganize the Armenian communities in the west. The Armenian Patriarch of Constantinople returned home from exile in February 1919. The Constitution of the Armenian community in Turkey was restored and the Armenian civic and religious organizations in the Turkish capital became reactivated. But the fate of Western Armenia remained in the hands of the victorious Allies who were now gathered in Paris to sign a peace treaty and redraw the map of the world after four years of fighting.

CHAPTER TWENTY-FIVE

TOWARD A NEW ORDER

The Armenians everywhere were encouraged by the prospect of a new order as the victorious Allies opened the Paris Peace Conference on January 18, 1919. With the defeat of Turkey, the path now seemed to be clear for the Allies to finally fulfill their promises and establish an Armenian homeland in Western Armenia.

A delegation headed by Avedis Aharonian represented the Republic of Armenia and another headed by Boghos Nubar Pasha, represented Western Armenia. Upon arrival in Paris a decision was made to combine the two delegations headed by the more sophisticated Boghos Nubar.

As the delegates of the foreign powers began to convene in Paris the U. S. State Department worked diligently to put an effective Armenian plan into execution. President Woodrow Wilson on his way to Paris received recommendations from the State Department to recognize the territorial rights of the Armenian people and grant the Armenians a homeland to include Cilicia and the six provinces of Western Armenia. The principal advocate of this recommendation was a young man, Walter Lippman, who was later to become one of the most pre-eminent newspapermen in the history of American journalism. Lippman told the President "the world should honor Armenia's claim for political self-determination and the United States should establish conditions that would right historic wrongs".

Similar recommendations were also made to David Lloyd George, Britain's Prime Minister, who upon arrival in Paris declared "Arabia, Armenia, Syria, and Palestine are entitled to a recognition of their separate national conditions and the complete emancipation of their people so long oppressed by the Turks. From the moment this war was declared Great Britain had it in mind that if we succeeded in defeating the inhuman empire of the Turks, our condition of peace would be the redemption of the Armenian territory from the bloody misrule of the Turks".

Many agreed that this was the least that the foreign powers could do, who for over a quarter of a century did nothing to promote the Armenian cause except making hollow promises and sending protest letters to the Sublime Porte. "Western Armenia for Armenians", people proclaimed everywhere. Others chose to link the fate of the Jews with that of the Armenians. "The world should help the Armenians immigrate into Armenia in the same way as the Jews needed to immigrate into Palestine. The Plains of Mount Ararat should be the national home for the scattered people of the Armenian race. Both the Jews and the Armenians should settle in their respective ancestral homeland".

To assure support for its ideas and expedite the process of negotiations, the British Foreign Office drew a map of the proposed Armenian homeland for consideration by the Great Powers. It was an ambitious blueprint of a new state covering territory from Alexandretta on the Mediterranean to the Black Sea in the north.

In February 1919 the Armenian delegation was invited to submit Armenia's claim to the delegates of the Peace Conference. After an exhaustive preparation, the Armenians presented a comprehensive and well documented paper with charts, maps, statistics, memoranda, and graphs. The documents included a summary of six centuries of Turkish repressive regime, violence, pillage, torture, rape, forced conversions, deportations, starvation, and wholesale massacre. They demanded the creation of an independent Armenian State to include the provinces of Van, Bitlis, Diyarbekir, Kharpert, Sivas, Erzerum, Trabizond, Cilicia, Erevan, Kars, Karabagh, and Zangezur. To protect the integrity of the new State the Armenian delegates urged the Great Powers to place Armenia under a protectorate of an Allied Power. As to the wholesale massacre of the Armenian people in 1915 (the word Genocide was not in use then. It appeared in the lexicon of Western languages during World War II) the Armenian delegates urged the Allied Powers to take necessary steps to apprehend and punish those who had perpetrated or participated in the crime. The Armenians demanded the payment of indemnity from the Ottoman government for the damages suffered by their people through massacre, deportation, and the devastation of their country. The memorandum on reparation and indemnity listed the total Armenian claims to be $3.7 billion which covered damages for physical properties, and compensation for physical injuries and deaths.

The Armenian delegates made their arguments and stated their case with an emotional appeal. "In the name of justice, in the name of the irresistible aspirations of the Armenian people, in the name of the inevitable historical necessity which sooner or later must triumph, we claim the absolute and the final solution of the Armenian Question".

The Allied response to the Armenian claims was positive but unfortunately inconclusive. The English historian Arnold Toynbee, acting as the principal formulator of the British position papers, advised His Majesty's delegates to accept the Armenian territorial claims with the exception of the district of Karabagh. He proposed instead to exchange the Armenian population of Karabagh for the Moslem population of Erevan and make Karabagh an integral part of Azerbeijan to give the Azeris more living space.

President Wilson assured the Armenian delegates in a private meeting held in his private quarters in Paris a few days after the conference that he would do his utmost to secure for Armenians the territories outlined in the Armenian document.

The delegates at the Peace Conference, while sympathetic to the Armenian cause, put the Armenian Question on the back burner awhile and directed their attention to the fate of the vanquished states of Germany and Austria.

The Armenian delegates continued their appeal. They asked the World Congress to recognize the newly formed Republic of Armenia to give the Armenian leaders the ability to negotiate for badly needed food and clothing. The new State had not yet been recognized by any nation and the government leaders in Erevan had no means to establish credit in the world market to float bonds for economic development. The refugee problem, while somehow ameliorated by American aid, continued to threaten the nation's political stability.

As the Great Powers continued to procrastinate over the Armenian issue the American delegation in Paris was deluged from people everywhere for American support for the establishment of an Armenian state in Western Armenia. Forty state governors, several hundred university professors, thousands of bishops and protestant ministers sent telegrams to President Wilson in Paris, urging him to help the Armenians, recognize the new Republic, and send arms if necessary to protect the Erevan government.

On the Senate floor some Senators urged the administration to send American marines to police the Armenian Republic and help the country to build its armed forces. Members of Congress and prominent American leaders, including the former Secretaries of State, Elihu Root and William Jennings Bryan; Charles Evans Hughes, Al Smith, Fred Panfield, Cleveland Dodge, John Sharp Williams, Charles Eliot, and others appealed to Wilson to restore Armenia's independence and help the Armenians militarily to defend themselves. "The American people are deeply interested in the welfare of the Armenian people and expect to see the restoration of the independence of Armenia", they wrote the President in Paris. "When the unspeakable Turks were perpetrating their diabolical crimes upon men, women, and children of Armenia, American hearts were stirred with impotent horror. But with the triumph of right over primitive barbarity, we had hoped that the Peace Conference in Paris would make it one of its duties to take necessary steps to put a stop to the agony of Armenia and recognize her fidelity and service to our cause. We urge that America send to the Republic of Armenia food, munitions, and supplies for 50,000 men to enable the Armenians to occupy the non-occupied parts of Western Armenia. We trust that it may be possible to secure prompt and full justice for Armenia."

Americans everywhere urged their representatives in Congress not to deprive Armenia of her ancestral lands. They warned their leaders that there will be sharp public reaction against the Peace Conference if the American delegates in Paris fail to recognize the territorial claims of the Armenian people. The Republican Henry Cabot Lodge, the President's most influential foe in the Senate and the powerful Chairman of the Senate Foreign Relations Committee, warned the White House that he would have enough votes in the Senate to deny the ratification of the Paris Peace Treaty if the administration "fails to defend the inalienable rights of the Armenian people".

Woodrow Wilson agreed. In response, he issued a statement in Paris and declared that "the protection of Armenia was a sacred trust of civilization". The other great powers and the associated participants of the Peace Conference expressed similar sentiments. "The Armenians have surely earned the right to have their own state, by their sufferings, their endurance, their unbroken spirit, and ambition, their industry, ability, and self-reliance", they declared. But despite their flamboyant statements and expressions of good will, the conferees in Paris did nothing for the Armenians. They even failed to recognize the sovereignty of the little Republic of Armenia lest they upset the Russian revolutionary forces which were then trying to crush the Bolshevik regime.

Bolshevik Russia was not a participant of the Paris Peace Conference and the Republic of Armenia was established on a territory which was since 1828 a part of the Russian Empire. The Allies continued to press for the restoration of democratic principles in Russia, supporting and financing the civil war campaign whose leaders had urged the great powers not to recognize the State of Armenia. As a result, irresolute and quarrelsome, the great powers deferred the recognition issue to a later date.

Meanwhile hundreds of thousands of Armenian refugees were gathered at the Turkish-Armenian border waiting for the world powers to make up their mind. They continued to struggle to survive for a seemingly hopeless future.

TURKS CONTINUE THEIR ATROCITIES

While the world was rejoicing at the approach of peace and the prospect of a new order, the Turks continued their atrocities against the Armenians. They began to harass the Armenian refugees who were bold enough to journey back to their homes in the Armenian provinces. Taking advantage of the Allied vacillation in Paris, the Turks began to exterminate the Armenian refugees and populate the Armenian provinces with Moslem elements. Huge numbers of Turks were forced to migrate to Western Armenia to prevent the Armenians to reclaim their homeland. A large influx of Moslem colonists began to settle in the abandoned Armenian villages through programs supported and financed by the Turkish government in Constantinople which was then under Allied supervision and control.

The U. S. Secretary of State, Robert Lansing, made some timid attempts, possibly to please the Armenophile political elements at home, to persuade the British to mobilize an expeditionary force to occupy Western Armenia and allow a safe passage to the Armenian refugees. Balfour, the British Foreign Secretary, rejected the idea of any British military engagement in the region. By then the British had already withdrawn all their forces from the Caucasus, evacuating their troops from Kars, leaving a weak Armenian army in direct confrontation with the mobilized units of the Turkish army. But not everyone in the British government was in agreement with Balfour. There were some who wanted to keep a British military presence to protect the Armenians. At a Cabinet meeting in London Lord Curzon, the Undersecretary for Foreign Affairs, remarked "We cannot take our forces away and have everybody cutting everybody else's throat". "Why not", retorted Balfour. "If they want to cut their own throats, we should let them do it. We do let other tribes in other parts of the world cut each other's throats in moderation".

In the case of the Armenians, cutting throats was not done in moderation. When the British decided to withdraw from the Caucasus, Armenia's Prime Minister told the British officer stationed in Erevan, "You are now leaving us prey to our enemies. You are now deserting us to be destroyed. There is no point in discussing the issue of repatriation of the refugees, for come winter there will be no more refugees to be repatriated. They all will die of starvation".

In August 1919 the Azeris and the Turks increased the intensity of their hostilities against the Armenians. Their aim was nothing less than the conquest of Armenia to open a corridor between Azerbeijan and Turkey. An Azeri revolt in Nakhichevan spread towards Erevan. Turco-Azeri bandits slaughtered helpless Armenians and butchered hundreds of orphans. The Turkish revolt reached its climax when the Azeri terrorists threatened to take the Holy City of Echmiadzin. The Armenians defended the city, rolled the Azeris back and flattened forty Azeri villages in Zangezur.

One of the most tragic episodes of this period occurred in a prehistoric town of Akulis where 26,000 Armenians lived a relatively quiet life. Akulis was an important cultural center for Eastern Armenians, located in one of the most beautiful regions of the Arax valley. The town was an unbroken paradise of orchards and majestic trees nestled in a land of spectacular beauty. Beyond the town there were the rolling plains from which rose an uninterrupted range of mountains.

Through the years the Armenians of Akulis had transformed the hillsides into terraces of blossom, and the fertile land offered an abundance of food at a time when other towns of Armenia were held in the tenacious grip of poverty. The city with its elegant buildings and palatial residences was the pride of Armenia, and its inhabitants represented the elite of the Armenian people who, somewhat docile in political affairs, never wanted to get involved in interracial quarrels. Then suddenly all came to an end. On December 17, 1919 the Azeris sacked the city and slaughtered the Armenian inhabitants one by one. Men, women, and children were forced into the streets and shot to death by machine guns. No one survived and the town was decimated, never to rise again.

The details of the Armenian tragedy became known around the world when the National Geographic Magazine published an eyewitness report in 1919 entitled "The Land of Stalking Death". According to the article, Armenia labored under the most precarious economic and political situation. Two hundred thousand out of a population of one million in the Republic died of starvation, disease, and massacres. Crowds of famished refugees roamed the streets begging for food, with children eating refuse in the streets, and old men dying of starvation and exhaustion. Human life had become intolerable and the people seemed to have reached the limit of their physical suffering. The leaders of the Republic had no economic means to grapple with the staggering problems of poverty, disease, and shortage of food. Their principal preoccupation was not to keep their sovereignty alive but rather to keep the people alive.

The government appointed special committees to deal with the economic problem of the State to give a new direction to the government. Alexander Khatisian, the former Mayor of Tiflis, was installed as the Head of the State and Prime Minister

in April 1919 to reorganize the country's representative government and with a valiant attempt establish democratic institutions. But the people who spent hours scavenging for food were
not interested in the principles of democracy and the blessings
of liberty and freedom. Their main concern was to have something to eat each day.

THE TURKS PRESENT THEIR CASE

As anti-Turkish sentiments spread around the world and the
delegates in Paris continued to vacillate over the Armenian issue, some British diplomats felt that the unbridled sympathy towards the Armenians would antagonize the Moslem sentiments
around the globe. While Turkey was a vanquished state, the
Sultan-Caliph of the Islamic world still resided in Constantinople. The British had millions of Moslem subjects in the Empire
and Agha Khan, the venerable Moslem leader in the east, had
made a personal appeal in Paris for the Great Powers to be lenient to the Turks.

A suggestion was made, therefore, to allow the Turks to
present their case to the Peace Conference in Paris. President
Wilson was at first against the idea of offering a forum to the
Turkish representatives since no such privileges were granted to
Germany. He later changed his mind and allowed the Turks to
be heard without the right of discussion.

On June 17, 1919, Damad Ferid Pasha, the Grand Vizier of
the Turkish government and Abdul Hamid's brother-in-law, told
the World Congress "We do not deny there had occurred misdeeds and crimes by the Turks which are such as to make the
conscience of mankind shudder with horror forever". The
blame rested not with the Turkish people he said, but with the
actual culprits, the Germans and the Young Turks, whose bands
of criminals had annihilated countless Christians.

Woodrow Wilson was appalled at the Turkish attempt to
absolve the Turks by holding some other group responsible for
the crimes. "Every defeated country can make the same statement", he said. He told his colleagues that the Turks had exhibited a complete absence of common sense and a gross
perversion of facts. In its official response to the Turkish statement the Great Powers declared, "The assertions that the Turkish people were not responsible for the massacres, whose

calculated atrocity exceeds anything in recorded history, cannot be acceptable by the civilized world. A nation is judged by the government it rules, which directs its foreign policy and controls its armies". The Allied Powers stated, "While the Turks as a people may have some good qualities, they could not find any among those qualities the capacity to rule over alien races. Neither among the Christians of Europe nor among the Moslems of Arabia, has the Turk done other than destroy whatever he has conquered; never has he shown himself able to develop in peace what he has won by war. The Turkish talent does not lie in that direction."

The Armenians were gratified with the Allied statement but the criminals of the Armenian Genocide were still at large. Despite their accusations of the Young Turks the new Turkish government failed to bring the organizers of the Genocide to justice.

THE TRIAL OF THE YOUNG TURKS

Shortly after the signing of the Mudros Agreement and the dissolution of the Young Turk Party in Constantinople, Sultan Mehmed VI, Abdul Hamid's brother, officially mourned the suffering of the Armenian people. "Such misdeeds have broken my heart", he declared publicly. "I have ordered an inquiry and justice will be done. We will never have a repetition of these ugly events".

The new Ottoman Council of Ministers formed ten regional committees to investigate the Armenian massacres and bring the criminals to justice. The government issued warrants to arrest the former leaders of the Young Turks. Most of the Turkish commanders who fought against the Armenians in the eastern front were apprehended, including Vehib Pasha, the commander who reoccupied the Western Armenian provinces and the infamous Khalil Pasha, the chief Turkish delegate at the Batum Conference.

The Turkish government set up a military tribunal to try the criminals but it soon became apparent that the judicial process was a sham. The new leaders showed no great haste to punish the former leaders of the country. They claimed there was insufficient evidence for prosecution. While they condemned the Young Turks as inept rulers, there was no real sentiment for holding them responsible for any criminal involvement. The Allied Commissioners protested against the government's laxity and exerted pressure on the Sultan to bring the criminals to justice.

In response to the Allied pressure, the Turkish Tribunal in July 1919 tried and sentenced to death in absentia, the three architects of the Armenian Genocide, Talaat, Enver, and Jemal, but the Pashas had fled to safety in Europe. Their whereabouts, however, were known to the Turkish intelligence. When the Turkish government made no attempt to initiate the proceedings of extradition and carry on the death sentences, the Armenians took the matter into their own hands, and lost no time to avenge the murders of their countrymen.

THE AVENGERS

A society of Armenian nationalists was organized to punish the perpetrators of the Armenian Genocide. The society, called Nemesis, named after the Goddess of Divine Retribution, meticulously gathered the names and whereabouts of the Turkish leaders who organized the mass murders of the Armenian people. Armenian men, haunted by the memory of the ghastly murders, turned to revenge to punish the murderers still at large. One of them was a young man, Soghomon Tehlirian.

Born of wealthy parents Soghomon was eighteen when the Genocide began in the spring of 1915. He witnessed the Turkish gendarmes rob his family, crack his brother's skull with an axe, rape his sister, and kill his mother. He was struck on the head and was thought to be dead, but two days later he found himself buried underneath the bodies of his family. With an injured leg, Soghomon began to walk, disguised in Kurdish attire, towards the Caucasus. He stayed in Tiflis awhile and returned to his hometown during the Russian occupation of the city to look for survivors. Finding no survivors and no Armenians in the town where 20,000 Armenians once lived, Soghomon returned to Tiflis, attended the Armenian College and traveled to Berlin in 1921 to study engineering.

One day when taking a walk on one of the busy streets in Berlin he heard three men walking behind him speaking Turkish. Two of them referred to the third as Pasha. Soghomon turned around and saw that the man who was being referred to as Pasha was Talaat himself, the principal architect of the Armenian Genocide. He followed the three men until Talaat and his company entered a house. Soghomon rented an apartment across the street to spy on Talaat and waited for an opportune moment to confront him. On March 15, 1921 he saw Talaat leave his house. Soghomon took his pistol and followed him. A few minutes later Talaat Pasha was shot to death. A German court exonerated Soghomon. A Turkish newspaper eulogized this murderer of the Armenian people as "a man of justice". Talaat was buried in Berlin, but during World War II Hitler ordered Talaat's body to be transferred to Turkey. It is now a national shrine in Ankara.

On June 19, 1921 Missak Torlakian in Constantinople assassinated Bahud Khan Jivanshir, the organizer of the Armenian massacres in Baku. On December 6, 1921 Arshavir Shirakian in Rome assassinated Said Halim Pasha, the former Grand Vizier of Turkey, who in 1915 signed the order to exterminate the Armenians in Turkey.

On April 17, 1922 Aram Erkanian and Arshavir Shirakian in Berlin, simultaneously assassinated the notorius Dr. Behaeddin Shakir, one of the organizers of the Armenian Genocide and Jemal Azni, the former Mayor of Trabizond, who had organized the systematic extermination of the Armenian children. Earlier Aram Erkanian had assassinated Khan Khoiski, the organizer of the Armenian massacres in Azerbeijan.

After hiding in Berlin awhile Enver Pasha went to Moscow to help the Russian Bolsheviks to assert their influence over the Moslem territories in central Asia. He dropped the Bolshevik cause, and moved to Turkestan to pursue his pan-Turanian ambitions. There he formed an army to fight the Bolsheviks, and he was called the "Emir of Bukhara". In May 1922, an Armenian nationalist, Hakob Melikov, spotted Enver in Uzbekistan and shot him to death on the spot.

After fleeing Turkey, Jemal Pasha spent some time in Moscow and then went to the Caucasus to try to unify the Turkic races and pursue the old pan-Islamic adventures of the Young Turks. He was discovered by Armenian nationalists. On July 25, 1922 Petros Der Boghosian and Artashes Dsaghikian killed Jemal Pasha in Tiflis.

AN AMERICAN MANDATE OVER ARMENIA

When Great Britain refused to send an expeditionary force to Western Armenia to allow the Armenian refugees to return to their homeland, a suggestion was made in Paris for the United States to assume mandatory powers over the entire region and send troops to protect the Armenians. By then the Great Powers had signed the Treaty of Versailles concluding the peace accord with Germany and President Wilson had returned home, leaving the rest of the American delegation in Paris to finalize a peace treaty with Turkey. The Armenian issue and the repatriation of the refugees were linked with the treaty of Turkey. Without guaranteed borders it was difficult for the Great Powers to create an Armenian State in a territory now mostly populated by the Turks. While forming an Armenian State was top priority among the Allies, the safety of the Armenians returning to their homeland was equally important. Forging a treaty was one thing but enforcing it was something else. There were indications of the emergence of virulent nationalism in the interior of Turkey.

Woodrow Wilson's intentions upon returning home to Washington, was to present the proposal of an American mandate over Armenia to the Senate only after the ratification process of the Versailles Treaty. Wilson anticipated difficulties in the Senate over the ratification issue since the Treaty contained covenants for the League of Nations, and the linkage of the mandate issue with the Treaty, he thought, would further complicate the political process. Over the years the President had gained a considerable number of foes in the Republican controlled Congress, prominent among them was the Senate Majority Leader, Henry Cabot Lodge, who had disassociated himself from those who favored the establishment of the League of Nations. A staunch supporter of the Armenian cause, Cabot Lodge was a member of the committee of prominent Americans dedicated to work for the independence of Armenia and had worked diligently to introduce legislation to send food and clothing to the Armenian refugees. While sympathetic to the Armenian cause, Lodge was vehemently opposed to the idea of an American mandate over Armenia.

When the Senate began its deliberations, the President decided to go around the country to rally support for the Treaty and the Armenian mandate. Beginning in September 1919 the President made emotional speeches to arouse the public's interest. He spoke about the sufferings and tribulations of the Armenian people. Prominent Americans joined the President and told the people that Armenia can no longer live under Turkish rule, as coexistence cannot be possible "between the murderer and the murdered, between the robber and the robbed". "The time has come to solve a problem that has plagued civilization for a long time. We must protect the Armenian people from the most revolting tyrants that history has ever known". "We must vindicate Armenia's right to freedom, otherwise we can never again persuade the world that our moral sentiments are anything but empty rhetoric".

The audiences were not particularly enthusiastic over the Armenian mandate issue. Not many Americans relished the thought of sending troops to the so-called "cesspool" of humanity, as some critics had begun to refer to this region. Armenia was a wasteland and a mandate over it would bring a tremendous fiscal and military burden on the United States. To act as the principal guarantor of peace over a region that will bring no economic benefit to the United States would be a costly blunder and a political folly, they claimed.

In every stop around the country Woodrow Wilson reminded his audiences about the poor people of Armenia. "At last this great people of Armenia after seeing their land stained with blood, are now given a promise of safety, and a promise of justice", Wilson said. "Safety and charity begin at home", retorted his Republican opponent, Warren G. Harding, "our armies, the sons of this Republic, the youth from American homes, are needed here".

The President's campaign about the Armenian cause came to an abrupt halt when Wilson, fatigued and exhausted, collapsed in Colorado on September 26, 1919. He was rushed to the White House and a week later suffered a stroke. For the next six months his wife shielded Wilson from the public, Cabinet, and the press. The President was incapacitated, hedged in by White House functionaries, and all efforts to establish an American mandate over Armenia came to an end. Even the ratification of the Treaty of Versailles was placed in jeopardy. Senator Lodge continued his attack and finally succeeded in convincing his fellow Senators to reject the Treaty. A few months later Cabot Lodge wrote "An American mandate over Armenia is out of the question. Congress would never assent to taking a mandate for Armenia. It cannot be done. The only way to help the Armenians is by direct help". It would be politi-

cally untenable, he feared, to have an Armenian State in an
area which by 1919 had become predominantly populated by the
Turks. No matter how much support the Armenians acquired
from America it would be militarily impossible, he felt, to contain armed Turkish and Kurdish bandits wandering around in
the Western Armenian provinces.

President Wilson formally submitted the Armenian mandate issue to the Senate in April 1920 but the Senators rejected it
a month later. Retreating to an isolationist cocoon, the Senators
had no taste to squander American lives and money in the vast
morass of Anatolian mainland. They could not plunge America
into a fresh military controversy. The men had already come
home after fighting in Europe and America needed to put its
domestic house in order. After the entanglement in the European war the United States wanted to stay aloof and adopt a
policy of isolationism, branded with neutrality and impartiality.
While the leaders of the country felt compassion for the suffering people of Armenia, their compassion had its limitations.
Sending food to a country of refugees was a form of humanitarian gesture, but putting America in a turmoil in a far away land,
threatened to undermine the public support for the Armenian
cause.

In the Armenian communities around the world there was
disillusionment and frustration. The inability of the world powers to establish an Armenian State shattered hopes for a better
life for the Armenian refugees. "This is nothing new", a newspaperman remarked. "Since the days of the Congress of Berlin
the civilized world has done nothing for the Armenians, and it
will continue to do nothing".

The promises to the Armenians were left unfulfilled but
the promises to the Greeks were fulfilled with no hesitation.

GREEKS OCCUPY SMYRNA

At the onset of the war the Allied Powers attempted to coax
Greece to join the coalition forces in their fight against the Central Powers. Greece's proximity to the Turkish waters had
made the country an ideal launching pad to attack the Turkish
mainland from the west. The Greek government wished to stay
neutral, however, and refused to participate in the conflict primarily because the King, Constantine, had married Kaiser Wil-

helm's sister and considered it inappropriate to fight his brother-in-law.

Things began to change a few years after the war started. A courageous Cretan, Venizelos, after rising to power as the Prime Minister of Greece, revolted against his King, formed his own government in Crete, and after obtaining some assurances and concessions from the Allies, declared war against the Central Powers in 1917. The Greek participation in the war was in exchange for a promise by the Allies that after the war the Greeks would acquire the entire western coast of Asia Minor including the city of Smyrna.

Smyrna, located on the edge of the Aegean Sea was the second largest city of Turkey after Constantinople, and since the days of the Byzantium Empire had a particular strategic importance as one of the most important commercial centers in the Middle East. Predominantly populated by Greeks, the city had an enormous Greek influence with cultural ties to Athens. Most of the large commercial enterprises were in the hands of the Greeks, who for centuries had controlled the international trade. As experienced merchants and sailors, the Greeks had made Smyrna the focal point of commercial traffic and a natural center for clearing goods from Europe and Asia. Its significance of being one of the most important commercial centers in the Levant had prompted John D. Rockefeller Sr. to open up installations of his Standard Oil Company on the waterfront of the city.

The Greeks were not alone. The city's prosperity was shared by a large population of well-to-do Armenians making Smyrna one of the most important cultural and cosmopolitan centers in the Middle East. The wealthy Armenians and Greeks had their villas on the waterfront with memberships at magnificent golf courses and country estates. They sent their children to European prep schools and universities and spent their summer months in southern France and on the mountains of Switzerland. The waterfront of the city was studded with fine department stores modeling the latest fashions from Paris. Near the Armenian quarter there were international colleges and prestigious institutions for boys and girls, notable among them was the American Collegiate Institute. The American YMCA and YWCA were not too far away. The city had an opera house and it had long become a haven for foreign performers and artists who regarded the city as the Switzerland of the

Middle East. Not far from Smyrna there was the flourishing town of Ushak where Armenian carpet weavers had made the town the center of Turkey's carpet industry. The carpets of Ushak were well sought after quality carpets throughout the world and their reputation at times surpassed carpets woven in Persia.

When the Paris Peace Conference was scheduled to convene, Prime Minister Venizelos rushed to Paris to put his territorial claim on the table. With a rare display of unanimity, the Allies authorized the Greeks to send their forces to Smyrna and occupy the city and its environs. This was a decision that will prove to be a serious political miscalculation, irrevocably changing the course of subsequent history with unfortunate consequences.

On May 15, 1919 Greek destroyers and battleships protected by British, American, and French naval power, appeared in the harbor. 20,000 Greek soldiers landed in Smyrna, blockaded the city, and amid cheers of welcome from the Greek and Armenian inhabitants, proceeded to the center of the city and occupied the government buildings where the Turkish troops were stationed. The Greeks began to shoot the Turks and the Greek residents, taking advantage of the situation, began to round up Turks in the streets and beat them with clubs. Soon violence broke out and in the melee hundreds of Greeks and Turks died within a few hours. The Turks were forced to yield the entire region and the Greeks became the *de facto* rulers of Smyrna. Venizelos took immediate steps to colonize the city, appointed one of his friends, a Greek extremist, to be the Governor of the region with a grand design to restore the former territories of the Byzantine emperors.

When the news of the Greek occupation of Smyrna spread in Turkey, the Turks were shocked and outraged. Their reaction was fast, violent, and spontaneous. Rumors spread like wildfire in the capital and the interior that the Greeks were massacring innocent Turkish civilians. Large crowds gathered in mosques and speeches were made with thousands swearing vengeance against the Greeks. Sultan Mehmed VI almost fainted when he heard the news. There were angry demonstrations in public squares protesting against the Allied policy of supporting the Greeks to occupy one of the most important centers of Turkey. The Turks couldn't get over the fact that it was the

Greeks, their former subjects, these "second class and inferior people", who had occupied Smyrna and not one of the Great Powers. Unlike the Allied occupation of Constantinople, which was meant to be temporary, the Greek occupation of Smyrna was designed to be a permanent annexation of the region to the Hellenic peninsula. Losing an important chunk of real estate was not acceptable to the Turkish masses. To them this occupation was an insult to their honor.

The Smyrna affair was the single most powerful event that generated a new wave of fanatic militarism in Turkey, galvanizing the nationalistic spirit of the Turks almost overnight.

FRENCH OCCUPY CILICIA

As the leaders of the United States were debating the issue of an American mandate over Armenia the French were preparing to occupy Armenian Cilicia to consolidate their hold in the Middle East. The French claim over Cilicia was principally based on the provisions of the Sykes-Picot Agreement signed by the Allied Powers in 1916.

In the fall of 1919, a few months after the Greek occupation of Smyrna, a French infantry regiment, mostly comprised of Armenian volunteers known as *Legion Armenien*, occupied Cilicia and made administrative arrangements to set up house in Marash. While Prime Minister Clemenceau proclaimed that the French occupation would be termporary since the Allies had already made up their minds to incorporate Cilicia into Greater Armenia, the French politicos thought that the control of the region in the heartland of Anatolia would give them enormous commercial benefits. Clemenceau's ulterior motive was to make Cilicia a French colony, similar to the French colonies in North Africa and Southeast Asia, with the prospect of controlling the Turkish tobacco industry along with the railway and mining, using the Armenians as tools to pursue the French colonial interests.

The French stationed garrisons at strategic points in Cilicia and placed a commandant, an incompetent second-rate military man, General Querette, in charge of the entire region. This was an ill-equipped colonial administration with poor military organization with no communications system, no airplanes, and no armored vehicles, making Cilicia an easy target for Turkish terrorist activity.

To populate the region with non-Turkish elements, the French government arranged that the Armenian refugees still in destitute condition in the desert of northern Syria, to repatriate to Cilicia and resettle in their commmunities. This was not exactly a charitable gesture. The French wanted to populate the region with people on whose loyalty they could rely, to better serve their colonial interests.

Around 150,000 Armenian refugees, supposedly shielded by French military power, began to march to Cilicia and settled in their homeland from which they were forced to leave four years earlier. The Armenians reopened their schools, rebuilt their churches and community centers, and even began publishing newspapers, making the cities of Hajin, Aintab, Marash, Urfa, Tarsus, and Adana, once again the vibrant centers of Armenian life. American citizens of Armenian descent were allowed, by a special consent of the United States government, to join their countrymen in Cilicia as volunteer soldiers together with the former mountaineer fighters of Mussa Dagh, to help the French army to protect the Armenian communities. The Catholicos of the Cilician See, after living in exile for several years returned home to reoccupy his throne in Sis. A bustling Armenian life began to take shape. Farmers began to cultivate their land and children were enrolled at schools. American missionaries reactivated the orphanages, American aid began to pour into the region, and the Armenian merchants reestablished their commercial links with Europe, serving French colonial interests and acting as intermediaries for western goods. The Armenians appeared to have finally broken the Turkish hold of Cilicia and with the help of their political parties began to formulate national policies to organize a political order.

Querette's notoriously inept military organization, the ill-planned program of refugee repatriation, and the hasty reactivation of the Armenian political organizations, made the Armenians once more the unfortunate victims of Turkish atrocities. The land that the Armenians reclaimed as their own was difficult to hold and there were not enough French and Armenian troops to guarantee the safety of the repatriated refugees.

As the Armenians began to resettle in their communities in Cilicia, the French army ordered the Turks to turn over the Armenian homes and properties to their rightful owners, and move out of Cilicia. The Turks resented this unexpected Armenian presence in their midst and decided that the time had come once again to put the Armenian "infidels" in their place.

THE REBIRTH OF TURKISH NATIONALISM

The Greek occupation of Smyrna and the Armenian presence in Cilicia emboldened the Turks to rise against the foreign powers and rekindled their desire to chase the non-Moslem elements out of the Turkish soil. They considered the Western Armenian provinces, Cilicia, and the coastal region of western Asia Minor vital to their interests and expressed their willingness in no uncertain terms, to fight to prevent the dissection of their country, which they claimed to have been theirs since the fall of Constantinople in 1453. A Turkish nationalist movement began to take shape to restore the Ottoman's territorial integrity.

Turkey was financially bankrupt and economically impoverished. The government was crippled, acting only as a puppet regime to Western Alliance with no freedom to function as an independent entity. The Turks were a demoralized people and their capital was fraught with a sense of despair. The non-Turks roamed the streets prepared to treat the Turks in the same manner that they were once treated by them. The Armenophile sentiments around the world had become so potent that even the least percipient Turkish politician knew that sooner or later Turkey would be deprived of its eastern provinces, turning over most of the Turkish heartland to the Armenians. A nationalist group called "The Association for the Defense of the Rights of Eastern Vilayets" was soon organized headed by one Suleiman Nazif Bey, with a program to disseminate literature proclaiming that Western Armenia was an integral part of Turkey and pledging to prevent the Armenians to gain control of the region.

The Association began as a political organization but soon acquired a military character. Kiazim Karabekir, the Turkish commander of the military campaign in Western Armenia in 1918, joined the Association and began to incite the Moslem leaders in Anatolia to fight to preserve the Turkish fatherland. He told Moslem political and religious leaders to defy the Allied orders and prevent the Armenians to repatriate to their homeland.

By mid-1919 there were only 40,000 Turks in the armed forces, all ill-equipped and ill-fed, with half a million deserters roaming around the country, carrying their guns, robbing, plundering, and killing innocent Christians. It was this group that Karabekir began to exploit extensively to organize his national movement. While Karabekir's incipient movement was powerful in conception, it needed a more charismatic leader to galvanize the forces of the malcontents.

Such a leader soon appeared whose spectacular rise to power will eventually design a new destiny for the Turkish race. The man was none other than Mustafa Kemal, the military genius of the Gallipoli campaign, who in mid-1919 began to establish the condition that later inspired the Turks to break the Ottoman mold and structure a new social and political order for the welfare of the Turkish fatherland.

THE RISE OF MUSTAFA KEMAL

Immediately after the signing of the Mudros Armistice Agreement, Mustafa Kemal was appointed as the Commander of the Turkish forces in southern Turkey. Frustrated by the Turkish defeat, Kemal used his appointment to bolster his standing in the army and used the forces under his command to pursue a war of independence of his own. As he witnessed the demise of the Ottoman Empire, Mustafa Kemal began to develop a new vision for the Turkish race in the heartland where his ancestors first settled. If Turkey was to survive as a nation, he declared, it must do so in Anatolia and nowhere else. He thus embarked on a journey to defend Anatolia proper and rid the territory of the non-Turkish elements.

Mustafa Kemal regrouped his army, removed officers who did not share his political views, and replaced them with nationalists prepared to fight a guerrilla war if necessary, to preserve the Turkish territorial integrity. He returned to private life after the war and lived in Constantinople, in obscurity for a while, but continued to pursue his nationalist plans and developed an alliance of interest with his comrade-in-arms Kiazim Karabekir operating in the east.

In the early months of 1919 the Turks and their Azeri cousins became concerned about the rapidly rising Armenian nationalism and the intention of the great powers to allow the

Armenian refugees to repatriate to Western Armenian provinces and create an independent state. Western Armenia had been thrown into a state of anarchy and the Allies had no military means to achieve an effective occupation of the region. Gangs of terrorists roamed the streets harassing people and plundering homes. Fearing that bands of fanatic Moslems will launch another frenzy of massacres, the Allied High Commissioner in Constantinople demanded that the Turkish government take necessary steps to curb the lawlessness in the region.

To comply with Allied orders the Grand Vizier, Damad Ferid Pasha, appointed Mustafa Kemal in April 1919 as the Inspector-General of the Turkish army, to rule Anatolia as a sort of military governor and establish law and order. The appointment suited Kemal's plans just fine. He would use his position to organize his nationalist movement and put his political ideas into practice.

As the Greeks were finalizing their invasion of Smyrna, Mustafa Kemal set up shop in Samsun on the Black Sea, and immediately made himself known as the leader of the nationalist movement. He organized mass meetings to inform the people about the injustices by the Greeks in Smyrna. He inflamed the people's spirit of nationalism and made it appear that his movement was the most passionate political issue for the survival of the Turkish race. He soon gained the loyalty and respect of the people and drew them into the support of his movement.

The news of Kemal's activities in Samsun reached the capital and the Allies were alarmed. The British put pressure on the government to recall Mustafa Kemal. The Grand Vizier ordered Kemal to relinquish his post and return to the capital, but Kemal ignored the order and moved his headquarters to Amasya to make his activities less conspicuous.

Meanwhile Kiazim Karabekir after establishing his headquarters in Erzerum, organized a conference on July 23, 1919 to legitimize his nationalist movement. Having found no suitable Turkish location to hold the conference, since Erzerum was an old Armenian town, the Turks held their conference in an Armenian school which was left vacant since the days of deportation.

The Erzerum Congress lasted two weeks, with Mustafa Kemal chairing the meeting. The delegates wrote the draft of a manifesto which later came to be known as the National Pact,

serving as the basis for Kemal's revolutionary movement, proclaiming the principles of self-determination, the preservation of
the will of the Turkish speaking majority, the prevention of foreign domination, and denial of privileges to the non-Moslems
with an implicit threat of their annihilation from the Turkish life.

To give the movement a national character, and to further
consolidate his power in the interior, Mustafa Kemal decided to
hold a second Congress in Sivas on September 4, 1919. The
Sivas Congress ratified the resolution passed in Erzerum and
gave Kemal executive powers with plenipotentiary authority to
represent the nationalist movement, making him the *de facto*
ruler of Anatolia.

The Nationalists began to conduct mass meetings throughout the country demanding the resignation of the government in
Constantinople. Unable to control the situation in the interior,
Damad Ferid Pasha resigned on October 5, 1919, paving the
way to Ali Riza to form a "cabinet of conciliation". Riza immediately sought the cooperation of Mustafa Kemal to work
together to organize a new Parliament allowing the Nationalists
to participate in the affairs of the State.

When a new Parliament was convened on January 16,
1920 Kemal's followers were found to hold the majority of the
seats. The Allied Commissioners were disturbed about the outcome of the election and the advent of the Turkish nationalist
fervor. They demanded the reshuffling of the cabinet ministers
and threatened to institute military measures to eradicate the
nationalist movement.

The Allied interference failed to deter Kemal's terrorist
activities in the interior. He mobilized his forces in the early
weeks of 1920 and began a reign of terror to chase the French
and Armenians out of Cilicia and Anatolia. He took Marash in
Cilicia as the starting point for his savage terrorist campaign.

ATROCITIES IN CILICIA

On January 21, 1920 Kemal's guerrilla units attacked the French
regiment in Marash. General Querette, in reckless desperation,
ordered to set the Turkish quarter of the city on fire. In reprisal
the Turks directed their attention to the Armenian community.
They stormed the Armenian quarter and began to slaughter Armenian settlers indiscriminately. They butchered men, women,

and children with knives and hatchets. They gouged out their eyes and cut off their tongues and genitals. They destroyed the Armenian church and stoned people to death with the stones from the destroyed church.

Unable to control the situation, Querette ordered his forces to withdraw from Marash. In panic around 3,000 Armenians gathered their belongings and followed the retreating French towards northern Syria. Before the Armenians reached the safety zone 1,000 of them perished, 1,800 who were left behind in Marash were butchered, and another 10,000 starved to death after the Turks refused to provide them with food.

Urfa, another city in Cilicia, proved to be a difficult obstacle for the Turks. The French army attempted to protect the Armenian community when the Turks began their attack on February 9, 1920. The French garrison together with the Armenian volunteers fought for two months against Kemal's terrorist bands. Finally with no food and arms left at their disposal, the French army officer promised to deliver the city and the Armenians to the Turks if his troops could receive a safe exit out of the city. The Turks agreed but when the French troops were a few miles away from Urfa, the Turks butchered them all.

The city of Hajin, situated amid rugged and impregnable mountains of northern Cilicia, was the next stop in Kemal's itinerary. Before the Genocide of 1915 there were about 30,000 Armenians living in Hajin, an Armenian enclave going back to the Kingdom of Cilicia. Most of them were massacred in the spring of 1915, 12,000 managed to escape to safety in the Syrian desert, of which 8,000 decided to repatriate after the French occupied Cilicia. After settling in Hajin the refugees rebuilt their community, their homes, churches, and put their children to school. But their resettlement proved to be short-lived.

After massacring the Armenians in Marash, Kemal's forces headed towards Hajin. On March 31, 1920 the Turks reached Hajin and surrounded the city. The Armenians organized a militia unit of 600 strong headed by a former officer of General Andranik's army and prepared to fight against numerically superior forces. The Turks dug trenches around the city and began to attack. The Armenians, well protected by massive walls, resisted the Turkish assault and prevented the Turks to enter the city. The Turkish siege lasted several months with neither side claiming victory. Things began to change. In late June 1920 the

Armenians launched an offensive, broke the Turkish line, and began to attack the enemy forces. The Turks retreated with heavy casualties, abandoned Hajin for a while but returned a few months later with fresh reinforcements. They surrounded the city once again and began their attack, this time more ferociously. Finally in October, 1920, after having fought for seven straight months, the people of Hajin decided to leave the city. They fled carrying their orphans and children. The Turks entered Hajin, burned it and leveled it to the ground.

The city of Aintab became the next target for Kemal's nationalists. After the Marash incident the Armenians in Aintab formed a national union to defend themselves against a possible Turkish attack. The Turkish assault began on April 1, 1920 and the Armenians fought back courageously. The battle lasted until October, 1920. Finally the French negotiated a peace treaty with Mustafa Kemal, agreeing to pull out of Cilicia. By then there were only 50,000 Armenians left in the region out of the group of 150,000, who had repatriated to their homeland a year earlier. Under a French escort these surviving Armenians left their homeland the second time around, never to return again.

Mustafa Kemal achieved his objectives, partially at least. He freed Cilicia from non-Turkish occupation. He now directed his attention to the east and the west. In the west there were the Greeks still occupying Smyrna and in the east there were the Armenians threatening to reoccupy Western Armenia. As he prepared to mobilize his forces against the Greeks, he told his friend Kiazim Karabekir, to take care of the Armenians in the east. Azeri, Kurd, and Turkish gunmen, organized and financed by Karabekir's army, attacked the Armenian villages in Nakhichevan and began to massacre the villagers.

THE ALLIED RESPONSE

Mustafa Kemal's terrorist campaign in Cilicia infuriated the Allied Powers, who now sought immediate measures to suppress the Nationalists. The British forces occupied the Parliament in Constantinople on March 26, 1920, arrested key nationalist deputies, and shipped them off to exile in Malta. The Grand Vizier, discredited and badly damaged in prestige, resigned and the Sultan called on his brother-in-law Damad Ferid once again, to form a new government. Ferid dissolved the Parliament and began to launch a vigorous campaign against Kemal's Nationalists.

The dissolution of the Parliament in Constantinople offered Mustafa Kemal an excellent opportunity to assemble his own Parliament. He saw a new opening for his movement. He shifted the focus of interest and ordered his forces to leave Constantinople, which had been dominated by foreign influence, and build a stronghold in the interior. He declared Ankara, a city built on the site of the old Hittite capital, as the capital of Turkey and prepared to carry on his fight against the government forces, with his new capital offering ready access to the Anatolian plains and the eastern frontiers of Turkey.

As a civil war began to rage between the Sultan's forces and the Nationalist group, the Allies decided to put the final touches on the peace treaty with Turkey to extricate themselves from the labyrinthine affairs of Turkey as expeditiously as possible.

THE CONFERENCE IN LONDON

The U. S. Senate's rejection of the Versailles Treaty forced the State Department to remove the U. S. delegation from the Paris Peace Conference, leaving the other powers to sign a treaty with Turkey without the United States' participation.

When the negotiations between the French and British began in February 1920 in London to finalize a Turkish treaty, the only surviving member of the original Supreme Council of the Paris Peace Conference was the British Prime Minister, David Lloyd George. Prime Ministers Orlando of Italy and Clemenceau of France had resigned their posts and President Wilson had withdrawn by virtue of the Senate rejection. The new conferees in London did not feel morally bound by the promises of their predecessors with regard to the Armenian Question. They removed Cilicia as part of the Armenian territorial claim, and reduced the size of the proposed state to include the provinces of Van, Bitlis, Erzerum, and Trabizond incorporated with the Erevan Republic.

THE TREATY OF SÈVRES

The representatives of Great Britain and France after concluding their conference in London presented their proposal to the

Supreme Council of the League of Nations, which met in San Remo to discuss the issue. The members of the Council signed a peace treaty with Turkey on August 10, 1920 proclaiming to have solved the Turkish issue and the Armenian Question once and for all. The Treaty, known as the Treaty of Sèvres, proved to be one of the most unenforceable documents of international diplomacy. It had the magic of words but no security arrangements to enforce its provisions. It demanded Turkey recognize the State of Armenia and called on the President of the United States to draw the map of Armenia to include Erzerum, Trabizond, Van, and Bitlis. The Treaty of Sèvres carved Turkey into several regions. Smyrna, Thrace, and several Turkish islands in the Aegean Sea were given to the Greeks, much of Anatolia was partitioned between France and Italy, and Western Armenia was given to the Armenians, leaving the Turks to occupy an inland territory in the heart of Anatolia.

The Treaty of Sèvres was presented to Sultan Mehmed VI who promptly signed it accepting its terms. But it was never implemented. Mustafa Kemal, having tasted the rewards of successful terrorist campaigns simply told the Allies that it would require another war for the Great Powers to impose the terms of the Treaty on Turkey.

The Treaty of Sèvres ignited the Turkish public opinion against the Allies and Mustafa Kemal made the most of it. Thousands of volunteers joined Kemal's movement and began to attack Allied strongholds. In retaliation the Allied and Greek forces prepared to invade Constantinople and occupy the Turkish capital. The Greek garrison in Smyrna advanced north and in July 1920 captured the city of Bursa, the former capital of the Ottomans, and chased the Turks out. The Greek occupation of Bursa, which was regarded as the holiest city of the Ottomans, rekindled the Turkish fighting spirit and strengthened their resolve, forcing Ferid's government to resign, paving the way for Mustafa Kemal to assure the leadership of the country.

GREAT POWERS RECOGNIZE THE STATE OF ARMENIA

As the Allies were deliberating the Armenian issue, the government in Erevan was finding new ways to improve its economic and political condition. The country now covering an area of 17,000 square miles had made tremendous strides since its inception. There was an expanded railway system and a new communications network. Consumer cooperative agencies had begun to proliferate, facilitating the production and distribution of agricultural products. There were food processing establishments and factories to manufacture shoes and leather goods, and the Armenian brandy had received an international reputation in the world market. Businessmen had begun to emerge into importance and merchants had founded agencies to clear foreign goods. The immigration of the Armenians from Georgia and southern Russia had given rise to a middle class which began to channel its resources into new opportunities and commercial ventures.

The government established a system of a five-year compulsory elementary education with a curriculum of languages, literature, history, geography, mathematics, music, and vocational training. The State University of Erevan opened faculties of history, philosophy, law, medicine, and physical sciences. "We are rebuilding our homeland," declared Nigol Aghbalian, the Minister of Culture, "without worrying about our enemies, who have always destroyed whatever we have built. This time we shall prevail, and the ship of the Armenian nation will weather the storm... We must grasp the sword in one hand and hold the pen in the other. The Turks have worn down our mountains and left only deserts in their place. But Turkey will sooner or later have its own day of reckoning."

To guarantee the exclusion of the Russian power from the Caucasus and insulate the region from the Bolsheviks the Great Powers decided to recognize the State of Armenia in January 1920. Armenia was finally admitted as a sovereign state in the community of nations. This was a tremendous news to the people who had suffered for so long. Erevan was swept with joy. Huge crowds gathered in the public squares and celebrated the occasion with military parades, fireworks, singing, and dancing in the streets. Prime Minister Khatisian spoke about the dawn of a new day. Armenians throughout the world celebrated the occasion and began to form societies to organize the repatriation of the refugees to the Motherland. The country was finally on the way to greater political stability with a marked advance in the direction of economic prosperity. Somehow the Republic had survived and the sick infant had left the incubator. The leaders of the Republic had won the test for endurance and the admiration of the people everywhere for their fortitude and stubborn tenacity. Even General Andranik agreed to accept the new State and praised the leaders for their accomplishments.

But the State was very fragile and there were forces on the horizon ready to crush it. The Red Army was fast approaching the Caucasus and Mustafa Kemal was in the process of mobilizing a formidable army on the other side of Mount Ararat.

CHAPTER TWENTY-SIX

BOLSHEVIKS OCCUPY ARMENIA

On May 28, 1920 the Armenians celebrated the second anniversary of the establishment of the Republic. The leaders were now confident that they were on the road to recovery. They had secured their borders and asserted the sovereignty of the State. There was a marked progress in every field of human endeavor and the course of economic growth, while still in its elementary stage, had been well defined. A reasonably sound monetary system had allowed the government to formulate economic policies in an attempt to establish a favorable parity with western currencies. The recognition of the Republic by foreign powers had enabled the government to establish credit abroad and make arrangements to float bonds for domestic projects. The supply of skilled labor and the immigration of technicians and engineers from abroad had greatly increased the production of raw materials, prompting the government to regulate certain industries and institute governmental monopolies in others. The annexation of Kars to the Armenian territory and the repatriation of the refugees made the region the granary of the Republic, encouraging the people to store excess provisions of grain, made possible by an effective economic planning and a system of distribution.

While economically the country seemed to be on the right track, politically the State continued to be susceptible to unstable political and economic conditions. Urgent problems faced the leadership. Internal strife and military pressure on the borders had created a problem in leadership. The old government had resigned and a new one had been installed. The danger from the Bolsheviks in the north and the Turkish terrorists in the west had become very real, threatening to upset the political order.

CONFLICT WITH THE BOLSHEVIKS

Russia refused to accept the *de facto* separation of Transcaucasia from its Empire. The territory in the southern flank of the Empire was an appendage to the Romanov domain, and it was well understood in the political circles in the north, that sooner or later the three republics will be forced to move back to the Russian hegemony. The hold of Russia on the Empire had weakened considerably, with Bolshevik leaders in Moscow in disarray, attempting to formulate a cohesive policy to preserve whatever was left of the Romanov Empire. The Bolshevik regime was hampered by revolt, the Russian continent was in turmoil, and the Empire was falling apart.

The Allied powers had sent expeditionary forces to the periphery of the Russian State to help the White Russians, and self-styled revolutionaries to topple the Bolshevik rule. A civil war was in full steam, raging on fourteen different fronts, and the White Russians had gained considerable political and military strength. There were anti-Bolshevik secessionist states created in Siberia, central Asia, South Russia, the Ukraine, Poland, Finland, the Baltic states, and the White Sea in the Arctic region, all financed and supported by the Allied Powers. The Czechoslovak soldiers had seized eastern territories, the Japanese had occupied Vladivostok in the east, and Admiral Kolchak had proclaimed himself as the Supreme Ruler of Russia in defiance of the Bolshevik rule in Moscow.

By early 1920 the situation changed rapidly. Events began to move in favor of the Bolsheviks. Lenin seemed to have consolidated his regime and the White Armies had recorded a series of crushing blows. Kolchak had been captured and executed, and Denikin had been pushed all the way to the south. Most of the conspirators were put to death. In the early weeks of 1920 the Bolsheviks launched an all out offensive to finish up the rebellious armies, causing the Denikin expedition to collapse, leaving only Wrangel fighting alone against the Bolsheviks with untenable frontier lines in the Crimean peninsula.

The Allies gradually removed their support of the White Armies and Lenin's Red Army moved closer to the Caucasus.

The leaders of the Armenian State chose to stay aloof from the political spectacle in the Russian continent. They only had some intermittent interest in the political revolution that had swept the Russian Empire and in the emergence of new ideas that prophesied to change the destiny of man. Their representatives in Moscow were instructed to maintain an amicable relationship with the leaders of the Bolshevik State with the hope that the Bolsheviks, after putting their house in order, will someday readjust their foreign policies and agree to recognize the sovereignty of the State of Armenia.

The Bolsheviks had different objectives, however. They wanted to crush the budding states of Transcaucasia and reincorporate the region with Mother Russia, through the use of instrumentalities of subversion and deception. There was a widespread terrorist and clandestine activity organized by J. V. Stalin who, acting as the People's Commissar of Nationalities, had infiltrated the region with Bolshevik operatives skilled in guerrilla warfare. Most of Stalin's agents were Armenian, chief among them was Anastas Mikoyan, who had established an Armenian Affairs Commissariat to educate the Armenian masses and lead them to Marxism, the only path to salvation. The members of this Commissariat were anti-Dashnak elements who were fond of referring to the regime in Erevan as "decadent bourgeois nationalist". They began to spread the Communist doctrine to topple the Dashnak government and install the Bolsheviks to bring Armenia once more under Russia's sphere of influence.

Stalin organized groups of Bolshevik saboteurs in the Caucasus and brandishing his Georgian background, played an active role in the organization and operation of subversive campaigns. He came into the political limelight in Transcaucasia in September 1918 when anti-Bolshevik agents in Baku, with the help of British intelligence, executed twenty-six Bolshevik Commissars, the elite of the Bolshevik movement, including Stalin's close friend Stepan Shahumian, the pre-eminent leader of the Bolsheviks in the Caucasus. Stalin retaliated by terrorizing anti-Bolshevik Transcaucasian elements in Moscow. He ordered the Armenian Affairs Commissariat to intensify its activities in the region and accused the Dashnaks of collusion with the British. Most of the Dashnak representatives in Moscow were put in jail and Armenian organizations and clubs in Russia that were affiliated with the Dashnak regime in Erevan were ordered to close shop.

BOLSHEVIKS IN ARMENIA

There were hardly any Bolsheviks in Armenia before the Russian Revolution of 1917. Their number began to increase dramatically when the Armenian Bolsheviks in Georgia and Azerbeijan fled to safety in Armenia as the two neighboring countries began to persecute Bolsheviks. In time the Bolshevik exiles organized a party in Armenia, and by the end of 1919 their number increased to five hundred.

Supported and financed by Moscow, the Armenian Bolsheviks began to make speeches and spread Marxist doctrines around Armenia. They told the people that the Dashnaks were lackeys to imperialist powers, an impotent lot, determined to oppress the workers and "suck the blood of the Armenian peasantry". The people were told that the Armenian Republic was a mocking insult to the Armenian workers and its leaders were nothing but "dogs", representing the dregs of society.

The problem was not with the "dogs" who were trying to run a crippled country in the most difficult circumstances. The problem was with the workers. There weren't any. At the time of the dissemination of the Bolshevik propaganda, impoverished Armenia, faced with shortages of food and hope, had a primitive agrarian society with no industry, and therefore, no workers. There were some in the railway system and a few in the factories. The country at the brink of physical exhaustion was not conducive to the development of the revolution of the proletariat, since there was hardly any proletariat. If the objective of the Bolsheviks was to achieve equality among the masses, that objective seemed to have been achieved in Armenia. Nobody had anything. They were all equal, including the leaders of the government, who were living in the most impoverished condition. The Head of the State had a small apartment above a drug store in Erevan, and the Commander-in-Chief of the Armed Forces lived in a one room house.

The Armenian political leaders generally ignored this Bolshevik propaganda and failed to accept the Bolsheviks as a serious threat to their political system. They let the Bolsheviks operate unchecked with no restrictions. The neighboring republics were not that lenient. The Georgian and Azeri police had begun to destroy underground Bolshevik cells and arrested hundreds of Communist agitators and party organizers.

The Armenian government's tolerance towards the Bolsheviks encouraged the Central Committee in Moscow to send veteran Bolshevik provocateurs to Erevan to strengthen the Bolshevik party network in the Caucasus and intensify the dissemination of the Marxist propaganda among the workers and peasants. The government leaders in Erevan were not concerned. Having found themselves isolated from their Allied friends, they planned to use the Armenian Bolsheviks to establish a favorable relationship with Moscow to persuade the Bolshevik leadership to press the Turks to leave Armenia alone and make arrangements for peace. There were signs of troop movement on the other side of the Armenian borders and Kiazim Karabekir was instructed to move his mobilized forces to the proximity of Mount Ararat.

Despite the good will Armenia had earned in Moscow by allowing the Bolsheviks to operate freely, Lenin dismissed the Armenian diplomatic pressure as a ploy to strengthen the Dashnak regime. By mid-1920 he had virtually crushed all opposition forces. Soviet power had been established in Siberia, Turkestan, and the Ukraine. Using the momentum of his victory, Lenin adopted a policy of *rapprochement* towards the Turks to chase the Allied Powers out of Russia's southern flank.

Mustafa Kemal, on his part, putting aside the traditional anti-Russian policy of the Turks, had begun to embrace Moscow openly to help him consolidate his power in Anatolia. In response, Lenin pledged to provide the Turks with financial and military support to enable Kemal to set up security arrangements to extricate Turkey from Allied occupation. The two leaders were drawn together by their common hatred of the Allied Powers. The motives of each were different, but their aim was the same. Lenin considered Anatolia as a fertile land for the revolution of the proletariat and Kemal wanted to use the Bolsheviks to preserve the integrity of the Turkish mainland. For Lenin Islamic Turkey was more important than Christian Armenia. He believed that an amicable relationship with the

Moslems in Turkey would strengthen his hand in central Asia, where the Moslems were the predominant element.

The Treaty of Sèvres signed by the Great Powers in August 1920 brought Lenin and Kemal even closer. Sèvres affected both. It threatened to carve Turkey into several regions, leaving only a landlocked territory for the Turks, and left Russia's southern flank exposed to foreign encroachments. Lenin denounced the terms of the Treaty which he proclaimed robbed Turkey of her important eastern provinces, and in an apparent demonstration to placate the Moslem sentiments, he promised to offer cultural and religious freedom to all the Moslems in the Russian Empire. Russia had millions of Moslem subjects who continued to look to Constantinople as the seat of Mohammed's successor, the Caliph.

Sèvres solidified the relationship between Lenin and Kemal, prompting both to establish a formal diplomatic tie with an exchange of ambassadors. The accord allowed the Soviets to put their claim on Azerbeijan and allowed the Turks to have the freedom to invade Armenia.

BOLSHEVIKS TAKE OVER AZERBEIJAN

With the Dashnaks accommodating the Bolsheviks to operate freely, the Armenian Bolsheviks had a field day in Armenia. They intensified their propaganda around the countryside, promising the people everything for everyone without distinction of class. They promised utopia, peace, stability, and food, promises that later proved to be illusion and myth beyond their capacity to deliver. In time the Bolsheviks crossed the Armenian border and infiltrated the Azeri territory in an attempt to topple the Azeri government.

As the Red Army began to march down the Caucasus, Mustafa Kemal instructed his operatives in Azerbeijan to help the Bolsheviks take over the Azeri government in accordance with the previously forged understanding with Lenin. Infamous Nuri Bey was still in Baku at this time operating as Kemal's principal agent in Azerbeijan. In March 1920 the Azeri government resigned, paving the way to the pro-Bolshevik forces to form a new government. The Bolshevik sympathizers floundered hopelessly amid a wave of uprisings. To expedite the process of takeover in April 1920 the Bolshevik hierarchy in Moscow, in collaboration with the Bolsheviks in Transcaucasia, formed a special bureau for the Caucasus called Kavburo with the Red Army acting as its military arm. On April 27, 1920 the Kavburo headed by Ordzhonikidze, Mikoyan, and Kirov, launched an all out offensive in Baku, demanding from the Azeri government to turn over the reign of the government to the Soviets. The following day Azerbeijan became a Soviet Republic, and the Communists began a repressive regime to suppress the Azeri nationalists.

With Azerbeijan safely in the Soviet orbit, Mustafa Kemal immediately moved to utilize the Azeri land as a corridor to transport Soviet arms into Nationalist Turkey. To facilitate the shipment of arms and to secure access to the Soviet frontier, he demanded from Moscow to have the provinces of Karabagh and Zangezur, which were still under Armenian control, to be handed over to the Azeris, making the region contiguous with the Turkish territory. Moscow staked out the territorial claim and began to apply pressure on the Armenian Republic, giving rise to open hostility between the Bolsheviks and the Dashnaks.

BOLSHEVIK REBELLION IN ARMENIA

During a May Day celebration in 1920 the Armenian Bolsheviks in Alexandropol seized an armored train and proclaimed a Soviet government under the command of Sarkis Musayelian. They arrested the venerable General Silikian, the hero of the Battle of Sardarabad and occupied several villages. To crush this uprising, the Erevan government immediately began to take appropriate political and military measures. Alexander Khatisian's government resigned and Hamo Ohanjanian was called upon to form a new cabinet with the Dashnak Bureau taking over the reign of the country. The Armenian forces headed by General Sebouh attacked the Bolshevik rebels and forced Musayelian to surrender. The rebellion proved to be premature. The rebels retreated to wait for a more opportune time to strike again.

This Bolshevik uprising was an eye-opener for the Dashnaks and served as a starting point of a new relationship with the Soviets. The appearance of a militant opposition to the leadership of the Republic provoked a new political orientation towards the Bolsheviks. The fundamental issue was the ques-

tion of survival. The Armenian leaders did not care about political ideologies or the Bolshevik hegemony in the north. The
problem was to protect the little state from Bolshevik encroachments. The leaders of the Republic realized that in order for
them to survive they needed to negotiate some sort of understanding with Moscow since the Allied Powers proved to be unreliable protectors and had deserted the Armenians to their
destiny.

A delegation headed by Levon Shant, a playwright, left
Erevan for Moscow with plenipotentiary powers to sign a treaty
with the Bolsheviks. Concurrently a Turkish delegation, representing Mustafa Kemal, left Turkey for Moscow to hold talks
with Lenin.

The Armenian delegates met with Chicherin, the Soviet
Commissar for Foreign Affairs, and proposed the following
terms as a basis for a bilateral treaty: The Soviet Russia will recognize the State of Armenia, will accept the annexation of Western Armenian provinces with the Armenian Republic, and will
not interfere in the internal affairs of the State of Armenia. Chicherin, after listening to the Armenians politely, spoke about the
importance of a cordial relationship between Nationalist Turkey
and Armenia, and suggested to Levon Shant that the Armenian
delegates meet with the Turkish delegates who were in Moscow
at the time to discuss the territorial disputes. Chicherin promised the Armenians that the Soviet government will do its utmost to get some Western Armenian provinces annexed to
Armenia, if not all.

In spite of these pronouncements and promises and extensive dialogues, no agreement was put on paper and no treaty
was signed with the Soviets. In mid-summer 1920, Levon Shant
returned home empty handed.

On July 5, 1920 Red Army units invaded Zangezur but
General Dro counterattacked and drove the Russians out. The
Bolsheviks tried again and this time the Armenians sued for
peace. On August 10, 1920, the day the Allied Powers signed
the Treaty of Sèvres, the Armenians and Russians signed an accord in which Armenia capitulated and accepted the Soviet occupation of Karabagh and Zangezur.

Meanwhile on the other side of Mount Ararat preparations
were being made to invade Armenia.

TURKS ATTACK ARMENIA

When the Turkish delegates met with the Soviets in Moscow, Lenin expressed the desire of taking Armenia himself, contrary to the arrangements that he had made earlier with Mustafa Kemal. Upon their return to Ankara the Turkish delegates told Kemal of Lenin's unexpected plan. Mustafa Kemal immediately began preparations to launch an attack to pre-empt Lenin. He ordered Kiazim Karabekir, who was anxiously waiting to start the gunfire, to forestall a conquest by the Bolsheviks by attacking Armenia first.

The Turks began their march on Armenia in September 1920 and on September 28, 1920 captured Sarikamish with ease. A few weeks later they were at the gates of Kars. The Armenian government appealed to foreign powers, but no help was forthcoming. The Armenians were left alone. In late October the Turks launched a massive offensive on Kars. They were so overwhelmingly powerful that their aggression was not met with resistance. The Armenian military commanders had their hands full with the Armenian Bolsheviks, who through an orchestrated program of subversion, were sabotaging the Armenian war efforts by helping the Turks indirectly. On October 30, 1920 Kars fell and the Turkish army entered the city, massacred the Armenians, plundered their homes, and took 3,000 prisoners of war, among them were prominent Armenian generals, government ministers, the Mayor of Kars, and a bishop, Karekin Hovsepian, who several decades later will be crowned as the Catholicos of the See of Cilicia. The Turks butchered men, women, and children, took young boys as slaves, and raped young Armenian girls. They burned the city, devastated the countryside, and made Kars an outpost of destitution.

As the rest of the Armenians began to flee to face a grim struggle of survival, Mustafa Kemal ordered Turkish farmers and peasants to move to Kars and settle in homes and properties vacated by Armenians to make Kars a Turkish city.

After taking Kars, Karabekir continued his march towards Alexandropol to repeat his predecessor's route of 1918. On November 7, 1920 Kemal's Foreign Commissar issued an ultimatum to the Armenians to move their forces to the interior, allowing the Turks to occupy Alexandropol. The ultimatum was rejected by the Armenian government. Karabekir occupied Alexandropol with no resistance and following a time-honored tradition, allowed his men to loot and plunder for three days. After establishing his headquarters in Alexandropol, Karabekir began to move his forces towards Erevan, the heart of the Armenian Republic. Alarmed by the Turkish advance, the Armenian government accepted Karabekir's terms and signed a cease-fire agreement on November 17, 1920. History was repeating itself. The situation in Armenia was now the same as it was during the creation of the Republic. The Armenian leaders were now faced with two problems. One was the Turkish threat to annihilate the Armenians and place a punctuation mark to their existence as a nation, and the other was the Bolshevik attempt to take over whatever remained of Armenia. It became abundantly clear to them to choose the lesser of two evils and thus directed their attention to the Bolsheviks. Hamo Ohanjanian stepped down as Prime Minister on November 23, 1920 allowing Simon Vratsian, known for his pro-Russian policies, to form a new government and negotiate a deal with the Soviets as soon as possible.

Vratsian formed a cabinet with considerable difficulty and immediately began his negotiations with the Soviets to obtain assurances for mediation with the Turks. But the Bolsheviks had conditions of their own. They wanted the Armenians to allow the Bolshevik forces to enter the Armenian territory in the pretense to stop the Turkish advance. Vratsian rejected the Soviet offer and sent former Prime Minister, Alexander Khatisian, to Alexandropol to negotiate with Karabekir.

Karabekir's demands in Alexandropol were similar to those of Enver Pasha in Batum in the spring of 1918. The Turks demanded that Armenia dismantle its military organization, leaving an army with no more that 1,500 troops to be deployed for internal security purposes only, and the Republic be a vassal state of Turkey, just like it was at the time of its creation two and a half years earlier.

THE FINAL ACT

The Turks and the Bolsheviks were now in a race to see who was going to get Armenia first. The anarchy in Armenia helped them both. Time was running short. The Turks were only a few miles away from Erevan and the Bolsheviks were in neighboring Azerbeijan within striking distance of Armenia. Both sides wanted nothing short of the complete conquest of Armenia.

On November 27, 1920 Joseph Stalin in Baku ordered Ordzhonikidze, Mikoyan, and Kirov to begin operations and "take Armenia at any cost". On the same day Lenin in Moscow ordered the Bolsheviks to issue an ultimatum to the Armenian government to surrender power to the Revolutionary Committee of the Soviet Socialist Republics. On November 29, 1920 Red Army units crossed the Azeri border, entered the Armenian territory, and declared Armenia Sovietized. Alarmed, the Dashnak Bureau met in an emergency session and decided not to resist the Soviet takeover. Meanwhile Karabekir in Alexandropol sought diplomatic measures to prevent a Bolshevik takeover. He pressed the Armenian delegates to accept the Turkish terms and sign the treaty without delay. With no hesitation the Armenian leadership decided to do both, to hand over the government to the Bolsheviks and simultaneously sign a treaty with the Turks. The Armenians were afraid that the Turks, deliberately ignoring the Soviet take-over, would seize the moment of uncertainty and unleash their forces towards Erevan and annihilate the people. The treaty with Turkey, they rationalized, would stop the Turkish advance.

Powerless, hopeless, and with broken spirit, Simon Vratsian resigned on December, 2, 1920 after being in power for only seven days and General Dro established a dictatorial rule as a regimen to avert chaos. Meanwhile the Armenian delegates in Alexandropol were continuing their negotiations with Karabekir for a treaty with the Turks. On December 2, 1920, they were informed that their government had resigned in Erevan and Dro, acting as an interim leader, had no legislative or statutory power to authorize a treaty. Alexander Khatisian, as the chief Armenian delegate, wired Dro for instructions with regard to the signing of the treaty. In the absence of a legitimate governmental body, General Dro instructed Khatisian to use his own discretion to sign or not to sign the treaty. Faced with a grave responsibility, the Armenian delegates decided to sign the treaty with the Turks on December 3, 1920, agreeing to declare the Treaty of Sèvres null and void, thus putting an end to the Armenian Question and renouncing the Armenian territorial claim over Western Armenia. With this treaty, the Turks finally crushed the half century Armenian struggle for political self-determination.

The Treaty with the Turks proved to be a meaningless and unenforceable document, since it was signed by a government not in existence. The day before, on December 2, 1920, the reign of the government was transferred to the Bolsheviks, and the State of Armenia had become a part of the Soviet Empire.

On December 7, 1920   Russian cavalry entered Erevan and General Dro unceremoniously surrendered the reign of the government to Comrade Gassian, the head of the Bolshevik Revolutionary Committee. The Bolsheviks took over the administration of the government, assailed "Bourgeois Nationalism", and appealed to the workers of Armenia to unite to achieve the victory of the proletariat.

Armenia became an integral part of the monolithic world of the Soviet hegemony. It was forced to embrace the doctrines of Karl Marx and become an accomplice to fulfill Lenin's prophecy of a Communist "Workers' Paradise".

Before the take over was completed someone made a speech from the balcony of the government building in Erevan exhorting "Long live Soviet Armenia. Down with the Bourgeoisie". An Armenian in the audience whispered to no one in particular, "Horseshit".

In an unusual twist of irony, two weeks earlier the civilized world had finally decided to solve the Armenian Question once and for all. On November 22, 1920 the White House announced that President Wilson had drawn the map of Armenia, as stipulated under the terms of the Treaty of Sèvres. Wilson awarded the Armenians a huge chunk of real estate covering 68,500 square kilometers with a stretched coastline on the Black Sea. The map included vast territories of historic Armenia including the cities of Erzinjan, Mush, Bitlis, Erzerum, the Lake Van region, Kars, and Trabizond to serve as an Armenian seaport.

The American award came too late and Wilson's map was destined to become a diplomatic fossil in the archives of the Smithsonian. By then it had become irrelevant to current realities, and the Armenians had ceased to be the masters of their own destiny. The bright expectations that had emanated from the Paris Peace Conference had now faded into bitter disillusion. Woodrow Wilson, the valiant humanitarian, who fought for the emancipation of the downtrodden people, was too late to help the Armenians. This great American visionary was the champion of the Armenian cause, and the exponent of individual dignity and freedom. He wanted to "make the world safe for democracy", but at the end failed to put his vision into practice. Mustafa Kemal and Vladimir Lenin had already agreed to guarantee that the Armenians never again be allowed to have an independent state and never again be permitted to exercise their inherent right of self-determination. Both, in their own way, had inflicted a tragic end to the Armenian dream.

CHAPTER TWENTY-SEVEN

THE AFTERMATH

The people of Armenia were happy about the change in government. The process of change had not been too painful to them. The Dashnak leaders felt that they could acquiesce in the situation without much loss of prestige. They were somehow relieved of their agonizing responsibility of trying to run a crippled country for two and a half years. They embraced the Bolshevik policy and expressed their willingness to cooperate with the new leaders to restore a badly needed political stability. This was not a political *coup d'état*. It was merely the result of a political breakdown and the inability of the Dashnak leadership to face two adversaries, one from the north and one from the west, at the same time. It was now the Bolshevik's turn to design a new destiny for the Armenian people. They were called upon to protect the country's borders from the encroachments of its neighbors and institute a program for economic recovery. They changed their gear, however, immediately after assuming the reign of the government. Instead of serving the interest of their people, they began to serve the interest of international Communism. They discredited the Dashnaks, stripped away their political privileges, established a police state under the aegis of the dictatorship of the proletariat, and brought a new surge of terror to the impoverished country.

The Soviet Secret Service, known as the Cheka, arrested political leaders and confiscated private properties. The country's food production and other industries were nationalized and private ownership of land was abolished. To crush political opponents, and there were none at the time, the Soviets fabricated stories and arrested Dashnak leaders indiscriminately and put them in jail incommunicado for many months. They interfered with the judicial system, suspended the state Constitution, and dismissed the Parliament.

The person who masterminded this Communist reign of terror was a twenty-four-year-old Armenian, Avis Nurijanian, who had been trained as a Communist hothead in the hinterland of the Caucasus. Politically immature and temperamentally impetuous, Avis assumed the control of the government and installed a political system patterned after the Soviet regime, with no regard to the Armenian interests. One of his biggest political gaffes, from which the State of Armenia continues to suffer to this day, was his decision with regard to the provinces of Karabagh, and Nakhichevan. Immediately after the Sovietization of Armenia, Soviet Azerbeijan, as a gesture of good will and brotherly love, offered to turn over to Soviet Armenia the two provinces which had been the cause of interracial hostilities and enmities between the two nations. After years of bloodshed and unsuccessful negotiations, the Armenians were being offered the disputed territories. But Avis rejected the offer. He was more concerned about the Turkish interest in the region and did not wish to upset the Turco-Soviet alliance that Lenin and Mustafa Kemal had forged earlier.

By January of 1921 most of the Dashnak leaders were put in jail, including former Prime Ministers Kachaznuni and Ohanjanian. Army officers were sent to exile and the popular General Dro was deported to Moscow. The Communist reign of terror prompted the Dashnaks, who still maintained a powerful organization in Armenia, to organize a rebellion against the Communists.

On February 12, 1921 a fierce fight broke out between the Dashnaks and the Armenian Communists. The Dashnak forces, headed by former Prime Minister Simon Vratsian, occupied Erevan and took control of the government. The success of the Dashnak uprising was primarily due to the fact that the Soviet forces, after occupying Armenia, shifted their attention to Georgia, which was yet to be Sovietized. The Red Army had moved its troops from Armenia to crush the Georgian Nationalist government, leaving only a small garrison in Erevan.

The Communists were forced to yield most of Armenia to the Dashnaks, and Vratsian immediately began to form a new government. The reaction from the Communists was swift and violent. Avis Nurijanian, unable to control the situation militarily, took drastic measures. He issued an order warning the Dashnaks that unless the rebellion is ceased immediately, all Dashnak leaders who were then held in jail in Communist cells "will be shot to death." Vratsian took this as a bluff and continued his rebellion. The Communists then executed fifty Dashnak prisoners in cold blood. When the rebellion continued, another group was shot to death the following day.

Armenia was now under a Dashnak government but the leaders had no place to go for help. The country was completely isolated. Azerbeijan was Sovietized, Georgia was about to be Sovietized and the Turks were on the other side of Mount Ararat, ready to exploit any political uncertainty to crush the Armenian State. The Dashnak leaders sent urgent messages to the great powers and the League of Nations pleading for help. But the Allies had no interest in such trivial matters.

After occupying Georgia on February 25, 1921, the Bolsheviks regrouped their army and marched back to Erevan. They surrounded the capital with heavy tanks and artillery and forced the Dashnaks to surrender. Meanwhile in the north the Turks and the Soviets signed a treaty of friendship on March 16, 1921, sealing the borders between Armenia and Turkey, and preventing each from undertaking subversive activities in the territory of the other. Stalin and Mustafa Kemal drew the mutual frontiers. Seventy thousand Turkish peasants who had fled Armenia during the Dashnak regime were allowed to return to Armenia. Nakhichevan became an autonomous Soviet region under the Azeri protectorate and the Soviet Union agreed to renounce the Treaty of Sèvres. By now Joseph Stalin had won possession of all the land south of the Caucasus. The Dashnak rebellion in Erevan caused some degree of consternation and threatened to disrupt the Soviet ambition. Stalin ordered the Bolsheviks to launch an all-out offensive and chase the insurgents out of the capital. On April 3, 1921, the Bolsheviks reoccupied Armenia. Thousands of Armenians fled to Iran and the less fortunate Dashnak leaders were captured and executed.

There developed some semblance of political order in Armenia under the Communist regime. For the first time in six years the people were guaranteed to have some tranquility. Moscow began to ship food and clothing to Armenia. Peace came to the plains of Mount Ararat with borders secured and shielded by the Soviet power. The Dashnak rebellion prompted Lenin to change Armenia's political organization. Avis Nurijanian was thrown out and a more somber and responsible man, Alexander Miassnikian, assumed the reign of the government with instructions to "bury the past" and practice moderation in transforming Armenia into Socialism. On December 13, 1922 Armenia became a part of the Transcaucasian Soviet Federated Socialist Republic, and in 1936 it became a Republic in the Union of Soviet Socialist Republics when the Soviet Union formally adopted its Constitution.

THE INTERLUDE

The Turco-Soviet Treaty formalized the relationship between the Soviet Union and Mustafa Kemal's Nationalist government. Kemal turned the Treaty to his own purposes to crush the last vestiges of the Ottoman government in Constantinople. With fresh supplies flowing from Russia, Kemal made his army a personal instrument to achieve his goals. He directed his attention to Asia Minor where the Greeks still held Turkey's western region with a clear desire to make it a permanent part of the Hellenic world.

Meanwhile, in Constantinople the Grand Vizier, Damad Ferid Pasha, had been badly discredited and his prestige irreparably damaged. He resigned his post, returned to private life and spent the rest of his days in Europe. Tevlik Pasha once again was called upon to form a new government. His new cabinet was forced to abandon the government's opposition towards Kemal's Nationalist movement. Exploiting the people's resentment against the Allied Powers, Tevlik began to cultivate a new relationship with Mustafa Kemal.

The single most important element that finally ended Turkey's civil war and brought the two factions together was the continued Greek presence in Asia Minor. Unlike the Armenian presence in the east, the Greek danger was real and affected the Turkish sentiments tremendously. The Greeks were in the process of organizing a huge military campaign in Anatolia. In the fall of 1920 the Greek Prime Minister Venizelos sent a message to the Supreme Council of the League of Nations that he would be willing to wage an all-out campaign against Kemal's forces and wipe out the Turkish Nationalist movement if his army was appropriately supported and financed by the Allied Powers. He assured his war partners that the job could be done within a couple of weeks. The Allies agreed and authorized the Greek expedition. Surprisingly enough the Greeks accomplished a series of impressive victories, forcing Mustafa Kemal to move his forces back to Ankara. The Greeks seized the principal cities in western Asia Minor and successfully disrupted the communications network and gained control of the railway system between Constantinople and Ankara.

The Greek military accomplishments did not sit well with Italy and France which had their own territorial interests in Anatolia, and did not want to have the Greeks dominate the political scene. The French and Italians preferred to have a weak Mustafa Kemal than a powerful Venizelos. They gradually discontinued their support and ordered the Greeks to stop the advance. Undisturbed by this change of policy, Venizelos continued to put his plan into execution. His minor victories over the Turks had inflated him with vanity, and encouraged him to forge his military campaign without Allied support. A monkey is about to change the course of subsequent history.

MUSTAFA KEMAL ON THE MOVE

In October 1920 young King Alexander of Greece died of blood poisoning from the bite of a pet monkey. His death threw Greece into a political turmoil. The king's brother refused to ascend the throne, forcing Venizelos to declare a general election to decide the fate of the Hellenic throne. People in Greece felt that the time was ripe for King Constantine, the dead king's father who had been in exile since 1917, to return home and occupy the throne. Venizelos miscalculated the outcome of the election. He was defeated at the polls and went into exile. Constantine returned home and ascended the Greek throne with popular acclaim, and took charge of the country's military affairs.

The return of King Constantine seriously aggravated the relationship of the Greeks with the Allies. Constantine had been implicated in collaboration with the Germans during the war, and his presence on the side of the Allies was considered abhorrent. While the King upon rising to power demonstrated his willingness to deal with the course of events that the Allies had designed for Greece and indicated support for the existing order, his prior relationship with his brother-in-law, the German Kaiser, had apparently alienated the Allies beyond repair.

The Great Powers warned the Greek government that they would no longer continue their financial and military support. Removing themselves from the alliance with Greece, the French and the Italians began to send arms to Mustafa Kemal to appease the nationalist leader in order to gain some commercial benefits from Turkey. The Allied alliance with Kemal seriously endangered the implementation of the Treaty of Sèvres, isolated Greece, and strengthened Mustafa Kemal's military and political organization. It failed to deter, however, the Greeks' ambitious drive to establish a permanent hegemony in Asia Minor, a goal that would soon prove to be a blunder of great magnitude.

As the Allies began to arm the Turkish Nationalists, King Constantine began to organize a formidable army to annihilate Mustafa Kemal's forces in the hinterland of Anatolia and enforce the implementation of the Treaty of Sèvres. With his treasury empty and his country's political structure seriously impaired, King Constantine decided to do it alone and continue his war against the Turks. Pulling the Greek forces out of Anatolia was out of the question. In doing so he would have left the Christian population of Asia Minor to the mercy of the Turks.

In January 1921 the Greeks began to reposition their military line in Asia Minor in an attempt to establish new lines of communication with their military command in Smyrna. Preparations were made to launch an all-out offensive against Kemal. The Greek army appeared to be well trained with an obvious enthusiasm to secure a permanent bridgehead in Anatolia. There were about 200,000 Greek soldiers stationed in Anatolia. They were far superior in potential strength, and Constantine's war machine appeared to be in good shape. His only problem was the divided structure of the military command. The hold of the Greek generals on the army had weakened considerably and there was some skepticism whether the Greeks would be able to carry the brunt of the war all by themselves without the Allied support.

In early 1921 the Greeks took the initiative and began their campaign with a daring raid on Afyon Karahisar. They captured the city and forced Kemal's forces to retreat with heavy losses. Unaffected by the Greek victory, Mustafa Kemal regrouped his army and gave the command to his trusted friend, Colonel Ismet. The Turks confronted the Greek forces at Inönü in the spring of 1921, fought ferociously, defended the city and forced the Greeks to abandon Inönü and retreat to Bursa. The Greeks fought with great courage but lost the battle.

The victory at Inönü boosted the Turkish morale immeasurably. This was the first Greek defeat after the occupation of Smyrna. Colonel Ismet returned to Ankara with cheers and celebrations. This was the first Turkish victory over the Greeks and it was a decisive one. It was from this battle at Inönü that Ismet Inönü took his surname later on.

The Greeks, faced with a prospect of total defeat, hurriedly reorganized their army and stretched their defense line over a 200-mile radius to protect their strongholds in Asia Minor. While they lost the battle at Inönü, they still held an important military establishment in Bursa from which another offensive might be launched.

After mobilizing their forces and obtaining fresh reinforcements from Smyrna, the Greeks launched an offensive on March 23, 1921 with a goal to proceed directly to Ankara. To give the troops moral support King Constantine sailed to Smyrna and with an illusion of grandeur ceremoniously entered the old Byzantine town as the supreme ruler of the Hellenic world, ready to conduct a war of conquest in the same way that Alexander the Great had achieved centuries earlier against the Persians.

The Greek campaign in Asia Minor was well publicized all around the world with correspondents ready to cover the war. Among them was a young American reporter, Ernest Hemingway, then a foreign correspondent in Anatolia for a Canadian newspaper. Hemingway would be the first to report the unexpected fate of the Greek army and the tragedy that was about to unfold.

A fierce battle took place in Eskishehir and the Greeks met stiff resistance from the Turks. The Greek forces floundered awhile but later decided to retreat, leaving a large stockpile of arms and ammunition for Kemal's use. The Greek King's presence on Turkish soil had infuriated the Turks and galvanized the nationalists to pool the country's resources to drive the Greeks out of Anatolia. The Greeks were not intimidated, however, by Kemal's show of force. They too reorganized their army and prepared to deliver a lethal blow to Kemal's power base. They continued their advance towards Ankara under the scorching sun, but they were not familiar with the terrain of the Anatolian hinterland. Soon the Greeks ran out of food and ammunition. Mustafa Kemal waited for them at the Sakarya River, not far from the home base at Ankara. As the Greeks approached the river, exhausted and ill equipped, Kemal put his men across the river, cut the Greek line of supply from the rear, and with a strong defensive posture, made a frontal attack, splicing the Greek army in two. The battle of Sakarya lasted twenty days. At the end the Greeks could not hold their defensive position any longer. Their elaborate military organization began to crumble. Thousands died and many more were taken prisoner. In mid-September 1921, the King ordered his troops to leave Sakarya immediately and retreat towards Smyrna.

This was a spectacular victory for the Turkish Nationalist movement and one that catapulted Mustafa Kemal to the international scene. He was now the illustrious hero of the Turkish people. His victory won the admiration of his people who upon his return to Ankara hailed him as their liberator and bestowed upon him the title Gazi–the conqueror of the Holy War against the infidel. While there was still a legitimate government in Constantinople with the Sultan as the constitutional monarch and the Grand Vizier as the head of the government, the foreign powers began to accept Kemal's government in Ankara as the real government in Turkey. Mustafa Kemal strengthened his military and political posture and obtained enormous supplies of arms and materiel from the Soviets and the Allies.

The victory at Sakarya opened the way to Smyrna. The Greeks were left alone, sulking in isolation. A rumor arose in the Western circles that the Greek army had been completely decimated and Kemal was on his way to Smyrna to smash the last vestiges of the Hellenic rule. The rumor was unfounded. Kemal wanted to wait a whole year to achieve that objective. First there was an urgent matter to be taken care of in Cilicia.

THE TURCO-FRENCH ALLIANCE

The Turkish victory at Sakarya sealed the fate of the Armenians in Cilicia. It prompted the French to adopt a pro-Kemalist policy. Taking advantage of the French policy of *rapprochement*, Mustafa Kemal demanded the French evacuate Cilicia and remove all the Armenian refugees from the region. There were still some 50,000 Armenians scattered around Cilicia attempting to defend their communities from Turkish attacks.

Immediately after the Battle of Sakarya, the French entered into an agreement with Mustafa Kemal in a blatant act of disloyalty to the Western Alliance, agreeing to remove the Armenians from Cilicia in return for some vague promises of commercial concessions that were destined never to come to fruition. The agreement formally repudiated the Treaty of Sèvres.

With the dream of political self-determination shattered, the Armenians began to march south once again to face the cruel realities of life in the deserts of Syria. As the Armenians evacuated the cities of Cilicia, the Turks moved in to settle on Armenian properties. Kemal ordered the indiscriminate destruction of Armenian churches and community centers to remove all traces of Armenian life in the region.

The control of Cilicia allowed Mustafa Kemal to strengthen his military machine, and transfer his forces from Cilicia to western Asia Minor to organize an assault against the Greeks.

As a gesture of good will the French left a valuable and enormous stockpile of guns and ammunition to the Turks. Hundreds of machine guns, thousands of rifles, mobilized cannons and armored vehicles, that were previously in the possession of Armenian volunteers, were given to Kemal. Former Mussa Dagh mountaineers, who had joined the French Legion as volunteers to defend Cilicia, were told to leave all their military equipment for the Turks, including their army uniforms, and march south to join the refugees in the deserts of Syria.

Fifty thousand Armenian refugees found themselves in the most desperate situation after reaching northern Syria. There was no help from abroad. Most of the American financial and economic aid in the Near East had already been allocated to various refugee programs and the new U. S. President, Warren G. Harding, who had earlier criticized Woodrow Wilson's pro-

Armenian policies, had no intention of expanding the foreign aid.

A DILEMMA FOR THE ENGLISH

While France and Italy signed separate agreements with Mustafa Kemal, England wanted to stay aloof. His Majesty's government wanted Kemal out but was incapable of putting him out. In the grand design of the post-war *real politik*, the government leaders of Great Britain had no intention to get involved with a dismembered Turkey. They had already captured the imagination of the world and through conquest, bloodshed, and exploitation appeared to have installed a new world order and built an empire that stretched over a million square miles of territory, from Capetown to Rangoon. There were some trouble spots, however. One of them was the Moslem Middle East. Their ability to control the region was constantly challenged and their military presence in the Middle East was occasionally threatened. Insurrection against Britain broke out in Egypt in 1919, followed by an Arab revolt in Iraq in which thousands of British soldiers died. These events took place during the period in which Mustafa Kemal was attempting to create a new order of his own in an effort to reverse the course of history.

While Britain refused to sign agreements with Kemal, as its two partners had chosen to do, it also refused to undertake military or political support of Greece. The British felt that the euphoria of victory in the Great War should not be stained by a mismanaged foreign policy in the Middle East. They feared that continued turmoil in the region may threaten to disrupt the delicate balance of power so meticulously put together in the mirrored halls of the palace of Versailles. Mustafa Kemal on his part did not need a British treaty. He had already woven a web of important ties with the Soviets, French and Italians and was ready to deliver the lethal blow to the Greeks to chase them out of Asia Minor.

MASSACRE IN PONTUS

After Sakarya, Kemal's next target was the enclave of Pontus on the coast of the Black Sea, where a large population of Greeks and Armenians had lived for centuries. The Pontic Greeks claimed descent from the former generals of Alexander the Great. A prosperous merchant class of Armenians and Greeks lived in Pontus. They grew in power and wealth in the Nineteenth century and played a prominent role in international commerce between Europe and the states surrounding the Black Sea.

For Mustafa Kemal this Christian enclave was a threat to his Nationalist movement. Pontus was part of Turkey and Christian presence on the Turkish soil was contrary to the provisions of the National Pact. After the elimination of the Armenians from Cilicia, the Turkish terrorists began a wholesale extermination of Armenians and Greeks in Pontus. Within a few months, over one hundred thousand Greeks and Armenians were massacred. By the end of the summer of 1922 the entire province was emptied of Christians and Pontus ceased to exist as a Christian enclave. Mustafa Kemal was now ready to turn his attention to the last Christian stronghold, Smyrna.

THE END OF THE HELLENIC RULE

The Turks began their attack on the Greek forces on August 26, 1922. Their goal was the Mediterranean. Within a few hours the Turkish forces annihilated the Greek army near Khoja Tepe, gained control of the railway, and found themselves on the main road to Smyrna. The Greek forces were taken by surprise. They began to flee towards the sea. By August 30th half of the Greek army was either decimated, slaughtered, or taken as prisoners. With the booty abandoned by the Greeks, Kemal continued his advance toward Smyrna. On the way to the sea the Turks butchered Armenian and Greek villagers and piled their bodies on top of each other. Soon the stench of the bodies became so unbearable that the Turkish troops had to divert the direction of their march.

Stench or no stench Mustafa Kemal ordered his army to push on before the Allies changed their minds and extended help to their Christian brothers. He did not need to be concerned. The Allies displayed no interest and the Greek army was in full retreat and made no attempt to defend Asia Minor. Most of the Greek commanders were captured and the officers were ordered to find any available means of transport to move the army to the shores of the Aegean Sea. Thousands of Greek soldiers managed to flee toward the Sea of Marmara but the French prevented their escape. Unable to retreat, the Greeks surrendered themselves to the French who promptly delivered them to the Turks, who later executed them.

The Allies were elated by the Turkish victory. To facilitate the Turkish conquest the French and Italians began to increase their military aid to Mustafa Kemal. Through the neutral zone in Constantinople they delivered large quantities of sophisticated weapons to Kemal's Nationalists. Supported by Allied power Mustafa Kemal moved his army to the hills surrounding Smyrna. He paused for a while to prepare for the final assault. The conquest of Smyrna would round off his occupation of the whole of Asia Minor and Anatolia, with the exception of Constantinople. He had already broken the Greek resistance and destroyed King Constantine's infrastructure in Asia Minor.

On September 8, 1922 the Greek soldiers left Smyrna by sea and their military command, headed by one Hadjianesti, an inept general with a mental problem, abandoned all attempts to defend the city.

As the Turkish victory became imminent, the Greek and Armenian community leaders appealed to the steamship companies and to the captains of Allied warships anchored in the harbor for a safe passage for their citizens. There were about two dozen Allied destroyers and battleships in the harbor of Smyrna, but the captains refused to help the Christians. Their instructions were to help only their own nationals. The U. S. State Department issued strict orders to the American Navy personnel stationed in Smyrna to extend help only to the American citizens who were employed by the Standard Oil Company, the American schools, the YMCA and the YWCA. The State Department made it clear to its representatives that the help was to be extended only to those who were native-born American citizens and not the naturalized U. S. citizens of which there were several hundred Armenians and Greeks.

By the first week of September the city was swarmed by hundreds upon thousands of Christian refugees who had fled the Turkish troops. An endless caravan of refugees had come from the surrounding villages where death and destruction had followed the Turkish invasion. With no help from the Allies, the Greeks and Armenians gathered at their respective churches to pray, a scene reminiscent of May 1453 when the Turks were about to enter Constantinople.

On Saturday, September 9,1922, the Turks entered Smyrna and placed their flag on top of the government building. Mobs of Armenians and Greeks gathered in front of the American consulate and schools to gain entrance and seek asylum. The Turkish soldiers dispersed the crowds and ordered the people to go back to their homes. The Turkish troops, assisted by the local Turks, began to loot, plunder and destroy Armenian and Greek stores. The following day Mustafa Kemal entered the city triumphantly at the head of a procession of cars and cavalry. Fifteen days after the start of their offensive, the Turks achieved their objective. To symbolize the attainment of their goal the Turks embarked on demolishing and destroying the city of Smyrna. Their first target was the Armenian quarter.

On Monday, September 11, 1922 the Turks entered the Armenian quarter and began to loot, plunder, and destroy. They went from house to house and took furniture, carpets, jewels, and anything they could get their hands on. They pulled Armenian women by their hair to the streets and raped them and later gave the women to the Turkish mob to finish them off. Armenian men were dragged to the edge of the city and butchered *en masse* and their bodies dumped into pits. Within a few hours the streets of the Armenian quarter were littered with bullet-riddled corpses. The survivors huddled together on street corners. But soon the Turks appeared, herded them to the edge of the town and butchered them with knives to economize on their bullets. Squads of Turkish soldiers ran through the streets and ransacked everything in sight. By Monday evening there were thousands of bodies piled up in the streets of the Armenian quarter, swollen, with their stomachs wide open and flies swarming over them. The Turks had apparently slashed their stomachs open to look for gold and jewels. The Turks decapitated a group of Armenian men and gave the heads to their children to play football with them. They carried away dismembered parts of human bodies from the Armenian quarter. Heaps of human heads, arms and legs were taken to the outskirts of the town and thrown in the field.

On the other side of Smyrna a Turkish mob grabbed the venerable Greek Metropolitan of Smyrna, the head of the Greek community, Archbishop Chrysostomos, dragged him down the street, pushed him inside a Jewish barber shop, put him in the barber's chair, tore off his beard, gouged out his eyes, cut off his ears, then his nose and hands, and using the Archbishop's miter, hit his stomach to pull out the entrails. They then tied the motionless body to the back of a carriage and dragged it in the streets of Smyrna. As the carriage entered the Turkish quarter, some Turks jumped on the carriage, plucking pieces of the Archbishop's body to keep as souvenirs.

In the outskirts of Smyrna the Turks pushed Greek men, women, and children into their church and set the church on fire, burning them all. The Turks made sure no foreign reporter witnessed the scene. Even Ernest Hemingway, who used to share a drink or two with Mustafa Kemal, was not allowed to enter Smyrna.

Directing their attention back to the Armenian quarter, the Turks blocked off the streets leading to the quarter, preventing people from leaving their homes. They brought wagons carrying gasoline tanks and parked them on the streets of the Armenian quarter. On Tuesday night, three days after the Turkish occupation, the Turks set the Armenian quarter on fire. Soon a gusty wind helped the fire to spread to the other parts of the city. The Turks entered the Armenian quarter to prevent the people from fleeing from their burning homes. Those who were courageous enough to attempt to escape were caught and slaughtered on the spot.

Earlier around 2,000 Armenians had sought asylum in the courtyard of the American Collegiate Institute located just outside the Armenian quarter. Within hours the fire reached the American compound and the people were forced to evacuate the buildings. They began to flee towards the waterfront. By Tuesday evening the entire city was on fire. Smyrna had become a veritable inferno. Thousands upon thousands of refugees, women wailing and children crying, thronged to the waterfront with nowhere else to go. Those who knew how to swim began swimming towards the big ships. Others committed suicide by jumping into the water. The entire city was ablaze, including the foreign consulates and the schools.

As night fell, the screaming Christians were pushed into the water. Many drowned, others swam aimlessly. A group of men stricken by panic jumped into the water to try to swim to a boat, but a Turkish soldier shot them, using the shoulder of an

English sailor as a prop for accuracy. A group of Armenian women jumped in the water and managed to get on board a small boat, but the boat overturned. Some women tried to swim back to the shore, but could not make it. A group of French sailors witnessing this incident thought it was amusing, the way the women were struggling to swim. Instead of helping them, they started to take bets on who was going to make it and who was not.

The fire now was two miles long and the quay appeared to be the only safe place. But soon the sweltering heat became so intense that people wanted to jump in the cool water and die. There were half a million people gathered at the quay, sandwiched between the sea and the fire. The people walked aimlessly in a fruitless search for food and shelter. Mothers threw their children on small boats, hoping that the Allied sailors would pick them up from the boats. Roving bands of Turks walked in the crowd, took young girls and boys and raped them as the parents watched in horror.

The Turks spotted an old man walking with his two grandsons, holding them by the hand. Earlier the Turks had killed the children's parents and now the old man was trying to take the children to a safe place. The old man walked straight to the Turks, pleaded for the life of his grandchildren with tears in his eyes, raising his hands in supplication. The Turks erupted into a loud laugh, looking at this pathetic man. They hit the old man, cut off his hands, and left. The children, too young to know, carefully picked up the bloody hands from the ground and said "Here, Grandpa, take your hands."

As the people were wailing for help, the warships of Great Britain, France, the United States and Italy made no attempt to rescue them. They did not want to upset Mustafa Kemal. The captains of these ships were instructed by their respective governments to help their own nationals only. By Wednesday morning the city of Smyrna had become a city of death and destruction, a smoldering wreckage, silhouetted against the sky. Some will describe this tragedy later as the greatest in the history of man, second only to the burning of Carthage. Twenty-five thousand buildings were destroyed. All that remained was Rockefeller's Standard Oil Company complex and the Turkish quarter with its inhabitants unharmed. The beautiful cosmopolitan city, the jewel of the Aegean Sea, was turned into ashes.

The aspiration of the Greeks to establish a Greater Greece with a territory on both sides of the Aegean Sea, a policy which had dominated their life for over one hundred years, went up in the flames of Smyrna.

Mustafa Kemal, after dismissing the event as a "disagreeable incident," began to move his forces to the north to remove the remaining vestiges of the foreign element from the Turkish soil. He issued an ultimatum to the foreign governments to evacuate all surviving Christians from Smyrna by October 1. Otherwise, he warned, they would all be deported to the interior of Turkey and used as slave labor. The Allies were forced to evacuate the refugees. Greek ships, protected by the American Navy, transported around 250,000 Greek and Armenian refugees to the Greek mainland.

The Allies were humiliated. The Turks were victorious and the Treaty of Sèvres was now completely dead. David Lloyd George was forced out of office and the shock of the Greek defeat paralyzed the government in Athens. A revolutionary committee took over the power of the Greek government, forced King Constantine to abdicate, arrested the King's cabinet ministers and executed them by a firing squad.

On October 19, 1922 Turkish Nationalists entered Constantinople amid cheers and celebrations, and the foreign powers withdrew from the Turkish capital. A few weeks later Tevlik Pasha, who was still the Grand Vizier of the Ottoman government, delivered the seal of his office to Sultan Mehmed VI. The Sultan, afraid for his safety, asked the British to help him escape. During a rainy night in November 1922, Sultan Mehmet VI Vahid-ed-Din, the thirty-fifth Sultan of the Ottoman Empire, was whisked out of his palace by the British and taken to the Island of Malta. Osman's dynasty came to an end after almost 640 years of continuous rule. Mustafa Kemal took over the reign of the government, abolished the Sultanate and the Moslem Caliphate, and established a Turkish Republic. For his meritorious accomplishments the Turks bestowed the title of Ataturk, the Father of the Turks, on Mustafa Kemal.

THE TREATY OF LAUSANNE

The humiliated Allies were now anxious to negotiate a peace treaty with Turkey. They hurriedly arranged a conference in

Lausanne. The foreign ministers of the Great Powers, with Is-met Inönü representing the Turkish government, sat down at the negotiating table on November 20, 1922. Ismet, with a talent for distortion and double-talk, deliberately delayed the proceedings, violated diplomatic niceties, even pleaded deafness at times, to get the best advantageous concessions for his government. At the outset of the conference a decision was made to have a compulsory exchange of population between Greece and Turkey. Greece had a Turkish population and Turkey had a Greek population. 1,250,000 Greeks together with 100,000 Armenians were sent to Greece and 390,000 Turks left Greece for Turkey. This compulsory exchange, the first of its kind in modern history, caused cruel hardship to the people involved. The Greeks and Armenians were forced to leave their ancestral homeland in which their forefathers had lived for 3,000 years. This was the end of the Greek presence, culture, and civilization in Asia Minor. The Turks will never again tolerate non-Turkish blood, non-Turkish religion, and culture in their midst.

The Armenians were mentioned only once at the Conference of Lausanne. When Lord Curzon, representing the British government, timidly wanted to introduce the Armenian Question for discussion, Ismet Inönü immediately jumped from his chair and declared that any discussion about Armenia would lead to the breakdown of the conference.

The Treaty of Lausanne was signed on July 24, 1923 and defeated Turkey imposed its own terms on the victorious Allies. The Allies waived all reparations from Turkey. The capitulations, which granted special privileges to foreigners, were abolished, and the Turkish territorial claims were all satisfied.

With the Armenians, Greeks and the Allies out of the way, Mustafa Kemal shifted the center of gravity of Turkish life from the Balkans to Anatolia. To design a new destiny for the Turkish race and mend the uncivilized legacy of his ancestors, he embarked on a vigorous campaign to reshape the historical background of the Turkish people. Kemal organized a Turkish Historical Congress in Ankara and proposed an outlandish theory that the Turks were in fact white Aryan people and the Hittites were their ancestors. He forced the Turkish "scholars" to accept and propagate the theory that the Hittites were Turks and they were in Anatolia long before the Armenians and Greeks. Anatolia, he said, had been a Turkish land since the dawn of civilization. This preposterous theory was the result of an elaborate campaign to give the Turks a more civilized historical background and improve their image, which had been irrevocably tarnished since the Armenian massacres of the late Nineteenth century.

The Lausanne Treaty did not end the Turkish terror against the Armenians. In 1929 the Turkish government deported 30,000 Armenian peasants from Kharpert, Diyarbekir and Mardin; and in 1939 23,000 more were thrown out of Alexandretta when that province was incorporated with Turkey.

While the United States was not a participant at the Lausanne Conference, the State Department reacted favorably to the Treaty to establish good relations with Nationalist Turkey. The American public, however, was opposed to pro-Turkish sentiments. Franklin Delano Roosevelt, then a Wall Street lawyer and a prominent policy maker in the Democratic Party, sent an urgent message to President Harding not to resume relations with Turkey "until the Turkish government shall have recognized the right of the Armenian people to an independent national existence."

Three and a half years after the signing of the Treaty of Lausanne, President Coolidge formally submitted the Lausanne Treaty to the Senate for ratification. On June 18, 1927 the United States Senate categorically rejected the Treaty, declaring that "it would be unfair and unreasonable for the United States to recognize and respect the claim and profession of Mustafa Kemal Pasha so long as he persists in holding control and sovereignty over Armenia, while nearly a million Armenian refugees and exiles are a people without a country."

Undaunted by the Senate's Constitutional block, the Coolidge administration recognized the Turkish Republic using executive powers and exchanged ambassadors. The first Turkish ambassador to Washington was Ahmed Moukhtar, a man accused of being an accomplice in the mass slaughter of the Armenian people.

CHAPTER TWENTY-EIGHT

NO PEACE FOR ARMENIA

As the Armenians were being killed in western Asia Minor, those in Armenia were trying to establish a state out of the ashes of destruction. While the country had no political independence and the policies were dictated by the Kremlin, the placement of the Armenian State within the political framework of the Bolshevik regime irrevocably eradicated the image of the Armenians as the perpetual victims of the Turkish oppression, and protected the people from the encroachments of their neighbors. In a matter of months the Armenian Communists stabilized the political situation, subdued the rebellious Dashnaks and began to build the country's economy with stubborn tenacity. They built factories and power stations, laid down roads and dug canals. Gradually Armenia's economy became industrialized and the volume of industrial production rose dramatically.

The rapid recovery was made possible by the New Economic Plan installed by Lenin in 1921. The plan called for a complete economic centralization, with the Communists controlling all aspects of industrial production and agricultural output. The new plan prompted a major overhaul of the country's economic organization, initiating a period in which private ownership virtually disappeared and commerce and industry came under direct governmental control. This was Socialism all the way, patterned after the Marxist Communist experiment in the north.

Politically the Communists' short term goal was to organize a stable form of government and establish conditions of peace and tranquility that the country needed so desperately. Armenia was still suffering from economic deprivation. In 1922 the harvest yielded less than 60% of the grain needed to feed the people, and the cultivable land was only one-third what it had been in 1914. There were still people dying of starvation. Household goods were sold for food and the peasants ate the grain rather than using it for sowing, and made bread out of filth picked up from the farms. Alexander Miassnikian, the First Secretary of the Armenian Communist Party, a somber man of intellect, assumed the reign of the government and promised the people peace and prosperity through Socialism. A dedicated Communist with a sharp sense of the political needs of the Armenian people, Miassnikian was able to deliver what he promised. Through administrative talent in the government and diplomatic skill with the Kremlin, he was able to increase consumer goods, expand the agricultural output, and provide food and clothing to the people. Out of ashes of poverty grew an industrial organization strong enough to develop commercial contacts with other countries. Miassnikian replaced turmoil and plight with restraint and tranquility, and restored the country to an economic well-being unknown before.

The people accepted their new leader with great enthusiasm and blamed the Dashnaks for having kept Armenia in poverty for so long. The Communists had no political opposition, organized or unorganized. The Dashnak Party was officially outlawed and its leaders were thrown out of the country. The Dashnak regime was advertised to be so deplorable that its repudiation brought visible and immediate dividends to the Communist regime. Economic recovery and political stability stimulated the growth of a cultural environment with the emergence of a new class of Armenian poets and writers, who began to write about the new political order and the fruits of Socialism. A new type of literature came into existence in which Communist heroes who were serving the goals of the Socialist revolution were praised, and those who were fighting to build a new world order were glorified. Objectivity, symbolism, and romanticism were discarded, and creative freedom was restricted. The artist was told to produce art within a rigid framework designed by the Armenian Communist leaders in accordance with instructions from Moscow. Art and literature had to serve a particular purpose they were told, based on Socialist ideology with optimism for the future and realism for the present.

Things began to change, however, when Lenin died and Joseph Stalin rose to power as the omnipotent ruler of the Soviet Union. Beginning in 1928 Stalin initiated a series of five-year economic plans to centralize the country's economic organization even more, in an attempt to increase the economic output. Marxist theories and Lenin's pragmatic ideas were blended into a new economic institution. The new catch-word was collectivization. Farmers were required to produce more, and workers were required to meet targets of industrial production. Stalin wanted to make the Soviet Union a world power quickly, forcing everyone to sacrifice for the State with an unflinching devotion to the Socialist cause. "We are a hundred years behind the advanced countries," he declared in 1931. "We must make good this distance in ten years." He did. In 1941 the Soviet Union was only ten years away from becoming the most advanced industrialized country in the Western world.

The rapid and miraculous transformation was made possible by the brutality of Joseph Stalin and the heroism of the Soviet people. The harsh measures of collectivization caused famine and economic upheaval in which millions died of starvation, thousands were exiled to Siberia, and millions of political opponents were arrested and murdered. Shortage of food and ineffective agricultural policy brought the country to the brink of economic depression. But Stalin achieved his objectives. He increased the industrial production, demolished obsolete plants and built new factories. He built dams to provide vital electricity for the uphill progress of the Soviet Union and produced energy resources in a way no other ruler of Russia has ever been able to achieve.

Stalin's economic programs proved to be painful to the Armenian people. Armenian officials were ordered to use harsh measures to subdue the Armenian farmers into a collective farm. Most of them resisted the program. The rebels were arrested and exiled, and others fled to Persia to avoid terror. Those who wanted to keep their private farms were almost completely wiped out, along with millions of Russian Kulaks in the north. By the early 1930's most of the Armenian farms were collectivized with their livestock and farm implements. But instead of placing their animals in a common pool, some farmers destroyed everything in their possession. The compulsory program of collectivization and deliberate slaughter of livestock resulted in famine in Armenia in the early 1930's. Thousands died of starvation; others fled the country in a desperate search for food.

Beginning in 1935 the forced agricultural programs began to produce some results. Agricultural techniques were mechanized and consumer cooperatives were developed. Cultivated land in the *Kolkhozes*, collective farms, and the *Sovkhozes*, state farms, began to produce enough crops to feed the people, and the country found itself on the road to recovery.

THE GREAT PURGES

While Miassnikian had gained considerable popularity and respect in Armenia and was largely responsible for giving the country a political and economic stability, he was not a member of Stalin's inner circle which generally ran the affairs of the Soviet Union. He was overthrown in 1930 and replaced with Aghasi Khanjian, a twenty-nine-year-old youth from Van, a true Communist and a friend to Stalin. Khanjian initiated a period of terror in Armenia, in which the so-called "enemies of the State and Socialism" were purged and executed. Writers and political activists who refused to follow the party line were either executed or shipped to Siberia, and those who had contact with them were discredited.

Khanjian's brutal rule forced the professional people, doctors, teachers, and scientists, whose skills Armenia needed so desperately, to flee the country. The centralist policy of the Bolshevik leaders paved the way for a Russification program in Armenia. There were people in the Soviet hierarchy, Stalin being one of them, who despised anything non-Russian. Russian became the official language of the State, and Armenian nationalist literature was banned in public schools.

Paradoxically, it was during this period of the Great Purge that Stalin introduced a new Constitution for the Soviet Union, a constitution with all the trappings of democracy, liberty, freedom, and human rights. It guaranteed freedom of speech, assembly, religious worship, and the propagation of the virtues of individual rights. The Constitution even allowed a Soviet republic to secede freely from the Union if it so desired. Stalin's

Constitution was a complete mockery. In spite of this clear-cut
stipulation in the Constitution, no republic dared to declare itself independent. The bicameral legislature, which pretended
to be a democratic institution similar to the U.S. Congress,
proved to be a rubber stamp assembly of men ready to carry
out Stalin's orders.

Khanjian's purges in Armenia were not effective enough,
however, for a Communist leader in Georgia who had become
increasingly anxious to win Stalin's confidence and act as the
supreme ruler of the Caucasus. His name was Lavrenti Beria,
the First Secretary of the Transcaucasian Communist Party.
Beria was jealous of Khanjian's close association with Stalin.
Motivated by a desire for power, he maneuvered his political
machine and through coercion and manipulation, succeeded in
accusing Khanjian of failing to comply with party directives.
Beria's men began to arrest Armenian government leaders and
Khanjian's political proteges. Ter Gabrielian, the Chairman of
the People's Commissars in 1935 was interrogated for seven
hours by NKVD agents, and was hit in the head with an iron
bar and thrown out of the window.

To make his accusations appear credible Beria prepared
show-trials in the Caucasus in kangaroo courts, and with a complete lack of evidence and trumped-up charges prosecuted most
of the people arrested. He accused Khanjian of collaborating
with the enemies of Socialism, a vague indictment with irrevers-
ible judgment. Khanjian was arrested in 1936 and brought to
Beria's office for interrogation. Beria upon entering his office,
took his revolver out and shot Khanjian in the head. But since
no prior approval had been obtained from the Kremlin, his killing of Khanjian was kept secret.

Stalin was violently enraged when he heard of Khanjian's
murder. He sent his trusted associates, Malenkov and Mikoyan,
to the Caucasus to investigate. Beria now concocted a story
about Khanjian's assassination. He accused the entire leadership of the Armenian Central Committee of the crime that he
himself had committed. Amatouni, the First Secretary of the
Armenian Communist Party, together with the Second Secretary, the Chairman of the Council of the People's Commissars,
the head of the local NKVD, and the entire leadership of Armenia's Central Committee, and the Council of People's Commissars were arrested as "enemies of the people" on charges of

organizing the murder of Aghasi Khanjian. About 3,500 Armenian officials were executed by firing squad without trial.

For the next three years Armenians were hit with Beria's terror. Fabricated charges against Armenian leaders sent most of them to Siberia. Stalin's henchmen liquidated (a fashionable word then) thousands of Armenians. Tens of thousands of Armenian men and women were put in jail and when the jails became overcrowded, they were shipped to Siberia.

Beginning in 1936 Armenia became a virtual prison camp in which nobody felt secure, from the Party Secretary to the common man. Death and suffering followed Beria's show-trials. An entire generation of Armenian Communist leaders was executed. People began to implicate each other to put themselves free of suspicion. Every member of a family was ordered to spy on the rest of the family. Even children were used to testify against their parents. Anybody talking to a relative of a person who was accused of being an "enemy of the people" was himself arrested and sent to Siberia. Wives were forced to disavow their husbands. Friends betrayed friends. Lots of them.

Armenian church properties were seized. Armenian priests were persecuted and molested. Most of the Armenian churches were ordered closed and atheistic literature was distributed throughout the country.

The properties of the Echmiadzin Monastery were confiscated, including the printing press, the museum and the library. The farm lands belonging to the Armenian Church were taken away and given to the collective farms. The Bolsheviks imposed a heavy tax on the Armenian monastery. Holy Echmiadzin found itself in the most desperate financial condition. The Catholicate was forced to sell farm implements and cattle for food. There was no food for the clergy.

Kevork V, the Supreme Catholicos of all Armenians appealed to the Armenians in the diaspora for financial aid. But gifts received from abroad were immediately confiscated by the NKVD. A wealthy Armenian from abroad sent the aging Catholicos an expensive car, but upon arrival in Batum the car was promptly delivered to Lavrenti Beria for his use.

Most of the priests were exiled to Siberia. The city of Erevan had only two priests, who were required to report to the NKVD office every day. Some Armenian churches were converted into movie houses, and others into warehouses and stables. If a village priest was bold enough to celebrate Mass, the NKVD agent prevented people from entering the church. No one was allowed to attend the church services at Holy Echmiadzin. When the Supreme Catholicos Kevork V died in May 1930 those who wished to attend the funeral were required to have a special permit from the NKVD. Kevork's successor, Catholicos Khoren, was murdered mysteriously eight years later.

The people who observed the Armenian religious holidays were punished. The Communist government substituted Lenin's Anniversary, January 21, for the Armenian Christmas Day, January 6. University students were forced to organize clubs to disseminate anti-Christian propaganda. Sunday, because of its religious connotation, ceased to be a weekly holiday. The workers were required to stagger their holidays, by taking one day off after working six consecutive days.

Beria's terror continued day after day, night after night. The people lived in an atmosphere of constant fear, conspiracy, lies, suspicion, intrigue, deceit, and physical danger. Nobody was certain when their time would come, whether there would be a knock on the door in the middle of the night, or if they might be taken away while walking on the street.

The NKVD network in Armenia had two types of operatives, called *Seksots*. One was voluntary and the other involuntary. The voluntary was the enthusiastic Armenian, the true believer, ready to denounce his parents, neighbors, friends, for the Communist cause. The involuntary *Seksot* was the one who had joined the NKVD ranks out of fear. Both were pressured by the NKVD high command to produce names and report people. Out of fear these stool pigeons reported people indiscriminately on imaginary, fictitious or false charges, just to save their skin. If the Armenian peasants were hoarding grain, instead of giving it to the *Kolkhos,* they were reported as the '"enemies of the people," arrested and shipped to Siberia. If the Armenian farmer refused to join the collective farms, he was reported and sent to Siberia. Twenty-five thousand such farmers were arrested and sent to Siberia. If the workers were slow doing their jobs, they were reported and put in jail. If the teacher was bold enough to lecture about the Armenian religion, he was promptly reported and sent to Siberia. If the director of a factory was caught using the state car for his personal use, he was arrested and sent to jail.

The Purge was an unprecedented criminal conspiracy, legitimized by laws and rules, organized and directed in the Caucasus by Lavrenti Beria, Commissar and Stalin's hatchet man. In time this conspiracy was transformed into a mass terror by its sheer process of association. Anybody associated with the accused person, even remotely, was himself accused and put in jail. People were accused at random. Past associations were distorted. Guilt came not only by accusation but also by association. A person accused of a crime carried with him an entire unit, organization, or a neighborhood. The first question a prisoner was asked when arrested was "Who are your accomplices?" From one arrest hundreds of others followed, producing a monumental mushroom effect.

Association with the Dashnaks was particularly fatal. To have had anything to do with the Dashnaks was enough reason for arrest. Even people having connections with the Dashnaks abroad automatically became suspect. An Armenian receiving a gift from a Dashnak abroad was arrested and sent to Siberia together with all the members of his family. He received an eight-year sentence, the family six years.

If occasionally an NKVD agent had shown some sympathy towards an Armenian prisoner, when caught for his act, he was promptly arrested on charges of "intolerable pity for the enemies of the people," and was sent to Siberia along with the prisoner. Failure to report a person was also considered a crime. An Armenian man was arrested for failing to report another Armenian for refusing to hang Stalin's picture in his living room. They were both arrested. But the first one received a harsher sentence.

Sometimes people were sent to jail for no reason at all, but since the prison authorities needed a manifesto of charges to accompany the prisoner, the ones arrested were beaten up to squeeze some crime out of them, any crime, no matter how insignificant the crime may have been, just to make the document look acceptable. Most people were sent to Siberia on charges of unspecified wrongful acts. "Enemy of the people" was good enough. There was no need for proof.

Bolsheviks decreed harsh and extraordinary penalties, including death sentences to 12-year-olds, throwing the country into the midst of a savage game of conspiracy. It was the constant changing of the rules of the game, penalties, decrees, codes or statutes that forced everyone to be on the alert. Their lives were at stake.

The entire country seemed to have been inhabited by people who appeared to be "dead people on furlough," as Lenin was fond of saying. The Armenians were exhausted by history's cruel fate. They lived in a perilous time. After being subjected to Turkish atrocities for years, they were now being subjected to a Communist oppression of unusual magnitude and intensity. The people were not even sure which one was worse, the Turkish massacres or Stalin's terror. Both had the same intensity and brutality. The massacres were final, but the terror was an ongoing process. For both Stalin and the Turks, it was merely an instrument of policy. Stalin's policy was to terrorize the people to force them to submit to his rule. The Turks' policy was to annihilate the people to eliminate the Armenians from their sphere of influence.

Since the Armenians were considered a minority in other parts of the Soviet Union, they were an easy target for extermination. In 1937 six hundred Armenians were massacred in Kharkov and hundreds of pockets of Armenian communities in the Crimea were eliminated. The people were either sent to Siberia or massacred. No one was certain.

The political experience of the Armenians and their national woes have inspired the Armenian writers to write about the national spirit, freedom, independence, and virtues of liberty. When Stalin's purge began, the Armenian writers were hard hit. They became the most vulnerable. The NKVD assumed that the Armenian intellectuals were conducting hostile acts against the Soviet system. The NKVD attack against the intellectuals began as early as 1927 and during the course of a few years, the writers were charged as ex-Dashnaks or ex-Mensheviks and arrested. The Bolsheviks labeled the Armenian intellectuals as political malcontents ready to overthrow the government at any time.

Any Armenian writer expressing any sentiments towards Armenian nationalism was interrogated for several hours before being sent to the firing squad or Siberia. The Armenian historians were exiled for failing to interpret the Armenian history in terms of Marxist-Leninist ideology. They were allowed to write only about those events that suited the Communist cause. The entire Armenian history was rewritten in such a way that the people's national struggle for survival had become "struggles for the proletariat" or "peasant uprising against the bourgeoisie nationalists." Events or episodes in the Armenian history which were considered reactionary were either omitted or changed to fit the Party line.

There were NKVD agents planted in every classroom at the University to inform on the professor. An entire generation of Armenians was born and raised without any knowledge about the Turkish atrocities or the Armenian Genocide. Writers were told to produce pro-Soviet conformist literature. The Armenian literature became contaminated by the most unpleasant adulation of Stalin and Beria. People writing about Armenian nationalism were shot or exiled to Siberia along with the editor who apparently was not diligent enough to scrutinize the work before publication. The objective was to eradicate ethnic nationalism.

Every piece of literature, art, or music was subject to intense editing and scrutiny. Yeghisheh Charents, a poet with considerable renown, was arrested and executed because one of his poems contained a message of Armenian nationalism. The editor, assigned to scrutinize the work before publication, had not detected Charents' message because the poet had cleverly hidden the message in the form of an acrostic by using the second letter of each line. Reading vertically from top to bottom, the message read, "Oh, Armenian people, your only salvation is in your united strength." This was a crime punishable by death.

A noted Armenian poet, Gourgen Mahari, was arrested in 1936 on trumped-up charges of nationalism. He was lucky. He survived the prison cells and the labor camps in Siberia. He was released in the late 1940's but re-arrested a few weeks later on fresh charges. He was finally released in 1954, after Stalin's death.

Some writers avoided the wave of the purge by acting tough with the NKVD agents. This was indeed a rare incident. H. Ajarian, the distinguished philologist, was arrested by the NKVD and interrogated for seven hours. Ajarian became enraged when at one point the NKVD agent tried to accuse him of espionage for the Turks. For an Armenian that was the ultimate insult. It was one thing to be an enemy of Socialism and the Proletarian cause, but it was another thing to be a spy for

killed. Fourteen out of sixteen army commanders were shot to death, all the admirals of the navy vanished through the night. Twenty-eight out of thirty-nine Armenian generals of the Red Army were executed by firing squads. Sixty out of sixty-seven Corp commanders were executed, and one hundred thirty-six out of one hundred ninety-nine Divisional commanders were shot to death. More than half of the army's officer corps were either shot or sent to Siberia. All these purges were to the delight of Adolph Hitler. With the backbone of the Soviet military might swept away, the Nazi leader was now ready to launch an all-out military campaign to invade the Soviet Union and execute his policy of *lebensraum*. By then he had already absorbed Austria and Czechoslovakia, conquered France and driven the British back to the British Isles.

THE GREAT PATRIOTIC WAR

Hitler's invasion of the Soviet Union was swift, sudden and unexpected. It began on June 22, 1941. Stalin was so stunned that it took him several days before he realized what was happening. He isolated himself in his *dacha* and regained his composure only several weeks later to supervise the military operations. Hitler's army was enormously powerful. Three million men, 600,000 armored vehicles, and 500,000 horses began to move into the Soviet Union across a front which stretched 850 miles from the Baltics to the Carpathians. Within a short period of time the German *luftwaffe* decimated the Red Army units and the German army placed itself at the outskirts of Leningrad, not too far away from the heartland of the Soviet Union. The Ukraine was gone, the Baltic republics were gone, and most of Byelorussia came under German occupation.

In a public address to the nation Stalin appealed to the conscience of the Soviet people to save the Motherland. Armenia's response was spontaneous. The smallest of the republics with a population of only a few million, Armenia's contribution to the war cause was tremendous. Half a million Armenian soldiers, 50 generals, and 3 admirals joined the Soviet force in the north, ready to crush the Nazi power. The Armenians in the diaspora contributed large sums of money to the Armenian army.

Not all Armenians were supportive, however. General Dro, the revolutionary hero and an important Dashnak leader, who had left Armenia immediately after the Communist take-over, recruited a commando unit of 20,000 Armenians and marched through the Soviet Union alongside the German army to reconquer Armenia and establish an independent state. For the Armenians this was a treasonable act against the Mother-land, even though most of them did not particularly cherish the Communist rule over their country. Just as the Americans have a saying "My country, right or wrong," the Armenians have similar sentiments about their country: "Whether it is in the right or in the wrong, it is my country, Armenia".

With German help, Dro was able to reach the northern part of the Caucasus, but could not proceed further. In a great offensive in the summer of 1942 the Germans were able to cap-ture Rostov-on-Don, pushing through southern Ukraine and placing themselves on the road to the Caucasus. If Dro wanted to recapture Armenia, Hitler wanted to reach Baku and take control of the Azeri oil fields. By then the Soviet military orga-nization was in a precarious situation. The morale of the fight-ing men was at the lowest and millions of Soviet soldiers were either killed or taken prisoner.

In July 1942 the German control of the Caucasus appeared to be imminent. The Western Allies were afraid that a succes-sful German push through the Caucasus would encourage neu-tral Turkey to join the Axis powers, invade Armenia, and proceed east to join the German forces near the shores of the Caspian Sea. This was not an outlandish speculation. Several days before the German invasion of Russia, Turkey signed a friendship treaty with Nazi Germany. When the Germans proved to be victorious during the early stages of the war, a Pan-Turkish Nationalist movement was organized in Turkey, supported by the government with the express purpose of in-vading Armenia, occupying Azerbeijan and gaining control of the Baku oil fields.

In this desperate hour Stalin issued a rallying cry, ordering every Soviet soldier and citizen to fight to the last drop of blood, in order to save the country. The Germans continued their push eastward, and in early September they managed to reach Stalingrad. This would be their last stop. They would not be able to proceed further.

Stalin's rallying cry spurred the Soviets to fight for their life. They began a massive counteroffensive in November 1942 and through a series of epic battles were able to break the back of the Nazi war machine and decimate the German military structure in the east. Three hundred thousand German troops were killed, and Hitler was forced to retreat. The Soviet victory at Stalingrad was the turning point of the war. It stopped the German threat to the Soviet heartland.

Dro and his Armenian commandos never reached the Armenian borders. They were thrown back with the Germans and in time vanished as a military organization. Most of the Armenian recruits were either killed or taken prisoner. The Soviet forces reoccupied the country piece by piece and chased the Germans to the west. The final Soviet offensive was launched in January 1945. By then most of eastern Europe was under Soviet occupation. The battle against Berlin began in April 1945. The city fell on May 2. It was the Armenian army headed by Colonel Safarian which made the first entry into Berlin. Aram Garents was one of the Armenian soldiers who fought their way through the gates of the Reichstag. Aram was the lad who was rescued by a Russian battleship in the Black Sea in 1915 when the Turkish ship carrying him and other Armenian refugees dumped the passengers in the sea after leaving the Trabizond harbor during the tragic days of the Armenian Genocide. Aram Garents became the first Allied soldier who climbed up the highest point of the Reichstag and mounted the Soviet flag symbolizing the end of the European war. Standing on top of the Reichstag which was once the symbol of the German war power, Aram screamed to no one in particular, "You Germans, you helped the Turks to kill my mother and my people in 1915. I have now conquered you to take my revenge."

POST-WAR PERIOD

The Soviet victory created the greatest public euphoria in the Soviet Empire. But the war had seriously damaged the country's economic infrastructure. Most of the productive capacity had been destroyed, and more than twenty million people had been killed. While the Armenian territory escaped the ravages of the war the country simply went hungry as the economic programs were geared towards the war effort. The victory changed the fortunes of the Armenian people, however. The leadership of the Kremlin never forgot the significant contribution of the small republic to the nation's war effort. More than twenty thousand Armenian soldiers were awarded medals for their bravery; one hundred of them became Heroes of the Soviet Union, and fifty of them became marshalls, generals, and admirals in the armed services.

Stalin ordered some Armenian churches to be opened, anti-church activities were toned down, the seminary of Holy Echmiadzin was reopened and Armenians were allowed to elect Kevork VI as the Supreme Catholicos of the Armenian Church in 1945. The seat had been left vacant since the murder of his predecessor in 1938.

It was during this period of euphoria that the Armenians throughout the world began to nurture their old dream of repatriation and territorial rights. In a personal letter addressed to Joseph Stalin, the newly elected Catholicos urged the Soviet leader to help the Armenians annex Western Armenian provinces still occupied by the Turks to Soviet Armenia and allow the Armenians in the diaspora to repatriate to their homeland. The letter created a tumultuous response in the Armenian communities around the world. About 120,000 Armenians from the Middle East, Europe and the United States immigrated to Armenia. The Armenian political parties, the Dashnak, Hunchak, and Ramgavar, organized a world-wide campaign to urge the world leaders to exert pressure on Turkey to release the provinces of Kars and Ardahan to Soviet Armenia. Some were even bold enough to demand the implementation of the map of Armenia issued by Woodrow Wilson in November 1920.

During the deliberations at the Potsdam Conference which was convened in July 1945 to reshape the post-war world, Stalin raised the issue of Kars and Ardahan but Churchill and Truman were vehemently against it. By then Stalin had already taken control of most of the territories he aspired for. At the Yalta Conference a few months earlier, the Allied powers had agreed to grant Stalin the right to occupy most of eastern Europe. Stalin was not too anxious, therefore, to press the Kars-Ardahan issue lest the discussion of new territorial claims would encourage London and Washington to reopen new discussion of the old territorial acquisitions. But if Stalin did not want to solve the Armenian territorial issue diplomatically, he chose to do it militarily. Tension reached a flash point when Stalin, after denouncing the Turco-Soviet Treaty of 1925, dispatched two armored divisions towards the Turkish frontier in the east while ordering Soviet forces in Bulgaria to advance south to exert military pressure on Turkey in the west. Stalin's military operation was inconclusive, however. He was forced to withdraw soon after on orders from the newly formed United Nations Security Council. But the Armenians in the diaspora did not give up. They continued to press the Kars-Ardahan issue through diplomatic channels.

In May 1947 a delegation of Armenian political leaders appealed to the U. S. Secretary of State, Dean Acheson, for the annexation of Kars and Ardahan to the Armenian Republic, but the U. S. government refused to encourage such changes in the *status quo* between Turkey and Soviet Armenia, and allow Stalin to have more land at the expense of the West. By then Turkey had joined the western camp and the cold war was in full steam.

THE BEGINNING OF A NEW ERA

Armenia became the center of teeming activity after Stalin's death. The new Communist regime in Moscow ushered in a new era of cultural and scientific achievement with a resurgence of hope for a better life. By the early 1960's Armenia became one of the most industrialized republics of the Soviet Union with a well-organized economic structure. In cultural and scientific accomplishments it surpassed most of the countries in the Communist world. Literature, opera, ballet, art were in full bloom. The poems of Yeghisheh Charents and other writers, whose works were banned during the purge of the 1930s, were reinstated. The Soviets built hydro-electric, thermal and nuclear power stations in Armenia, expanding the country's industrial capacity. Irrigation projects were put into operation. Canals were constructed utilizing the water from the Arax River. Cotton textile factories were established. Armenia became an important producer of electric motors, power transformers, machine tools, instruments, computers, leather goods, carpets, textiles, high quality cognac and wine, and food preserves. The economic growth was made possible by the more liberalized administration of Nikita Krushchev.

Life in post-war Armenia became less harsh. Consumer products helped the people to raise their standard of living.

The rationing of basic commodities was discontinued and new technical and scientific research institutes were established to enhance industrial technology. Agriculture became mechanized, with more land in cultivation and new irrigation systems were put in place.

New schools, colleges, theaters, museums, and libraries were opened, and philharmonic societies were established. Armenia made tremendous strides in the field of science: astrophysics, stellar astronomy, chemistry of silicates and polymers, with scientists such as Victor Ambartzumian achieving a worldwide reputation. The Armenian Academy of Sciences made Erevan one of the most important centers of scientific research in the Soviet Union. Composer Aram Khatchadourian received an international reputation. A new cadre of poets, writers, artists, composers, and architects came into existence. If the motto of the great Communist Revolution that swept Armenia in 1920 was "everything for the good of men, in the name of men," the revolution appeared to have achieved its goal in the 1960's. Stalin and Beria were gone, and the Armenians began to congratulate themselves for having endured the harsh regime of the 1930's.

There was something lacking, however. The favorable treatment accorded the Armenians did nothing to satisfy their thirst for nationalism. The Soviet society was still a monolithic closed society and the Communist rigidity continued. Krushchev, while projecting himself as a lovable ruler with enlightened domestic and foreign policies, proved to be as dictatorial as his predecessors. The Armenians were still prevented from observing their national holidays, and manifestations of religion were oppressed. While traditionally they preferred authoritarian rule over anarchy, the moment the rule was relaxed, they were the first to press for freedom and liberty. This has been the case throughout their political experience, as they were forced to live under a variety of despotic rulers. The somewhat relaxed policies of Stalin's successors and increase in dissent encouraged the Armenians to do just that. It began in 1965 when the entire population of the Armenian capital, over a million people, went on strike and marched in the streets of Erevan in defiance of Soviet orders to mark the fiftieth anniversary of the Armenian Genocide. This was a mass demonstration of nationalism unheard of in the history of the Soviet Union. The Kremlin could do nothing to stop it. There were some outbreaks of hostilities between the Soviet police and Armenians, but the demonstration went on as planned. In retaliation Moscow fired the First Secretary of the Armenian Communist Party, and installed a new government, mostly dominated by the Russians, with instructions to place restrictions over the Armenian affairs. The fire of nationalism had already been ignited, however, and it was difficult for the Soviets to put it out.

The number of Armenian political activists and nationalists increased considerably when Brezhnev came to power. In the 1970's the cozy relationship with the West had made modern ideas and practices more alluring to the Soviet citizens. Manifestations of nationalism forced the Kremlin to relax the policies on nationalities, and Brezhnev's new Constitution emphasized the multi-nationalist nature of the Soviet Union. The Kremlin even allowed the Armenians to erect a monument on top of a hill, called Dzidzernagapert, the Castle of the Sparrows near Erevan, to commemorate the Genocide of 1915. The monument, with its 12 stone slabs representing the 12 Armenian provinces lost to Turkey, came to symbolize the rise of Armenian nationalism.

It was during this period in the early 1970's that the Armenians urged the Kremlin leaders to reconsider their territorial claims over the province of Karabagh, which was taken away from them during the reshaping of the Caucasian republics.

KARABAGH

Since the 1920's, the province of Karabagh, administratively known as Nagorno-Karabagh (mountainous Karabagh in Russian), had been under an Azeri jurisdiction with Armenians constituting 85 per cent of the population. To weaken the legitimacy of the Armenian claim over the territory the Azeri government, during the post-Stalin era, had begun to colonize the province with Azeri Turks. This was the same policy that the Azeris had successfully implemented earlier in the province of Nakhichevan, another historic Armenian territory, tilting the demographics of the region in their favor, making Nakhichevan a *de facto* Azeri territory, thus preventing the Armenians from placing claims over the land.

The Azeri encroachments into areas predominantly dominated by Armenians prompted those in Armenia to press for the annexation of Karabagh into the Republic of Armenia. It was not easy for Moscow to honor such requests. While some of the Soviet hierarchy considered the Armenian claim legitimate, they feared that the remapping of the Caucasus would open Pandora's box of other demands by other groups for territorial alterations.

The pro-Armenian sentiments in the Kremlin in the early 1970's were generally made in deference to the veteran Armenian Communist, Anastas Mikoyan, who had earlier served as Chairman of the Supreme Soviet. At the time Mikoyan was the only surviving member of the original team of 1917 Bolshevik Revolutionaries, and as such had a considerable influence in the Moscow Politburo. His survival was a remarkable achievement. He had been a member of the Politburo since 1926, and a full member of the Communist Party's Central Committee. He had worked closely with Stalin in the Caucasus during the early stages of the Communist Revolution, and had never been in favor of Stalin's decision to place Karabagh under an Azeri jurisdiction.

Mikoyan played a significant role in the Caucasian Bureau of the Communist Party and had been able to convince the members of the Bureau at a meeting held in July 1921 to vote in favor of Armenia and decree to transfer Karabagh to Armenia. But the following day Stalin illegally reversed the decision in favor of the Azeris.

Mikoyan survived Stalin's purges of the 1930's principally because of his versatility and clever diplomatic skill in keeping his thoughts to himself and siding always with the winners. As a true diplomat, he knew how to keep his loyalty to the people around him, particularly when his personal interests were at stake.

In spite of his important position in the Communist hierarchy, Mikoyan was a type of man who had never been bold enough to press his own convictions on the affairs of the government. He was an indispensable counsel to Stalin, but he seemed to be more preoccupied with his personal struggle for survival in the rough and tumble of Soviet life than with the nationalist struggle of his countrymen. During his association with General Andranik in the Armenian revolutionary period, Andranik liked to chide Mikoyan for his lack of courage. "Anastas, you intellectuals, you cannot even shoot a mouse.

You are afraid that a group of mice would come and attack you," Andranik used to say.

In 1953 Mikoyan proved Andranik wrong. Immediately after Stalin's death in 1953 the evil man of the NKVD, Lavrenti Beria, began to refurbish the image of the Soviet intelligence to expand his influence in the Politburo. His action raised the possibility of new purges. The memory of the old purges was still fresh in the minds of the rulers who succeeded Stalin. Nobody felt secure with Beria around. A decision was made, therefore, to get rid of him, and there is widespread belief that Mikoyan was chosen to do the job. While the official version of the circumstances surrounding Beria's death was a trial and execution in December 1953, Krushchev told an Italian delegation in 1954 that Beria was actually shot to death on the spot in June 1953 at a meeting of the Presidium and that it was Mikoyan who had emptied his revolver into Beria's head.

Mikoyan's deed was never forgotten, and things began to change rapidly. With his renewed prestige, Mikoyan began to act in the interest of the Armenian people. During his tours around the world in the late 1950's, Mikoyan visited the Armenian communities in the diaspora and urged the Armenians to repatriate to their homeland. He protected the Armenian interests, at times surreptitiously, and represented the Republic of Armenia in the Soviet hierarchy. He could have been called the father of Soviet Armenia, because he was the one who persuaded Joseph Stalin in 1936 to make Armenia one of the republics of the U.S.S.R. During the framing of the Soviet Constitution Stalin had planned to deny the status of republic to Armenia, since the country had less than one million people at the time. Mikoyan's influence did not last long, however. Just when the Armenians needed him the most, he decided to retire from public life in 1974, leaving the Armenians unprotected. With Mikoyan's retirement, the Karabagh issue went into remission.

THE ERA OF GLASNOST

The territorial dispute over Karabagh came back to life in the mid 1980's when Mikhail Gorbachev assumed the leadership of the Soviet Union and introduced the terms of Glasnost and Perestroika in the Soviet political lexicon. The era of Glasnost promised to bring political and economic reforms and a new surge of confidence to the Soviet people. Glasnost invoked the people to assert their national identities, and the Armenians were the first to jump on the bandwagon. In adopting the policies of Glasnost, Moscow created the conditions for nationalities to organize their own political force. Before Glasnost, they were all Soviet citizens, living in the brotherhood of the "Worker's Paradise." But Glasnost changed the multi-nationalist nature of the Soviet Union, giving the people the freedom to seek political self-determination within the framework of the Soviet Union.

Gorbachev's new era of openness and freedom of expression, which professed to signify a period of rising expectations, proved to be an illusion with no expectations for the Armenians in Karabagh. They saw no difference between Stalin's rule and Glasnost. They were harassed by the Soviet KGB (the new name for the NKVD) and the Azeri police. The Armenians in Karabagh were, in effect, faced with double jeopardy. Not only were they required to conform themselves to the Soviet authoritative rule, but also suffer indignities of life caused by their Azeri governors. They were prisoners in their own home. Nobody cared to respond to their plight.

Late in 1987 the Armenians in Karabagh petitioned Moscow to allow the annexation of their province with the State of Armenia. Armenians in Erevan organized mass demonstrations in support of their brothers in Karabagh, but Moscow was quick to suppress such nationalist movements, and promptly arrested the leaders of the Armenian community in Karabagh. In a terse statement issued in February 1988 the Kremlin declared that Karabagh belonged to the Azeris and the Armenians had no right to the land.

Moscow's statement enraged the Armenians. Over one million people poured into the streets of Erevan to protest against the Kremlin's decision. Panicked by this public outrage, Gorbachev called the Armenian leaders to Moscow. He used flattery to try to pacify them, but promised nothing and the meeting proved to be fruitless. The Armenians returned home empty-handed, and Moscow refused to reverse its decision. Mass demonstrations in Erevan continued, and the Armenians went on a general strike to paralyze the government's operation.

In the Soviet political experience the Russians are not noted for having the skill to solve historical disputes, particularly

those caused by their own people. At the onset of the Communist Revolution Lenin thought that the problem of nationalities
would eventually go away and the Soviet people would unite,
not as Armenians or Ukrainians, but as workers or citizens of a
common united country, similar to the process of assimilation of
the great melting pot of the United States. National boundaries
meant nothing to him, since the proletariat of the workers would
eventually triumph and national identities would fade away.

While Lenin planned for a universal identification of people, blending them in a Communist loyalty along class lines,
Stalin worked for the disappearance of nationalities through oppressive and military strength. Both of them failed. The proletariat did not win. The moment Gorbachev allowed the
nationalities to speak out, they all rose, almost in unison, to demand political self-determination.

For the Armenians if Glasnost spurred dissent and offered
them courage to pursue their political aspirations, it also provided the spark that ignited such a fierce nationalistic movement
that it almost became unmanageable for Moscow to contain.
The National Security Advisor to President Carter once wrote
that Karl Marx referred to the Czar's Empire as a prison of nations. Stalin made it the graveyard of nations and Gorbachev
made it the volcano of nations. It was not too surprising to see
that Armenia, the smallest of the republics, would be the first
volcano to erupt when Gorbachev ushered in the new era.

Seven decades of Communist rule were enough to convince the Armenians that the time had come for them to seek
another political structure, this time based on the principles of
democracy and the virtues of liberty and freedom. Glasnost
gave the Armenians an awareness that Communism had failed
socially and politically and had lost its sense of infallibility.
While it was able to transform underdeveloped Armenia into a
modern state, it eroded Armenia's sense of dignity and made
the Armenian person a mindless robot in the monolithic world
of the Communist ideology.

Glasnost was both a blessing and a curse to the Armenian
people. It gave many the opportunity to pursue their political
aspirations, but it gave others the opportunity to leave the
homeland and build a new life elsewhere. If Mikoyan urged
the Armenians in the diaspora to return to the homeland, many
already in the homeland, decided to leave and go to foreign

lands in quest of safety. They were too exhausted to continue their struggle for survival in the harsh realities of the Soviet regime.

THE EXODUS TO THE DIASPORA

Since the latter part of the 1970's there has been a steady outward flow of Armenians to foreign lands. Thousands of Armenians have emigrated from Armenia and settled in the Middle East, Europe and North America. The debilitating aspect of life in the Soviet Union had made life in the diaspora sweeter and safer. The Armenians felt no guilt in leaving the country of their ancestors. When meeting other Armenians, born and raised in the diaspora, who looked at them with contempt for deserting the Motherland, they simply suggested that perhaps it was now their turn to go and live in the Armenian homeland and endure the harsh realities of life that had been their fate for all their life. After decades of repressive regimes in which they saw themselves as strangers in their own home, these people preferred to continue to live as Armenians without the geographic attachment to the Motherland. They thought it would be easier to be an Armenian in France than an Armenian in Armenia. But they were mistaken.

The long and crowded history of the Armenian diaspora is a sad one. Going back to the period of the Armenian emigration to Poland in the Eleventh century, rarely has there been an Armenian community in a foreign land that has been able to maintain its identity and preserve the national heritage on a sustained basis. They lived in separate communities at first, bonded together by common language and tradition. They built their churches and schools and continued to glue themselves to the Motherland. They observed their national holidays and occasionally sent contributions to Holy Echmiadzin, but in the end they failed to flourish as an independently separate group of people. They lost their passion to continue to preserve the national identity when forces of assimilation in the foreign land proved to be overwhelming. The Armenian institutions that they brought with them merely delayed the process of assimilation but never stopped it. In time the body of the Armenian traditions and values lost its attractiveness and the community lost its instinct to continue the struggle for survival.

If at first they regarded themselves as a nation in exile, gradually they changed their status and became a mere ethnic group in a foreign community. They lost their ethnicity shortly thereafter, drifted away and forever lost their Armenian identity.

The unique characteristics of the Armenian people, such as language and religion, that for centuries built a defense mechanism to help the people preserve their identity, gradually disappeared, and the people were absorbed into the communities of other people. For the Armenians in Poland, the Middle East, India, the Far East, or Europe, the diaspora was never an enduring phenomenon. Unlike the Jews, the Armenians refused to live in ghettos or segregated communities in the midst of other people. They regarded themselves more cosmopolitan and less nationalistic and wanted to remain an integral component of the community in which they chose to live, as long as the host country allowed them to do so. There were some who even chose to sacrifice their national identity and obliterate the signs of being members of a minority group. They did not want to be regarded as persons in exile. They wanted to feel at home. If for a period of time they were able to retain their identity, they did so principally because of the memory of their tragedies, which somehow helped them glue themselves to their heritage. The memory of their sufferings hardened their will to survive. But that hardening was not potent enough to provide them with the stamina or the spiritual resistance to force them to continue the struggle for survival. When the memory of the national woes faded away through succeeding generations, they lost their impulse to continue the struggle.

Beirut became the center of Armenian culture and political life in the Middle East. With the Armenian Catholicate of Cilicia nearby, the Armenians were able to spearhead a national movement, whose leaders claimed to be the legitimate representatives of all the Armenians in the diaspora. The Armenian General Benevolent Union, the largest and the most prominent Armenian benevolent association, headquartered in New York, spent millions of dollars, built schools, and organized Armenian youth clubs. The Armenian political parties, the Dashnak, Hunchak, Ramgavar, organized political movements, with the Dashnaks playing a more dominant role. It was the Dashnaks who made the Cilician Catholicos at Antelias, a suburb of Beirut, their political instrument in 1956, and began to dominate the political life of the Armenian diaspora. They encouraged the Cilician Catholicos to expand his ecclesiastical jurisdiction over areas previously held by the See of Echmiadzin, and even attempt to challenge the authority of the Supreme Catholicos of all Armenians.

The cosmopolitan life of Beirut and the often archaic nature of the Lebanese government encouraged the Armenians to make Beirut a thriving Armenian community with an intellectual ferment unmatched anywhere else in the diaspora. But at the end the Armenians failed to foster a permanent foothold. While they considered themselves forever entrenched on the Lebanese soil, they had no awareness of the fragility of their existence in the Middle East. The political turmoil of the region finally disrupted their national life, forcing them to move out and become exiles the second time around. Beirut was not their home and it was never intended to be.

In other parts of the diaspora the Armenians succeeded in forming organic communities powerful enough to sustain their traditions. They were connected with the legacy of their ancestral past and felt proud of the accomplishments of their countrymen in Armenia. There was a communal linkage, a feeling of fraternity and kinship between them, one fighting to preserve the land, the other supporting him to fight harder. For both Armenia was the center of the Armenian universe, and the acquisition of their ancestral land was the ultimate reality and the culmination of their dream. It was the land that gave both the unifying force to fuse them to their identity. There was an undeniable union between land and people, an unending love affair that helped them reinforce the uniqueness of their heritage. For them the land was the essential part of the history of the Armenian people. The land was the place from which the people emerged as a nation. The people did not precede the land and Armenia did not precede the people. The formation of the Armenian people occurred only after an amorphous group of people, the remnants of the Hittites, the Hayasas, the Azzis, the Phrygians, the Thracians, the Melids, the Luwians, and the Urartians settled in the plains of Mount Ararat and forged what came to be known as the Armenian nation. The sacredness of this land has been ingrained in the psyche of the people and has become part and parcel of the Armenian consciousness.

The history of the Armenian people is the history of the land. It is the land that has offered them the most auspicious reason for their longevity. This is the place where their ances- tors developed a legacy that has endured for over 3,000 years. This is the place where the Armenians felt vindicated after all their sufferings and tragedies of centuries past, and this was the galvanizing, raging force that pushed them to fight for whatev- er little they had been allowed to keep. They lost Western Ar- menia to the Turks, they lost the provinces of Lori and Pambak to the Georgians, they lost Nakhichevan to the Azeris. But Ka- rabagh was the last stop. They chose to fight to keep Karabagh for themselves. They felt that the redemption of the Armenian people cannot be complete without the land of Karabagh.

ARMENIAN - SOVIET - AZERI CONFLICT

Despite the policies of Glasnost, which became an essential part of the Soviet life after 1985, the Armenians rarely enjoyed the freedom to create an independent political organization. They declared the State of Armenia independent in August 1990, and changed the name of the country from the Armenian Soviet So- cialist Republic to the Republic of Armenia. But that was only on paper. The Kremlin never allowed them to exercise the right to govern their country independently from the Soviet Union. The movement for Armenian independence led the Kremlin to suppress nationalistic activities. Political activists were put in jail and the Soviet police prevented the people from organizing mass demonstrations. The Armenian independence movement was taken by the Kremlin as a sign of massive civil disobedience. Soviet tanks and armored vehicles appeared in the squares of Erevan, ready to crush the rebellious Armenians. Glasnost may have tolerated freedom of expression, but the freedom to organize a communal resistance against the Kremlin and sever ties with the Soviet Union was too much for the lead- ership of the Kremlin to stomach. The Armenians wanted total and unqualified liberation of Karabagh, a claim that the Azeris did not accept and the Russians did not honor. This territorial dispute has precipitated violent ethnic hostilities between the Armenians and the Azeri Turks with the Kremlin on the side of the Azeris in an attempt to crush the Armenian nationalist movement.

In February 1988 the Azeri Turks organized a pogrom against the Armenian residents of Sumgait, an industrial city on the Caspian Sea northeast of Baku. Thousands of Azeris dressed in black, carrying clubs and Turkish flags, marched in the streets of Sumgait yelling "death to the Armenians, death to the Armenians." They moved to the Armenian quarter and began to ransack Armenian homes. They burned people alive and raped women in the public square. An Azeri mob dragged an Armenian woman to the street, forced her to strip naked, slashed her breasts, raped her, and left her mutilated body on the street.

The pogrom was the Azeri response to the petition that the Armenians in Karabagh had presented to the Supreme Soviet a few weeks earlier, requesting Moscow to transfer the province from the Azeri jurisdiction to the State of Armenia. The Azeris wanted to keep Karabagh under their control. They formed a nationalist party called the Popular Front to pressure the Armenians to leave Azerbeijan. So did the Armenians. An Armenian nationalist movement was organized in Erevan to recruit men to chase the Azeris out of Armenia, and annex Karabagh to Armenia by force if necessary. Both sides began to hijack Soviet weapon stores and procured enormous amounts of arms and machine guns. The Armenians organized guerrilla units and began to attack Azeri villages located on the border of Armenia and Azerbeijan to avenge the Azeri pogroms. The situation deteriorated. Moscow grew impatient. Gorbachev ordered Soviet troops to move to Erevan to suppress the nationalist movement and guerrilla activities. Meanwhile the Azeris blockaded the roads and railroads leading to Armenia and began to terrorize the Armenians in Baku. Bands of Azeri Turks ransacked the Armenian homes and beat up the Armenians. They grabbed several hundred Armenian men, women, and children, took them to the harbor, crammed them in a ship like cattle and ordered the captain to take them to the other side of the Caspian Sea and dump them someplace. Sixty-eight Armenians were killed and thousands of Armenian homes were destroyed.

Continued violence in Azerbeijan forced the Armenian residents to flee Azerbeijan. Baku had about 200,000 Armenian residents. Very few remained. In November 1988 117,000 Armenian men, women, and children fled the Azeri terror, moved to Armenia and settled in Leninakan, Armenia, hoping to build a new life under the tranquil skies of the Armenian homeland. That tranquility lasted only a few weeks. In the recesses of the earth underneath their new settlement the forces of nature were about to tremble with an unprecedented ferocity.

THE EARTHQUAKE

It happened on December 7, 1988. The ground trembled shortly before midday. In 200 seconds thousands of Armenians died, hundreds of buildings crumbled, cities were destroyed, and 500,000 Armenians became homeless. Spitak, a town of 30,000, was the epicenter of the Earthquake. It became the symbol of death and destruction. Schools, buildings, hospitals were destroyed and workers at factories were buried alive. Children were trapped in piles of rubble. The Earthquake toppled buildings within a radius of 30 miles, an area where 700,000 people lived. Cities of Leninakan, Kirovakan, and Stepanavan were destroyed with 48 villages surrounding them. Most of the victims were the Armenian refugees from Azerbeijan. Pictures of stricken Armenians appeared in the world press and the response was spontaneous. Rescue workers and medical teams from all over the world rushed to Armenia. Armenians around the world organized fund drives and raised millions of dollars for the victims. Even the Turks felt compassionate and sent convoys of food, clothing, and medicine across the border to the Armenian victims. But not their Azeri cousins. As the rescue workers sifted through the debris for signs of life, the Azeri thugs in Baku continued their atrocities against the Armenians. "Allah finally punished the Armenians," the Moslems proclaimed.

This was a tragedy beyond comprehension. It was a catastrophe of monumental proportion. But this luckless land was well acquainted with the grief of such destruction. Armenia is situated on top of a structural knot of interactions of plates that occasionally had caused violent tremors in the past. In 735 AD 10,000 perished in an earthquake, and 20,000 died in 893. In 1687 80,000 people lost their lives in an earthquake. In 1840 Armenian villages were destroyed by an earthquake on the slopes of Mount Ararat, and in 1939 30,000 perished.

The Earthquake of 1988 made Armenia once again "*Voghpi Hairenik, Vorpi Hairenik*" - "a fatherland of sorrows, a fatherland of orphans," a phrase the Armenians use whenever tragedy hits the country.

CHAPTER TWENTY-NINE

ARMENIA TODAY

The tragedy caused by the Earthquake did not end the hostilities between the Armenians and the Azeris. In 1990 there were more Azeri atrocities against the Armenian villagers. Farms were destroyed, people were killed, and men were taken away during the night. The Karabagh issue continued to dominate the political scene of the region and has taken precedence over other pressing problems that beleaguered the country since the Earthquake. The centuries old hostilities continued and Moscow, on the pretense of establishing order, found it convenient to level off Armenian villages bordering Azerbeijan and massacring the Armenian villagers. The Kremlin sided with the Moslem Azeris primarily because of the Islamic fundamentalism in central Asia. There were fifty million Moslem subjects in the Soviet Union and five out of fifteen republics were Moslem. The bloody feud continued and the ethnic unrest threatened to transform the country into a Caucasian version of Lebanon.

The continued social unrest in Armenia and communal violence, coupled with staggering economic problems forced more Armenians to leave their Motherland and migrate to the west or to other parts of the Soviet Union. Moscow favored such Armenian emigration and even encouraged the people to move out. During the Azeri pogroms in Azerbeijan, thousands of Armenian families were forced to resettle in the interior of Asia. Their migration had been sponsored by Moscow. In the aftermath of the Earthquake of 1988 thousands of Armenian orphans were taken away from Armenia and dispersed in various parts of the Soviet Union.

Armenia today is a maelstrom of strangeness. While life in the rest of the disintegrating Soviet Union is unpleasantly boring and dull, life in Armenia is somewhat charming and relaxed. In spite of the political problems, the scars of the Earthquake, and the impoverished condition of the economy, the Armenians have somehow managed to make their country cosmopolitan, with dynamism and vitality not seen anywhere else in the vastness of the Soviet Empire. There is an on-going process of rebuilding Armenia in a spirit that defies ideological and political dogmas. That spirit has transformed the country into a vigorous modern state, with a brave determination to snatch victory out of tragedy and convert failure into success.

Erevan is a city older than Rome, founded 800 years before Christ, but it is more modern today than most of the newer cities in the world. On one side there is art, music, and literature that continue to thrive and the villagers who continue to sing and dance to the tune of Armenian music. There is the beautiful Lake Sevan against the backdrop of a chain of hills, where the sunset gives the visitor a breathtaking experience. There is the everlasting presence of Mount Ararat, albeit located on a foreign soil. But on the other side there are the homeless of the Earthquake, huddled in their makeshift camps, in a desperate search for food and shelter. It is both exhilarating and depressing.

There is a strange feeling of optimism in Armenia today. The people voted for independence on September 21, 1991, unequivocally severing their ties to Soviet colonialism. They are now free to design their own destiny in their own land without the interference of the "Big Brother" in the north. The people no longer talk about the traumatic years of yesterday, the Turkish pogroms, the Genocide, and the atrocities. They now talk about freedom and the virtues of liberty and independence. While they are exuberant about the prospect of a new dawn they express in simple candor the economic hopelessness that has dominated the region since the late 1980's. They talk about the Azeri economic blockade in which the Azeris refuse to send Armenia the essential commodities for daily sustenance. They talk about the principles of democracy and human rights, but they also talk about their limited resources and a dwindling population. They talk about freedom and liberty, but they also talk about the emigration of their countrymen to foreign lands and the continued encroachment of the Azeris to colonize the Armenian villages left vacant by the departing Armenians. They talk about independence, but they are also worried about the security of their country. They talk about the possibility that the disintegration and the declining prestige of the Russian power may someday encourage the Turks to sweep in from the west, walk over Armenia and achieve their centuries old ambition.

In spite of the public utterances to the contrary, there is no reliable evidence that Turkey has abandoned such goals of Pan-Turkism. Armenia's Moslem neighbors, who have made their country the breeding ground for hostilities, regard Ankara as a potential protector against non-Islamic powers. Turkey has always been agile to exploit signs of weakness among its political rivals and pursue its goal at the expense of others. The dismemberment of Armenia from the Russian hegemony and the demise of the Soviet Union may make the country an easy prey for the Turks. This would be a disastrous price to pay for independence.

Throughout the crowded history of the Armenian people rarely have these people been able to sustain their sovereignty without the protective umbrella of a great power. For 3,000 years their cumulative genius has helped them weather the setbacks, defeats, oppression, and genocide, and preserve their priceless legacy and pass it on to the succeeding generations, primarily because they were shielded most of the time by a great power which felt charitable enough at times to leave them alone.

In view of this historical experience it is vitally important for the present leadership of Armenia to separate fact from fiction, emotion from political realism, and guide the nation with wisdom and prudence. This is the second time since 1918 that the leaders of Armenia are being called upon to design a new direction for the Armenian people. If they want to make Armenia safe and fit for the Armenian people and establish a truly democratic society, they must try to remember the lessons of the past. Their task to build a new order in the Armenian homeland extends far beyond the limits of their political experience. They seem to be so fascinated by the demise of Communism and the extinction of the dream of People's Paradise, that they tend to overlook the monstrous responsibilities ahead of them. To build capitalism from scratch is not an easy undertaking in an environment that has never witnessed the fruits of capitalism, the free-enterprise system, and market economy. The absence of Communism would not guarantee an automatic restoration of economic well-being. The country needs industrial production, investment capital from abroad, and markets for its products, before it can truly enjoy the fruits of its labor. Freedom and sovereignty can only be achieved if there is a reliable economic program. Evolution from Communism into Capitalism may be a more formidable task than defending the country from foreign intervention. Armenia's ominous commercial dependence on their hostile neighbors makes the job extremely difficult.

Perhaps there is a new approach in store for the Armenians. If in 1918 the hostility of their neighbors towards their newly formed republic forced the Armenians to adopt a belligerent policy to protect Armenia's national interest, three quarters of a century later the Armenians may need to formulate a new policy and find ways to live in harmony with their neighbors. This may be the true test of leadership in this troubled age. Wisdom is a better substitute for emotion, and sobriety is better than belligerence. Armenia's neighbors are there to stay; so is Armenia. They all have the same predicament. All of them are in the process of unchaining themselves from the Kremlin and finding ways to offer a better life to their people. If in the past the deep-rooted Armenian subconscious drew inspiration from defeat, there can be no inspiration in a country where incessant warfare has made life intolerable.

Throughout their history the Armenians have suffered from wishful expectations that their national problems can be solved by passion, fortitude, and warfare. They have gone to war to defend their faith, country, and people. But when they came out defeated in battle, they celebrated the defeat as a victory. Their history is full of such victories. The subconscious transformation of the actual defeat into a moral victory has been ingrained in the Armenian character in such a way that until today most of their national holidays are celebrations of defeat or remembrances of sufferings. In these convoluted times of the post-Communist era perhaps the Armenians need to school themselves in a different belief and pour their energy and determination in ways that would open the doors of negotiation rather than warfare for the defense of their national interests. If the future sits in judgment of the past, perhaps in hindsight the Armenians should have done things differently. If the past offers guidance to design the destiny of the future, the recollection of the national woes may be instructive to adopt a new national policy to draw inspiration from victory for a change and not defeat.

Could this be done? Of course. There is nothing irreconcilable, including deep-rooted conflicts, if there is determination on both sides to solve issues peacefully and with reason. This is the era of change in the world. Yesterday's enemies are turning to be today's friends. The Armenians should not be imprisoned by their past, even if the painful memory of the past defies solution of today's issue with reason. To turn Armenia into a Lebanon would be such a cruel destiny that it will destroy everything that the Armenians had built during the last one hundred years. The rigidity of the Maronites turned Lebanon into a nightmare and chased the Christian leadership out of the country. To seek accommodation with neighbors and to solve international problems by peaceful processes are signs of strength, not weakness.

The Armenian leaders must be bold enough to take risks but wise enough to avoid them, if necessary, without violating the spirit of self-determination or jeopardizing their national interests. Armenia is a small nation. It was before and it is now. As a small nation it is vulnerable. As a measure of protection it must stay in partnership with other nations. It is only in partnership that it can protect its fragile existence and be a viable member of the world community. It may have been necessary in the past to use force to assert its will, but today's world is too complicated, and no small nation would have sufficient resources to enforce its will or protect its vital interests through the use of force. In the context of our times it is inconceivable for any nation to survive in self-imposed isolation from the global family. The unification of Europe and the formation of economic blocs around the globe are manifestations in that direction. Mutual economic and political arrangements have become an indispensable part of the strategy of the great powers in running the affairs of their people.

In their passionate search for the culmination of their national interests, if the leaders of Armenia choose to solve their conflict with their neighbors by military means, they will throw the people back to the same predicament as they were in the troubled times of the first quarter of this century. The Armenians rarely have been able to bring their military conflicts to a decisive finish. Violence can no longer be an instrument to settle accounts.

Armenia's neighbors should also understand that the Armenians can live under dictatorships, the Armenians can live in poverty, the Armenians can deprive themselves from the niceties of life, the Armenians can dismantle the old systems, the Armenians can uphold the primacy of international laws, but the Armenians will never give up their pursuit to fulfill their dreams, even if the dream exceeds the means to achieve it. International collaboration or political dialogue does not mean capitulation or appeasement. For the Armenians the ownership of the land is a birthright and not a privilege. Their love of their land comes from the suffering of the people, and they will never forget that.

Recklessness leads people to anarchy and anarchy threatens the political stability. Civil disorder is a great obstacle to the establishment of confidence and the advancement of democracy. If the Armenians want to emancipate themselves from the chains of totalitarianism, as they must, they must attack it with a rational alternative, but staying always in partnership with others. Together they may succeed. This may be a revolution in itself, a new kind of revolution, a revolution of mind and spirit, a revolution based, for a change, on the dignity of men and respect of others.

The drama continues. In the harsh realities of modern life it is difficult to predict the future of this proud race whose ancestors crossed the Bosporus 3,200 years ago on their way to form the Armenian nation and make their country the cradle of man's civilization. One can take solace only in the reassuring words of the Nineteenth century Armenian writer, Khachadour Abovian, "If the Armenian nation were a mountain, it would have crumbled. If it were iron, it would have melted. If it were a sea, it would have dried up, but the God-loving Armenian nation stood up to all these and kept its identity."

It was the land that kept them going. As long as they are able to hold on to the land, no matter how small it is, they will be able to keep their identity. It is the land that has kept them alive. It is the land that has given them the passion to build and the passion to preserve. It will also be the land that will give them the stamina to build their future. The day when the Armenians no longer consider their land essential in their struggle for survival, that will be the day when they will find themselves on the road to extinction.

*   *   *

Such is the story of the Armenian people.

Perhaps someday there will be another writer who will continue the chronicle of this ancient race, and perhaps someday there will be a leader who will lead these people back to their homeland, the Plains of Mount Ararat.

INDEX